# THE WAY WE LOOK

## DRESS AND AESTHETICS

# THE WAY WE LOOK

## DRESS AND AESTHETICS

### SECOND EDITION

**Marilyn Revell DeLong**

*University of Minnesota*

Fairchild Publications
*New York*

Director: Pam Kirshen Fishman
Senior Editor: Olga Kontzias
Photo Library, Fairchild Publications: Delcima Charles,
Assistant Editor: Lori Applebaum
Art Director: Mary Siener
Production Manager: Priscilla Taguer

Copyeditor: Colleen Corrice Clifford

Interior Design: Ellen Pettengell

Cover Design: Lisa Klausing

Library of Congress Catalog Card Number: 97–77480

ISBN: 1–56367–071–2

GST R 133004424

Printed in the United States of America

# CONTENTS

# EXTENDED CONTENTS

*Chapter Six*

# Materials of the Apparel-Body-Construct 137

*Chapter Seven*

# Visual Definition Within the Apparel-Body-Construct 165

*Chapter Eight*

# Organizing the Apparel-Body-Construct  207

| | |
|---|---|
| *Chapter Nine* | # Interpreting the Apparel-Body-Construct 251 |

| | |
|---|---|
| *Chapter Ten* | # Evaluation Within the Aesthetic Framework 297 |

# PREFACE

**T**HE REASON FOR THIS EDITION WAS SUMMARIZED BY a student upon completion of the course for which it was designed: to overcome tunnel vision. Both my research and teaching have helped in formulating the topics. Students have had input throughout the entire process.

Aesthetics is defined as understanding how we perceive forms of dress, their characteristic features, and our reactions to them. This includes:

1. our relationship to the entire form and its meanings;
2. understanding the characteristics of the audience and such specific relevant information as age, gender, education; and
3. the context, including both the immediate viewing circumstance and the constant reference of the specific cultural milieu.

Understanding our response includes an awareness of its basis and assumptions and how it may differ from that of a client. The reader is addressed as viewer, wearer, and professional with varying interests, such as retail merchandiser, clothing designer, or fashion journalist. These interests can be understood in relation to dress through the book's approach to viewing the entirety of the apparel-body-construct (the ABC).

This book is a revision of *The Way We Look: A Framework for Visual Analysis of Dress*, but this version differs significantly. Professional relevance is addressed and includes applications for the design, manufacture, and merchandising of apparel. Boundaries between various professional roles, such as design and merchandising of apparel, are not as great as they once were. The apparel industry is ever changing, and those preparing for careers within this industry must acknowledge the transformations taking place. Understanding aesthetic response is becoming increasingly necessary.

*The Way We Look: Dress and Aesthetics* is based upon the need to adopt a professional viewpoint and to understand the aesthetic responses of our audiences. It explores what it means to be aware of how we respond aesthetically and to encourage certain practices, such as the viewing reference of the apparel-body-construct. A process for learning and understanding is offered through response to the apparel-body-construct to develop the sophisticated evaluation essential for the apparel professional. In the beginning, the concepts are outlined and explained for application. Patterns of viewing and their influence upon the visual effect are then explained, including elements of line, shape, point, color, and texture, and compositional aspects, such as coherence of the unit, proportion, and balance. The visual form and its attendant meanings are investigated in terms of potential visual relations and their interpretation, inherent in the context of the whole, the apparel-body construct, the viewer, and the situation of viewing. These visual relationships influence the process as well as the outcome of the visual effect.

Aesthetic concepts include those related to the unit of the apparel-body-construct and to the meaning and how each derives from personal and cultural sources. Viewing the apparel-body-construct is emphasized, including what contextualizes it, i.e., wearer/viewer, immediate physical background, degrees of understanding within one culture, and relationships within and outside of the apparel-body-construct. We need to understand our views and what makes them ours, but also we must understand the aesthetic views of other cultures and their relevance to the market. Increasingly the aesthetic codes and responses of another culture are important to understand. The marketplace for apparel has become globally oriented.

The skills to become a discerning and educated viewer are stressed through exercises. Application exercises are numerous and included within each chapter to encourage active learning and to engage the reader in visual imagination and thinking. Application exercises focus on a wide range of topics related to the text and are both verbal and visual. Sometimes application is individually oriented, sometimes group oriented, with the objective of stimulating the reader's imagination while also giving a context in which concepts can be further understood.

1998                                              Marilyn Revell DeLong
                                                 St. Paul, Minnesota

# ACKNOWLEDGMENTS

The second edition of *The Way We Look* could not have been developed without the response of the undergraduate and graduate students at the University of Minnesota. They helped me see what I did not see and let me know when they did not understand.

A special thank you to the reviewers of the manuscript. In its early stages reviewers at the University of Minnesota were: Patricia Hemmis and Nancy Nelson. In later stages a number of external, reviewers read carefully and made valuable comments and suggestions.

Other reviewers selected by the publisher were also every helpful. They included: Nancy O. Bryant, Oregon State University; Diane Frey, Bowling Green University; Jane Hegland, New Mexico State University; Janet Hethorn, University of California—Davis; Susan Michelman, University of Massachusetts—Amherst; Karen Robinette, California State University—Northridge; Diane Sparks, Colorado State University.

A valuable resource for photographs was the historic costume collection of The Goldstein at the University of Minnesota. Supporting work of students in Design, Housing, and Apparel included their generous loan of photographs from their own design and research: Elka Stevens, Colleen Gau, Barbara Sumberg, Masami Suga, Susheela Hoefer, Hazel Lutz, Marlene Breu, Janel Urke, Isa Freeman. Pat Hemmis photographed Jane Hegland who graciously and generously allowed use of much of her personal wardrobe. Thank you to Key Sook Geum and Joanne B. Eicher for their understanding and help with needed resources. Thank you to Fairchild for the many visual materials from their archives. To Olga Kontzias from Fairchild Publications, who became my friend in the editing process.

Finally, for the personal support of my husband, Max, whose understanding and insight into the process never failed, thank you.

# Chapter One

# YOUR AESTHETIC RESPONSE

*After you have read this chapter, you will be able to understand:*

- The meaning of aesthetics and the aesthetic response.

- How culture influences people's perceptions of what is aesthetically pleasing in clothing, and how both the collective and the personal influence aesthetic judgments.

- The difference between subjective, objective, abstract, and concrete responses to dress.

- How form, context, and viewer are dynamically interconnected in the aesthetic response to clothing.

A S YOU LOOK THROUGH A MAGAZINE ADVERTISING apparel, what is it about a photograph that catches your eye—a special look, a color, a beautiful model, an unusual message? It could be that you find a picture of just the look you like, such as "the return of the 1970s" with straight hair and hip-hugging pants with flared legs. In the 1990s, the 1970s look is influenced by music groups, the fashion industry, and vintage clothing. You may be drawn to a photograph of a model wearing the latest fashion and your eye scans the lengths and takes note of how the jacket fits the body. You may be attracted to a unique color combination, or even a fabric that looks as though it would be pleasing to touch and wear on a cool morning. Often what you notice is what you relate to in a personal way and from which you derive pleasure. This is your **aesthetic response**—your involvement in looking and your resulting experiences stimulated by looking, such as pleasure or satisfaction. Consider Figure 1.1 and how you can become involved in your looking.

## PURSUING THE AESTHETIC

Your relationship to what you evaluate as excellent and as having value in your life is vital. How you appreciate and express the relationship has to do with life's very essence—what we sometimes refer to as the quality of life. Experiencing and understanding this response in you and in others is the study of **aesthetics**.

To pursue the aesthetic involves continual reference to what people value. Some feel that although aesthetics matters, it is an extra after basic needs are met. But Tuan (1995) writes about aesthetics, ". . . the pervasive role of the aesthetic is suggested by its root meaning of 'feeling'—not just any kind of feeling, but 'shaped' feeling and sensitive perception. And it is suggested even more by its opposite, anesthetic 'or lack of feeling'—the condition of living death" (p. 1). He believes the more attuned people are to the beauty in the world, the more they feel alive and enjoy living.

Traditionally aesthetics has been equated with the ultimate "oohhh" and "ahhh" experience. This means you are connecting with what you are seeing and sensing. That is, you are becoming engrossed in colors, textures, shapes, and the way they are combined. But what you are experiencing may remind you of something from the past, or it may be just delightful because it completely meets your current expectations. Thus, aesthetics implies interest and involvement in what you sense and feel. Aesthetics also relies significantly on the time and place in which you live, to who you are, and to the social groups to which you belong.

Aesthetics includes the act of evaluation. This is why we often use words such as "ideal," "ultimate," or "epitome" in aesthetic judgments because they designate yardsticks by which people measure goals. Specifically, the study of

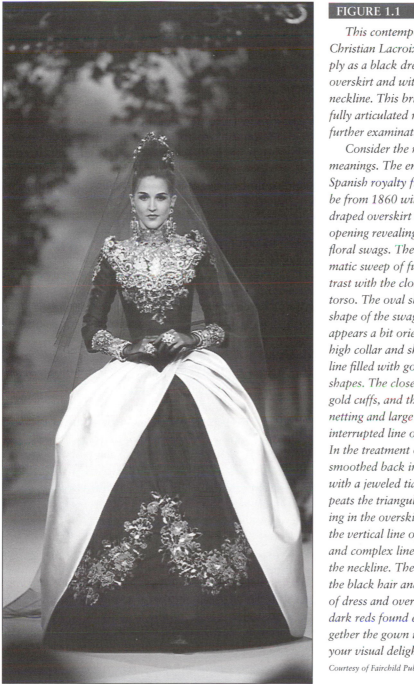

## FIGURE 1.1

*This contemporary creation, designed by Christian Lacroix in 1992, can be described simply as a black dress with a contrasting creamy overskirt and with much gold concentrated at the neckline. This brief description, however, is not a fully articulated response that would come with further examination.*

*Consider the myriad details and their possible meanings. The ensemble resembles an image of Spanish royalty from the past, and the skirt could be from 1860 with its bell shape and elegantly draped overskirt that results in the center front opening revealing black fabric festooned with floral swags. The diaphanous skirt creates a dramatic sweep of fullness at the hem in sharp contrast with the closely fitted shape of the upper torso. The oval shapes of the neckline repeat the shape of the swags in the skirt. The upper torso appears a bit oriental as well as historical with its high collar and shoulder-wide, oval-shaped neckline filled with gold and multicolored floral shapes. The closely fitted sleeves end in heavy gold cuffs, and the hands are covered with black netting and large golden rings to continue an uninterrupted line of black on the arms and hands. In the treatment of the head, the hair is smoothed back in an upward thrust and covered with a jeweled tiara and veil. The veil shape repeats the triangular shaping created by the opening in the overskirt. Her large earrings continue the vertical line of the head as well as the many and complex lines and shapes of gold found at the neckline. The personal colors of the model, the black hair and creamy skin, repeat the colors of dress and overskirt. Her dark red lips echo the dark reds found elsewhere in the ensemble. Altogether the gown is truly a masterpiece created for your visual delight.*

Courtesy of Fairchild Publications.

aesthetics and the presentation of the body and how it is arranged for viewing implies relating what is valued to the mode of dress. In other words, people are concerned with what they value, and this is reflected in their goals regarding their appearances and how they desire to look. How human beings dress and choose to appear reflects a relationship between themselves and the various forms of dress available within their given cultures. When people remark about an item of clothing, "That looks like you," they are connecting clothing characteristics with personal characteristics. But they are also indicating a value—the desirability of a connection between the clothing and the person.

How the dressed body appears at any given time period is influenced by historical perspective. For example, fashions of the 1990s evoke the social and political climate of the decade. But according to Hollander (1978), ideas about past eras are formed through persistent images presented in the media. Then the viewer's perception may be altered so as to expect something different than what was actually worn during a given historical period. By examining theater costume, one can sometimes see a variation from what was actually worn than what has become an expected cue to that era, but is actually a part of today's fashion. Thus, 1990s appearances may influence dress worn to depict a previous era. In how many weddings in the 1960s did the bride actually wear a simple muslin dress and fresh flowers in her loosely flowing hair? Probably not as often as we see in movies featuring the 1960s. Media such as the theater, film, and television all portray history through the appearances of the actors and actresses, and this helps viewers identify various periods and form ideas about them. For example, the decades of the 40s, 50s, 60s are all related by viewers, or the populace, to the visual images the media associates with them. With exposure, images become set and the audience comes to expect certain conventions associated with those images, though such appearances may not portray an accurate picture of what was worn during that time.

Consider aesthetics further. Until this century much of the work in aesthetics involved only the dominant aspects of a culture and equated them with an absolute called "beauty." In the eighteenth century, aesthetics was considered to be the study of beauty, unity, harmony, or repose and the result was a standard for the way all things, including clothing, should appear (Binkley, 1963). Beauty, in a philosophical sense, is that which we believe portrays excellence. However, what is called excellent changes over time because our definition of beauty changes according to the changes in shared cultural values.

Today the study of aesthetics is mainly concerned with the ideology and culture of the individual viewer and how this translates to the image. In aesthetics we are more concerned with expressions of diversity than with everyone preferring the same image. A viewer may not think about or use words like "beauty" but instead may use words like "cool," "awesome," "outstanding," or "radical." The subject of aesthetic inquiry is how the body is clothed to be most attractive to the eye, and this is subject to time and interpretation and the values of different periods. The viewer may relate excellence more to modernity and what makes us appear modern, or to a postmodern look. Here postmodern refers to an aesthetic expression viewed as parallel or in contrast to the modern. An appearance that is postmodern often embodies diverse values and disparate features of clothing and a mixing of aesthetic codes (Morgado, 1996). An example would be putting new and vintage clothing together to form a creative combination of the past and the present (Henderson, 1995).

Thus, aesthetics is about learning what visual qualities people are attracted to and make evaluative judgments about. Aesthetics relates what is valued as an ideal and how people desire to look according to the dominant images of the time. Such ideals evolve slowly from one image to another based on perceived cultural cues. **Culture** is defined as those symbolic and learned aspects of a unified societal group (Marshall, 1994). A cultural grouping can be formed around a nation, race, or school and can vary with time and place, so that over a lifetime a person can relate to a number of different cultural identities. Learning can be passed on through material artifacts or nonmaterial teaching and traditions. Culture from an individual perspective is viewed as a kind of secondary environment that influences one's perceptions, thinking, and overt behavior (Lachmann, 1991). Within any one culture there are many personal variations as well as traditional conventions. People cue into these conventions depending on their social and economic positions within a given culture.

By now you may be asking, "Why should we want or need to understand not only our own aesthetic response but also that of others?" It is both fascinating and important to explore and understand why people take pleasure in what they wear. If you work with clothing and the outward appearance of yourself and others, you will necessarily be involved with aesthetics. Professionals within the apparel industry may be involved in many activities related to clothing—designing, producing, and merchandising. For example, you could write about fashion, buy or design clothing, help a client shop for clothing and dress attractively, create ensembles to communicate a message for a fashion show, or create visual displays that portray an inviting message. To learn how to communicate about clothing and appearance as a professional, you must understand the aesthetic response of both yourself and your audience.

The study of aesthetics will be of interest to others besides apparel professionals.

## UNDERSTANDING AESTHETIC RESPONSE

**Aesthetic response** is a personal expression—it involves what people select and thus becomes an expression of their tastes and preferences. It is personal in that it is:

- an expression of how people take pleasure in the world around them.
- an involvement of the relationship of human beings with the various forms of dress available to them.
- a decision on how people choose to communicate their identities to others through what they wear.

Aesthetic response also includes a shared or collective expression of groups to which people belong. Think of a time you shared ideas about clothing, hairstyles, and makeup with friends. You agreed on many points and you enjoyed sharing and playing those ideas off of each other. But at the same time, you realized that you and your friends did not agree on everything. You may have even disagreed about what was being featured as the current look. Many other factors were involved, such as different personalities and the varied experiences that added a diversity to your responses.

Your culture influences your aesthetic response. Cultural influence involves the sum total of your past experiences. This may include both your culture of origin, that is, the one you were born into, and the present culture you live in that impacts your experience. Even if your culture of origin is not currently part of your experience, it can be continually influential through family traditions.

Aesthetics includes the domain of the personal, as well as the collective thoughts and feelings you share with others. The realm of the collective culture involves a kind of overarching cultural influence, which includes responses that are different from your own. Think of others outside your usual sphere, a group very different in age but that is still within your culture. Consider teen-aged skate punks, residents of a retirement home, or members of a little league baseball team. Though you recognize that the members of such a group are quite different from yours, you have noticed that they are similar to others with whom they associate who are of similar age. They have different shared experiences and thus different expectations than your own. Knowing that their experiences are unlike yours and those of your friends, you can understand that the members of this group express themselves in their appearance differently and may have different needs and desires than yours. People in this group express their different values and goals in the way they appear, though relatively speaking the resulting appearance may be more similar to the way you look than you realize. Certainly groups within one culture are more identifiable visually than those from a completely different culture.

*Application Exercise 1.1*

Think of your personal response to the clothing you wear. What about your clothing gives you pleasure? Is it when you touch the surfaces of clothing, glance at yourself in a mirror, or receive a compliment about how great you look? How do you express your delight and satisfaction? Now think back to an earlier time in your life. Can you remember your thoughts and feelings about clothing at that time? How have you changed from then to now in the way you respond to clothing?

One reason why aesthetics is so fascinating to study is that the ways people choose to dress and appear reflect themselves and the cultures they live in and also help to shape them and their cultures. On the one hand, clothing and appearance help identify people's personal attributes, social affiliations, cultural values, and place in history. On the other hand, such clues help influence the behaviors of these people and of others toward them because they constitute identifiable images or variations on such images.

There are times in one's life when these images are more important and thus we pay more attention to them. Sometimes we understand our own images by looking and comparing them with others. For example, when you travel to a completely different locale (e.g., a foreign country) you may become much more aware of your own appearance because it differs from that of the people you are traveling among.

Sometimes you evaluate without much reflection or understanding of your response. In my research on perception, individuals presented with an ensemble of the dressed body—an image in a photograph, slide, or on a clothed mannequin—almost instantly made personal judgments. This evaluation included whether or not and how much they liked what they saw, whether they would wear it, and maybe even what was wrong with the dressed body, for example, too ho-hum, dull and boring.

Such evaluation involves a quick, often emotional, subconscious assessment of the image of the dressed body. There may be a number of reasons for this:

1. People react more quickly to images than to written messages. The phrase, "A picture is worth a thousand words," is appropriate because we can attribute, absorb, and assess personal meanings very quickly.

2. People connect easily with images that are collective—that form a public memory, as noted by Rubenstein (1995). Such images come to them from everywhere—from exposure within their own cultures and from the influence of other cultures. Tapping this public memory is like tapping a well of already formed ideas, models, that provide people with cues and conventions—codes for shortcuts to a response. For example, any time you respond that an image is "up-to-date," you are probably referring to such a collective image based upon other images you have seen in current movies, on television, and in newspapers and magazines, as well as in stores and on people at events you attend.

3. People form images in their minds about those things they value personally, that is, how they desire to look and what is in fashion at the moment. What you value serves as a quick reference for evaluation and you react immediately with your emotions. The response is voiced as "great," "cool," or "lovely"—whatever they feel expresses the overall result. Though people can make judgments instantaneously based upon their feelings, to do so does not require much reflection about what they see. That is, the mind helps people by processing certain conventions of seeing—codes and shortcuts that cue them into already developed images—whether they are personal or collective.

*Application Exercise 1.2*

Read the following descriptions of the aesthetic responses of three different individuals of different ages and cultural experiences. How do values influence their ideas of what defines excellence and what they consider to be exemplary?

- What I consider important is what looks good on my body and what complements my personality. What I mean is that the clothing should fit me comfortably and smoothly without wrinkling. I want to select colors and textures to reflect my personality. However, I recognize that what is good for me is not necessarily attractive on others.
- My clothing must reflect the current fashion but also my individual features. It should fit me properly and be proportioned to my body. The colors of my clothing should relate to the colors of my body, that is, my skin tone and hair and eye color. I want to know I look great!
- Being from China, I can accept various types of beauty from different time periods, races, cultures, and ages. It is important to me to look neat and clean at all times. But to me, true beauty comes from within. According to my Buddhist belief, the internal character of a person must shine through.

# ARTICULATING AESTHETIC RESPONSE

People respond to clothing in many ways—from subjective to objective, from concrete to abstract. In *subjective* responses, the viewer tunes in to how he or she feels personally about clothing. In *objective* responses, the viewer reasons or analyzes more about clothing that he or she is wearing. In *concrete* terms, the viewer responds to perceived information and in *abstract* terms the meaningful information that arises from knowledge and experiences. In the following brief passage this person is expressing a highly emotional response to a favorite piece of clothing.

> *My starry jacket: It lives in my closet like a discrete primitive deity. Like an allusion to night. We watch over one another. Sometimes I wear it; sometimes it wears me . . . my jacket manifests the luminous presence of the night, up above and in my closet. The Great Outside is also inside. (Cixous, 1994, p. 95)*

This wearer expresses strong feelings about this black wool jacket and is paying tribute to the designer Sonia Rykiel. The jacket comes alive in her description, but the concrete details are left to your imagination. Responses like this are expressions of a very personal and subjective nature. Others may reveal less feeling and more reasoning in response to their clothing, such as the following: "I own a black wool jacket that I wear a lot. It has a collar that works well with many combinations of shirts and sweaters. I think it complements me because it repeats my hair color and puts a finishing touch on many separate pieces that I put together in my wardrobe."

Many wearers' responses are a mixture of subjective and objective language. Both types play a role in an aesthetic response. The subjective contributes spontaneity and excitement, and the objective includes logic and reasoning. Realizing what is subjective and what is objective is necessary to understand aesthetics. Can you find each in the following response? "I really love my black wool jacket. When I first tried it on, I knew instantly it was meant only for me. It is me! I find it works with many different outfits and is comfortable to wear because it fits my body in just the right places, through the shoulders and across the back. Besides, it was on sale, a real bargain."

Our aesthetic response must be considered dynamic and continuously evolving. Aesthetic response involves (l) form, (2) viewer, and (3) context—all are dynamically interrelated and influential (Figure 1.2). Particularly as a

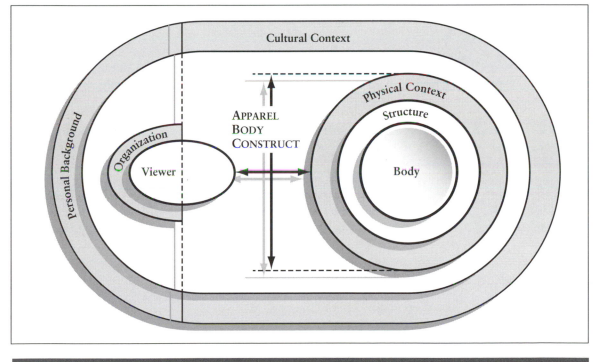

### FIGURE 1.2

*The aesthetic response is an interaction involving what the viewer brings (including personal background, organizational skills, knowledge) and the form of the apparel-body-construct. Contexts important in the viewing process are the immediate physical surround and the cultural context of the viewer.*

*A wedding dress of the 1930s that could have been worn by two generations of brides—the grand-mother as a bride and her granddaughter, a present-day bride. No matter when such a dress is worn, aesthetic response demands considera-tion of the form, viewer, and contexts.*

Courtesy of Charles Kleibacker.

professional, it is important to examine aesthetic response because it greatly influences not only decisions and actions but how one communicates with others. But there are times in one's life when such a decision warrants careful thought. First, let us examine the aesthetic response of a young bride as she makes a decision and then follow with a more thorough discussion of the three aspects of aesthetic response—form, viewer, and context.

This bride, planning her wedding, is deciding whether or not to wear the dress worn by her grandmother, who was married in 1939. The dress is similar to the one in Figure 1.3. First she considers what she thinks about the dress and how she will appear in it. She loves the dress and has always admired the vision of her grandmother in the dress in her wedding portrait. To her, the dress is elegant in its simplicity and appears on her as a vertical column of off-white silk satin as it skims the body surfaces. The rounded neckline and shaped sleeves extending to the wrist add to its elegance. Upon examination, the surfaces are a bit yellowed, but this gives a certain patina to the dress. The dress fits her remarkably well and requires few alterations. The headdress is not available, but it could be reproduced through the use of the photographs. Perhaps a slightly modified version is called for to give the desired visual effect, given the bride's current hairstyle.

The bride views herself wearing the dress, but also thinks about others involved: her groom, her close friends and family, and all of those guests who will be attending the wedding. In this regard, the bride examines herself in the mirror wearing the dress and considers the similarity in her appearance to that of her grandmother. She has a close relationship with her grandmother and would like to wear her dress. The bride also considers how her husband-to-be and the audience of guests will respond. She imagines they will respond positively as they glimpse her for the very first time in the dress as she enters the church.

Next she thinks about where she will be seen wearing the dress, in this instance at the church ceremony and reception. The dress will complement the simple church interior where the wedding will take place. Its dark-wood altar and deep, red-pile floor covering will contrast with the creamy surfaces of the dress. The wedding will be in the evening and the candlelight provided during the ceremony will enhance the shimmer of the surfaces. At the hotel reception there will also be low lighting and candlelight.

Because this decision is very important to her, she reflects how tradition is regarded within her circle of family and friends. The family thinks that wearing the dress would be a positive symbol of family tradition, unity, and continuance and would provide many wonderful memories. At the present time, within her community, a number of her friends have chosen to wear wedding dresses formerly worn by family members. Thus, news of her intent to wear her grandmother's dress would surely reach enough of those attending the wedding to create a stir of anticipation.

As the bride considers all of the preceding influences in her decision, she will experience more fully the implications of her aesthetic response. One or the other may become a priority and influence the decision of what to wear. For example, the consideration of context is slightly different with each decision made, and it influences the form and viewer.

The process of learning about the components of aesthetic response is rewarding because of the discoveries that can be made and the understanding that results. Consider further the influence of cultural context. Let us examine a different cultural context. In Osaka, Japan, the wedding could take place at a Shinto shrine or the entire wedding could take place in a hotel. In this scenario, the bride is involved in elaborate changes of dress from traditional kimono to a long, white dress with a veil similar to what might be worn in the United States—what is called "Western" style. A typical series of changes may be as follows: a white wedding kimono and headdress with face painted white and with special facial makeup defining certain facial features for a Shinto ceremony; a red kimono covered with elaborate motifs of a symbolic nature; then a switch to a full-length Westernized, white wedding dress with a veil; then a second full-length, festive evening dress of a brilliant hue, that is, blue or gold (Suga, 1996). The groom has fewer changes of dress, but would wear two ensembles corresponding to the traditional Japanese dress and tuxedo or other formal, Westernized dress (Figure 1.4).

## ANALYZING AESTHETIC RESPONSE

As mentioned earlier, we experience our aesthetic response through a three-way interaction of: (1) form, (2) viewer, and (3) contexts of viewing. Even though we can set aside or even ignore the influence of any one of these determinants, understanding the effects of each is critical to understanding our response.

### The Form

The **form** for our purposes is not limited to details of clothing, but includes the body and how the clothing and body interrelate. Viewing clothing details is necessary to our understanding, but the term "form" also refers to how

**FIGURE 1.4**

*Japanese wedding in Osaka, Japan, 1993. To understand the aesthetic response of those attending a wedding means learning about the customs and traditions of the culture. The clothing of the bride and groom is only one of several changes throughout the ceremony.*

Courtesy of Masami Suga.

details relate within the whole, which involves the interaction of the clothing with the body of the wearer, including body proportions, hair shape, skin texture, and color. The visual form is a whole with a structure of parts related to other parts. This includes not only color of jacket or the line of silhouette, but hair, skin, cosmetics, and shoes. All materials arranged on the wearer's body are considered, as well as manipulations and modifications of the body: shapes and sizes, textures and colors.

Form information includes both *figural*, that is, what is perceived and concrete, as well as *semantic,* that is, abstract information that gives meaning (Guilford, 1977). To describe a form, we traditionally speak of the particular lines, shapes, colors, and textures, such as those specific to swim- or skiwear, or we may even describe what we perceive in such terms as number of clothing items, that is, a three-piece ensemble of jacket, shirt, and trousers. Such details of the form are important to notice and describe. In addition, the interplay of the detail within the form needs to be considered for maximum understanding of the semantic information.

The form is defined by the interaction of lines, shapes, textures, and colors. The character of these details is critical in defining the form. For example, shapes with hard edges are perceived as different from shapes with soft edges (Figure 1.5a and b), one shape as different from many, a horizontal line as different from a vertical one. Such details combine in unique ways to become visual units within a whole. These units of perception are affected by such factors as number, size, and visual weight, which we will study in subsequent chapters.

A form is a distinctive arrangement of colors, textures, lines, and shapes that creates a particular and characteristic look. The visual result is this particular look, the style. **Style** is defined as the characteristic manner of expression, the distinguishing way in which the parts are put together. The term can define one form or imply repetition of several forms. Style can identify a category, such as the current fashion, the Italian style, or the traditional style of a particular culture, such as the saris of India. In this instance, use of the term "style" refers to a synthesis that becomes recognizable as a form pattern that persists through an accumulation of images. Thus, the assembly of details defines the parts, creates a look, an image, that is not defined by individual details alone. Though two leather jackets are the same in all details except the surface of one is brown and the other is black, the potential meaning is immediately different because of the cultural messages that result. For several decades wearing a black leather jacket has not been the same as wearing a brown leather jacket, despite their similarities. The black leather jacket may

a                                        b

**FIGURE 1.5A & B**

*Differences in visual effect based upon hard- and soft-edged shapes. The shapes with hard edges in Figure 1.5a contrast with the use of shapes with soft edges in Figure 1.5b. Think about the resulting contrasts and how they affect your aesthetic response.*

Courtesy of Fairchild Publications.

"There's the look. You know the look. There it is. *That* look."

### FIGURE 1.6

*An entire form is viewed as a whole and creates meaning differently than viewing any one of its details. Note the caption: "There's the look. You know the look. There it is.* **That look.** *" Viewing this overall look involves expressive and referential characteristics.*

*Drawing by Cline; © 1994, The New Yorker Magazine, Inc.*

### FIGURE 1.7

*Consider how you as the viewer describe in detail this apparel-body-construct. Does this description help you to become more aware of the form?*

*Designed by Giorgio Armani. Courtesy of Fairchild Publications.*

be associated with rebellion, conjuring up the 1950s images of Marlon Brando or James Dean, or more recently the combination of black and leather may also represent power, danger, mystery, or chic simplicity. They become something more when viewed together by the viewer; they become a whole form that is viewed and creates meaning differently than any one of its details alone (Arnheim, 1974). Thus, we often refer to the "look" (Figure 1.6).

Viewing the form in terms of its style includes consideration of its overall look that can derive from its expressive and referential characteristics. **Expressive characteristics** are the result of viewing the form features directly. *Expression* is defined as the external manifestation of states of mind, that is, that feeling of excitement or calmness derived from the features themselves. For example, we often feel excitement upon seeing red-orange, but in contrast we feel calm when we see light blue. Expressive features are those that arise directly from what we see in the form through a feeling that often emerges spontaneously and immediately without prior thought.

The form is also influenced by reference to semantic information that gives meaning. **Referential characteristics** are inferred relationships of the form that cannot be understood by directly viewing the form. They are known by indirect causes that arise because of shared values within the context of viewing. Such references may be symbolic within a culture. For example, in the Korean culture wearing rainbow colors in a striped sleeve pattern is symbolic of happiness, while rocks, cranes, and pine trees indicate the wish of a long life for the wearer. All of these symbols are related to the cultural priority for members to live long and happy lives (Geum and DeLong, 1992). While we can directly see motifs such as rainbow stripes, their meaning is not fully determined until this cultural reference is understood.

Look at a photograph with clear details of clothing, such as Figure 1.7, and describe what you see, giving as much information as you can. Consider how the form is viewed in terms of the whole, that is the style imparted.

Example: The form could be described as a man wearing a clothing ensemble consisting of several components: a black T-shirt, a middle-value vest, a jacket, and a pleated, full pair of trousers. His vest has a center front opening with all five buttons buttoned closed. The roomy jacket of the same value as the vest has a lapel but no collar. His hands are in his pockets, which further emphasizes the fullness of the trousers. The viewer can notice the play of light and shadow on the middle-value ensemble of jacket, vest, and trousers, contrasting with the dark hair slicked back and the dark T-shirt and shoes. His face is clean shaven and his hair is pulled to the back and tied at the nape of the neck. Expressive characteristics include a calm look defined primarily by similarity of the three parts of the ensemble and their integration by light and shadow, but also by the dark value found in the upper and lower extremities of the body, i.e., the T-shirt, hair, and shoes. The eye moves between the dark contrasts over the surfaces of the suit. All in all, the wearer seems to enjoy the way he looks. Referential character could include reference to the subtleties observed in the break from tradition: the texture evident in the three-piece suit and the variations from the traditional suit in the open, casual look of the jacket with lapels but no collar; the long, roomy, and comfortable-looking trousers; and the contrast of the dark T-shirt rather than the more traditional collared white shirt and contrasting tie. This ensemble gives meaning to the concept of soft tailoring for which the designer, Armani, has become famous.

*Application Exercise 1.4*

The study of aesthetics involves seeing and understanding sensory data about the form, taking in detail that can be described from direct observation, for example, the swishing movement of a skirt as the wearer walks by or the shape and color of a jacket on the body. It also entails value and meaning that one must understand indirectly by association. One's aesthetic response to the total form is focused upon its directly perceived features and indirectly experienced content.

## The Viewer

The **viewer** is the observer of the form. The viewer may be the wearer of a clothing ensemble looking in a mirror or the viewer of a form other than self, for example, a friend, stranger, photograph, or even a mannequin. We bring to this interaction both personal, individual traits and experiences, as well as those shared through our humanness and our position within a culture.

Individual viewer traits include those relatively stable and slowly evolving, as well as fleeting thoughts and moods. Stable traits include personality, age, gender, physical stature, stage of maturation, and special aptitudes. As an adult, a trait such as a person's height is quite a stable factor and can affect our viewing. A viewer who is small in stature may experience a tall form differently than a viewer who is as tall as the form being viewed. Other relatively stable traits include our accumulation of experience and education. Living and sharing certain experiences among those of similar age can result in similarities of response. However, such age-related perspectives need to be appreciated because they can create misunderstandings across generations if their origins are not understood.

Preference, or the favoring of one thing over others, is a part of our learned appreciation of clothing. Apparel preferences affect how we think about and behave toward our clothing. They develop from our combined knowledge, experiences, sensory perception, and expression of likes and dislikes. Ordinarily our preferences are stable yet slowly evolving traits.

---

**FIGURE 1.8**

*Guidelines for how we wear clothing are often learned from family members.*

CATHY © Cathy Guisewite. Reprinted with permission of UNIVERSAL PRESS SYNDICATE. All rights reserved.

Traits that change more rapidly include a person's interest and activity at the time of viewing, mood, likes and dislikes, and momentary expectations. Think how your perception changes if your mood is angry, fearful, proud, euphoric, or happy.

Expectations also enter into what we see. We anticipate based upon our past experiences. For example, our anticipation of the various seasons is influenced by our past experience of each season; similarly, we form anticipations of the various holidays within each season based on past experiences of them—our expectations of a coming Christmas or New Year's Day will be based on our recalled experiences of past Christmases or New Years.

Our response is interpreted through our ideology, a set of internal guidelines based on learned ways of doing, values, and resulting ideals. Such guidelines include how we desire to look and how we measure this. For example, our desired way to look could include consideration of body type, our personality, gender, age, and how we value the new versus the familiar. Such guidelines are comparatively stable; however, as we continue to see new forms we are introduced to new ideas, new ways of putting combinations together of textures, colors, proportions. If what we see over and over again differs from our internal guidelines, we eventually may expand or alter our guidelines to accommodate the differences. For example, our internal guideline may dictate the use of only one pattern with all of the other surfaces plain within an ensemble. However, if we see a number of examples of pattern combinations, such as in quilting or in sportswear, eventually our guideline may include certain combinations of patterns. Our personal expectations also gradually adjust to what we see.

Values as reflected through appearance may not be immediately apparent from observation alone, but upon reflection can become clear. For example, members of a group who wear particular clothing may exhibit their values through their appearances. Those who wear oversized, tattered, basic flannel shirts over blue jeans are making a statement visually, and they may be expressing an affiliation with a particular group. Upon further reflection, however, the values may be more complex than that. During the early 1990s such clothing was part of an appearance called the "grunge" look, so a person wearing such clothing may have been following fashion. But that person may also have worn such clothing because of a belief in recycling secondhand clothing, a disinterest in public display of the body, or an effort to protest commercialism. Values are seldom simple to uncover.

---

Think about a rule for putting together an ensemble that has guided you in the past (Figure 1.8). This is a personal guideline if you use it to compare with what you see. Do you find your guidelines changing over time? If so, how? Was this shared with family or friends or just personally useful?

Example: I learned not to combine plaids and stripes in the same ensemble, but as I see many examples of plaids and stripes together I alter my guideline. For example, plaid and stripe of the same colors and size or scale are acceptable to me.

*Application Exercise 1.5*

Though our personal guidelines help us to interpret what we see, we are often attracted to clothing that has some aspect that is new to us, that breaks with our expectations. This is why new colors and combinations are so important in defining a season or a year. Introducing small but apparent changes can disrupt our expectations and help to make us more aware without too much upheaval. However, because we often prefer the familiar, we may resist what is totally new or unexpected. We may respond most positively with just the right combination of the familiar and the new. This is our personal "cutting edge," so to speak, because the combination acknowledges the internal guidelines but breaks away to create excitement and new interest.

The **viewer as wearer** needs to be considered in the aesthetic response. These two perspectives of viewer and wearer are interrelated. The perspective of the viewer just discussed focused upon how the apparel-body-construct appeared visually. Some viewers appreciate clothing regardless of whether or not they would wear it. A fashion editor, however, probably would do well to consider personal wearability as less important than interpretation of the particular look for an audience. The perspective of wearer is concerned with experiences of wearing, that is, how clothing feels physically, how it moves on the body. The two perspectives may merge, that is, the wearer looking at himself or herself in a mirror may be considering both. Our experiences also influence merging the two perspectives by including both, such as how clothing looks like it feels on the body. Such mergers derive from past experience and influence response. Ultimately both perspectives need to be considered. Problems arise when both are not considered, such as when we try on shoes that are exquisite looking (viewer) but do not consider how physically uncomfortable they are (wearer).

## The Context

Two contexts that affect aesthetic response are the immediate physical surrounding and the cultural milieu that impacts our viewing. The **physical context** is simply the immediate physical space or environment and how all aspects of this space interact with the clothed body. This includes lighting that surrounds and affects viewing, as well as textures and colors of the surrounding space and their relationship to the silhouette of the apparel-body-construct, a reminder to pay attention to the entire unit we view. The **cultural context** includes date, time, and place, as well as the values and ideals of a society. A context shared among members of a society would be location within a country and time period. For example, those living in the Twin Cities of Minneapolis, Minnesota, and Saint Paul, Minnesota, share the physical context of climate and terrain that affect the clothing they wear. A number of winter activities, such as skiing, ice skating, and sledding, result in clothing forms that are prevalent in this area. In addition, those living in the

Twin Cities during a particular time have a number of similarities of cultural context, such as experiencing the same media, politics, activities, and events.

Many examples of the influence of immediate physical space can be cited. Looking in the mirror at yourself in a new clothing purchase while still at the store often differs markedly from the image you see when you try on the clothing at home. The fluorescent lighting and surroundings in a dressing room and such factors as a hasty try-on in the small space may create a distinctive in-store response.

The effect of the immediate physical space, including the surrounding area, the lighting, and neighboring objects, can be illustrated by the example of a man in a black suit and white shirt. If the suit appears within a dark background, similar to the dark surface of the suit, the silhouette edge would be less visible and therefore less noticeable. Because the white shirt would be the area of most contrast against the black lapels of the jacket, the upper center of the torso would attract attention. Boundaries between the silhouette and background influence the way the form is viewed in Figure 1.9. The similar white jacket and surrounding space create an undefined outline in the area of the upper torso. A more clearly defined boundary is the black pants contrasting with the surround, and the striped, black-and-white T-shirt contrasting with the open jacket and the head shape. These contrasts become more influential in viewing the structure of this apparel-body-construct and cause the viewer to concentrate more upon the body center.

The broader cultural context includes tastes, values, and timely uses of the visual form. Fashion has been valued in some cultures for a number of centuries. **Fashion** is a look, a style, identified as what is current with the times. It is what is recognized by people of a particular era to be an expression of their time. Consequently, the look must change regularly. If such a fashion context strongly influences our perceptions, we will discard clothing that we consider to be unfashionable. The clothing has not changed but the context has. Thus, fashion within a culture is a source of numerous referential characteristics of the form.

Today we call out-of-date clothing "vintage" when it is not yet antique but old enough to necessitate regaining its value to our eyes. An example would be a cocktail dress from the 1950s, like the one worn by Audrey Hepburn in the movie *Sabrina* (Figure 1.10). The original garments may be sought after for both historical value and as a current statement. Such a dress, once laid

**FIGURE 1.9**

*The way boundaries of the silhouette are variously defined influences the viewer: the relative lack of definition between the white jacket of the upper torso with the surround and the contrasting boundary of the black pants with the surround.*

Designed by Valentino. Courtesy of Fairchild Publications.

FIGURE 1.10

*Audrey Hepburn
played Sabrina in the
movie of the same
name. Her pixie
personality and
dresses such as this
one, with its perky
bows on either side of
a high, horizontal
neckline, were a
popular detail of the
1950s cocktail dress.*

Courtesy of The Kobal
Collection.

aside as out-of-date, is perceived with new appreciation. It becomes fashionable and may be identified with a revival of the cocktail party. Thus, what appears unfashionable at one point may become attractive again to our eye after a lapse of time. Then memory and current images change sufficiently to give us a different perspective. James Laver, costume historian and author, wrote that with the passage of time, our response to what our eye sees changes (Laver, 1945). Thus, we may consider clothing that is decades old to be beautiful.

This cultural context is more complex to comprehend and requires an ability to consider the pervasive but evolving influence of time upon the form characteristics. Consider the example of the tuxedo. Even though a tuxedo as a form is fairly constant through the twentieth century United States, the experience of this form has varied depending upon the occasion. In the nineteenth century, the tuxedo was introduced as an option to formal wear for men. Along with the form was a strict convention of where, how, and by whom it was worn (Russell, 1983). Today in U.S. society, the tuxedo is considered formal and is often worn to a formal event such as a prom. However, its form has changed somewhat; it can be worn in a number of colors and is often selected to coordinate with the colors of the man's partner, for example, a blue evening gown and a blue tux. Even though a man is expected to wear a tuxedo to a formal event, we might pay more attention to a man in a tuxedo in an unexpected informal situation, such as seeing a man in a tux at a shopping mall. We might even reason that this young man is going to a prom and just stopped off on his way to buy a forgotten item. In this way, our expectations shape our reactions when viewing clothing in a specific social context.

What about the category of formal dress, that is, clothing worn to a special, highly ceremonious social event? In other cultures such a formal category often exists. But formal dress may be defined quite differently. In some cultures "formal" is a reference to traditional dress; for example, the Kalabari in Port Harcourt, Nigeria, who wear their own version of formal dress (Figure 1.11).

Because our culture influences aesthetic response to such a great extent, learning about one's own history and roots provides a rich background for our understanding. Refer back to Figure 1.1 and consider the contexts of the immediate physical surroundings and the cultural context. The mood of the immediate surrounding is dark and romantic, with colors of the background repeating those of the dress. The shadows of the leaves in the background repeat the gold filigree of the neckline and floral swags on the skirt. The cultural context involves details that remind the viewer of a wedding—the veil, the full and attractive skirt that would certainly call attention to a bride. Designers of French couture often conclude a major showing of their work with a wedding gown—sometimes a magnificent tongue-in-cheek rendition, never seriously considered for actual wearing. Would this ensemble ever be worn for a real wedding? Consider the symbolism surrounding the wedding—the commitment of a couple to lifelong bonding for better or worse. What type of dress is desirable for such an occasion? Certainly the look here is one of such somber and ornate elegance that this ensemble could easily have been worn by royalty for a coronation. The wearer does look splendid and elegant, but almost untouchable. Compare this dress with the 1930s wedding dress in Figure 1.3. Both are visually stunning, but consider the meaning of a wedding within your present culture. Is there evidence in the details of these gowns that calls to mind a wedding? How would you consider each ensemble in the context of a present-day wedding where you live?

Visiting another culture and observing closely what people wear and how they wear it not only helps us appreciate that culture but also helps us gain perspective of the codes and conventions of our own culture. Each culture provides a unique context, and subgroups living within that larger group will

**FIGURE 1.11**

*What is defined as formal dress may differ from one culture to another. This Kalabari man and woman wear formal dress, which references traditions of their African culture.*

Courtesy of Joanne B. Eicher.

develop different expectations for clothing the human body, that is, differences in the presentation of the body, color and texture combinations, and expectations for combining ensembles. For example, in England black has traditionally been a color for mourning the death of a loved one, whereas in some Asian countries white is used for the same purpose. In Japan white is a symbol of death and for this reason is used for the initial stages of the traditional wedding ceremony in which the bride separates from her family of birth. Wearing white at first symbolizes the death of the bride from her family of origin and then, wearing a second colored kimono, she becomes reborn into her husband's family. Therefore, the same color—white—becomes a source of different associations of meaning in different cultures. An awareness of such differences can help identify the various cultural meanings of clothing. Such observations can only add to the richness of one's understanding of how humans respond aesthetically and stress the importance of learned contextual expectations associated with belonging to groups.

*Application Exercise 1.6*

Form, viewer, and contexts are three parts of the aesthetic response that interrelate and influence each other. Think of an example where the immediate context would influence the viewer of a form. Now think of how the form can influence the mood of the viewer as set by the context. For example, a festive occasion is often more memorable because of what we wear. Can you remember an occasion by the clothing you wore? Finally, describe a situation where you, the viewer, influenced the form, for example, helping a customer interpret the completion of an ensemble with a final accessory that helps focus and define it.

In summary, the aesthetic response needs to be approached through its intense, three-way interactions of form, viewer, and contexts. You need to understand your aesthetic response through your own perspective, but communicating with others requires relating to their perspectives as well. If you understand yourself first, you can learn to be mindful of the responses of others. If you recognize and understand their aesthetic responses, you can understand their decisions based upon their aesthetic goals.

## Summary

- The aesthetic response to dress is connected to what people evaluate as excellent and important. Aesthetics is highly influenced by the cultural context, including images of the historical past, and by the collective thoughts and feelings you share with others, as well as by personal feelings.

- Aesthetic responses to dress may be *subjective, objective,* or *concrete, abstract,* or a mixture.

- We experience the aesthetic response through the dynamic interaction of form, viewer, and contexts of viewing.

The *form* involves the clothing and the body and how they interrelate. A form is a distinctive arrangement of colors, textures, lines, and shapes that create a characteristic look. *Style* is the distinctive manner of expression, how the parts are put together. The *viewer* is the observer of the form. Viewers have preferences and both stable and momentary traits. Both the *physical* and the *cultural context* are important. *Fashion* is a look identified as current with the times.

## Key Terms and Concepts

aesthetic response
aesthetics
cultural context
culture
expressive characteristics
fashion
form

physical context
postmodern
referential characteristics
style
viewer
viewer as wearer

## References

Arnheim, R. *Art and Visual Perception: A Psychology of the Creative Eye,* 2nd ed. Berkeley: University of California Press, 1974.

Binkley, T. P. "Contra Aesthetics." In Weitz, M., ed., *Problems in Aesthetics.* New York: Macmillan, 1963, 80–99.

Cixous, H. "Sonia Rykiel in Translation." In Benstock, S., and Ferriss, S., eds., *On Fashion.* New Brunswick, NJ: Rutgers University Press, 1994.

Geum, K. S., and DeLong, M. R. "Dress as an Expression of Heritage: Exploring Korean Costume." *Dress, 19,* 1992, 57–68.

Guilford, J. P. *Way Beyond the I.Q.: Guide to Improving Intelligence and Creativity.* Buffalo, NY: Creative Education Foundation, 1977.

Henderson, B. "Teaching Aesthetics in a Postmodern Environment." In DeLong, M. R., and Fiore, A. M., eds., *Aesthetics of Textiles and Clothing: Advancing Multi-Disciplinary Perspectives.* Monument, CO: ITAA Publication No. 7, 1994, 1994.

Hollander, A. *Seeing Through Clothes.* New York: Viking Press, 1978.

Lachmann, R., ed. *The Encyclopedic Dictionary of Sociology*, 4th ed. Guilford, CT: Dushkin, 1991.

Laver, J. *Taste and Fashion*. London: Harrap, 1945.

Marshall, G., ed. *The Concise Oxford Dictionary of Sociology*. Oxford: Oxford University Press, 1994.

Morgado, M. "Coming to Terms with Postmodern: Theories and Concepts of Contemporary Culture and Their Implications for Apparel Scholars." *Clothing and Textiles Research Journal, 14*:1, 1996, 41–53.

Rubinstein, R. *Dress Codes: Meanings and Messages in American Culture*. San Francisco: Westview Press, 1995.

Russell, D. A. *Costume History and Style*. Englewood Cliffs, NJ: Prentice-Hall, 1983.

Suga, M. "The Japanese Wedding Package." Unpublished Ph.D. dissertation, University of Minnesota, 1996.

Tuan, Y. F. *Passing Strange and Wonderful: Aesthetics Nature and Culture*. New York: Kodansha International, 1995.

*Chapter Two*

# PERCEPTION: INTERPRETATION OF FORM AND MEANING

*After you have read this chapter, you will be able to understand:*

- The visual aspect of perceiving the apparel-body-construct, including the contributions of sensory data, past experiences, and education.

- The concept of visual part and the meaning of the Gestalt in relationship to perceiving the importance of viewing an item of clothing as a whole entity.

- How order is perceived, including the concepts of grouping and separating as they apply to the clothed body, and the perception of relationships in dress, including the figure-ground concept.

- The importance of shape, color, and texture in the clothing ensemble and the relationship of the body with clothing.

- The meaning of physical and cultural contexts.

- The importance of relationships of form and meaning within the apparel-body-construct.

A FULLY ARTICULATED AESTHETIC RESPONSE, BROADLY conceived, includes understanding your response based upon personal, shared, and cultural influences. When you consciously comprehend the viewing process, this sets the stage for subsequent steps in understanding the response process. You need to be aware of how you weave all these facets together.

In this chapter, terminology will be defined and the nature of the viewing process is discussed, focusing on the potential relationship between form and meaning. You will examine how form is perceived as a unique entity with elements and relationships that define and characterize your viewing experience. You will learn how meaning is derived from the form and its relationships to the viewer and to physical and cultural contexts.

## THE VISUAL ASPECT OF PERCEIVING THE APPAREL-BODY-CONSTRUCT

Perception is active and interpretive: We *actively* search for order and regularity through our sources of data. We *interpret* based upon the data. However, our senses do not necessarily provide us with a completely detailed and accurate picture of our world. For one thing, ordinarily we take in only a small amount of what is available for us to see, enough to negotiate and function within our environment. Seeing in order to understand a visual result is not usually our ultimate goal. Thus, the first step is to strive to understand and not take for granted what is seen.

Throughout this book we will use the term **apparel-body-construct** to refer to this form, the subject of our viewing. Apparel-body-construct is a term the author has posited. It is a construct defined as the way structural information is perceived and organized by the brain. The term serves as a reminder of the entire unit you will focus on, of the interaction of the body with the clothing assembled upon it. You will also be reminded to pay attention to the interaction of the viewer with the perceived form. This definition implies the importance of the interaction of the viewer with the form. In popular terms, the apparel-body-construct is the "look," the "presentation," or the "appearance" of the body, clothing, and accessories as a visual unit. Perceiving this unit involves relationships within the clothing ensemble itself and also those of the clothing to the body and to one's cultural context. Figure 2.1 illustrates relationships within the apparel-body-construct.

Data are received from three interrelated sources—our senses, our past experiences, and our knowledge or education (Myers, 1989). The first data, **sensory data,** are what we take in from the eyes (seeing), ears (hearing), nose (smelling), skin (touching/tactility), and mouth (tasting). Seeing, hearing, smelling, and touching are all used at various times while perceiving the apparel-body-construct, that is, in grasping its essential nature. Think of

### FIGURE 2.1

*Relationships in this apparel-body-construct are interactions within the clothing ensemble, the clothing to the body, and those of the cultural context. Within the clothing ensemble are the dark and soft pile surfaces, rounding shapes of the two-piece jacket and pants (i.e., buttons, collar), and the all-over motifs of the rounded teddy bear shapes in a lighter value. Interactions of the clothing to body are the continuation of the idea of soft and rounded with this child's small, rounded face and features and her hair pugs that somehow resemble the shaping of the head of the teddy bear she holds. By now the viewer has grasped the idea of the teddy bear repeated in several different ways, from more obvious to subtle. Contextual relationships include the wearer actually holding a teddy bear. But additionally knowing the cultural origin of the teddy bear enhances the pleasure in viewing this image. The teddy bear was named after Theodore Roosevelt, president of the United States from 1901 to 1905. The play with this consistent visual theme occurs within the clothing, the clothing to the body, and finally from the knowledge of the cultural context.*

Courtesy of Fairchild Publications.

instances when each sense might be used and when one sense is primary in perceiving the apparel-body-construct.

Data from our senses are related to our **past experiences**. We constantly compare what we presently view to past experiences stored in our memories. This memory storehouse is a remarkable, interwoven network. It is from this network that we respond with feelings such as familiarity and nostalgia, and with well-developed preferences for certain goods over others, and with ideas of what we have experienced that we want to repeat. Past experiences influence present expectations and these in turn influence our viewing.

Finally, **education** increases knowledge and the ability to respond. Knowledge provides information about and increased awareness of what we see. By increasing our perceptual abilities we learn what is important to focus upon in our response. For example, if you know who designed the apparel-body-construct you are looking at, and for what time period, you have greatly enriched your perception through education. You have learned two possible sources of consistency related to designer and historical time frame. You then have some knowledge that could influence not only this result but future experiences.

The three data sources—sensory data, past experiences, and education—are interrelated. For example, you can learn that certain color complements balance via sensory data and whether your eye will find the balance stimulating and satisfying based upon past experience. Thus, you perceive a visual scheme through your senses, and you understand its effect on you as a viewer based on education and prior experience.

## The Importance of the Whole

Visual perception is a repeated process of scanning and focusing. Human beings focus upon what separates from their field of vision, and that depends on the definition of form, its specific characteristics, and how they relate to potential meaning. Gombrich (1979) points out the importance of framing, or what we set apart for viewing and how that affects what we see.

Each feature of the form can be viewed and understood separately, but its significance is dependent upon the contextual relationships that in combination make for a unique whole. Once the whole is defined, what separates from the whole as a perceptual unit is defined as a visual part. An apparel-body-construct can have a number of visual parts. These parts are each composed of line, shape, color, and texture that initially provide definition and expressive characteristics such that the part is separated for viewing from the remainder of the apparel-body-construct. Thus, the visual part in Figure 2.2a is the center area of white in the upper torso that is surrounded by contrasting dark values.

*Application Exercise 2.1* | What could be changed about the visual part, the jacket in the apparel-body-construct in Figure 2.2a, to decrease its dominance as a visual part? What could be changed for it not to be perceived as a visual part at all?

The viewer must understand the elements of line, shape, color, and texture and the influence of each in defining the character of the apparel-body-construct. For example, think of the expressive difference in using the color red as contrasted with a tint of blue or the difference in using round or square shapes on the body. Though each element can be separated and described, its effect can only be fully appreciated by considering it in a particular instance, a particular whole. For example, imagine a sweater differing in only one feature from another sweater—the first is lime green, the second is black. This feature, color, is an elemental component that visually defines and characterizes the surface. The difference in this one feature influences not only perception of surface and its expressive character, but its relation to the whole. The viewer will relate each of the sweaters in a very different way within the whole.

Gestalt psychologists have stressed the importance of referencing the whole. A premise of the **Gestalt** is that the whole is more than the sum of its parts (Ellis, 1955). Taken together, parts influence viewing in a different way than each would separately. What we learn in the process of combining clothing separates into an ensemble is an experience of the Gestalt. For example, within one combination, a particular jacket blends with the trouser (Figure 2.2a) and in the other it stands out in contrast (Figure 2.2b). It is the same jacket, but the relationships to the whole make it appear differently. In Figure

2.2a, b, c, and d, the jacket is the same, but the relationship to the whole is different depending upon what is combined with it. The relationships among the parts characterize the structure of the whole.

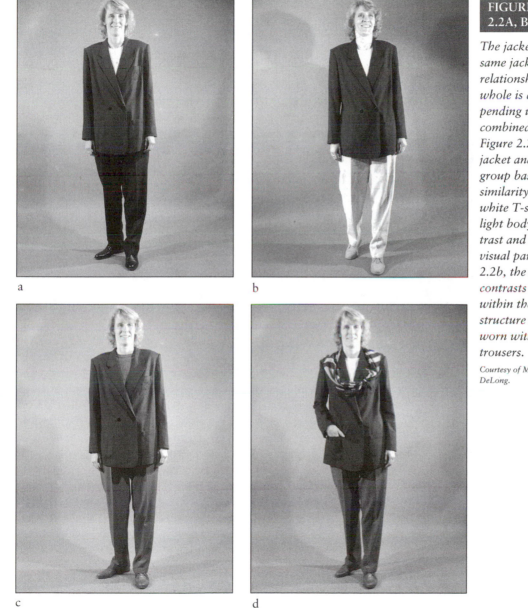

a

b

c

d

**FIGURE 2.2A, B, C & D**

*The jacket is the same jacket, but the relationship to the whole is different depending upon what is combined with it. In Figure 2.2a, the black jacket and trousers group based on similarity, and the white T-shirt and light body parts contrast and separate as visual parts. In Figure 2.2b, the jacket contrasts as a part within the whole structure because it is worn with white trousers.*

Courtesy of Marilyn Revell DeLong.

## Viewing the Structure of the Apparel-Body-Construct

How the viewer is attracted by, pays attention to, and then interprets the form depends upon its particular visual structure. **Structure** is defined as the way the parts are ordered within the whole. Perceiving the apparel-body-construct means perceiving structural relationships. The structure provides an essential function of the form. Since perception involves an insistence on taking in meaning, we strive to perceive the apparel-body-construct as an organized structure whenever possible.

We perceive the order of an apparel-body-construct based upon its structure. The visual effect is explained by the line, shape, color, and texture and by the way they combine to form parts. Structure is the way in which the parts are combined to give the apparel-body-construct its qualities as a whole, that is, its Gestalt.

We first notice contrast or change within our field of vision, for example, edges that contrast with the surrounding area. This could be the silhouette of the apparel-body-construct, if edges contrast to create a boundary with the surrounding area. We then search further for relationships, such as patterns that involve simple all-over repetition on the surface of a shirt or sequences such as rows of buttons. Gradually we take note of certain overall relationships provided by the structure. At first this needs to be deliberate, but eventually this will be part of a disciplined approach. As the eye notices more and more, it becomes educated to the details—size, length, color, texture—within the structure of the whole. For example, we may note the relation of the colors of fabric surfaces to the physical coloring of the wearer. Eventually, when looking at two images, the eye may compare the proportions of the one with the proportions of the other. Such self-education occurs when people take an intense interest in what they see and pay close attention to the form structure.

In Figure 2.3 the apparel-body-construct consists of an overblouse, pants, and a jacket. At first the viewer will most likely focus on the upper body because of the dark and round shaping of the head and hair and the surface texture, which is more visually definite in the jacket and overblouse than in the pants. The light and dark contrast continues in the remainder of the ensemble. The pants appear as similarly textured to the other pieces, but with less value contrast than the overblouse and jacket so that they appear related but not the same. Footwear is a sandal with two crossed straps that attract the viewer's eye.

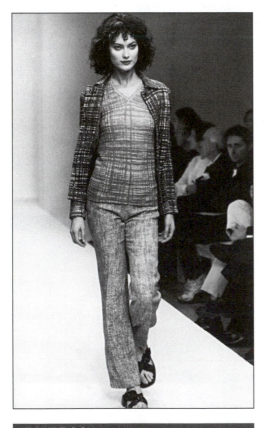

**FIGURE 2.3**

*A variety of relationships can occur within an apparel-body-construct.*

Designed by Prada. Courtesy of Fairchild Publications.

Relationships of angularity are created from the many lines within the garment surfaces, the sandals, the outline of the silhouette, and hemlines of the overblouse, jacket, and pants. Relationships also occur due to the roundness of the head and hair and the body. The body is perceived as rounding because of the all-over treatment of the surfaces, which causes the eye to be attracted to the three dimensionality of the body surfaces. Order of the whole is also perceived because of the dark and light contrast at the upper and lower body extremities of the head and face and the dark sandals crossing the light skin of the feet. Thus, many relationships contribute to the perception of the whole.

## Perceiving Order

Visual structure of the form is created by a specific arrangement of parts, perceived to be an organization, a composition, or a design. We strive to see the simplest and best organization possible and ordinarily are attracted to simple, unambiguous forms that can be interpreted in one way (Arnheim, 1974). For example, following signs on a freeway is a pleasure if they are simple and direct and a nightmare when they are not. In like manner, when we see an apparel-body-construct that is simple and direct, we often find an immediacy and pleasure in viewing it.

**Coherence** is how the unit holds together and is usually considered to be a highly desirable goal. Coherence is perceived as a consistent unity with enough variety to make it interesting. Perceiving such coherence of the apparel-body-construct can provide pleasure and satisfaction, often without our knowing what planning was involved in the design. Viewing the structure of the apparel-body-construct is diagrammed in Figure 2.4.

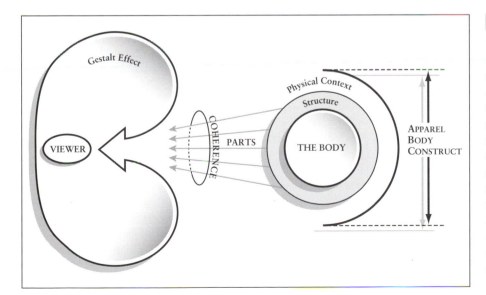

**FIGURE 2.4**

*Viewing the apparel-body-construct involves the body structure, the structure of parts, and the influence of the immediate physical context. The viewer who perceives this unit is influenced by the Gestalt effect, that is, the relationship of the parts within the whole unit.*

**FIGURE 2.4**

*Visual complexity and coherence can result from patterned surfaces. These young girls are dressed to celebrate their Igbo heritage.*

Courtesy of Janel Urke, 1996.

Coherence is not the same as simplicity, although most apparel-body-constructs that appear simple are coherent. Complexity can also relate to coherence because an apparel-body-construct with a precise visual order is often quite complex. But the ordering of the parts makes it simpler to view. When perceiving artistic forms, the viewer frequently enjoys those with a degree of complexity. In Figure 2.5 the surface patterns provide a degree of complexity while maintaining a consistent order upon the body.

## Ordering of Parts

Gestalt psychologists have identified very basic perceptual processes used in organizing a form. Our perception of structural coherence, the feeling we get of the order of the design, is a direct result of the way we view it. For example, because of the way the form is ordered, it is possible to suggest certain directions to lead the eye of the viewer throughout the form or to keep attention within a small, focused area. In Figure 2.6 the woman's sari has both dominant vertical lines of the silhouette and diagonal lines across the upper torso to direct the eye.

**Grouping** and **separating** are viewer activities in perceiving the form of the apparel-body-construct by its visual parts. Through the processes of grouping and separating, the viewer is directed to the visual relationships of the structure of the apparel-body-construct. These processes of grouping and separating are based on the premise that the viewer strives to perceive order at its most simple level (Arnheim, 1974). **Grouping** is what the viewer does when similar visual units are simpler to see together than separated. On the other hand, units may appear to **separate** into visual parts when that is the simplest organization.

In Figure 2.7, the silhouette is a definite boundary to frame the apparel-body-construct, and the eye follows the straight lines of this topcoat. Order in viewing the details of the coat strongly relates to the center: the double row of buttons march in groupings two by two up the front and then the six buttons may group as a long, vertical rectangle. The shirt collar is similar in width and color to the buttons, which provide a continuous line. In addition, the head forms a grouping with the collar because of similar color and width. Thus, the head and neck are grouped as a focal point and the remainder of the coat is viewed as separate.

A more complicated example of the perceptual processes of viewing structure is illustrated in Figure 2.8. Some units are grouping while others are sepa-

**FIGURE 2.6**

*(Above left) The woman wearing the Indian sari is pictured with a dominant vertical line of the silhouette and the diagonal lines of the crossover and banding provided by the fabric borders in the upper torso. Together these lines suggest a direction for the eye of the viewer.*
Courtesy of Hazel Lutz.

**FIGURE 2.7**

*(Above right) Order influences how we view. The straight lines of the silhouette are a boundary and frame, and the buttons and shirt collar provide a continuous center focus.*
Designed by Matthew Batanian. Courtesy of Fairchild Publications.

**FIGURE 2.8**

*(Left) The perceptual processes of grouping and separating occur within the apparel-body-construct.*
Designed by Donna Karan. Courtesy of Fairchild Publications.

rating and, what is more, some can interchange and be viewed alternately in one and then another relationship. The upper body provides focus with the dark and light contrasts of the scarf and the play of light on its surfaces. These are less defined than the definite shapes of the sunglasses, hair, and head, but nonetheless create a general attraction to the upper body.

On the lower body are dark leggings that primarily define the body outline. The close fit of the leggings is in contrast to the more bulky shape of the coat and its pile surface. Finally, the contrasting chain belt creates a horizontal line across the body, centered in the opening of the coat that relates to the glistening of the scarf, and a vertical line as it hangs downward. The belt's lighter value and contrast cause the viewer to search for additional relationships in viewing the whole, and the connection could be made with any or all of the following: the horizontal line of the neckline, sunglasses, and hairline or the horizontal line of the hem of the coat.

This process of grouping and separating needs to become part of the viewer's consciousness. For example, pockets that treat the left and right side of the body the same may be perceived as a grouping if they are simpler to see this way than separated and perceived as two parts. Grouping is automatic in perception. We do not have to be conscious of the process for it to occur. In Figure 2.8 there are many such relationships that are so obvious and automatic that the viewer must bring them to awareness to recognize them, for example, left and right legs with similar treatment and left and right hang of the scarf.

When the viewer focuses on a particular apparel-body-construct, the process of grouping and separating is taking place. This process occurs constantly, simultaneously, and automatically. Each time you group you also separate. We take for granted the process of grouping and separating and do not have to be conscious of the process for it to occur. But bringing the process to consciousness is necessary in order to understand how human beings organize visual information. This entails becoming aware of what is grouping and what is separating in the field of vision.

## Viewing Figure-Ground

A particular spatial relationship that is primary in our perception is the one of **figure** to **ground**. **Figure** is what we focus upon in the form. Figure is what has "thing" or "object" quality and appears to lie above or in front of the ground. It is also a visual part in our perception because it separates as a focus from its surroundings. **Ground**, in the figure-ground relationship, is what appears to lie around, behind, or under the perceived figure. Because ground does not have "thing" or "object" quality, it is not included in our conscious processing, unless we make it conscious.

For example, in Figure 2.9 the skin is revealed as figure because of the shapes of the neckline oval and head and their contrast with the lighter tank dress and coat. Though the viewer knows the dress may be perceived as figure in another body view, in this one the body parts are perceived as figure.

The figure-ground relationship is sometimes expressed as positive versus negative space. We constantly seek meaning by discriminating figure from ground, or positive from negative space. Separating figure from ground is essentially separating what has object quality and definition, as such, from what does not. When many parts are included, what becomes figure is essential to the grouping and separating processes. In addition, the relationship of figure to ground is considered in the perception of the "simplest" and "best" structure in the grouping and separating processes.

The brain ordinarily disregards whatever does not become figure. However, for the educated viewer, understanding the relationship means being aware of both—what becomes figure and what becomes ground. In addition, the educated viewer understands why. For example, in Figure 2.8 the figure is perceived in the dark hair, sunglasses, leggings and top, jacket or scarf and belt. By contrast, as shown in Figure 2.9, the skin is revealed as figure at the neckline oval and head, which contrast with the lighter tank dress and coat.

Any relationship found in a particular apparel-body-construct is important to notice. For example, the relationship of the surrounding space to silhouette affects the viewing of the form itself, but we rarely consider its influence separately. Thus, we usually focus on the apparel-body-construct or its parts as figure rather than the surrounding space as figure in the figure-ground relationship.

The figure-ground relationship can shift as we scan and focus in the process of perceiving the apparel-body-construct carefully. We may first view the entire silhouette as figure. Then we may shift and focus on a distinct part within the upper torso area as figure with the remaining upper torso as ground. Then the lower torso may become figure and the upper torso ground. Thus, what has figure quality in the process of looking can change. Some apparel-body-constructs are designed and organized to be perceived in alternative ways. For example, we first notice color relationships, then shapes, and these alternately become our focus in perception.

When figure and ground can be interchanged easily, the apparel-body-construct may be visually ambiguous. Usually we are first attracted to order that appears simple and has the least ambiguity. Then, if the apparel-body-construct captures our interest, we pay further attention and appreciate the complexity of other arrangements. Though such a design is just one organization, it can be perceived in a number of orderly arrangements. For example, in viewing this apparel-body-construct in Figure 2.10, we may first perceive the body-skimming jumper, the similar texture and value of the stockings and shoes,

**FIGURE 2.9**

*A figure-ground relationship is created by the body parts, ivory tank dress, and coat.*

Designed by Donna Karan. Courtesy of Fairchild Publications.

FIGURE 2.10

*An example of the figure-ground relationship of clothing and body parts that can be read as interchangeable.*

Designed by Isaac Mizrahi. Courtesy of Fairchild Publications.

and the coat worn off of the shoulders. However, upon further examination, the body parts, in their contrast with the clothing, can become figure.

A visual element is what separates figure from what surrounds it. A visual element can also be viewed within a grouping. For example, if the viewer focuses on three buttons in a row on a sleeve, they may be perceived first as a grouping of the three buttons and then each may be focused upon separately. Remember that at the same time the three buttons are being grouped, they are also being separated from the remainder of the sleeve.

## Viewing Relationships

**Relationships** are the important connecting links between elemental components and parts by which the viewer perceives the structure of a form. From the viewer's perspective, relationships within the apparel-body-construct can be directly perceptible and/or inferred. **Directly perceptible relationships** result from comparisons of the form itself with the elements within it. **Inferred relationships** depend upon what past experiences, knowledge, and expectations the viewer brings to the experience of seeing. Meaning results from connecting these directly perceptible and inferred relationships. In Figure 2.11 the directly perceptible relationships include the man in the khaki, body-skimming trenchcoat. He wears a dark suit and shoes and white shirt and tie, and he is carrying a camera. The woman, on the other hand, is wearing a blue, satin-weave coat and scarf over a long, red skirt. Both people have similar physical coloring, that is, dark hair. In inferred relationships, knowing that this is a Korean couple makes the viewer realize that both are wearing contemporary formal Korean dress. He is wearing Westernized business dress, and she is wearing Korean traditional dress consisting of an outer wrap, *chogori*, and *chima*.

*Directly Perceptible Relationships.* Lines, shapes, colors, and textures are all elemental components that are directly perceptible in the apparel-body-construct. Each element has many characteristics that are the source of relationships. Surface textures can be rough or smooth, matte or shiny. The eye connects many such elemental similarities as shiny with shiny. Lines can be straight or curved, vertical or horizontal, and they may exist in combinations such as straight and vertical lines or straight and horizontal lines. Lines and shapes are also related in characteristics such as position, size, and direction.

How viewers perceive the apparel-body-construct depends upon the relationships of contrast and similarity. Contrast is usually what we notice first. Such contrast often results in the creation of a visual part or element, that is, contrast is required for a visual part to be separated from the whole. A part that is separated from the whole causes the viewer to pause and focus his or her attention. Relationships of similarity are very satisfying to the viewer because of the visual linkages that result. Such linkages can be simple or more complex and can still be directly perceptible. Relationships of similarity are a source of coherence because they can connect the parts within the whole. In Figure 2.2a the black jacket and trousers group based upon similarity and the white shirt is a separate contrasting part that becomes figure, along with body parts, in the figure-ground relationship. In Figure 2.2b the contrast of values of light and dark create a part that can appear as figure interchangeably, i.e., the black jacket or the white trousers and T-shirt can become focus. But in either interchange, the white parts are grouped.

The relationships among parts cause them to group and separate. There is, however, another way to consider relationships in terms of their potential for ordering the whole. They can be repetitive, sequential, or hierarchical. Parts that are perceived as the same or similar can be **repetitive**, such as a textile pattern that includes a number of similar small motifs. Sometimes a simple motif that is repetitive will be grouped with other such motifs. We note one motif and then the remainder repeat in an overall figure-ground relationship. Repetition is often satisfying to the viewer because the eye moves from one motif to another; this movement is sometimes called rhythm. Repetition can also occur with other attributes of surfaces and edges. Parts are perceived as **sequential** where they share common traits and are thereby ordered because of their shared commonalities. An example is shapes that are similar in many respects, that is, they occupy a similar amount of space, but due to the placement on the body they are perceived in an ordered way. The reason for order may be inherent in the parts, for example, shapes varying from larger to smaller perceived in order of size. Parts can also be **hierarchical**, that is, they may be arranged in ascending or descending order, where one part is perceived as having more visual importance than another. For example, in Figure 2.2d the head and neck area are important visually. In examining why this is so, the viewer can take note of the relationships of similarity—color of hair and scarf motif and

**FIGURE 2.11**

A Korean couple in contemporary formal dress. The man is wearing Westernized business dress, while the woman is wearing Korean traditional dress consisting of an outer wrap, chogori, and chima.

Courtesy of Marilyn Revell DeLong.

trouser that group together. Figure 2.2d, however, differs from Figure 2.2c in that a hierarchy is created in Figure 2.2d, including the color grouping of the head and neck area.

Let us consider the three types of relationships, using a jacket as an example. Imagine the surface has a checkered motif woven in black and white, repeated throughout the body of the jacket (*repetitive relationship*). A series of five buttons on the jacket front closing may be perceived in a row from top to bottom, moving from the one at the neckline to the one at the hem. But they may also be perceived in reverse, from bottom to top. In other words, the order is not set by either the buttons or their placement alone (*sequential relationship*). The jacket lapels are black and the pocket flaps are the same black-and-white checkered motif as the remainder of the jacket. Thus, the contrasting lapels are perceived before the pocket flaps because they have more visual importance (*hierarchical relationship*).

In the process of organizing, one part may be perceived in several ways. In the jacket example imagined previously, the buttons are considered at two levels. At one time the buttons are perceived as a group of five, but if they were all brass, they may also become part of the hierarchical order of details. For example, we could view the jacket in this order: (l) lapels, (2) brass buttons, (3) pocket flaps. In Figure 2.12 the relationships of the narrow stripes are repetitive upon first consideration. But they are placed upon the body in such a way that they interact with the silhouette, making each stripe different in length. A sequence is created with the narrower stripes and wider white strip outlining the neck, sleeve, and hem of the dress. The viewer perceives a hierarchy of the light colors with the dark because of the figure-ground ambiguity of viewing light on dark and then viewing the dark areas as figure. As you scan the whole image, your eye perceives the dark areas as figure and this creates a hierarchy of large, dark areas in the upper torso and a smaller area of dark at the hemline. The sunglasses and beret cue us into this ambiguity. If your eye first takes in the beret, it is led to the shapes created by the silhouette and the narrow shoulder area. Conversely, the sunglasses suggest the dark as figure and lead your eye throughout the dark areas.

**Gradation** is a term used for a series of just-perceptible steps in the variation of elemental aspects of the apparel-body-construct, such as line, shape, color, or texture. An example of a relationship based upon gradation includes shapes varying in measurable quantity—in size or number. A set of nested measuring cups would exemplify the notion

## FIGURE 2.12

*The relationships within one apparel-body-construct can be perceived as examples of repetition, sequence, and hierarchy. Repetition is in the width of the horizontal stripes, sequence is in the two widths of the stripes, and hierarchy is in the variously sized areas of dark, including the beret and sunglasses to cue us to the dark areas.*

Designed by Yves Saint Laurent. Courtesy of Fairchild Publications.

of gradation when placed in a row according to size. As the viewer perceives a gradation within the apparel-body-construct, the eye will strive to complete the sequence and so will move along from one step to the next.

In the apparel-body-construct, sensory data presented in an orderly arrangement are called a *sensory scheme*. Sensory schemes are created through relationships of attributes. Hues can be presented in a natural array as they appear adjacent on the hue circle, of yellow to orange, then red, purple, blue, and green, coming full circle back to yellow. In this order, a sensory scheme of closely related hues is presented, a rainbow effect.

The range does not need to represent the complete array, but it must be in sequence to be perceived as a gradation. For example, color has attributes of hue, value, and intensity, all of which can provide order. Color *value*, the lightness-darkness attribute, can provide sequence through a range of pink to red to maroon or vice versa. A gradation may exist upon the surface of a dress, such as a striped pattern moving from light to dark. Sometimes this is called an *ombre effect*, which means shadowing. Within an apparel-body-construct, gradation provides order. For example, the gradation may begin with light-value skin and hair at the top, gradating to medium-value shirt and dark-value trousers and shoes and stockings. Location within the apparel-body-construct influences how we direct our viewing and is a powerful influence in viewing the whole. Figure 2.13a and b illustrate a variety of sensory schemes of gradation and contrast along with an example of grouping and segregating visual units.

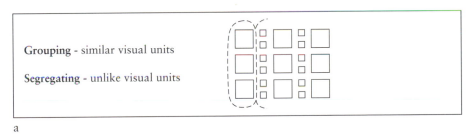

a

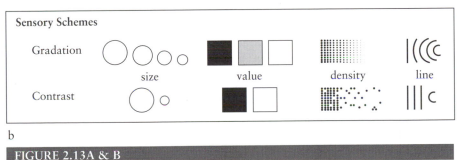

b

**FIGURE 2.13A & B**

*A variety of sensory schemes, a grouping of similar visual units, and separation of unlike visual units.*

*Inferred Relationships.* Inferred relationships are not directly perceptible but are nonetheless a vital link in understanding the apparel-body-construct. Inferred relationships range from simple—for example, a star shape may be related to a flag and patriotism—to more complex—for example, the relationships of certain body proportions to the ever-changing ideals of body appearance. The latter might be the relation of torso and leg lengths to hip and waist circumferences that change over time. Inferred relationships are based upon a viewer's past cultural experiences. In Figure 2.14 a man and woman, a married couple from Nembe, stand in front of their house. While the proportions of lengths and widths of each ensemble differ when compared, the proportions are nonetheless typical for their respective genders within the cultural context.

Understanding inferred relationships requires knowing something about cultural context. Relationships that are directly perceptible can be linked easily within the form structure, but inferred relationships may be as elusive as trying to determine exactly what provides pleasure and satisfaction. In this way they can reflect past experiences and, at the same time, influence present expectations. For example, as shown in Figure 2.8, the idea of wearing leggings with a jacket is a common enough experience that many viewers within the United States are not surprised at the combination. What people pay attention to is often related to cultural expectancies—for example, a certain look is predictable when often met within our cultural experience, but we may be surprised when we see one that is not.

An inferred relationship can involve the association of a particular form structure with an activity. Think of some events you attend and what you would consider an appropriate apparel-body-construct at that event: a tennis match, a movie, the theater, a birthday party, a vacation. Specific social expectations accompany each event. Think about what you take for granted. Many factors come to mind. What is appropriate can also depend upon a person's role at that event. Expectations are also related to place and time, for example, a July vacation on a warm beach as contrasted with one in a large city.

All of these examples are translated into our perception of the form and potential inferred relationships. In advertising media, such relationships are often emphasized in a planned theme so that the person interprets the apparel-body-construct within that designated theme. For example, a model in a swimsuit is pictured in a catalog in a tropical setting with the caption, "Come to the Islands." The tropical theme is carried through in the description and even the colors are named for tropical fruits, like passion pink or pineapple yellow. What the viewer desires—imagining himself or herself taking a tropical vacation in the middle of a harsh winter—has appeal within that context.

**FIGURE 2.14**

*This couple from Nembe are wearing traditional dress in differing proportions that are typical for their respective genders.*

Courtesy of Barbara Sumberg.

Select an apparel-body-construct. Examine it for as many relationships as you can find. Then sort out those that are directly perceptible and those that are inferred. Explain the difference. How might a person from another culture interpret each type of relationship?

*Application Exercise 2.2*

## Where to Find Relationships Within the Apparel-Body-Construct

Relations of the part to the whole can occur between the entire form (the apparel-body-construct) and the immediately surrounding space, between the clothing and the body, and between the units within the clothing ensemble. These are all directly perceptible relationships. To consider the extent of the possible relations, the viewer must adopt as a frame of reference the apparel-body-construct in its entirety (Figure 2.15). If taking note of all of the relationships of the apparel-body-construct is not a viewing habit, then learning to do so will require a conscious effort.

*The Clothing Ensemble.* There are many potential visual relationships within the clothing ensemble itself. Surfaces can be related by any of the elements—line, shape, color, or texture. It is useful to begin with one element first, such as shape. Clothing shapes are created by cut and fabric manipulation and include collars, sleeves, cuffs, and pockets. Shapes can originate from gathers or pleating and the play of light and shadow on the fabric surfaces as they drape on the body. Shapes are also created by motifs printed on the surface of fabrics, such as dots, stripes, or floral motifs.

Shapes can be related in many ways: in their angularity, roundness, size, direction, or location on the body. Shapes can be combined through the use of collars, sleeves, and cuffs put together into a shape we call a jacket, blazer, or shirt. A jacket is also related to other garment categories that combine to make a suit, such as to a shirt, a skirt, or shoes, all of which provide their own shapes. Shapes can then be related and noted as to their proportions when placed together.

In addition to shape, line, color, and texture can have potential interrelationships within the apparel-body-construct. The colors, textures, lines, and shapes of clothing can group or separate. An example of grouping is shown in Figure 2.16 where six buttons are spaced at center front. They appear to group as a

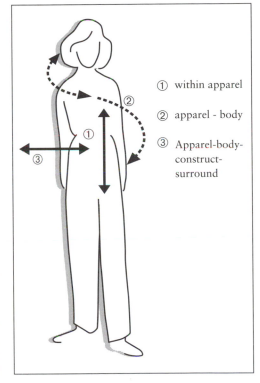

① within apparel

② apparel - body

③ Apparel-body-construct-surround

**FIGURE 2.15**

*Where to look for relationships within the apparel-body-construct: within the apparel, between the apparel and the body, and between the apparel-body-construct and the surround.*

**FIGURE 2.16**

*Spacing of six buttons both vertically and horizontally influences how they will be perceived. Similarity of width of buttons and spacing at the neck area create a grouping.*

Designed by Nautica. Courtesy of Fairchild Publications.

rectangular shape in Figure 2.16. Depending upon the spacing, they can appear more as horizontal pairs of buttons (as in Figure 2.7). These buttons can also relate to other features. For example, in Figure 2.16 the area created by the neck and filled in with the shirt and tie contrasts with the dark coat lapels but is similar in width to the double row of buttons. The similar value of the dark coat and hair create a continuous line, especially because of the way the hair is shaped to frame the face to continue the lines of the coat collar. The light skin can group with the similar value shirt and can be perceived as a unit. In addition, the light value of the trousers and buttons keep your eye moving in a vertical direction. In the process, parts are grouping and separating within the whole. For example, the buttons are easily perceived as figure, and then the grouping of the neck and head also become figure in their relationship with the buttons. However, when the coat is perceived as figure because of the strong silhouette, the hair frame also becomes figure and the remainder of the apparel-body-construct is ground.

*The Clothing and the Body.* An understanding of the apparel-body-construct includes an awareness of the interaction of clothing with the body attributes, which also have their own line, shape, color, and texture. Any element can be a source of relationships. For example, the shape of hair adjacent to a jacket with a neckline of a similar shape or a vertical line of buttons down the center front of a jacket can repeat body verticality.

Noting such relationships between clothing and body is rewarding. When a person tries on clothing and stands before the mirror, he or she may recognize that by comparison one garment is more attractive on the body than another, but may never think about the association explicitly. The surfaces placed upon the body can interact with the body surfaces through color or texture. Likewise, the lines and shapes interact with those of the body. Clothing can be perceived as a grouping with body parts or as separating from body parts. In Figure 2.17 a grouping of the hat and collar with the face is created because of the continuation of the line of the collar with the hat. The similarity of round shape, value, and texture aid in this process. Separation of the full skirt with the legs occurs with the young girl in the center because of the contrast of horizontal hemline with the vertical lines of the legs. However, the separation is not extreme because of the light value of the stockings, shoes, and skirt.

A sensitivity to the interactions taking place between body and clothing can be encouraged. A black jacket and dress will not look the same next to

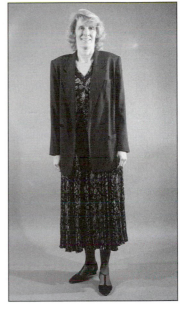

**FIGURE 2.17**

*This apparel-body-construct illustrates how clothing and body parts can group and separate. For the model in the middle, the similar light value used throughout and the similar rounded shapes of the collar, hat, and hemline help to create a grouping. A separation occurs at the hemline due to the contrast of the line of the hem and the legs. For the model on the left, the buttons and draping of the coat fabric create a more vertical line of the coat with the legs and feet.*

*Courtesy of Fairchild Publications.*

**FIGURE 2.18**

*A dress and jacket of similar dark-value group will create soft edges between surfaces. The contrasting light hair and skin create a part.*

*Courtesy of Marilyn Revell DeLong.*

different body colors. On a model with dark hair and skin, the surfaces of hair, skin, jacket, and dress would be similar in value and would create a soft edge between the surfaces. The silhouette of the apparel-body-construct would offer a continuous and defined outline of hair and dress. In another instance, the identical black ensemble is worn by a different model with blonde hair and light skin. The similar hue and value in hair and skin contrast with the black surface of the jacket and dress, and the hair and skin create a more definite edge and separation from the dress, as in Figure 2.18.

It often helps to envision the effect of one item in its relation to others and as they would be positioned on the body. Awareness of the visual interactions helps in the imaging process. The selection of a belt for a specific visual effect provides an example. The belt can be considered in combination with other items to be worn, such as shoes and trousers. The viewer considers how the belt will be viewed, perhaps as a focal point because of its size and contrast as in Figure 2.8, or perhaps with the buckle and leather belt portion blending with the shirt, or the belt may relate to a body part, such as the color of the belt in relation to the wearer's hair. A belt may be a source of focus or a background item that only varies with texture—a smooth matte leather with the same color wool trousers. It may function as a part of the visual structure of the apparel-body-construct as well as serving to hold up the trousers, or it may function only to hold up the trousers. The placement of the belt, along with its color, size, and texture as related to the body and clothing, all affect how we view the apparel-body-construct.

## The Contexts

The context includes, first, the immediately adjacent physical space, which affects how we view the apparel-body-construct. Second, the cultural context includes the viewer's cultural knowledge and past experiences and also affects how the apparel-body-construct will be perceived and interpreted.

*The Physical Context.*  An important visual relationship while viewing the apparel-body-construct is the one with the immediately adjacent surround. This spatial orientation of the apparel-body-construct is directly perceptible but nevertheless difficult to keep in mind. At first it may seem unnatural since we must scan the outline, or silhouette, to perceive the apparel-body-construct as figure. Scanning requires observing the nature of the adjacent area because of its effect on the definition of the apparel-body-construct. For example, a mostly white apparel-body-construct would have a different sort of boundary—and therefore visual impact—when the space surrounding it was also white as opposed to a contrast of green or black.

Much of the visual impact of the apparel-body-construct at a distance derives from the frame created by the silhouette. The apparel-body-construct can be visually separated from the immediate background or can seem to blend with the space around. A boundary can also seem to disappear at times because of a blending of two adjacent surfaces. This phenomenon is known as "vanishing boundaries." For example, a chameleon has the capacity to change its body color to blend with its environment and become virtually undetectable. If the apparel-body-construct is viewed as separated from adjacent space, it must have distinct boundaries or edges. The difference in viewing a visually distinct silhouette can be due to the character of the silhouette or may be the result of the relation of the apparel-body-construct to the space around it. Either the form or the space can be manipulated. In Figure 2.19 the form and surrounding space on the left are similar in value and consequently the silhouette is not defined for the viewer. However, on the right side, the jacket silhouette is distinctly defined against the lighter surround.

The relationship of silhouette to surrounding space is a powerful influence on viewer perception and is controllable in a photograph or other staging of

**FIGURE 2.19**

*On the left side, the jacket visually blends in with the immediate background. On the right side, the sleeve of the jacket is distinctly defined against the lighter surround of the tree trunk. This difference in viewing the apparel-body-construct creates visual interest and a focus upon the contrast of the vest, shirt, and tie at the body's center.*

Courtesy of Fineberg Publicity.

the apparel-body-construct. For this reason photographers and theatrical designers are particularly aware of the surrounding space and its relation to the apparel-body-construct. In fashion photography, a silhouette is often set apart from an appropriate context to draw attention to the clothing. In the theater, the character we are supposed to attend to is often set apart within the context. For example, the actor pausing before a brightly lit doorway is framed just as he enters.

In everyday situations, surroundings are not controlled, but it is useful to consider the apparel-body-construct as it would fit into its most likely setting. For example, a dark business suit with its straight and vertical lines usually has a defined, hard-edged boundary as its silhouette. The typical surrounding space is a light-to-medium value office setting, and this provides enough of a contrast to create a distinct silhouette most of the time. However, the surroundings for an evening of dancing with dimmed lighting and evening attire can include soft boundaries and some blurring of the silhouette.

Some apparel-body-constructs involve extremes in the surrounding spaces they are likely to occupy. For example, the silhouette of a ski suit composed of dark-value surfaces looks quite different on a snowy slope from how it looks in a dimly lit ski lodge. In the former instance, the silhouette is a sharply defined boundary against the snow, and in the latter, softened and perhaps even blurred and indistinguishable at times.

*The Cultural Context.* The cultural context includes relationships that arise from the cultural milieu, that is, those relationships to people, time, and

*Color is often related to time of year. For example, this suit looks more like spring in a four-season climate than the suit in Figure 2.2a.*

Courtesy of Marilyn Revell DeLong.

place. Cultural context is an inferred relationship. Colors can visually go together and connect by both formal elements, that is, what is there and directly perceptible but also connect because of meaning—earth tones are muted hues found in nature. We label other combined colors with meaning: ice cream sherbet colors, colors on the dark side, colors related to gender, colors related to time of year, colors fashionable this season. Colors in Figure 2.20 could relate to time of year in a four-season climate. In Figure 2.20 colors are light for spring as compared with colors on the same model in Figure 2.2a that appear darker for winter. Some of these may be common across cultures, but some are unique to one culture.

Another level of complexity within the apparel-body-construct is meaning that would derive from knowing the subtle differences in how and where to wear clothing. Think of the changes that have occurred in a work image and casual image in the twentieth century in the United States. Close your eyes and imagine an apparel-body-construct that is defined by the places where you live and work that would be appropriate as a work image. Think about how that image has changed over time within your culture. Knowing in this instance means recognizing subtleties within the cultural context.

We tend to notice what is familiar, especially if it has a touch of unfamiliarity, and take note of similarities and differences. When we see something new, however, we may compare what we see with our mind's images and ideas and find it puzzling.

## THE MEANING ASPECT OF PERCEPTION

The same visual stimuli that give character to the form also provide meaning. All apparel-body-constructs are made up of both the form structure and meanings that derive directly or indirectly from their features and relationships (Hillestad, 1994). Understanding the structure of the apparel-body-construct and recognizing how the viewer makes relationships that provide meaning is vital information for understanding aesthetic response.

Form consists of interrelated components that define surfaces and edges which create structure and directly perceptible meaning. At the individual level, such meaning may be a stated preference—for example, "I like this"— whereas at the collective level many relationships may create a shared inferred interpretation—for example, "This is up-to-date." Directly perceptible and inferred relationships prevail at both individual and collective levels. Meaning can be a response from any one or a combination of these perspectives.

Meaning associations range from direct sensory experiences—for example, this is red (visual) and is exciting (meaning)—to more indirect and abstract ones—that is, this looks like a new trend. Deriving such indirect meaning requires an astute ability to recognize the right form relationships in reference to time and place. In a variety of ways we associate meaning with visual forms. Even though surfaces and shapes are automatically perceived and identified as shoes, fur, apples, and people, our responses are specific to the contour, shape, size, color, and movements. We do not confuse a shirt with an apple; neither do we need to see them in any detail to recognize them. What we do is learn those salient cues that define shirt and apple and match them with our mind's images of shirt and apple. We then respond from our categories of what forms constitute shirts and apples.

We are aware of visual information that has meaning to us. Perception is creating or attaching meaning to what we notice through our senses. This involves the recognition and naming of what we see. To recognize and name what we see involves our past experience, that is, comparison with images stored within our memories. As previously stated, each of us has a collection of accumulated mental images from our past experiences that serves as a defining model which evolves with experience and knowledge. We match what we see with such definitive models. For example, such a mental image could be proportions that are fashionable this year.

A primary way that we learn about things and objects in our environment is not only recognizing and naming them, but also classifying them. This is a basic way to provide meaning. Each of us uses many categories that are both personal and collective. Categories are individually and culturally based. For example, we may categorize clothing based upon the part of the body on which it is worn. For example, shoes, sandals, boots, and rollerblades are all worn on the feet; trousers, shorts, skirts, and sarongs are worn on the lower torso. We categorize clothing according to the sequence of layers on the body. For example, underwear includes T-shirts, briefs, and hosiery, while outerwear includes jackets and topcoats. We further categorize based upon place and event, generally as formal, casual, or, specifically, as something to wear home to visit family. We are more comfortable with the familiar rather than the unfamiliar in terms of people, places, and events in clothing selections. Personal categories may include categories related to excellence, quality, what you like to wear, and what you do not like to wear. Your categories may not be identical to those of your friends, but they are basic to your understanding of clothing. You accumulate them from childhood through adulthood and change them when the category no longer works for you. They provide information for your memory storehouse, and you continue to learn based upon your categories.

Think of categories into which you organize your clothing. If this is difficult, begin thinking about one ensemble of clothing in your closet. In what ways do you think about and categorize it? Then examine several ensembles and consider further the categories into which they fall. What do you learn about your clothing from the way you categorize it?

*Application Exercise 2.3*

When we create a category from a formula based upon too broad a generalization, we often call it a stereotype. **Stereotypes** are a particular category where the same repeated action is produced from a set of cues that may not be sufficient. When we do not see nuances or small differences in an object, we classify broadly rather than from an awareness of what makes the difference. The stages from unfamiliar to familiar may be marked by a series of stereotypes in the learning process. There is, however, a danger in not noting the nuances or small differences in creating a formula or category too prematurely. This stops awareness and stifles creativity.

Form structure and meaning are intimately interacting and interconnected. Many examples illustrate the connections of meaning with directly perceptible features. For example, a youthful apparel-body-construct may call to mind smooth textures, intense or contrasting colors, and many small interdependent parts that result in much visual activity as the eye moves from one part to the other.

Some viewers are more aware of the form, being attracted to specific colors, textures, or lines and shapes within the clothing. Other viewers may be less aware of the interrelationships of form and meaning and immediately look for message. They believe they make a statement with their clothing first before connecting the form with that message and may only concern themselves with the form if it underscores the desired meaning. An example is the viewer who, upon viewing an apparel-body-construct, immediately responds by saying, "But it is so richly elegant!"

Relationships need to be considered in the process of learning about and interpreting visual forms. Such associations can be relatively simple when confined solely to identification of an apparel item, as when we name and categorize according to structure and what body part is covered. For example, the term "blazer" refers to a type of covering for the upper torso with specific tailored lines and shapes. Associations, however, can be complex when expanded to include an inferred relationship between the apparel-body-construct and the cultural context (O'Neal, 1994). With an example of the T-shirt, a relatively simple visual structure, associations can include who wears it in your society and connotations that reference the specific wearer. Thus, the T-shirt may include not only descriptive, identifying features, including what is printed on it, but also call to mind an image of ways of wearing it and with what. For example, one student may wear the T-shirt with jeans, another adds a blazer, while someone else wears it with a two-piece suit.

Meanings for a specific feature can be both individual and shared. You may have a category called "favorite color," and blue is at the top of the list. You may be quite specific as to its exact hue, value, and intensity. Not everyone shares this same blue as a favorite color, yet many have "favorite color" as a category in their memory storehouses. If a poll of "favorite colors" were taken, you probably would find certain ones favored by many individuals within a given culture. Though a favorite color is an individual matter at one level, the idea or concept of favorite color is a shared experience at another level of category. Meanings are shared because they are connected to our humanness and to our culture.

We must relate form and meaning each time we see an apparel-body-construct, not only meaning inherent in the form structure, which is directly perceptible, but more complex interactions from inferred associations with our environment or culture. Categories of people who become known by what or how they wear clothing can create shared mind images, like Jackie Kennedy or Mamie Eisenhower in Figure 2.21. Some of these images from one culture become recognized in others as well, but often they are primarily understood within the culture of origination.

Two designers, Anna Sui and Arnold Scaasi, provide examples of contrasts in their work that are directly perceptible in the form as well as inferred from their design intentions (Orlean, 1994). Each has a different idea of how the modern woman should look. Compare a Scaasi design with a Sui design in Figure 2.22a and b. Scaasi states that he designs clothing to "make a woman look beautiful." Thus, he has become a master at designing evening gowns, draping sumptuous columns of silk jersey to fall regally to the floor and show off the curves of the body or enfolding the body in cascades of tulle. On the other hand, designer Anna Sui greatly admires teenage girls, and she considers it a high compliment for her clothing to be called "so teenage girl." She describes her clothing as sassy and cute with features that reflect nostalgia for past eras like the decade of the seventies.

Not all cultures have the same beliefs and values. Thus, ideals in appearances also vary from culture to culture. In some cultures, the relationships of formal aspects of the apparel-body-construct do not seem as important as their meaning in combination. For example, Michelman and Eicher (1995) found in their

**FIGURE 2.21**

*Consistency and distinctness in the dressing patterns of Mamie Eisenhower and Jacqueline Kennedy were easily recognized and referenced as shared images of the 1960s.*

*Courtesy of Fairchild Publications.*

FIGURE
2.22A & B

*In Figure 2.22a, Arnold Scaasi believes that he designs to make a woman beautiful. In Figure 2.22b, Anna Sui designs clothing to look "so teenage girl."*

a                                                    b

research in Nigeria that fabric surfaces were combined within an ensemble because of their similar cost. In the United States, surface combinations are seldom based on cost similarity; rather surface combinations are considered in combination more according to their visual effect and spatial orientation—in combination they may blend or create contrast and focus.

The degree to which an experience is shared is the amount of communication that will take place. The role of shared knowledge within a culture is vital to understanding. We need to consider how our experiences are shared with others. For example, we may personally abhor blue. Blue may be associated with a bad experience, and every time it appears it triggers the bad experience. This is a personal mental image, because not everyone has that feeling. In other words, another viewer will not experience blue in the same way. On the contrary, blue is a relatively desirable hue to most viewers and usually does not elicit such negative feelings. A cultural preference for blue is apparent when a foreigner travels to the Scandinavian countries, as this color is used in many public interior spaces.

Meanings evolve and change with time and circumstance. For example, the Beatles haircut was worn primarily by youth in the 1960s, but the cultural associations have changed as the hair length became more acceptable to a variety of ages. Royal blue was originally a color worn primarily by royalty.

Today the chief among the Nembe of Nigeria wears a white robe. Velvet, the pile fabric considered luxurious at an earlier time, was limited in who could wear it as dictated by sumptuary laws in the sixteenth century. In the twentieth century, velvets became a source of widely available sensuousness and were used for trim or full garments (Lutz, 1994). Traditionally, fabrics such as satin that are shiny or cast light and shadow are used for more formal, "dressed up" affairs, while fabrics such as denim are used for more casual, "dressed down" affairs. Previous to 1960, they would not have been considered in combination—their meaning associations were so different. In the past 20 years, however, we have witnessed the combination of satin with blue denim as a textural variation.

| | |
|---|---|
| Any visual artist attempts to engage the viewer in an emotional experience. The degree to which this experience is shared with others is the amount of communication that can take place. Page through this book and find an illustration of an apparel-body-construct that could communicate a shared experience and explain why. | *Application Exercise 2.5* |

## Summary

• A fully articulated aesthetic response is based on personal, shared, and cultural influences.

• Perception is *active* and *interpretive*. The term "apparel-body-construct" designates the object of perception.

• Sensory data, past experiences, and education influence our perception.

• Gestalt psychology stresses that the visual whole is greater than the sum of its parts; the visual part may be distinguished from the whole.

• Visual structure is the way the parts of an item of clothing—shape, texture, color, line—are ordered within the whole. Coherence, grouping, and separating are activities related to perceiving the whole of the apparel-body-construct by means of viewing its parts.

• The figure-ground relationship is a spatial relationship that is important to perception.

• Relationships are the connections among parts that may cause the parts to group or separate. Relationships may be perceptible or inferred, and they can be repetitive, sequential, or hierarchical. Relationships found within the apparel-body-construct include both form and meaning.

• The physical and cultural contexts are important in viewing dress and in assigning meaning to elements of clothing.

## Key Terms and Concepts

apparel-body-construct

coherence

directly perceptible relationships

education

figure

Gestalt

gradation

ground

grouping

hierarchical

inferred relationships

past experiences

relationships

repetitive

sensory data

separate (separating)

sequential

stereotypes

structure

visual part

## References

Arnheim, R. *Art and Visual Perception: A Psychology of the Creative Eye,* 2nd ed. Berkeley: University of California Press, 1974.

Ellis, W. *A Sourcebook of Gestalt Psychology.* New York: The Humanities Press, 1955.

Gombrich, E. H. *The Sense of Order: A Study in the Psychology of Decorative Art.* Ithaca, NY: Cornell University Press, 1979.

Hillestad, R. "Form in Dress and Adornment: The Shape of Content." In DeLong, M., and Fiore, A. M., eds., *Aesthetics of Textiles and Clothing: Advancing Multi-Disciplinary Perspectives.* Monument, CO: ITAA Publication No. 7, 1994, 80–83.

Lutz, H. "From Wealth to Sensuality: The Changing Meaning of Velvet 1910–1939." In DeLong, M., and Fiore, A. M., eds., *Aesthetics of Textiles and Clothing: Advancing Multi-Disciplinary*

*Perspectives.* Monument, CO: ITAA Publication No. 7, 1994, 105–119.

Michelman, S., and Eicher, J. "Dress and Gender in Kalabari Women's Societies." *Clothing and Textiles Research Journal, 13*(2), 1995, 121–130.

Myers, J. F. *The Language of Visual Art: Perception as a Basis for Design.* Chicago: Holt, Rinehart & Winston, Inc., 1989.

O'Neal, G. S. "African-American Aesthetic of Dress: Symmetry through Diversity." In DeLong, M., and Fiore, A. M., eds., *Aesthetics of Textiles and Clothing: Advancing Multi-Disciplinary Perspectives.* Monument, CO: ITAA Publication No. 7, 1994, 212–223.

Orlean, S. "The Talk of the Town: Fashion Designers Uptown and Downtown Get Ready for this Week's Shows in Bryant Park." *The New Yorker,* November 7, l994, 71–78.

# Chapter Three

# STUDYING THE AESTHETIC RESPONSE

*After you have read this chapter, you will be able to understand:*

- The four-step method of observation, differentiation, interpretation, and evaluation for understanding aesthetic response.

- The importance of increasing awareness and developing perceptual skills, and learning how to apply them to perceive apparel more clearly.

- How to apply perceptual ability to your area of professional interest—be it customer relations, design, merchandising, or other apparel skills.

Most of us have been involved with clothing to some extent throughout our lives. We see images of clothing on the body via photographs or store displays, in the media, or on people who walk by. We dress ourselves each day. In the process we often examine the images of ourselves in the mirror for confirmation of the results we desire, for the ways we want to look. As we stand in front of a mirror getting dressed, we deliberately try on and take off clothes until we "get it right." The image in the mirror is our cue for making judgments. The eye can quickly take in and judge. Often the result is based upon intuition and emotion that does not involve reflection and reasoning. In fact, much of our response is instantaneous, and we evaluate our choices in a way that bypasses conscious reasoning.

This mode of operation is not sufficient for the professional who must communicate with clientele, as a designer, buyer, or personal shopping assistant at a store. Such a perspective involves expanding beyond the personal to an awareness resulting from fully developed perceptual skills. Perceiving fully means understanding the communication between the audience and the product—its form properties, message, and meaning. Understanding aesthetic response helps us to know and understand the differences in customers' responses and define our market. Thus, aesthetics offers a vital link in the marketing chain.

To continue to develop an understanding of aesthetic response, full perceptual awareness and self-education may be achieved by the four-step method detailed in this chapter. The four steps include:

1. Observation
2. Differentiation
3. Interpretation
4. Evaluation

## A METHOD AND PERSPECTIVE FOR VIEWING

Understanding how we see can be aided by a methodology that helps us to be more objective in our viewing. This is accomplished by conducting our examination in definable, incremental steps aimed at slowing perception and the making of instant, intuitive judgments. The observer is engaged in an active, seeking process of discovery using a system that offers a repeatable process and a definable language.

The objective in introducing this methodology is to analyze the form of the apparel-body-construct and its relationships to the viewer and the contexts. The apparel-body-construct has a structure made up of perceptible parts organized within a whole. Such parts may be observed and differentiated. The apparel-body-construct has meaning and conveys a message, which are considered in the interpretation.

The four steps will teach you to observe the character of the whole, to separate it into visual units in order to study their makeup and interaction, and then to put these units back together (Figure 3.1). By means of becoming absorbed in the process of viewing the form, the viewer differentiates the part surfaces and edges. The observer begins and ends observing the apparel-body-construct as a whole in order to understand it in a more complete way.

Becoming fully aware of the visual and then describing or writing about what you see is an optimal way of reinforcing what the eye sees and learns. When one reinforces the other, communication of ideas begins. In this way, the mind can discover what the eye is doing and can use the appropriate words to describe the experience. Communicating to yourself and with others about products through analysis involves learning to think of the connection between what you see, say, and write. Working effectively to clothe the human body and spirit entails understanding how you respond and then using words to make this knowledge explicit to yourself.

A word of caution is needed about the viewer's response as the steps are explained. Viewers do not always see exactly the same thing, nor do they interpret it in the same way. The apparel-body-construct as presented suggests viewing based upon the organization, but the viewer can always respond based upon individual preferences and other influential past experiences. Pay attention to the process, and do not worry if you do not see in the same way as someone else. The first time through, the point is to be flexible and open to the way you are seeing the form, but at the same time be as thorough and precise as possible in understanding why. The process is based on the idea that the form is designed

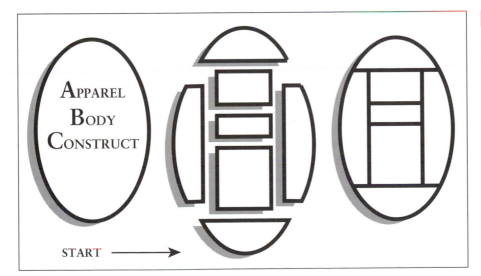

FIGURE 3.1

*Perceiving the apparel-body-construct as a whole, separating it into its constituent parts, and putting it back together.*

in a certain way and that relationships can create a dynamic visual effect. Relationships of the apparel-body-construct may be considered in one or a number of ways. For example, depending upon the type of relationship, a relationship of equality is viewed differently from one resulting from a hierarchy of parts. The suggestion of order is stronger in the latter relationship.

To explore the method, the first apparel-body-construct selected needs to be static, captured in a photograph or slide, so that you can spend the time necessary to process it through the four steps. Eventually the apparel-body-construct in movement will also be understood, such as the way the surfaces drape and move on the body.

## Steps in the Process

How do you begin? A thorough examination of the form demands attention. First learn to look with new eyes and really see what you typically ignore or take for granted. This approach involves a conscious effort to detach from your own self-interests and viewpoint. This means spending the time to examine thoroughly and not let personal reactions influence your viewing. By following the steps the viewer is forced to pause and examine not only the conspicuous features, but also the less conspicuous ones, and the function of each part within the whole.

The first step in the process is **observation**, paying attention to the total visual form, the apparel-body-construct, and describing what you see. The next step, **differentiation**, requires identification of the visual parts and then an awareness of their relationships—how each part influences the other parts and the whole. The third step, **interpretation**, consists of looking for the themes and associations of meaning that seem to summarize and explain the form, again describing it fully. The fourth and final step, **evaluation**, concludes the process with explicit criteria for making a judgment that includes but goes beyond the personal (Table 3.1).

At first, selection of more than one apparel-body-construct for processing may give better insight into the one being examined. One apparel-body-construct serves as a focus of examination, while the other provides a comparison.

*Step 1: Observation: Paying Attention to the Form.* In this step, the goal is to observe and describe what is immediately apparent. Select one apparel-body-construct and experience the entire form. How much space does it occupy? Observe the silhouette, that is, the outline of the entire apparel-body-construct. Does the silhouette become a distinct boundary or an indistinct outline? Describe its shape. Does it flare outward from the body in an A shape or create an H shape? Does it create a horizontal or a vertical line? What details of lines and shapes do you notice? Are edges distinct or subtle? Are there few or many? Where are they located? Is your eye directed throughout the form or does it remain in one area?

| Step 1 Observation | Consider the entire form. Describe what you see and identify any information you can glean about the form—for example, the ordering in which you see visual parts 1, 2, 3, etc. |
|---|---|
| Step 2 Differentiation | What are the parts? What makes the parts appear separated? Are the parts equal? Is one part dominant? What are their relationships? Are they similar in color, texture, shape? How do the parts combine? Why did you see the order of parts in Step 1? What is the visual result? What degree of simplicity/complexity? |
| Step 3 Interpretation | What are the visual themes? How is the form characterized—that is, what is its character and quality, who wears the form, how it is worn, etc.? Then, how is it summarized? What is the relation to intention/function: suitability for purpose? How is intention communicated? With what clarity? |
| Step 4 Evaluation | How does the apparel-body-construct relate to the individual, visual culture, fashion, time period, place, location? How is appearance defined according to culture's values? How does the apparel-body-construct fit within the culture and time period? Describe relation to personal and cultural ideals. How is the apparel-body-construct excellent? Unique? What about it gives you pleasure and satisfaction? |

**TABLE 3.1**

*Steps to Aesthetic Analysis of the Apparel-Body-Construct*

Do you notice colors and textures of surfaces? Is there a play of light and shadow on the surface? Does the surface appear flat or rounded? Does it appear to be deep and thick, or thin? Do you notice the body or the clothes? How do they interact? Do the clothes cause you to focus your attention on certain parts of the body? How does this happen? Do parts appear to come forward and others remain in the background?

The viewer always plays an important role in how the apparel-body-construct is viewed. As you compare your descriptions with other viewers, you will discover this. By stressing the reasons why, you will understand your responses and those of other viewers.

The vocabulary is important in such an account. In this step, try to use descriptive rather than evaluative language. For example, label a shape rectangular or oval rather than lovely or grotesque, the edge of a contour sharp or indistinct rather than harsh or harmonious. In this way you can describe with clarity. Precision and absence of judgmental language allows for communication to take place. In this way you will learn to describe first before evaluating.

Now consider an example. In Figure 3.2 the two apparel-body-constructs occupy approximately the same amount of space. The physical surround is identical. Both silhouettes are defined by their outlines, though the one on the left (Figure 3.2a) is more distinctly defined. In other words, there is a greater difference between the edge and the surrounding area. The eye is directed to the outline in Figure 3.2a, first noticing the tubular shape of the dark trouser and vest, and then is attracted to the texture of the jacket with the light threads on the otherwise dark surface. The eye is also attracted to the value contrast of the light-gray band of the vest and the similar value of the shirt. In Figure 3.2b the eye is directed to the vest at the upper center of the torso and to the dark-value hair and shoes.

***Step 2: Differentiation: Part Identification and Part Relationships.*** In this step, the form structure is examined by separating the whole into its *visual parts*. Visual parts are units within the whole that separate for viewing. These can be body parts and clothing parts, or parts that include body and clothing. It may be necessary to cover the photo with tracing paper to remove value contrast and quickly trace lines and shapes that separate in some way, that is,

**FIGURE 3.2A & B**

*Comparing two similar apparel-body-constructs.*

Courtesy of Marc Joseph, photographer.

a                                                        b

through a different surface, shape, silhouette, or edge. After identification of the parts, the concern is the influence of one part on another and how the parts affect viewing of the whole.

What part separates first for attention? How many separate parts are there? Is the sequence of parts important? Which parts are noticed first? Number the parts in the order in which they are viewed. Consider why you were attracted first to part number 1, second to number 2, and so forth. How is each part similar to the whole form—by color, texture, size? How does it differ?

Now describe the relationships of part to whole (Figure 3.2a and b). How do the parts function within the form? For example, are they repetitious or singular, regular or irregular? What is the influence of line, shape, color, or texture in the relationship of the parts to the whole? Describe their use in the form and how this affects viewing. Consider each part individually and then consider the visual parts in relationship to each other. A description should be as complete and objective as possible, so that another observer can follow the reasoning.

The silhouette is noticed more in Figure 3.2a than in Figure 3.2b. In Figure 3.2a, the apparel-body-construct is viewed as a whole first. Then the contrast of light value at the neck and down the center front attracts attention to the body's center. The light value of this one dominant area is repeated in the jacket, but the minute areas of light value adjacent to the dark value make these appear as a different value. The shape of the hair surrounds the head as the suit does the body. In Figure 3.2b, the whole is viewed first, but for a different reason. The surfaces of the jacket and trousers and hair are noticed because of the variation in texture and value and the play of light and shadow on the surfaces. In both apparel-body-constructs the round head shape is in contrast with the horizontal line at the shoulders. The head is related to the focus at center front. The value relationship between the shirt and trousers is less contrasting in Figure 3.2b than in Figure 3.2a. There is a centering effect in Figure 3.2b because of the focus on the vest and then the buttons and space between the legs and the V-shape of the neckline. The shape of the hair is similar to that in Figure 3.2a, but the relationships to skin and vest and shoes all make for more connections between body coloring and the clothing. Another focus after viewing these parts is the lighter value of the shirt, collar, and trousers.

In Figure 3.2a the similar values, or the degrees of lightness-darkness, between the hair and other items of the ensemble relate visually. In Figure 3.2b there is a similarity in hue of the skin and hair, and a similarity in the value of the hair and other parts of the ensemble, like the vest and shoes.

*Step 3: Interpretation: Summarizing the Form Is Impression and Meaning.* The goal of interpretation is to look for the relationships and associations that summarize and explain the form. What seems to fuse as the pervasive and connecting linkage? Which visual relationships become priorities as observed in the form? Does an idea, or concept, seem to connect the parts of the form?

First, look back on your descriptions from the first two steps. Record all word associations that come to mind. As you begin, consider all alternatives without judgment. Complete the sentences:

- This reminds me of . . .
- This looks like . . .

Now consider your recorded impressions. Which seem to be possible and probable? For example, you could comment and then begin interpretation in this way: Figure 3.2a looks like a man with authority who is organized and efficient. The ensemble looks like it would be comfortable to wear for winter. This outfit looks like casual clothing of the 1990s. It is at this point that impressions are linked to the form and the culture. Interpretations that are personal may be compared with those likely to be shared.

Second, step back from your impressions as noted. Consider what within the culture is valued and of high priority. Craik (1994) describes fashion as the playing out of various tensions within a society, such as status, gender, occasion, the body, or social regulation. What tensions are being played out here? Work versus play has been a dynamic contextual trend within the United States for most of the twentieth century. Along with the trend toward casual clothing has come a term like "weekend wear" to differentiate clothing worn both to work and for leisure. Now Friday is becoming a time when it is acceptable to wear casual clothing in the workplace. Men and women who work in offices and schools sometimes wear more casual clothing on Fridays than clothing worn Monday through Thursday. This has been noted as a contextual trend within U.S. culture in the 1990s. The form in Figure 3.2 could be related to such a trend as it diverges considerably from the traditional male suit.

Specifically, how does the form relate to such impressions and cultural values? For example, the silhouette of Figure 3.2a is viewed immediately as a solid, dark outline defined by edges. Surfaces attract immediate attention and the ensemble offers a focus at the head and neck and at center front of the upper torso. A whole-to-part relationship is apparent, and the apparel-body-construct is organized with the upper torso dominant in viewing. The clothing-to-body relationship is somewhat looser than in a traditional suit, that is, the clothing fits the model with ease. The casual impression here is derived from the attention to the softened surfaces and looser relation to the body. Thus, recorded impressions can be based upon the direct perception of the apparel-body-construct itself, as well as cultural values.

Test your impressions on others, accept their suggestions, and formulate what you believe to be the main contextual influences upon the apparel-body-construct.

***Step 4: Evaluation: Considering the Visual Effectiveness.*** Evaluation needs to be postponed until each of the other steps of the process has been completed. Much can be overlooked in reaching a conclusion when evaluation is

Continue examining Figure 3.2b for Step 3 applications. Go back and add information to Steps 1 and 2 from insights concerning Figure 3.2a. Then proceed to examine Figure 3.2b in like manner, using the questions in the four steps as a guide.

Example: The outfit in Figure 3.2b looks softer, more approachable, friendly. A greater number of values of light to dark are found in the apparel-body-construct surfaces. The middle value carries light and shadow so that the parts such as the jacket lapels are noticed. More parts are perceived. Here the parts dominate more than in Figure 3.2a and, although there is a strong visual connection between them, they are viewed first as more discrete. Perhaps the casual interpretation of Figure 3.2b derives from these more independent parts and light-value surfaces.

*Application Exercise 3.1*

not preceded by careful observation, differentiation, and interpretation. There is an old folk adage in American culture: "Don't put the cart before the horse!" This is useful wisdom when following the four steps: observing, differentiating, interpreting, and then evaluating the apparel-body-construct.

Consider the visual merit of the form. A comparison with other known forms helps evaluation. To evaluate visual merit, consider such criteria as the following: Did the apparel-body-construct attract? Did it hold your attention? How did it attract and hold your attention? How does it rank with similar forms? Is it unique in conveying visual relationships or messages?

Other evaluative criteria need to be specified, such as, is the message of the form clear and congruous, or is it mixed? Is it consistent with other forms of the designer or manufacturer? Is it acceptable, desirable, to a large diverse audience, or to a small select audience? How does it express the time in which it was created? As you notice, these criteria are not absolutes, that is, one form may be for a large diverse audience and another for a small one. However, one is not necessarily better than the other.

Figure 3.2a is evaluated as attracting attention because of the dark value of surfaces and the distinct edges. The silhouette is distinct, which is typical of a formal business suit. It is closed to the physical adjacent space. The man, however, is dressed more casually, because the fuller trouser and jacket texture soften an otherwise closed silhouette. The focus at the neck is a contrast, but it is also unusual. A more traditional treatment for formal clothing would be a focused tie, and for casual clothing, an open neck or possibly a patterned scarf.

Evaluation of an apparel-body-construct often centers around the audience—those likely to appreciate and respond to it. How many could or would be wearers? Who would be interested in viewing the apparel-body-construct? Few viewers? Many viewers? What is the appeal of the form to satisfy the unique-to-me needs of specific people, as well as the collective needs of many? If your professional perspective is merchandising and you are a buyer for a store that would have clothing such as that pictured in Figure 3.2a, how many ensembles like this would you order? Would this look be popular with your clientele?

The "forgiving look" was the label given in the description of these apparel-body-constructs in Figure 3.2a, referring to the fact that both were designed to hide the slightly overweight male body successfully. To apply this idea to a specific store, how many in your audience shop to hide figure flaws? Would this be an appealing idea to them?

Those involved in the merchandising of apparel are interpreters of the apparel-body-construct within a culture. Those successful in merchandising consider how their audience will want to look and stock what will achieve that look—again dealing with the whole apparel-body-construct. They display those images and realize the value of advertising the image—the look. They know their clientele.

*Application Exercise 3.2*

Continue with Figure 3.2b for this step. Examine, using the questions in the four steps as a guide.

Example: In Figure 3.2b the softened edges of the silhouette attract less attention to the apparel-body-construct. The form appears more open to the surround and even though it is still a suit, it is more casual than in Figure 3.2a. The nuance of the light to dark and the texture of surfaces are played out and make this apparel-body-construct pleasant to view. Figure 3.2b attracts immediate attention to parts in the upper and lower torso, the hair and vest, and shoes. This suit looks more like the traditional three-piece suit. The apparel-body-construct still appears to be ordered, but in a more random way. The apparel-body-constructs could be worn for similar purposes, but the season may differ due to the heavier visual weight of Figure 3.2a as opposed to Figure 3.2b. Due to the dark value throughout, the apparel-body-construct in Figure 3.2a looks more appropriate for winter and the lighter values of Figure 3.2b are more the colors of another season, such as fall or spring.

As you begin to understand Figure 3.2b, try another apparel-body-construct. Select an apparel-body-construct of your choice—an entire visual form for study. The form needs to be in full view and stationary to allow sufficient time to follow the procedure. A clear, color photograph from a magazine or another figure from this book is a good place to start. After you have made your selection, take note and record the reference where you found the photograph and any accompanying information, such as season, designer, and other editorial remarks, and then proceed with the four steps discussed previously.

## Learning This Approach to Develop Aesthetic Response

What does it take to understand the apparel-body-construct? Following the four steps of observation, differentiation, interpretation, and evaluation begins a process of discovery. Initially the process may seem overly deliberate, but with continued use this disciplined approach will yield increasingly useful results. The first time through is the hardest. If you persist in developing perceptual skills using this approach, you will become more perceptually aware because of a lasting curiosity. Eventually, you can acquire a full perceptual ability, the ability to observe and understand the apparel-body-construct and its visual relationships.

All of the skills developed in this systematic approach will not come simultaneously or be understood immediately. If you successfully proceed through the system with one apparel-body-construct, you will understand the system more thoroughly. However, the discovery process is continuous. As you become aware of each feature and component, such as color, shape, or line, you will learn to understand its influence within a particular context. While learning to understand color, you may ignore shape. But in continuing with this approach, the whole apparel-body-construct will remain the viewing reference and eventually both color and shape will be understood.

Looking at the apparel-body-construct with the whole as the frame of reference is not as easy as it sounds, but to continually view the whole is necessary to maximize discovery of structure and relationships. If viewing is a controlled searching process, then relationships of context and meaning will become more apparent. The expert viewer becomes skilled in understanding how past experiences and present expectations influence the apparel-body-construct. An active viewer will continue to question the visual effect. Patterns in viewing, how form structure repeats from one viewing experience to another, will become obvious.

The viewer who learns to understand one apparel-body-construct, then another, will achieve not only understanding, but will begin to accumulate a mental information bank. Exposure to more visual forms, plus practice analyzing them using Steps 1 through 4 previously, will broaden your comprehension, which will become more complete over time and with repeated use of these steps.

What other incentives are there to continue? What are the rewards if you are introduced to this approach and continue to work at developing perceptual skills? The following are a number of additional possible outcomes:

- Educating for perceptual awareness
- Developing visual thinking skills
- Making the connections
- Applying your perceptual knowledge to your profession

*Educating for Perceptual Awareness.* The more experience and knowledge you gain concerning the apparel-body-construct, the more you develop a discrimination for particulars. For example, a color can be evaluated as to how intense or subdued it is, or how it looks in combination with other colors. You may also discriminate based upon relationships of texture to cultural context: one texture may be appropriate for a dress for a young girl, another for a mature woman. Paying attention to such nuances of the particular can enhance your aesthetic response as well as educate your vision.

Perceptive is an adjective used to describe persons who see well in the sense of interacting with a given apparel-body-construct—actively absorbing its colors, textures, placement in space, how it relates to personal and cultural values and meaning—everything that contributes to its exact appearance. Some people do perceive more than others. They observe and reason about what they see in an open and active way.

Learning to perceive means taking in more completely with awareness of our conventions and cues, that is, assumptions and internal guidelines. When people grasp fully the meaning of our experience, they understand what they take in, the influence of the form within the culture, and how they respond. Examining the basis for our response is the beginning of our understanding.

Developing perceptual skills offers an invitation to become less passive, to examine the nature of viewing as a dynamic interaction. It offers an expansion of understanding of the results, the aesthetic response. Understanding your personal response can help you to become more objective about the responses of others.

The language used throughout this process is standard. Much of the language is the same as that which is used by artists—but this is a viewing language used to define visual concepts and to learn about them. The discoveries you make using such a language can be communicated to your client, but when a client's frame of reference is not yours, the same language is not appropriate.

We are aiming to learn to question what we see, to slow down the process to fully understand our response and those of others. We can educate our eyes to perceive fully and recognize visual relationships: the whole and its parts, its images and ideas, and the way they are combined and interrelated into purposeful units within a cultural context. We can then develop our professional role of helping others become aware of the importance of such relationships through designing, buying, and marketing apparel.

*Developing Visual Thinking Skills.* Visual thinking is the ability to reason in visual terms. As you become more skilled perceptually, you will gain a new understanding of forms and their relationships. For example, surfaces can be important because of pattern or texture, but their relationship can provide an unusual result. If you learn how details of the form tend to be viewed you can begin to think beyond one form, from those already experienced to those as yet not created.

Understanding the potential of a medium comes from full awareness of the apparel-body-construct in context. Look at the two apparel-body-constructs in Figure 3.3a and b. There are a number of similarities, such as the amount of space each takes, but there are differences too—what attracts first and how the

a                                                    b

**FIGURE 3.3A & B**

*Comparing and imagining substitutions using the "what if" approach.*

Designed by Bisou Bisou. Courtesy of Fairchild Publications.

viewer orders the form. Comparing the two for similarities and differences is a useful exercise in learning how surfaces and their placement affect the result.

Practice taking mental pictures. As you establish a mental picture of the form as it exists, you can analyze its parts and whole. Imaginative powers develop as you think and reason in visual terms. Then you can begin to use such knowledge in the process of creating new forms.

A "what if" attitude helps in developing an ability to visualize or imagine the apparel-body-construct and its relationships. Think about substitutions. The "what if" attitude comes about when you try to imagine what would happen if one detail were substituted for an existing one. What would the difference be? What changes in viewing would occur? For example, refer back to Figure 3.3. Begin imagining an exchange of the heads of the two models. What difference would this make? Then consider a change in one of the surfaces, such as the skirt. First try to imagine the apparel-body-construct with an exchange of skirts, leaving the top the same. Then try imagining the substitution of a one-color, dark-value skirt instead of either of the skirts pictured. What would this change accomplish in viewing?

Analyzing and comparing apparel-body-constructs when a constant such as color or silhouette is repeated in each is also useful. Examine the suit in Figure 3.4a, b, and c. A constant is the jacket and model, which are identical in each example. In two of the three examples there are two additional pieces that are identical—the vest and trousers. Beyond this, important details complete each apparel-body-construct. In the example shown in Figure 3.4a, the man is wearing a high-collared shirt of the same value as the suit itself. The focus is thus more on the wearer and the texture of the suit. Only three of the six buttons are closed on the vest, and the opening at the waist of the vest gives a slightly more casual appearance. In Figure 3.4b, the additional hat and more formal shirt and tie create more focus on the head and neck. The hat brim and the width of the jacket lapels, and the contrast of the tie with the V-shape of the vest, help to attract attention to the upper neckline of the vest. When the five buttons are buttoned, more notice is given to the similar shape of the lower edge of the center front of the vest—an inverted arrow. The apparel-body-construct in Figure 3.4c diverges in that the only repeated piece of clothing is the jacket. The silhouette is outlined with the dark of the leather jacket and trousers. The wool tailored jacket becomes the contrast and, because it is covered by the leather jacket, it acts as a centered focus upon the body. The plaid shirt repeats some of the values from the dark and light surfaces of the ensemble and thus does not stand out or become the focus itself. Now imagine an interchange of the pieces. Try one at a time at first. For example, shift the hat in Figure 3.4b to the outfit shown in Figure 3.4c. In this instance, the hat would repeat the dark value of the leather jacket and echo the collar of the jacket. Keep interchanging the clothing to practice imagining the substitution of one clothing item for another.

*Application Exercise 3.3*

Adopting a "What If" Approach

A "what if" attitude helps in developing visual thinking skills. This is the ability to visualize or imagine substitutions:

- What would happen if this color were to be substituted for that?
- What would the difference be in the apparel-body-construct?
- What changes in viewing would occur?

By opening your awareness in this way, you may better understand the complexities of the visual form of dress, the apparel-body-construct. Select an apparel-body-construct and practice imaging substitutions.

***Making the Connections.*** If you continue active attention and reflection, you will develop an educated eye, perceptual skills, and the language to think about, describe, and arrive at solutions. The use of precise language for viewing can lead to increased awareness through use. Your capacity develops to see more because the language defines the concepts. As you proceed through the chapters in this book, additional language will be introduced and explained that will apply not only to each of the four steps of the methodology introduced previously, but also to the perceptual concepts of viewing.

a

b

c

## FIGURE 3.4A, B & C

*Analyzing and comparing dress when constant articles of clothing are repeated.*

Courtesy of Fairchild Publications.

Analyzing many apparel-body-constructs will broaden your viewing potential and enable perception and interpretation of the unfamiliar. As the analysis of one apparel-body-construct is understood, comparisons and substitutions can be made. This ability to interpret familiar and unfamiliar apparel-body-constructs has a number of applications. You can analyze existing forms for various trends. For example, trends often develop based upon the structure of the apparel-body-construct and the way it is viewed. In the field of fashion apparel, new forms are continually offered for viewing consideration.

<table>
<tr>
<td>Application Exercise 3.4</td>
<td>Flexibility in viewing is a by-product of subjecting oneself to a great variety of apparel-body-constructs, both familiar and unfamiliar. Find an apparel-body-construct that appears strange to you personally, separate the background from the form, and imagine how it would look. Follow the steps of the framework.<br><br>• What audience would you identify for the apparel-body-construct?<br>• How would you market the product?</td>
</tr>
</table>

***Applying Your Perceptual Knowledge to Your Profession.*** This perceptual ability can be applied in your area of professional interest. The process of imaging the whole apparel-body-construct and the relationship of parts is needed at each level or stage of designing, manufacturing, and merchandising. Eventually you will adopt a perspective based on your particular professional goals. If your focus is on marketing a product, you will consider not only how it looks, but also who the audience might be and how to relate with that audience. If your focus is as a designer of clothing, then you identify a target audience for whom you imagine and create new forms.

Think about the objectives of apparel-related careers. For example, a fashion journalist provides coverage of topics related to dress. A fashion editor plays a parallel role of interpreter of the apparel-body-constructs of our time to communicate how trends relate to an audience. In a career such as visual merchandising, the retailer is buying, selecting, and assembling clothing on racks, mannequins, and shelves. Window displays in a retail setting may strategically combine apparel marketed separately to develop a message. For example, mannequins in a window, clothed in citrus-fruit colors of lime green, lemon, and orange, could give a color message for spring and summer.

The apparel professional can consider the point of view of clientele but also how the consumer picks up on those trends. The retailer in a fashion-based store can better understand the market through a continual awareness of his client and what is being offered. You can aid the customer by communicating to him or her about the product's potential (Figure 3.5). If you center on the perspective of your targeted customer, you can evaluate each apparel-body-construct for its intended audience.

a

b

Wardrobe consulting requires an ability to interpret the apparel-body-construct for specific persons and situations. Through processing and understanding a number of apparel-body-constructs, the wardrobe consultant can learn about the relationship of the clothing to the body, the physical coloring, and the shape and proportions of the client. The consultant who continues to analyze and interpret the apparel-body-construct will understand how many associations there are of clothing to cultural context (Figure 3.6) and help to set the stage for dressing appropriately within the culture. Visual impact can be communicated directly and explicitly. Specialists such as the wardrobe consultant, the color analyst, and the hair or body stylist interpret cultural trends for individuals. Those clients who seek such consultants often do not have the time, knowledge, or inclination to pursue an optimal individual appearance. Such aid is often welcome to the client who does not care to take time to imagine the visual effect of an ensemble or the relation of the apparel-body-construct to the cultural context.

The designer can use analysis in the creative process to imagine visual results based upon knowledge of the part-to-whole relationship. For example, one designer can begin with an idea and the basic materials of fabric of the apparel-body-construct and produce an entire ensemble. Another may design single items that must blend and be consistent together, such as a slip with a skirt or a belt with a trouser. The accessory designer, too, needs to consider not only the particular design of a hat, but the relation of crown to brim, surfaces of color and texture, and also the way that hat could be worn with a hairstyle or an ensemble.

**FIGURE 3.5A & B**

*Figure 3.5a illustrates the professional perspective of visual display at Hecht's, Washington, D.C. Another example of visual display in Figure 3.5b at Dayton's, Minneapolis, Minnesota, when Dayton's launched a promotion for "work day casual," and the theme of dressing casually for business.*

Courtesy of: (a) Fairchild Publications. and (b) Dayton's, Minneapolis, Minnesota.

**FIGURE 3.6**

*The professional perspective of showing designer clothing within a cultural context. Here a client is examining the work of Icinoo, a Korean designer, who incorporated the rolling hills of the Korean landscape into her jacket.*

*Courtesy of Marilyn Revell DeLong.*

A professional who puts a number of apparel-body-constructs together for a presentation to create a unifying message could be an interpreter of apparel-body-constructs—for example, a stylist for fashion shows or photographic advertising. To understand the potential of the apparel-body-construct in staging and character portrayal, a designer of costumes for the theater or film is involved with the form, viewer, and context.

A major task for the student becoming an apparel professional is to communicate with clientele. Clientele are the audience for products. Understanding your clientele means promoting satisfaction by being responsive to their needs. By listening and asking directed questions, you can understand their responses and then can use your knowledge and experience to gain insight as to how to serve them. Much of what the customer ultimately purchases is based on what is perceived as desirable, what looks and feels good, and what gives personal pleasure. If the professional can give voice to the process of communicating, the customer is more likely to feel satisfactorily served.

## Summary

- The four-step method of understanding aesthetic response consists of: observation, differentiation, interpretation, and evaluation.

    1. *Observation* involves paying attention to and describing what is immediately apparent.

    2. *Differentiation* involves examining the whole and its relationship to its visual parts.

    3. *Interpretation* has as its goal looking for the relationships and associations that summarize and explain the form.

    4. *Evaluation* involves considering the visual content of the form and its relationship to the clientele.

- It is important to develop your perceptual skills, such as practicing taking mental pictures and developing the "what if" attitude when looking at the apparel-body-construct.

- Perceptual ability can be applied to your area of professional interest—be it design, customer relations, merchandising, or other apparel professions.

## Key Terms and Concepts

differentiation
evaluation

interpretation
observation

## References

Anderson, T. "The Content of Art Criticism." *Art Education*, 44(1), 1991, 16–24.

Arnheim, R. *Visual Thinking*. Berkeley: University of California Press, 1969.

Berlyne, D. *Studies in the New Experimental Aesthetics: Steps Toward an Objective Psychology of Aesthetic Appreciation*. Washington, DC: Hemisphere, 1974.

Craik, J. *The Face of Fashion: Cultural Studies in Fashion*. London: Routledge, 1994.

Crozier, W., and Chapman A., eds. *Cognitive Processes in the Perception of Art*. New York: Elsevier Science, 1984.

DeLong, M. "Analysis of Costume Visual Form." *Journal of Home Economics*, 60(10), 1968, 784–788.

Ettinger, L. "Critique of Art Criticism: Problemizing Practice in Art Education." *Controversies in Art and Culture*, 3(1), 1990, 30–41.

Guilford, J. *Way Beyond the IQ*. Buffalo, NY: Creative Synergetic Association, 1977.

Hamblen, D. "In the Quest for Art Criticism Equity: A Tentative Model." *Visual Arts Research*, 17(1), 1991, 12–22.

Hillestad, R. "The Underlying Structure of Appearance." *Dress*, 6, 1980, 117–125.

Kaplan, S., and Kaplan, R. C*ognition and Environment: Functioning in an Uncertain World*. New York: Praeger, 1982.

Margolin, V., ed. *Design Discourse: History, Theory, Criticism*. Chicago: University of Chicago Press, 1980.

McKim, R. *Experiences in Visual Thinking*. Boston: Prindle, Weber, and Schmidt, 1980.

Munro, T. *Toward Science in Aesthetics*. New York: Liberal Arts Press, 1956.

Papanek, V. *Design for the Real World: Human Ecology and Social Change*. Chicago: Academy Chicago Publishers, 1985.

Van Gundy, A. *Creative Problem Solving: A Guide for Trainers and Management*. New York: Quorum, 1987.

# Chapter Four

# OBSERVING THE SPACE OF THE APPAREL-BODY-CONSTRUCT

*After you have read this chapter, you will be able to understand:*

- The difference between the two significant ways of perceiving the apparel-body-construct: the visual world and the visual field.

- The steps and opposite word pairs that aid one in observing and describing the space occupied by the apparel-body-construct: closed-open; part-whole; figure-ground integration, figure-ground separation; flat-rounded; determinate-indeterminate.

- The opposite word pairs described previously can aid in observation and description and help the apparel professional assess visual goals of coherence and order. They can even be the start of a significant new look.

THINK ABOUT WAKING UP ONE MORNING AND DECIDing, while still in bed, that you are going to take in every detail of what you see from that moment on. If you seriously set out to accomplish this task, you might never get any further than the edge of your bed. The reason you can accomplish what you do each day is because you basically ignore most of what is in your visual field, that is, information about the visual space you perceive is taken in but only on a subconscious level. Habit takes over and you learn to ignore detail in order to survive. The task is now different. You must overcome this natural and learned tendency and find a way to observe every bit of detail within the apparel-body-construct you choose to evaluate.

Viewing the apparel-body-construct depends not only upon its form but also upon the position and perspective of the viewer. The viewer who slows down to take in all of the information in a systematic way will begin to ask, "How do I take it in? Do I start at the head and work downward, and if so, what about the features causes me to process visual information in this way?" Usually the viewer, upon reflection, will discover that the apparel-body-construct has been designed to create focus areas that relate to each other in a structured way, and this influences the order of viewing. The form is also designed to relate to cultural context and to draw upon specific personal and cultural meaning.

When observing the apparel-body-construct, much of the character and impression we receive depends upon how it occupies space. The silhouette, the outermost outline that defines the frame of the apparel-body-construct, can appear softy blurred and mysterious, or hard-edged and assertive. Whether we pay attention to the upper or lower section of the body is dependent upon the way the form is structured. A certain part or parts may be strongly figural and dominate viewing. This explains why the viewer may focus on a large brass belt buckle at the waist, then take in a plaid headband encircling the face, before even noticing a dark blue T-shirt, denim jeans, and vest.

How space is viewed is dependent upon an observer's perception of the apparel-body-construct (Barratt, 1980; Collier, 1967). Two orientations of the observer when responding to the apparel-body-construct are the **visual world** and the **visual field**. Being aware of both, and being able to develop the viewing orientation of the visual field, is important in order to achieve a full understanding of the apparel-body-construct.

## TWO VIEWING ORIENTATIONS

To consider the perception of space, you need to think about how you see, but not in the sense of the obvious—eyes open and focusing on the subject, with sufficient light. We will assume these primary factors. Consider two significant ways to **perceive** the apparel-body-construct through the:

1. Visual world
2. Visual field

Becoming aware of differences in these two orientations is vital to one's understanding of space and ultimately developing your aesthetic response.

## The Visual World

The visual world is described by Gibson (1996) as that familiar space in which people ordinarily operate—an unbounded and extended environment filled with solid objects of constant and learned features. People focus on these solid objects for meaning and action and recognize without perceiving them in any detail. People often rely upon what they know from memory and take for granted what they see. Minimal cues are developed for what they need, and our memories can be jogged into recognizing an object or a person with only a minimum of visual cues.

People usually receive their information via our orientation to the visual world. This means using a minimum number of cues and relying heavily on our memory storehouse. For example, when you are taking the bus, what cues do you need? When the bus is on a route and you take it regularly, you do not have to look for such details as how many windows or tires it has, or what are details of its exterior shape or where it is going. You know where it is going because of the time it arrives at the corner bus stop. You can recognize it from past experience from the front, side, or back, or even a small patch of the bus coming around the corner behind another vehicle; in other words, with a minimum of visual cues.

This visual world remains the same when the viewer moves about. It is a surround extending beyond what can be immediately seen to what we know exists from experience. It is the world perceived under ordinary circumstances and is based heavily upon people's past experiences. Their memories allow them to connect those experiences with their actions in the present or future. They then take those memories for granted. Constancy of an object's attributes is a fact of the visual world—a book viewed from across the room appears as the same book as it does when the viewer is close by. It remains the same book regardless of our position relative to it, because all you need to do is recognize that it is a book and that you have seen it many times before. If asked to describe a plate, a viewer whose perspective is the visual world describes it without considering from what perspective the plate is viewed. It may be described according to function: We put food on a plate. Thus, the plate is the same constant object no matter how it would appear to change if you examine it from the top, side, or bottom.

From the perspective of the visual world, the viewer sees space as having no center or periphery. It is a world that we move about in, not a particular field for viewing. If the viewer does focus on the objects in the space, they are viewed as figure. The viewer does not need to attend to the ground in the figure-ground relationship. The viewer looks for just enough meaning in order to understand what actions to take. In Figure 4.1a, b, and c, the viewer can see the models "Mary and Sara" and recognize them regardless of the position from which they are seen. If one knows them well, one would recognize them even if they were seen in less detail or wearing different clothing.

Development of an aesthetic response means one must learn to observe and analyze the details and nuances of what is seen, and this requires the perspective of the visual field. Appreciating takes time, knowledge, and attention to detail (Dondis, 1973; Eisner, 1972). A friend may advise you, "You need to learn to stop and smell the roses!" What this usually means is, "Stop! Slow down to examine the objects that surround you. Be ever mindful of their very essence. Savor those perceptions because they are good for the soul." Look to the visual field for this to happen (Paramenter, 1968).

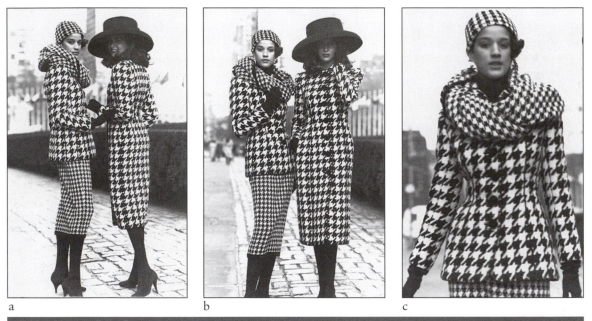

a                    b                    c

**FIGURE 4.1A, B & C**

*The apparel-body-construct in the visual world/visual field perspective. In the visual world the two models would appear the same to the viewer who might say, "There are Mary and Sara." However, from the visual field perspective, what the viewer notices and sees is different. For example, in Figure 4.1a the two models are facing the viewer, in Figure 4.1b what you see is a side, full view of both, and Figure 4.1c is a close-up of only one of the models.*

*Designed by Oscar de la Renta. Courtesy of Fairchild Publications.*

## The Visual Field

When you want to be completely conscious of what you see, how do you ensure that your eyes will take in a manageable quantity of data? The orientation of the visual field involves viewing from a fixed position exactly what is in front of you and examining it in great detail. Think about taking a photograph with your camera. In many respects the visual field is like the result of a photographer who examines the surround carefully to select the very best shot. This is a learned orientation for the person who wants to be educated visually. However, the visual field is less familiar than the visual world because it is only observable through special effort. We must raise our awareness to what we have long since taken for granted.

We orient to the visual field by fixing the eye, then examining what can be viewed from that specific perspective (Figure 4.2). It takes time and a special attention to hold what is before you, observe the whole and the details of what you have focused upon, see fully, and appreciate the structural relationships involved. Imagine you are going to draw what you see before you. All of a sudden you must take in more deeply exactly what is before you—the shapes and sizes, the way light and shadow play upon the surfaces (Gibson, 1966).

From a fixed position, consider what you can see out to your visual periphery without moving your head or eyes. This scene has boundaries and therefore differs from the visual world. The field or picture should appear clear and sharp at the center and less clear at the edges. Try closing one eye to remove the effects of binocular vision (depth). When one eye is closed, your nose

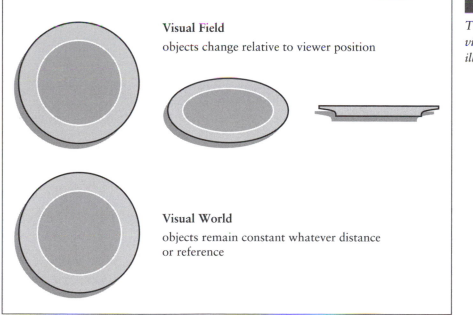

**Visual Field**
objects change relative to viewer position

**Visual World**
objects remain constant whatever distance or reference

appears at the periphery of this oval-shaped field. The visual field is approximately 180 degrees horizontally and 150 degrees vertically. That is our field of vision. If you persist, the scene will resemble an oval-shaped picture with areas of colored, flattened surfaces divided by edges and contours. You can learn a great deal of the subtlety in what you see by fixing your position.

A viewer whose perspective is the visual field would describe an object such as a plate by the way it appears relative to viewer position. Depending upon how far or near the viewer is to it and the position, one time the plate may appear elliptical and small, and another time round and large. Remember you are looking intently, as though you are going to draw what you see before you. In the visual field one object can eclipse another when it is positioned to partially overlap the other. If the plate is partially covered by another object in front of it, the viewer would take note of exactly what is in view and how this cues to perceiving depth.

A comparison of the conditions of observation of the visual world and visual field indicates differences in perception of shape and size. In the visual world, objects remain a constant size and shape, whatever their distance or position from the viewer. Surfaces of the three-dimensional form in the visual world remain constant from any viewing location. This is due to the effect of memory and how we learn to interpret objects in space with a minimum of cues. Objects must appear constant to us in order for us to recognize and name them. This is important for learning about the world we live in, but this perspective does not foster the attention to detail needed for an aesthetic response.

In the visual field, objects are not perceived as constant. They change based upon our position relative to them. We pay attention to their inconstancy and for what we can learn from their changing nature by fixing upon one view. They are larger when close to us and smaller at a distance. Just as the apparel-body-construct in Figure 4.1a is different from our view in Figure 4.1b or Figure 4.1c, we would take note of this difference. Shape is defined by the outlines of the object viewed as projected on a plane (Gombrich, 1979). Details such as highlighting and shading on the surface are noticed. As expected, this planar shape changes with a change in viewing position. Even though the surfaces are not totally flat, they approximate depthlessness and take on a pictorial quality of flatness or two dimensionality.

Thus, if one views the apparel-body-construct from the reference point of the visual world or from that of the visual field, it makes a difference in what is seen and what is taken for granted. In the visual world experience, there is an unbounded totality of vision, all of which is taken for granted; in the visual field experience, there is a bounded experience of visual cues and nothing is taken for granted.

For full awareness of the visual field you must learn to differentiate among various subtle visual qualities by attending to the details (Bloomer, 1976). This attention to detail depends upon past experience and knowledge. For example, a young child experiences only the greenness of a tree, but the botanist notices the type of tree in great detail—for example, if it is a birch or an oak.

The botanist who is concerned with tree types is seeing differently than a person mowing the lawn, who only sees trees to avoid running into them. Paying attention to the details of the visual field teaches discrimination.

Examine a simple object that you know well, such as a book, from four different viewing locations.

- How do its characteristics affect viewing?
- How does context affect viewing (e.g., if the book is placed on a bookshelf with other books of similar features or if it is lying flat on a table)?
- How many different views could you have of it?
- What is the one view of the book that offers the most information?
- What is the view that offers the least information?
- What happens if the book is partially covered or hidden from view?

Now try this with a person very familiar to you. Consider and describe this person as an apparel-body-construct from the perspective of the (1) visual world and the (2) visual field. What can you discover about the difference? A question to ask yourself for the visual world perspective is how little can you see and still recognize the familiar person—his or her manner of walking or a small area of the person's head. Now, from the visual field perspective, look at that familiar person standing still before you or look at a photograph of him or her. What can you learn about such aspects as body proportions or physical coloring that you did not notice before?

*Application Exercise 4.1*

## SPATIAL PRIORITIES IN VIEWING THE APPAREL-BODY-CONSTRUCT

When observing the apparel-body-construct in its entirety, in order to discover the most information, you must take the perspective of the visual field and examine the apparel-body-construct thoroughly from one point of view at a time (DeLong, 1988). Consider the space occupied by the apparel-body-construct and how the adjacent area influences its silhouette. Consider the space that separates the form and yourself as the viewer (Figure 4.3). The form may be perceived as having space in several directions—forward, backward; side to side; and up, down. What is foreground, or figure, and what is background space? Spend some time looking at what is before you. Now look further. If you become very aware of the way you view the apparel-body-construct, you will begin to notice certain visual priorities—the differences in the way certain elements occupy space—and this can affect what you perceive. For example, the silhouette can appear as a hard edge with the focus directed to the outline itself. Such a silhouette is viewed as a boundary, immediately defining and setting off the apparel-body-construct from the surround.

FIGURE 4.3

*The space occupied by the apparel-body-construct.*

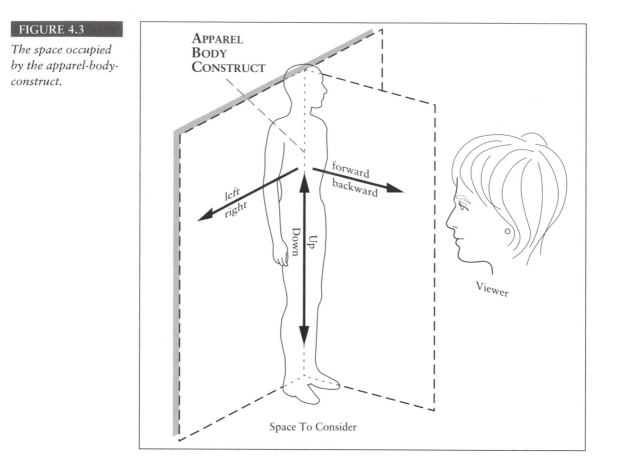

This characteristic would create an immediacy for the observer. The silhouette can also appear as a soft, even blurred, outline that does not act as a boundary at all. Picture several layers of printed chiffon. This may cause the viewer's focus to be directed elsewhere, that is, to more definite parts within the apparel-body-construct.

Let us consider a language that was developed to define spatial priorities in viewing the apparel-body-construct. The following vocabulary is intended to aid the observer in becoming aware of the way the apparel-body-construct occupies space in terms of a visual field perspective. It is a cumulative procedure that starts with the silhouette, then moves inward to observation of parts within the boundary of silhouette, and finally describes the surfaces of the apparel-body-construct. The steps in observing the space of the apparel-body-construct are:

Step 1 **Closed-open.** Observe the silhouette and how its *boundary* is defined within the space.

**Step 2  Part-whole; figure-ground integration/figure-ground separation.** Observe the way parts relate *within the silhouette* of the apparel-body-construct; what aspect separates first for viewing?

**Step 3  Flat-rounded; determinate-indeterminate.** Observe the way the *surfaces appear*, first with relation to the way the body's surfaces appear and then the way apparel-body-construct surfaces appear to the viewer.

The preceding terms are meant to help you move away from personal biases in examining the relationships and notice the particular way a form occupies space. Persistence in using the vocabulary will enable you to consider how certain combinations affect not only your viewing but your understanding of how spatial priorities of forms are associated with meaning. For example, the character of an apparel-body-construct in a particular historical time period is influenced by the way it occupies space. Thus, the apparel professional can achieve a fuller understanding of the design of the apparel-body-construct.

The vocabulary is couched in extremes: that is, it is presented as polar opposite terms. The use of such descriptors serves to call attention to the extremes in how an apparel-body-construct occupies space. The terms that are opposite in meaning (e.g., flat-rounded) are placed at the two ends of a continuum, and any apparel-body-construct can be seen as being within such a continuum. There are two reasons for this. First, learning the extremes (e.g., flat or rounded) allows any apparel-body-construct to be identified. Second, the continuum calls attention to the many subtleties of form that exist between the polar opposites. To begin to really understand the use of this vocabulary, the viewer must go beyond recognition of extreme forms to their subtleties. For example, one apparel-body-construct can be both closed and open: closed on the lower portion of the body and open on the upper portion. But then the viewer needs to go further and determine what this does to the visual effect.

## Closed or Open

Historically, one of the most important identifying features of the dressed body has been its silhouette. The way the silhouette influences the viewer is based upon how much space is occupied and how it occupies space. In the nineteenth century, the silhouette of female fashion was characterized as bell, tubular, and bustle—all labels that reiterated the importance of the silhouette and the shape it creates. For example, characteristic of the 1850s is the voluminous bell-shaped skirt of the female that contrasts with the corseted upper torso. The interaction of these two factors—the amount of space occupied and the way space is occupied—is key in studying characteristics of historical periods. In the early twentieth century, although silhouette continued to be a defining factor, the emphasis that defined the silhouette was concentrated more on the hemlines that were in fashion in each particular season. How the silhouette defines the form is a factor in how the apparel-body-construct occupies space and attracts our attention; it can appear very distinct and independent from the surround or indistinct and interdependent with the surround. **Closed** and **open** are expressions of difference in the relationship of the apparel-body-construct to the surrounding space. These differences alter the visual effect of the apparel-body-construct, possibly causing the silhouette to appear as a frame for the apparel-body-construct or at times directing the eye to parts with more definitive edges within.

A **closed** form is self-contained with a hard-edged silhouette, and this creates a boundary. This effect of boundary is often a controlling factor in perception. When one views a closed form, the silhouette of the apparel-body-construct appears set apart from the surrounding space with a terminal edge, that is, an edge that does not invite viewing beyond the boundary of the silhouette but contains viewing within it. The contrast between the silhouette and the surround in Figure 4.4a creates a closed form. A continuous silhouette edge often defines the apparel-body-construct as an envelope. The type of line that frames the boundary is also important. Often the closed form is mostly a continuous straight line or slightly convex as in Figure 4.5a. Convex

a                    b

outlines appear to enclose more than do concave ones. An outline that is concave or discontinuous appears to incorporate the surround more, as in Figure 4.5b. Visual eye movement of the viewer in taking in the apparel-body-construct of a closed form is contained within the envelope of the silhouette. The viewer does not consider the space around the form because the form appears quite separate and distinct. A closed apparel-body-construct is taken in more immediately by the viewer and is much simpler to perceive because of its clarity in relation to the surround. Thus, a closed apparel-body-construct appears more immediate and nearer to the observer than does an open form.

In an **open** form the apparel-body-construct and the surround appear to interact. An open form does not appear self-contained. The form and the surrounding area are interdependent. The outline of the apparel-body-construct does not enclose as a boundary or an edge but can appear to belong as much to the surround as to the form, as in Figure 4.4b. This can occur, as in Figure 4.4b, because the edge is not distinct and clear, for example, where the silhouette has transparent edges or is the same color as the surround. The silhouette may also appear open because it has many discontinuous lines that seem to incorporate the space around it. It may be ambiguous or may even seem to

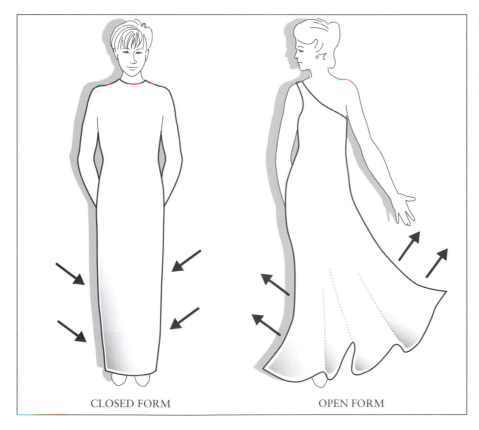

CLOSED FORM                    OPEN FORM

**FIGURE 4.5A & B**

*The outline of a closed form is often continuous and only slightly curved inward toward the body, but that of an open form can be discontinuous and curved outward from the body. Thus, the silhouette of the closed form appears as an envelope and that of the open appears to incorporate space around.*

disappear. The silhouette often does not direct the viewer to essential information in framing the apparel-body-construct. Instead the viewer may be directed to the central axis, for example, or to the surface itself. In Figure 4.6b the silhouette is not a dominant force in framing the whole and the eye is directed to the surface. As a result, the open form may seem more distant from the observer. Figure 4.6b with more open characteristics appears farther away than Figure 4.6a, which is more closed.

When the apparel-body-construct is moving, the viewer is attracted to the movement itself. It is harder to attend to a moving apparel-body-construct, because in motion it has different capabilities for interaction with the surround and can appear closed or more open because of the effect of movement. A closed form in motion may become more open because of the materials and their relation to the apparel-body-construct. For example, a two-piece business suit contrasting with the surround would ordinarily appear closed. An open form in motion can be enhanced by a lightweight fabric floating away from the body, which can interact further with the surround. In Figure 4.7 there are two women in long coats: one (a) that is more closed to the surround and one (b) that trails out from the wearer slightly and thus, both still and in motion, would appear to interact more with the surround and become a more open form.

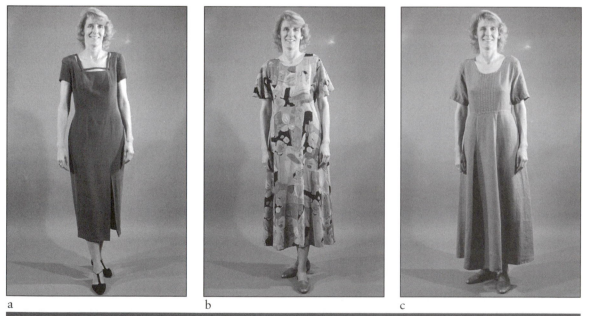

a                                    b                                    c

**FIGURE 4.6A, B & C**

*The apparel-body-construct in Figure 4.6a appears more closed than the one on the Figure 4.6b and c because of straighter lines of the silhouette and contrasting surface. The pattern of the surface of Figure 4.6b becomes more important structurally than the silhouette and thus appears more open.*

Courtesy of Marilyn Revell DeLong.

FIGURE 4.7A & B

*Two women in long coats illustrate closed and open. Figure 4.7a is more closed to the surround because of straighter lines of the silhouette and contrast with the surround. Figure 4.7b is a more open form because of its lighter value and greater interaction with the surround as the body moves.*

Designed by Claude Montana. Courtesy of Fairchild Publications.

a                                        b

    Closed and open fall at either end of a continuum of visual effects created by extreme differences in how the observer views the relationship of the apparel-body-construct to the surround. At the extreme end of closed, the boundary of the silhouette appears totally separate from the surround. At the extreme end of open, the actual boundary of the silhouette may be difficult to distinguish. It may be blurred or disappearing as it interacts with the surround. Most apparel-body-constructs fall somewhere along the continuum between closed and open. Examples include an apparel-body-construct with a direct and simple shape on the lower torso but a more complex and indistinct outline on the upper torso, or a silhouette that appears closed but does not capture attention because of dominant foci within the apparel-body-construct.

    Each viewer will expand his or her understanding of closed and open with the experience of perceiving a wide range of apparel-body-constructs. You will be aware of the influence of the character of the silhouette. The continuum looks like this:

**Closed** ←————————————————————————————→ **Open**

| | |
|---|---|
| Distinct convex edge | Vague concave edge |
| Continuous simple line | Discontinuous complex line |

Think about the most extreme example of an open apparel-body-construct that you have ever seen. Then think of the most extreme example of a closed apparel-body-construct. Now think of examples that are not at the extremes. Fill in the continuum with apparel-body-constructs that fall between the two extremes.

## Whole or Part

In this spatial priority, it is assumed that the viewer references the apparel-body-construct as a whole. The difference is whether the viewer takes in the apparel-body-construct as an entire ensemble first or as a relationship of first one part, then another. Whether you first view the apparel-body-construct **whole-to-part** or **part-to-whole** is a matter of the way features are related within it. Organizing means perceiving or taking in the apparel-body-construct by some visual path. Generally the apparel-body-construct is designed to involve the viewer in ordering of parts as they relate to the structure of the whole. The way the apparel-body-construct and its details are put together can make a difference in what is viewed first—whether the whole or the part stands out in perception. Since the viewer takes in the entire apparel-body-construct, upon prolonged examination, both the whole and its part relationships are revealed.

A **visual part** is defined as a unit of the whole that has a measure of separation or distinction from the rest of the apparel-body-construct (Arnheim, 1974). A part can be as small as one button, as large as the upper torso of the body or the entire outline of a minidress. What initially separates for viewing may be the whole apparel-body-construct or one or more smaller parts. The question to ask when examining a form for **whole** or **part** relationships is: "What separates first for viewing?"

**Whole-to-part viewing** occurs when the observer sees first the whole and then the parts. This process occurs as the observer scans the apparel-body-construct, consciously taking in its entirety. However, the process of **viewing** depends not only on the **viewer** but also on the form. Instances when the form is likely to be viewed as a whole first are numerous. If the silhouette is distinct, as it is in Figure 4.8 where it creates a boundary for the apparel-body-construct and all parts blend with soft edges between surfaces, the whole is likely to be viewed first. When the apparel-body-construct is all matte black and the surface does not

**FIGURE 4.8**

*An apparel-body-construct that is viewed whole-to-part because of soft edges that blend from one part to another. The darker hair becomes a distinguishing part by contrast with the clothing.*

Designed by Alexander Julian. Courtesy of Fairchild Publications.

subdivide into parts within the silhouette, the whole will be viewed first. When the surface is covered with a small, distinct, repeated shape and the silhouette is the most important continuous shape, the whole will again be viewed first. Though the whole is viewed first, there is no excuse to terminate looking for other relationships.

The apparel-body-construct will also be viewed first as a whole when parts are completely interdependent. An example of this type of whole-to-part viewing occurs when an apparel-body-construct has a number of visual parts that have soft edges because of a textural but not a noticeable edge difference as in Figure 4.9. Looking "all of a piece" can be accomplished by selecting one color that is similar to personal coloring for an entire ensemble that only varies because of layout of collar, pockets, and other details. For example, if hair and skin are light in value and the hue of golden blonde, dressing in a creamy white matte surface overall can create a blending whole-to-part look. Soft edges create blending between the body and the apparel within the silhouette of the apparel-body-construct.

**Part-to-whole viewing** takes place when the observer views the parts first and then the whole. Part-to-whole viewing is largely due to parts that are relatively independent within an apparel-body-construct, that is, clear edge definition of shapes or contrast of surface that overrides the effect of the silhouette as a whole as in Figure 4.9b. In Figure 4.10 the apparel-body-construct offers

a                                                                b

**FIGURE 4.9A & B**

*The apparel-body-construct in Figure 4.9a is viewed as a whole first because parts are soft edged and interdependent, while Figure 4.9b is viewed part-to-whole because parts have edge definition and a contrasting surface.*

Designed by: (a) Giorgio Armani and (b) Ermenegliko Zegna. Courtesy of Fairchild Publications.

**FIGURE 4.10**

*Part-to-whole viewing is primarily due to the independence of parts, including leather jacket, skirt, stockings, and boots.*

Designed by Byblos. Courtesy of Fairchild Publications.

part-to-whole viewing and primarily a closed silhouette. Parts include the leather jacket, the skirt with the diagonal plaid, the center front opening revealing the dark stockings and boots, and so forth. The examples in Figure 4.11 are both part-to-whole but for different reasons. In the example to the left, the dark skirt and boots on the lower half separate from the upper half of the body, which includes the jacket and shirt of similar value. In the one on the right, the parts include body parts such as the legs and the area of head and neck. The light at the center of the apparel-body-construct with the contrasting darker-value parts at the upper and lower extremities creates part-to-whole viewing.

Body coloring can create visual parts. For example, when an ivory skin-toned, flaxen blonde wears dark purple, her head (both skin and hair), arms, and legs become visual parts because they separate from the rest of the apparel-body-construct as in Figure 4.6a. The same part effect could be created with dark hair and skin contrasted against a light-value surface near the head and neck. Lapels or other details often contribute to part-to-whole viewing phenomena. The part could be extended from the dark hair and skin to include dark lapels on an otherwise light-value jacket.

The use of the term "separates" usually refers to the visual effect of viewing parts first and then the whole. In this case, parts usually refers to garment categories, such as shirts, shorts, and jackets, that may be planned as a coordinated ensemble, but not a totally matching one as in Figure 4.9b. But parts can also be motifs or patterns, as on the jackets in Figure 4.11. Then, the parts that are perceived as figure include the patterns created on the fabric surfaces. However, in the example on the left, the jacket surface has more distinct parts. In the apparel-body-construct on the right, the jacket pattern is less regular, and the stronger contrast is the shirt with the jacket, pants, skin, and hair.

The part-to-whole relationship is also considered on a continuum. Those apparel-body-constructs that are viewed as parts first usually have several distinct foci that direct the observer, such as contrasting velvet lapel, pocket flaps, and buttons. There are other combinations of part-to-whole relationships—the form may have only one distinct visual part as a focus. This often happens with the business suit where the addition of a shirt and tie create an area near the face that contrasts in value and/or hue, pattern, or texture. The remainder of the body, which fits one's expectations of a business suit, is only scanned. Some details that are similar and expected may go unnoticed.

The continuum of what is viewed first with reference to the part looks like this:

**Whole**                                                                                    **Part**

Indistinct parts                        One distinct part                        Distinct parts

## FIGURE 4.11

*Both apparel-body-constructs offer part-to-whole viewing when the viewer takes in both clothing and body as parts, but in the one on the left, the parts (i.e., jacket, shirt, belt, pants, and head/hair) are more subtle. On the right, stronger parts are created because of the greater value contrast in the upper torso between the white shirt and jacket, dark pants, and head/hair.*

*Designed by Emanuel Ungaro. Courtesy of Fairchild Publications.*

## Figure-Ground Integrated or Figure-Ground Separated

The term **figure-ground** is a way to express the spatial relationships of forward-backward space. The silhouette is the frame of reference of the visual field from which the parts of the apparel-body-construct can project toward the viewer at different levels or planes. Thus, the space between the viewer and the form enters awareness and is expressed as the planar relationship of figure to ground.

**Figure** was defined as that which has object quality, meaning, or "thingness" in our viewing. It is what we focus upon. This is very different from figure referring to the body of the wearer. **Ground** provides a frame of reference for the figure, appearing to surround and lie behind it. In essence, the ground provides the context for the figure. Generally, the figure will appear to exist to some degree in front of the ground. How far the figure appears to lie in front of ground determines whether it distinctly separates from ground or integrates with it. Remember that we are speaking of a visual relationship as opposed to an actual spatial relationship.

When parts are an integral aspect of a single surface it is termed **figure-ground integration**. Whole-to-part viewing can occur with lines or shapes integrated upon the surfaces of the apparel-body-construct when viewed on one level. In Figure 4.12a the stripes of the vest combine the slightly different values of the shirt and pants. Thus, the whole is viewed as figure-ground integrated. Sometimes parts are organized to appear in more definite levels or layers, such as a surface with a pattern that appears to lie on a level well

**FIGURE 4.12A & B**

*In Figure 4.12a, the vest, shirt, and pants are figure-ground integrated. Though a gradation of value exists between the long shirt and pants, the vest includes both values. In Figure 4.12b the long shirt contrasts more with the light pants and appears more figure-ground separated.*

*Designed by Alexander Julian. Courtesy of Fairchild Publications.*

a                                          b

above another. In Figure 4.12b the long tunic with the dominant pattern creates **figure-ground separation** from the lighter value pants. The example in Figure 4.13 is a part-to-whole relationship with figure-ground integration. This occurs because the ground is constant in the knit shirt and trousers, and the stripes of unequal but regular widths allow the figure-ground relation to occur gently.

Figure can relate to ground at different levels of apparent closeness. Figure can appear on a level very close to the ground, and, therefore appear integrated with the ground. This can occur with closely graded values or intensities or with similar small shapes. For example, motifs or shapes on a surface can appear to lie just barely in front of the ground, especially when in a value similar to the ground, as in Figure 4.14. In this apparel-body-construct, the upper torso has textures of knit and leather that are very similar in value. The lower body is covered with a meandering print of slightly lighter value but in the same color family and also similar to the model's hair color. This creates a part-to-whole relation that is figure-ground integrated.

Figure and ground can also appear relatively separated. The level where the figure lies can appear at a distance from the plane of the ground as in Figure 4.15. Here the eye jumps, especially between light and dark contrasts. In a contrasting pattern of shapes on a surface, this has sometimes been called a *spotty effect* (Gombrich, 1979), especially if not organized with the wearer in

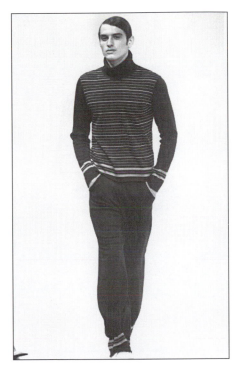

### FIGURE 4.13

*(Above left) Figure-ground integration occurs in this knit shirt and trouser ensemble.*

*Designed by Dolce & Gabbana.*

### FIGURE 4.14

*(Above right) Integration of figure-ground occurs here with similar values but different textures of knit and leather in the upper torso. The lower torso is integrated with the apparel-body-construct through repetition of the same color family and with the model's hair color.*

*Designed by Bill Blass. .*

### FIGURE 4.15

*(Left) Separation of figure-ground occurs because of contrasts in the shapes of the hat, scarf, sweater, and skirt; light and dark value contrasts; and striped patterns on the stockings and scarf.*

*Designed by Ghost.*

*Figures 4.13–4.15 courtesy of Fairchild Publications.*

**FIGURE
4.16A & B**

*Examine figure-
ground separation
and integration in
these examples.*

Designed by Alexander Julian.
Courtesy of Fairchild
Publications.

a                                          b

<table>
</table>

*Application
Exercise 4.3*

Examine the ensembles in Figure 4.16a and b in terms of figure-ground integration
or separation.

- Which is figure-ground integrated? Why?
- Which is figure-ground separated? Why?
- What effect does this have on viewing the remainder of the apparel-body-
  construct?

mind, because it presents to the viewer a separation of figure from ground.
However, in this apparel-body-construct (Figure 4.15), the viewer is attracted
to the contrasts in value of both the striped pattern of the scarf and leggings
and the areas of light and dark values throughout.

The relationship of figure to ground can change as the viewer focuses on
different areas of the apparel-body-construct. What is figure in an initial viewing may become ground in the refocusing process. In Figure 4.15, when the
viewer focuses on the area of the light skirt, the other light areas advance as
figure and connect with each other. When the viewer focuses upon the head
and the dark hair, which flows into the dark sweater, these black parts—the
hair, the sweater, and dark legs and feet—are then organized together.

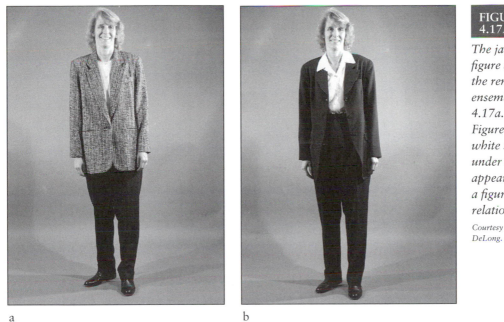

a                                                    b

**FIGURE
4.17A & B**

*The jacket appears as
figure and on top of
the remainder of the
ensemble in Figure
4.17a. However, in
Figure 4.17b, the
white shirt, though
under the jacket,
appears on top in
a figure-ground
relation.*

Courtesy of Marilyn Revell
DeLong.

Figure has also been referred to as positive shape, or focal viewing, and ground as negative space, or contextual viewing. The context here is the surrounding area for the figure. The viewer usually picks out simple positive shapes to focus upon because they are what make the most sense or carry the most visual meaning. It is more difficult to maintain an awareness of the location of ground in viewing. But to maintain an awareness of what is figure and what is ground is critical in the organizing process. There are certain features of the apparel-body-construct that tend to be viewed as figure, such as simple shapes that appear to enclose and separate, from the adjacent space. Every time the viewer distinguishes, separates, and views figure, the relationship of figure to ground is an influencing factor.

In applying the figure-ground concept, the viewer is not bound with what is actually on top but with which surface appears to advance visually. For example, in Figure 4.17a the jacket both appears and actually is on top. However, in Figure 4.17b the jacket is physically the outer layer but appears as ground while the shirt beneath the jacket appears as figure in the area of the jacket opening. Appearing as figure, the shirt in such an instance could be a more intense, warmer color than the jacket, or it could be a shinier, softer material that advances visually.

To become aware of what can be viewed as figure is valuable, especially for the designer. Viewing as figure means understanding whether a neckline is perceived as defining the body or the clothing or perhaps either or both. Figure 4.18a shows an ambiguous figure-ground relationship—Is it two faces or a goblet?

Think of a historical time period when the neckline framed and defined the body as figure first. For example, think of the off-the-shoulder horizontal line of the mid-nineteenth century or the straight portrait neckline often seen on a bridal gown. The shape of the neckline in Figure 4.18a, b, and c varies and creates an interesting figure-ground relationship. The neck can be viewed alternately as figure or ground.

When we view the apparel-body-construct, the body or clothes may vary in their visual priority because of what is perceived as figure. Either the clothing or the body can provide the figure or focus in the figure-ground relationship. The examples in Figure 4.18b and c are interesting in this regard, as the body parts can become figural in the organization. Consider other examples. When viewing a model in a bathing suit, the body itself may function as figure in the figure-ground relationship, but not always. Amount of body covered, degree of curvature of shape, or value contrast are factors in whether the body or the clothing is viewed first.

| *Application Exercise 4.4* | Find an example of a swimsuit where the body becomes figure and the suit the ground. What about the combination made this happen? |
|---|---|

Reversals in figure-ground may occur because the character of the apparel-body-construct and the surround do not automatically create a clear, unambiguous relationship. **Figure-ground ambiguity** is the term used when this relationship can easily be reversed or switched by the viewer. This can occur because the cues for "figuredness" are not clear or because as the viewer focuses equally on various parts of the apparel-body-construct, there is not dominance of one or the other. This reversal may be stimulating or somewhat disturbing, depending upon the orientation of the viewer. We have all experienced an alteration of meaning in two-dimensional examples, such as the face or goblet in Figure 4.18a. In the apparel-body-construct, the reversal may change the meaning as is illustrated in 4.18a. Cues for figuredness are often introduced in the design of an apparel-body-construct to make clear the figure-ground relationship.

In the scanning-focusing process, what is viewed as figure and ground can become a conscious act. In other words, the active viewer can become skilled at understanding what is first seen as figure and what is ground, but also what cues provide for perception of figure and in what order we attend. For example, initially we may focus on the entire apparel-body-construct as figure and the space around as ground. Then we may focus on one part that attracts our attention as figure. The surrounding area becomes ground. Often the viewer can force reversals, even though the figure-ground relationship is

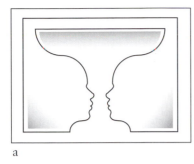

a

## FIGURE 4.18A, B & C

*Figure 4.18a is an ambiguous figure-ground relationship, depending upon focus on the faces or the goblet. Is the neckline in the examples in Figure 4.18b and Figure 4.19c defining the body, the clothing, or both?*

*Designed by Valentino. Courtesy of Fairchild Publications.*

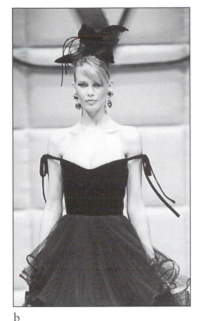

b

c

relatively clear. This practice of making reversals can lead to a better understanding of what cues play an important role in a particular figure-ground relationship. Both figure and ground are important to the visual effect of the apparel-body-construct, but since noting such relationships is not ordinarily necessary for carrying on life events, they are overlooked. The visually attuned viewer needs to make a conscious effort to perceive the intricacies of the figure-ground relationship.

In a relationship of parts, all may appear relatively close together, separated from a ground but not jumping out at the viewer. This is often the look of a two-piece suit with top and bottom of the same fabric. Such a suit with a similar value shirt would be experienced as figure-ground integration. However, the apparel-body-construct may appear more separated with the trousers, shoes, and hair of dark value and dull finish, and the top jacket of a shiny, light fabric. The top is viewed as figure first with the bottom as ground, because of the lightness of color and the shiny finish of the fabric. The viewer would label this apparel-body-construct as figure-ground separated since various distinct levels of surface are experienced.

**Figure-Ground Integrated**                          **Figure-Ground Separated**

◄─────────────────────────────────────────►

Indistinct edges                                              Distinct edges

Interrelated shapes filling surface          Discrete shapes dispersed on surface

## Flat or Rounded

The way surfaces occupy space needs to be differentiated by the viewer (Rothschild, 1960; Munro, 1970). From the perspective of the visual world, we know the body is a three-dimensional form in space. From the perspective of the visual field, the body of the wearer may or may not be a rounded surface. We may perceive its surfaces as either three-dimensional with rounded surfaces, as in Figure 4.19a, or essentially as two-dimensional with flat surfaces, as in Figure 4.19b, depending upon their nature within the apparel-body-construct.

At any one time you can only see one side of an apparel-body-construct as a visual unit. If you take note of silhouette—the outermost perimeter of the apparel-body-construct that can be viewed from one side—you are viewing a two-dimensional, flat aspect. If you take note of how a shiny-surfaced fabric interacts with body curvature, you are viewing a three-dimensional or cylindrical aspect of the surfaces of the apparel-body-construct. The form can give three-dimensional cues, which direct viewing of surface as a cylinder. This depends on the manner in which the body is treated with the surfaces and shapes of the garment and the configurations that can be applied to a conforming material, such as fabric, by easing, gathering, or pleating. Compare Figure 4.6a and c, where the shapes of the necklines appear two-dimensional, and the skirt in Figure 4.6c, which appears three-dimensional because of the deep folds of fabric.

**FIGURE 4.19A & B**

*The surfaces of Figure 4.19a appear rounded and three dimensional, while the surfaces in Figure 4.19b appear flat and two dimensional.*

Designed by: (a) Gianni Versace and (b) Patricia Underwood. Courtesy of Fairchild Publications.

a

b

The surfaces will always influence how the viewer will perceive the apparel-body-construct. Some surfaces do not reflect the body's curvatures and will appear more two-dimensional, flat, and essentially on a plane parallel to the viewer. Think of such a surface as a rectangular piece of paper held before the viewer, or the effect of a cookie cut from rolled dough. These surfaces can be viewed as essentially flat, even though the viewer knows the body is a cylindrical surface. The surfaces of the garment can hang straight down from the shoulders because of gravity. They can skim the body surfaces and not interact with the body curves. When a surface appears to be relatively unoccupied, without texture or light reflectance, the eye perceives the area as a block of color and edge becomes a priority. This occurs in a matte black that does not call attention to surface contours but rather to area and edge.

The apparel can also appear to emphasize the rounded contours and curves of the body. Surfaces are often hypothetically extended around the body simply because the viewer knows they are there from past knowledge and memory of other visual world experiences. The viewer can also be made conscious of the rounded body surface through its interaction with fabric surfaces. This can be accomplished in various ways. Fabrics can be wrapped around the body to emphasize the rounded body surface, such as with a sari or sarong. In these cases, diagonal folds add to the contouring effect. A diagonal ruffle circling the body can emphasize the three-dimensional nature of the body and make the viewer aware of a visual path.

Attention can be called to the rounded surfaces of the body cylinder by a shiny fabric reflecting at different angles or by a printed surface that is somewhat distorted from regularity by the cylindrical nature of the body. For example, picture a print of circle shapes. As the fabric covers the contours of the female body, some of the circles will appear incomplete and others elliptical. This creates an awareness of the body cylinder or, if the shapes are perceived independently, they may take over in a figure-ground relationship on the surface. Surfaces can also appear rounded because of layout structuring, gathers, or pleats. Light and shadow effects will enhance awareness of the body cylinder. For example, in the dress in Figure 4.20 the skirt alternates with varying light and shadow effects and emphasizes the body as a cylinder, whereas the bodice appears relatively flat.

The continuum of flat or rounded surfaces looks like this:

**FIGURE 4.20**

*Light and shadow enhance the body cylinder. Here the bodice appears relatively flat while the skirt alternates light and shadow effects to increase the awareness of its three-dimensional qualities, also enhanced by its shape.*

Designed by Valentino. Courtesy of Fairchild Publications.

| Flat | Rounded |
|---|---|
| Smooth, nonreflecting surfaces | Curved, reflecting surfaces |
| Two-dimensional shapes | Three-dimensional shapes |

## Determinate or Indeterminate

The final set of polar terms refers to a second characteristic of the surfaces of the apparel-body-construct. Determinate or indeterminate refers to the apparent thickness of the surfaces of the apparel-body-construct and thus their apparent distance from the observer. Reference is to the immediacy of surfaces for the viewer, that is, how near or far away they appear and how easily they are assimilated by the viewer. This is different from figure-ground integration or separation because this relationship involves surfaces and does not deal directly with visual parts.

**Determinate** describes surfaces that appear definite, sharp, regular, and clear-cut. There is no doubt about what is figure and what is ground. If shapes are present, they are few and large, simple or repetitious overall. The shapes are easily perceived as figure, while at the same time the viewer clearly perceives ground. The surface has relatively few planes or levels in viewing that can be ordered by the viewer, as in Figure 4.21. A determinate surface usually has little visual texture and carries little potential for interplay between light and shadow. The observer takes in the determinate surface quickly because of the immediacy in the way it occupies space.

In contrast, an **indeterminate** surface appears less definite in the way it occupies space. Indeterminate surfaces often appear blurred, soft, or with infinite levels or ambiguity of figure to ground. Shapes are irregular and soft edged. The surface appears thick because of overall visual texture, as in Figure 4.22. In this apparel-body-construct the layers are undefined by boundaries and the edges next to the body are mostly undefined. The main focus is the slightly more dominant patterned jacket and head. Another example of indeterminacy is a transparent surface, such as would occur with layers of printed chiffon over a printed undersurface. This would occur when the transparency was not backed with an opaque surface, such as the lower torso in Figure 4.22. Still another example would be a reflective surface that creates a myriad of different, interrelated light and shadow surface effects, as in Figure 4.19a. Gathers or pleats that carry light and shadow effects could also aid in the appearance of indeterminate surfaces.

Printed surfaces can create an interesting effect when they do not have a specific figure-to-ground relationship. This can occur when the motif is integrated somewhat with the ground, as in Figure 4.22. In this instance, the surface with the motif may be viewed as slightly thicker than the surface minus the motif. The viewer may read such a surface as indeterminate when the motif does not separate

**FIGURE 4.21**

*Determinate surfaces appear definite, sharp, and clear-cut with defined levels of viewing.*

Designed by Marziotto/Accento. Courtesy of Fairchild Publications.

**FIGURE 4.22**

*(Left) Indeterminate surfaces can appear soft and blurred with infinite levels or ambiguous figure-ground relationships.*

Designed by Oscar de la Renta. Courtesy of Fairchild Publications.

**FIGURE 4.23**

*(Right) Printed surfaces without a specific figure-ground relationship can simply appear thicker.*

Designed by Arnold Scaasi. Courtesy of Fairchild Publications.

clearly and is not read as figure-ground. Boundaries created by edges at sleeve, neckline, and hem often become important as a cut-off and therefore a source of structure, and often the surface gathers or other manipulations add to the indeterminacy. In Figure 4.23, the motif also does not separate into figure-ground, but the medium-value surfaces do carry the light and shadow. What is more, the surfaces of the dress with the small, regular, checkered pattern are not hard to separate within the dress because they change direction. The dark hair and leggings contrast with the indeterminate qualities of the dress and offer a grounding effect when viewing the apparel-body-construct.

As you may have guessed by now, many apparel-body-constructs effectively combine a variety of determinate and indeterminate surfaces into one ensemble. In Figure 4.11 the jackets are somewhat indeterminate, but the remainder of the ensemble is more determinate, repeating the color values used in the jacket. The result is a strong, dark centering of the body's verticality in the example on the left and a part-to-whole effect in the example on the right.

The continuum of surfaces defined by determinate to indeterminate looks like this:

| Determinate | Indeterminate |
| --- | --- |
| Plain, smooth surface | Much surface texture |
| Few but regular or no shapes | Many irregular shapes |
| No light and shadow effect | Much light and shadow |

# USING THE VOCABULARY OF SPACE

The vocabulary describing the space of the apparel-body-construct consists of opposite word pairs that characterize how space is occupied. Discoveries can be made by slowing down and thinking about the viewing process related to the five continuums to understand spatial relationships and how they influence structure and organization. Asking yourself *how* and *why* you are viewing the apparel-body-construct in this way is essential to learning about spatial character.

Each word pair represents, first of all, a spatial phenomenon. The viewer learns about the apparel-body-construct by first locating the extreme examples at the ends of a continuum. However, each apparel-body-construct can be most usefully considered as representing a range of spatial phenomena. Apparel-body-constructs can be compared using this vocabulary and decisions can be made about the visual effectiveness of any one apparel-body-construct according to a particular visual goal. Examples can be found placed all along each continuum. Furthermore, all four sets of word pairs can be applied to each apparel-body-construct. For example, in Figure 4.16 the apparel-body-constructs can be compared on all the continuums. Figure 4.16a is whole-to-part, and Figure 4.16b is more part-to-whole. Comparing figure-ground, Figure 4.16a is integrated within the ensemble, whereas in Figure 4.16b the figure-ground is separated. The surfaces of both are somewhat rounded and determinate.

*Application Exercise 4.5*

Use the examples of apparel-body-constructs in Figure 4.25a, b, c, and d, which initially appear very different. Now consider where each would appear on the line of five continuums of visual priorities as shown in Figure 4.24. Begin with the silhouette and work toward part definition and then surface definition. Placement on the continuums is a first step. The next step is to understand how to manipulate and control the space. Look at one apparel-body-construct using the vocabulary of space, and then relate it to another if necessary. Adopting a "what if" approach often helps, that is, what if this surface were altered? What difference would it make in the way it occupies space?

**FIGURE 4.24**

*Visual priorities of the apparel-body-construct.*

| Closed | Open |
|---|---|
| Whole | Part |
| Figure-ground integrated | Separated |
| Flat | Rounded |
| Determinate | Indeterminate |

a

b

c

d

**FIGURE 4.25A, B, C & D**

*Plot each of the four apparel-body-constructs on each of the five continuums of visual priorities in Figure 4.24 by placing along each line the letter a, b, c, or d. Compare the results. What do you learn about the use of space in each of the examples?*

*Designed by (a) Oscar de la Renta, (b) Yves Saint Laurent, (c) Bill Blass, and (d) Giorgio Armani. Courtesy of Fairchild Publications.*

This vocabulary is meant as an aid to description and imagination. In other words, a certain apparel-body-construct could be described as *closed*, *whole-to-part*, *figure-ground integrated*, *flat*, and *determinate*. By this description, you will soon be able to imagine or picture in your mind some of the characteristics of such an apparel-body-construct and how it will appear. There is nothing inherent in the vocabulary that is meant to be construed as a negative or positive visual experience. The terms help you assess and evaluate an apparel-body-construct for the look you like and its appropriateness to a given client or situation.

In addition, the word pairs interrelate when applied to apparel-body-constructs. As the viewer considers the apparel-body-construct according to each set of word pairs, certain combinations tend to reoccur together. Over time, a certain relatedness between the concepts will emerge as the terminology becomes familiar and each of the word pairs is applied repeatedly. For example, closed and determinate are often connected in the same apparel-body-construct. But are they always linked together in the same way? The answer is: No! Unusual combinations may be found, possibly giving the viewer certain expectations in applying the vocabulary. For example, an apparel-body-construct can be closed and indeterminate. Look for one. The viewer who applies this vocabulary with fresh awareness each time may be surprised by an unusual apparel-body-construct. Such a visual form may be the start of a significant new look.

a                    b                    c

## FIGURE 4.26A, B & C

*The apparel-body-construct within a given culture can appear to have characteristic relatedness of certain concepts. For example, Figure 4.26a and b are front and back views of a woman wearing traditional dress from Turkey. The many layers of related surfaces create visual parts in a part-to-whole and indeterminate relationship that is more flat in the front view (a) than the back view (b). The form is open primarily because of its similarity with the surround, and figure-ground is integrated because of the combinations that are color-related as well as incorporate light and shadow. In Figure 4.26c, the veil worn to cover the face increases the indeterminacy.*

Courtesy of Marlene Breu.

Within a given culture, certain combinations of visual priorities often occur, especially with traditional dress that, by definition, occurs in familiar and similar apparel-body-constructs. For example, in Figure 4.26 there are front and back views of traditional dress worn by a woman from Turkey. Consider how certain combinations occur together: open—closed, part—whole, figure-ground integrated or separated, flat—rounded, determinate—indeterminate. Variations of the dress, as in Figure 4.26c, where she is wearing a veil to cover her face, can create more of a characteristic of indeterminacy.

Finally, application of the word pairs can help the viewer assess visual goals—coherence and order. As you remember from Chapter 2, coherence was defined as how the unit holds together visually, and order can provide a visual path for the viewer to take throughout the structure of the apparel-body-construct. For example, the viewer may prefer an apparel-body-construct with different visual priorities than what appears: one that is a stronger visual presentation or one that is more complex but appears to be ordered in a hierarchy. By analyzing the part-to-whole relationship the viewer can make changes in the apparel-body-construct toward a desired visual goal of a whole-to-part relationship. The viewer-turned-designer can also modify any apparel-body-construct so it is oriented toward one or the other end of the continuum.

Application of spatial priorities in a retailing setting can be rewarding. Walk through a children's store or department and consider how spatial priorities influence a display and the theme of the display.

*Application Exercise 4.6*

## Summary

- Two significant viewing orientations are the **visual field** and the **visual world.**

- The *visual world* is the familiar visual space in which people perceive solid objects with constant and learned features. People focus on these objects for meaning and recognize them from memory without perceiving them in any detail by means of minimal cues.

- The *visual field* is the totality of the visual experience—what the educated observer takes in by paying special attention to everything that is in his or her field of vision.

- A special language consisting of opposite word pairs helps in observing the space occupied by the apparel-body-construct. These word pairs are organized in steps:

  **Closed-open:** How the silhouette and its boundary are defined within the visual space. Example: A transparent blouse has an open silhouette.

  **Part-whole, figure-ground integration, figure-ground separation:** How the parts relate to the whole within the silhouette; what separates first for viewing. It is important to learn to distinguish figure from ground.

  **Flat-rounded, determinate-indeterminate:** The apparel-body-construct can call attention to the rounded surfaces of the body or can make the body appear relatively flat. Determinate surfaces appear sharp, regular, clear-cut; indeterminate or soft-edged surfaces appear less definite in the way they delimit space.

- These word pairs or steps greatly help the observer in perceiving the apparel-body-construct and can even help in designing significant new looks.

## Key Terms and Concepts

closed
closed-open
determinate-indeterminate
figure
figure-ground ambiguity
figure-ground integration

figure-ground separation
flat-rounded
ground
open
part-to-whole
perceive

viewer
viewing
visual field
visual part
visual world
whole-to-part

## References

Arnheim, R. *Art and Visual Perception: A Psychology of the Creative Eye*. Berkeley: University of California Press, 1974.

Arnheim, R. *The Power of the Center*. Berkeley: University of California Press, 1982.

Barratt, K. *Logic and Design*. Westfield, NJ: Eastview Editions, 1980.

Bloomer, C. *Principles of Visual Perception*. New York: Van Nostrand Reinhold, 1976.

Collier, G. *Form, Space and Vision*. Englewood Cliffs, NJ: Prentice-Hall, 1967.

DeLong, M. "Clothing and Aesthetics: Perception of Form." *Home Economics Research Journal*, 47, 1978, 214–224.

DeLong, M., and Larntz, K. "Measuring Visual Response to Clothing." *Home Economics Research Journal*, 8, 281–93.

Dondis, D. *A Primer of Visual Literacy*. Cambridge, MA: MIT Press, 1973.

Eisner, E. *Educating Artistic Vision*. New York: Macmillan, 1972.

Gibson, J. *Perception of the Visual World*. Boston: Houghton Mifflin, 1950.

Gibson, J. *The Senses Considered as Perpetual Systems*. Boston: Houghton Mifflin, 1966.

Gombrich, E. *The Sense of Order: A Study in the Psychology of Decorative Art*. Ithaca, NY: Cornell University Press, 1979.

Munro, T. *Form and Style in the Arts*. Cleveland: Case Western Reserve University Press, 1970.

Paramenter, R. *The Awakened Eye*. Middleton, CT: Wesleyan University Press, 1968.

Rothschild, L. *Style in Art*. New York: Thomas Yoseloff, 1960.

# Chapter Five

# THE BODY AS A PREEXISTING STRUCTURE

After you have read this chapter, you will be able to understand:

- The potential influence of the body structure on the organization of the apparel-body-construct.

- The effect of historical ideals on idealized body forms and how this relates to the way we dress.

- The universal similarities in the physical structure of the body and how body views (front, side, back, body-in-the-round) affect the design of clothing.

- The impact of bilateral symmetry of the body—and the impact of focal points such as where wrists and lower hip meet—on clothing design.

- How planar and depth effects affect how the body is viewed and how this impacts clothing design.

- How the body affects the apparel-body-construct in terms of how clothing emphasizes or deemphasizes body contours, accentuates the relationship of body parts to each other, extends body parts, reveals or conceals body parts, and underlines body movement or stasis.

- How the body serves as a medium of cultural expression via dress, emphasizing such characteristics as age or gender-specific dress.

EVERYONE'S BODY IS UNIQUE. A PERSON WOULD NOT be recognizable without his or her individual qualities. In our usual viewing of the body of another person, we are interacting with a structure fundamentally similar to our own. We compare what we see to ourselves and to others, noting similarities and differences. For example, we assign gender; we may view a form as shorter, taller, fuller, or thinner than ourselves; or we may determine both general and specific age categories, such as categorizing someone as a teenager approximately 14 years of age. As the term implies, the apparel-body-construct is a framework to look at the interaction between the apparel and the body. This chapter begins a more thorough examination of this interaction by concentrating on the body.

In the visual world people become experts at recognizing other individuals with a minimum of visual cues. Yet, if you are sensitive to variations in visual effect, you will be quick to notice changes in someone's appearance, like a new haircut. Sometimes you notice a change even though you do not identify what that change is. For example, asking a friend hesitantly, "Did you just get new glasses?" is a sign that you know some aspect of her features is different, but you are not sure exactly what has changed. People are so intimately acquainted with the body—our own and others—that they do not stop to think about what it offers visually. You constantly interact with other people who influence your actions, without thinking much about their body structure and its relationship to the apparel-body-construct.

For purposes of visual analysis, it is important to alter the habit of using a minimum number of cues to accomplish recognition, that is, the visual world orientation. It is important to separate oneself from reacting to the familiar and concentrate on identifying and recognizing the specific attributes that make up the body. The body will be discussed as a generalized visual structure and then its various features will be delineated. In this way you will understand in more detail the complexities of visual relationships.

The body, considered as a basic visual structure, has many universal aspects that everyone shares as members of the human race—upright posture, a trunk or torso, and four extremities. Viewing the body in this way will enable you to set aside the qualities that make the body individual to concentrate on the body as a generalized form. You will concentrate on what you see, not what you know. This will help you to see beyond your own body and consider the body structure and its effect upon various arrangements of materials. Then you will be able to understand the potential influence of the body structure upon the organization of the apparel-body-construct.

Viewing the body for its potential as an apparel-body-construct is a useful objective. A designer's success is often measured in the dressing room when the client tries on the creation for the first time. The designer has succeeded if what is viewed in the mirror flatters the body according to the wearer, fulfilling expectations of the way the client wants to look. Many consultants selecting clothing to enhance body type instruct the client how to dress toward

a

b

c

some goal without making it explicit. Goals, however, change with time and culture. This discussion of the "body as potential" will clarify and make explicit such goals.

In every historical period, there exist ideals for body structure. This can change based upon the society's motivations and resulting characteristic forms of dress. In general, we strive for what we hold up as a desirable body type and that relates to the apparel-body-construct prevalent at the time. At the turn of the twentieth century in the United States, the Gibson Girl expressed a wholesome, athletic type. The Gibson Girl was described as having a long, swanlike neck that related to the high, closely fitted collar of her "waist" or "bodice," giving her a patrician look, and a small waist circumference in relation to a broad shoulderline. Her hair was swept up in a full teapot shape that further emphasized the neck by contrast. In the 1960s, on the other hand, Twiggy epitomized a body image desired by many—a tall, slender, and very youthful androgynous form with an expression of innocence that originated from large, wide eyes and short, cropped hair. The "Twiggy" form was enhanced through the clothing, which consisted of simple minidresses that skimmed the body curvatures. Visual parts were often contrasting, small details in rounded, self-contained units and body extremities. Eye makeup further focused the viewer on the wide-eyed expression. Thus, the body itself and all the clothing, hair shapes, etc., that make for the total appearance relate and reinforce the image of the time. In the 1990s in the United States the perfect body continues to be defined by models. One

**FIGURE 5.1A, B & C**

*Examples of ideals of body structure: The Gibson Girl as sketched by Charles Dana Gibson (a); a womanly ideal of the first decade of the twentieth century (b); Twiggy (c), who became an ideal of the 1960s with her slender and youthful androgynous body and wide-eyed, innocent face.*

example, according to Barnette (1995), is Italian-born Carla Bruni, described as having 34–23–35 1/2 inch measurements with long legs, narrow hips, and broad shoulders.

According to McCracken (1988), females have at times striven to appear like their male counterparts in a business setting. Thus, they wear suits with shoulder pads, constructed from no-nonsense fabrics, and the focus is upon the upper torso and head through contrast. At the same time, males have become less gender-specific, especially in their casual dress. Colors that have been designated as feminine are now worn by both males and females. Many younger males and females have adopted body piercing and jewelry. Perhaps we will look back at this time as a loosening of the restrictions, limitations, and ideals of gender dressing that took on such polarized forms in the late nineteenth and early twentieth centuries.

Many cultures have different ideas of the ideal body, such as number of body rings or degree of portliness. In some societies obesity means wealth because it denotes privilege. In other societies wide hips give the appearance of fertility, an important characteristic for marriage. Ideal in one culture are small feet and in another culture big feet are prized. Our task in this chapter is to consider the body as a preexisting visual structure and recognize its potential for the apparel-body-construct. First the body will be described as an existing physical structure, then as a component of the apparel-body-construct. Finally, the body will be considered as it suggests associations that affect our viewing of the apparel-body-construct.

## THE BODY AS A PHYSICAL STRUCTURE

The physical structure of the body is a vertical unit, consisting of a head, torso or trunk, and four limbs or extremities. The upper portion of the body is generally considered to have more visual interest than the lower portion. The arms are configured similarly to the legs, only shorter in length and smaller in circumference. The head is predominant in our viewing of the body primarily because of the eye-to-eye connection. We often think the eyes are a window to the soul and this brings about a focus on eyes, regardless of whether or not we interact with the person. The head offers other form-related features—the most visual detail—and its size, rounded shape, and position, centered on the body, make it a natural focal point. Also, the contrast of the head shape with shoulder width forms a triangular shape which increases the importance of this area as a center of attention.

The head can become dominant in the proportional relationships of the remainder of the human body, as the unit of visual measure. The head is one way of measuring the body proportions, with the head length of a particular body used for measuring the lengths of the remainder of the body (Figures 5.2 and 5.3). Thus, the entire body can be described as a certain number of heads

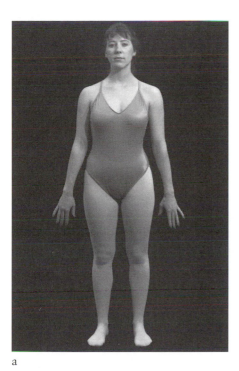

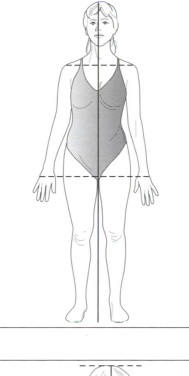

a

b

FIGURE 5.2A & B

*Head length may be used to measure body proportions and thus is expressed as number of heads high, e.g., 7 1/2 heads high. This is because in the viewing process the head becomes a unit of measure for the remainder of the body.*

Courtesy of Marilyn Revell DeLong.

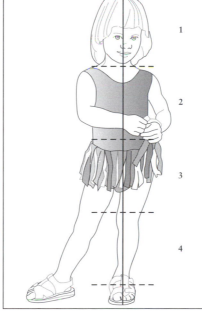

a

b

FIGURE 5.3A & B

*In the same manner as an adult, the proportions of a child's body are measured as number of heads high, e.g., 4+ heads high.*

Courtesy of Marilyn Revell DeLong.

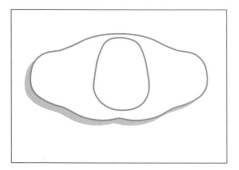

FIGURE 5.4

*The body is a convex shape when viewing a cross section from the top down.*

high. Though the average body is 7 1/2 heads tall, the proportions of the body of a model whose function is to display clothing is at least an additional head length visually. We appear taller or shorter, in part, because of the proportion of our heads. Two identically sized bodies, one with a larger and one with a smaller-sized head, would create quite a different sense of proportion, which in turn would affect the overall appearance of each. The reason for this variation in appearance is that the viewer's eye uses size within the context of that entire body as a means of comparison.

The body torso is a convex surface. A cross section viewed from the top down would appear as an oval or ellipse (Figure 5.4). A cross section of any body segment would vary in circumference depending upon where the cross section was taken. The body limbs are also convex but smaller in size than the torso. The curvature of the surface affects the appearance of a covering placed upon it. A body cylinder has a flatter curve when viewed from the front or back and a fuller curve when viewed from the side.

FIGURE 5.5A & B

*The body viewed as a unit from the perspective of the visual field. In viewing the front body view, the body has bilateral symmetry, that is, the left and right halves appear similar. Noticing the varying widths of the silhouette and body configurations, i.e., the relation of head to shoulders, arm to torso are important to the design of the apparel-body-construct.*

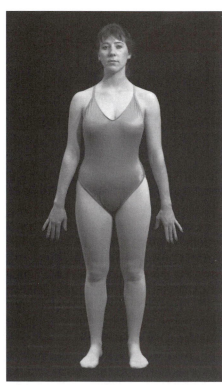

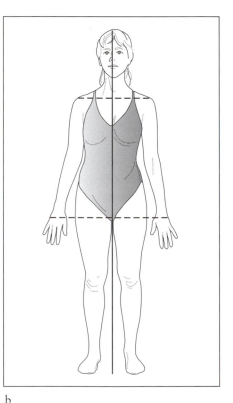

a

b

## Body Views

An observer of the body knows of its structure but may not have thought about its visual effect in terms of **body views** (Figure 5.5a and b). We take for granted what we see frequently because of our reliance upon memory and what we know about the way the body appears from many viewpoints. In other words, we see it from our visual world orientation (discussed in Chapter 4) in which the body moves about and we do not focus on any one body view. However, what can be viewed at any one time depends upon the relationship of the observer to a particular body structure. This constitutes the observer's view of the body from the visual field orientation. The extent of the body that can be viewed at any one time influences the units of the body that are available to the clothing designer.

A visual field, as you will remember, is that portion of the visual world that can be perceived by an observer from a fixed position. As the observer or the object moves, the visual field changes. Imagine a model in a fashion photo shoot moving about and posing for a series of shots. Each one of these photo views presents the apparel-body-construct differently. To understand the apparel-body-construct from any one viewpoint requires that an observer first focus on it and then observe its details and how it becomes a component of the apparel-body-construct. This requires concentration.

From the reference of a visual field, the body is viewed as having visual units or views as in a photograph: front, back, and side views. The front view is the visual unit of the body that receives much of the attention of both designer and viewer. We interact as one human to another mostly from the front view, and this often influences how the apparel-body-construct is designed to be viewed. The head, the frontal position of facial details, the body symmetry, and the way the body moves forward are important to this front view. However, examples of apparel-body-constructs can be found that emphasize other body views or even an in-the-round treatment of the body. In Figure 5.6, the child has one body view treatment of contrasting details on the front T-shirt and toes of his shoes. This will make him appear different, according to the body view. The man, in contrast, has a flowing robe which extends the body length and would appear similarly in all body views. Minor features that suggest one body view include the beads and neck detailing at the front. Also, the dark walking stick provides contrast against the white robe and will emphasize more of one body view, depending upon how it is carried. In this example, the body itself provides the major cue to visual units.

**FIGURE 5.6**

*The child is dressed to emphasize the front body view and the man to emphasize the length and breadth of the front and back views. This contemporary Igbo man and child are celebrating their heritage in St. Paul, Minnesota.*

Courtesy of Janel Urke.

## Body Views from Front or Back

The body structure is a symmetrical form about a vertical axis when viewed from the front or back. In other words, the left half and the right half of the front or back are viewed as more or less the same: This is called **bilateral symmetry** (Figure 5.5). It looks more stable from either front or back views than it does when viewed from the side. One body view is often treated as a dominant design focus and in various historic periods this view can differ depending upon the cultural context. For example, in the United States during the 1930s, a woman's back was often used for quite exotic treatments in evening gowns; low, cleverly shaped necklines as in Figure 5.7a; or a back fullness centered at the hip (Figure 5.7b). Due to the popularity of pairs dancing, the front of the female torso was less in view than the back. A 1990s treatment of the back in Figure 5.7c extends interest in the front and back body views through asymmetry.

The body has several points along the silhouette where more visual information occurs, that is, where change or contrast is greatest, such as at the waist, crotch, fingertips, at the axis of the shoulder and arm, head and neck, and so forth (Figure 5.8). Since these points of change are noticed more than

a                                          b                                          c

### FIGURE 5.7A, B & C

*Front and back views of a 1930s Schiaparelli design are represented in Figure 5.7a and b. A contemporary version of back interest created through an asymmetric treatment of the front and back body view is depicted in Figure 5.7c.*

Courtesy of: (a and b) The Goldstein Gallery, University of Minnesota, and (c) Designed by Calvin Klein. Fairchild Publications.

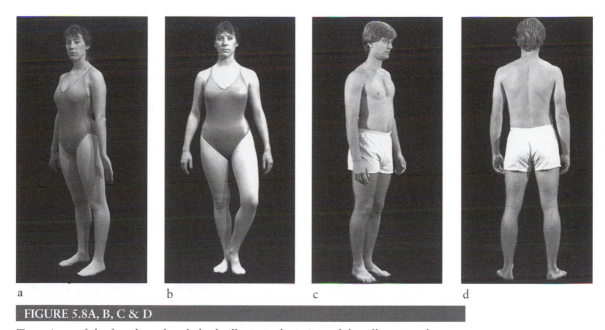

a      b      c      d

**FIGURE 5.8A, B, C & D**

*Two views of the female and male body illustrate the points of the silhouette where much visual information occurs because of change in body conformation, i.e., head, shoulders, arms, waist, crotch, fingertips, and feet.*

Courtesy of Marilyn Revell DeLong.

where no change occurs, they become important in the apparel-body-construct. As one views the body, the outline that helps to frame the apparel-body-construct can follow the body outline or alter it.

From the front or back view, the shoulder width contrasts with the head width. The shoulders then can become a focus which can be enhanced through various shoulder treatments, such as shoulder pads or large sleeves. The famous Letty Lynton dress worn by Joan Crawford in a 1930s movie with its large sleeves, slim waist, and gently flaring skirt was actually reported to be designed to camouflage her broad shoulders in an unusual way (Figure 5.9). The volume of the sleeve created a viewing emphasis at the shoulder, thus calling attention to the large sleeve. The result of this "visual deception" or "illusion" quickly moved into the mainstream market.

A natural point of focus on the body is the area where the wrists and lower hip meet when the body is still and the arms are hanging in a relaxed position. The female body is wide at the hipline and, when the body ideal does not include or enhance such an area, the usual treatment is to visually minimize it. Thus, to be photographed, we are often instructed to place our hand up at the waist or stand at a three-quarter angle view to the camera to lessen this width by concealing one arm from view. These points along the body silhouette are often emphasized or deemphasized through contrasts in

*Joan Crawford wears a dress that attracted much attention in a 1930s movie and was copied widely. As an actress, she played the role of Letty Lynton and wore a dress with sleeves of such volume that the attention of the viewer was drawn to the large sleeves rather than to what she considered a defect, her broad shoulders.*

Courtesy of The Kobal Collection.

width in clothing. A jacket whose length ends at the hipline can deemphasize by contrasting a full jacket with a slim skirt or trouser. Such contrasts appear often because of their success in controlling the visual result. These points of change are critical in perception and clothing can be used to alter or enhance the body at these points.

The body usually appears grounded and balanced in modern design. Modern dance of the twentieth century makes the viewer aware of this grounding through choreography. The longer lower limbs are often slightly spread to balance the body either standing still or in movement with the body trunk rising from this grounding. The concept of grounding of the body can be aided and abetted, visually and literally, in the design of the apparel-body-construct. A figure skater or ballet dancer uses skate blades or small, close-fitting shoes to create an airy, ungrounded movement and appearance. Shoes and stockings can be light in value and shaped delicately to deemphasize visual weight of the foot. By contrast, the stable boots of a mountain climber ground the body visually, as do Doc Martens and other visually heavy shoes worn in the recent decade. In addition, taking wide, aggressive steps relates the body movement to the concept of grounding through the footwear.

## Body Views from the Side

When the body is viewed from the side, it is asymmetrical with respect to the vertical axis (Figure 5.10). This can create an unbalanced appearance that is not often emphasized as a body view. However, there are some examples of the side as a body view for design, that is, the band uniform with a contrasting shoulder

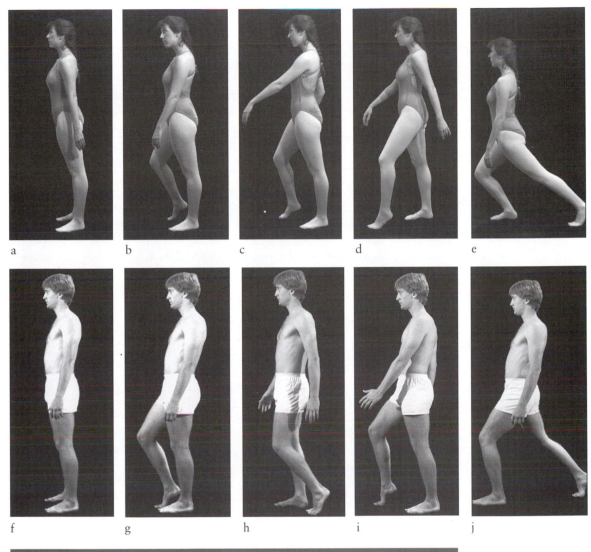

a   b   c   d   e

f   g   h   i   j

## FIGURE 5.10A THROUGH J

*The body viewed from the side is asymmetrical with respect to a vertical axis, that is, an imaginary line drawn through the center of the body.*

Courtesy of Marilyn Revell DeLong.

The changes apparent from the side view are not often emphasized by clothing. But there are some exceptions. Can you think of some? Example: The skier who races often has a side leg treatment to emphasize body movements.

*Application Exercise 5.1*

epaulet with gold fringe and stripe down the side of the leg to emphasize precision marching. The 1970s saw the beginning of blue jeans individually decorated, and the side seam was and still is used for lacing, side zippers to create a close shaping to the leg, or godets of fabric inserted to create a flare from the knee to ankle.

Of course, the side view must be considered for its influence even though it is not often a point of focus or a body unit selected for designing. Shoes with a side buckle often are a minor but complementary focus in the apparel-body-construct. Ponytails, where the hair is drawn up to the back or the sides of the head and secured, call attention to the body in movement when they swish from side to side.

A designer can choose to treat any side of the body as the most important unit for viewing. For example, a man's suit relies on a typical front view treatment with the center front lapels of the jacket opening to reveal the shirt, tie, and belt buckle as points of focus. Viewing the trouser, we may observe the waistline, pleats, and vertical column of the legs as silhouette, if the jacket is

a                    b                    c                    d

### FIGURE 5.11A, B, C & D

*A velvet dress and coat, dated 1908, is an ensemble designed to be interesting from different body views. Details of the front and back provide variation and visual continuity. The neckline treatment, the three front buttons on the lower skirt, and the combination of fabric surfaces that drape into folds in the upper torso of the dress add to the variety of interest. The train extends backward and creates interest in viewing the side, especially when the body is moving. The coat features a front asymmetric opening, fur trim around the neckline and sleeves, and a back contrasting panel that continues to the front shoulders.*

Courtesy of The Goldstein Gallery, University of Minnesota.

unbuttoned. However, you may also pay attention to the space between the legs as a continuation of the center front treatment, which can extend the vertical eye movement for the observer, forming a triangular "negative space." Another example is a velvet dress and coat in Figure 5.11, circa 1908, designed to be worn together and to be interesting from each side. The front and back body views provide interest through details and yet also provide a continuity of views. The dress features the neckline treatment, the three front buttons on the lower skirt, the combination of fabric surfaces that drape into folds in the upper torso, and the back train (Figure 5.11a and b). In movement the train would extend backward and create interest in viewing the side. The coat also appears interesting from various body views: the front asymmetric opening, the fur trim around the neckline and sleeves, the back contrasting panel that continues over the shoulder to the front (Figure 5.11c and d).

## The Body-in-the-Round

The body can be treated as though it has one body view to be emphasized or it can be designed with the whole body in mind—the **body-in-the-round**. This creates interest in viewing all sides of the body treated as a rounded cylinder. The Indian sari is an example of the influence of diagonal folds of fabric encircling the body, creating a cylinder. The fabric border on many saris further emphasizes viewing the body-in-the-round. The border also encircles the body but with each view offering a different interaction with the border; the viewer may feel compelled to view the entire rounded surface to see where the border goes.

The design can also lead us to view the body as a rounded surface. The treatment of the body surfaces can enhance the rounded effect. For example, a line continuing around the body, diagonal stripes that are not too dominant, or a reflecting surface smoothly contouring the body call our attention to the rounded contours (Figures 5.12). The viewing unit may not even appear to be complete from only one side of the body. An observer may feel a strong urge to follow around the body to satisfy curiosity and discover how a line is continued or simply fill in mentally by continuing the line from memory or imagination.

There are events and times when viewing the body-in-the-round is especially important. Most designers of dance attire consider the effect of the entire body in motion. The formal attire for dancing of white tie and black tails, made popular by Fred Astaire in the 1930s, is an example of abstracting the structure and body surfaces to create interest in body movement from all body views. The front view is interesting

**FIGURE 5.12**

*The smooth surfaces of the jacket and pants reflect light and call the viewer's attention to the rounding body contours.*

Designed by Hermés. Courtesy of Fairchild Publications.

*Fred Astaire dancing with his partner, Ginger Rogers, became famous in the 1930s for their coordinated movements in dancing. The clothing of the pair was designed to display their body movements. The tails of Fred's clothing move with his body almost magically, and Ginger's dresses emphasize her every movement.*

Courtesy of The Kobal Collection.

because of the contrast of the stiff white shirt and neck treatment with the black jacket, as well as the body contours shaped with the close-fitting jacket and trouser. The back is interesting to view because of the tails centered on the body and, when in vigorous movement, especially via the dancing of Fred Astaire, the tails do magical things as in Figure 5.13. Finally, the side view is interesting because of the stripe of fabric down the side seam that reflects light and calls further attention to the leg in motion.

***Planar and Depth Effects.*** From the standpoint of the visual field, the body structure can present two general form characteristics—**planar** and **depth effects**. A planar effect is the body viewed primarily in terms of flat surfaces skimming the body to take on their own shape, and surface depth is viewing the body as it exists forward and backward in space from the viewer, its contoured relief from the silhouette (Figure 5.14). Though both aspects are present in the apparel-body-construct, the viewer ordinarily does not separate these two characteristics to fully understand their influence.

When the body is viewed as a silhouette, you are focusing upon a planar or flat effect. This is a "cookie cutter" effect of viewing the body outline. In this way the silhouette of the body does not depend upon the surrounding space and thus the viewer focuses attention on or within this out-line. This silhouette, in conjunction with the assemblage of clothing, achieves an essential framing for the apparel-body-construct.

The observer is viewing surface depth when the body is considered for its three-dimensional contours. In this way of viewing, shape consists of varying rounded surfaces that protrude from the silhouette, extending toward and away from the viewer. Clothing may obscure the actual body contour, as when a long jacket skims over the waist, ignor-ing the contour between full chest and hip, or the Japanese kimono, which creates a pillar shape of the upper and lower torso. Aspects of the body contours also may be em-phasized, as when women of the nineteenth century wore corsets that constricted the waistline, in contrast with skirt treatments such as a bell shape or back bustle. Body con-tours may be emphasized with a Wonder Bra®, a smooth leather belt, or with shiny fabrics that reflect the body an-gles and curves.

The overall appearance of planar and depth effects of the body can be affected by their treatment of surfaces placed upon them. The surfaces can appear flat or rounded through clothing fabrics as discussed in Chapter 4. If the planar shape of the silhouette is especially emphasized, the form may appear closed and flat; if deemphasized, the ap-parel-body-construct may appear more open or integrated with the surround. If the body shape is emphasized, the form appears three-dimensional.

Traditionally, with the increasing use of the business suit in the nineteenth century, the male form has been deemphasized according to depth and em-phasized through its planar effect. However, at certain times the contours of the male body have been emphasized, as in the 1830s Romantic Period (Fig-ure 5.15a). In female dressing, depth effects were emphasized. Perhaps the shocked reaction by some to the silhouette of the 1920s flapper occurred in part because of a reversal (Figure 5-15c). The emphasis of planar effects in the simple tubular silhouettes was quite a reverse of the depth effects and

**FIGURE 5.14**

*Contoured relief from the silhouette is featured when the rounded body sur-faces are emphasized by the clothing.*

Designed by Valentino. Cour-tesy of Fairchild Publications.

Planar and depth effects are both present in the apparel-body-construct and affect each other; however, awareness of their separate effects aids in our understanding. Imagine or find an example of an apparel-body-construct and focus first upon how the body appears according to its planar aspects and then its depth effect. Is one or the other more dominant in viewing? How do they influence each other?

*Application Exercise 5.2*

## FIGURE 5.15A, B, C, D, E & F

*Examples of planar and depth effect. In Figure 5.15a, an example of emphasis on the contours of the male body from 1834. A wedding dress from 1894 in Figure 5.15b emphasizes depth effects. A 1920s example of emphasis on simple, tubular silhouettes with flat surfaces that hang directly from the shoulders (c). The smooth, bias-cut surfaces of female dresses in the 1930s (d) often emphasized the female contour and body curvatures. Wartime restrictions limited fabrics used in clothing in the 1940s, resulting in practical casual clothing (e). The "New Look" of post-World War II once again emphasized the body's contours (f). This was accomplished by elaborate cutting and shaping, longer skirts, features that required padding hips, and built-in belts to constrict the waist.*

Courtesy of: (a) Petite Courrier des Dames, March 1834, Picture Collection, New York City Public Library; (b, c, and d) The Goldstein Gallery, University of Minnesota; (e and f) UPI/CORBIS-BETTMANN.

contours emphasized at the end of the nineteenth century. Then, when the decade of the 1930s arrived, again a reversal, to the bias cut of female dresses which emphasized the female contour and body curvatures (Figure 5.15d). Some writers have linked this emphasis to a response to the economic realities of the Great Depression, when limited job opportunities forced many women from the job market. In the l940s, with the wartime restrictions of limited fabrics and women entering the work force, designers created a more planar silhouette with pants that hung full and straight. Following World War II, the New Look created by designer Christian Dior again emphasized depth and the contours of the female body through a cinched waist, longer skirt lengths, and emphasis of hips with peplums or padding (5.15e, f).

## THE BODY AS POTENTIAL FOR THE APPAREL-BODY-CONSTRUCT

The apparel-body-construct is often considered as a variation and an interpretation of the body structure. In the preceding discussion, the body in its relationship to the apparel-body-construct has been suggested. Questions to ask in understanding its potential are: How is the body affected by what is placed upon it? How does the body help to determine the forms of appearance? What limitations of the apparel-body-construct are imposed because of the body characteristics?

The relationship between the body and what is arranged upon it depends upon how the arrangement is essentially similar to or different than the body. In one instance, a natural centering occurs when the centrality of the vertical axis of the body is repeated by a center line of a jacket. This is taking full advantage of the power of the center, a term defined by Arnheim (1982) for the centering or convergent effect present in artistic forms. In another instance, the body verticality is contrasted by the horizontal width of a large sleeve. The body contours may be evident because of a material stretched over the body surface, as in a leotard. While the contours become more evident, the body textures, such as body hair and kneecap lines, are covered and minimized and often replaced with the structure of the fabric of the leotard. Thus, surfaces can repeat the body curvatures and at the same time cover the body textures, eliminating visual differences of surfaces.

The entire body may be emphasized for its height and width. For example, the viewer may perceive the body as primarily a form onto which fabric is draped. The apparel-body-construct may change the relationships of the body structure by combining body segments. The legs and the trunk of the body can be combined visually by wearing a floor-length skirt that extends the shape of the trunk vertically. A hood can change the relationship of the head and neck to the shoulders (Figure 5.16). A cape covering the body from shoulders to hipline has the effect of combining the arms and torso, which in turn extends the visual effect of the trunk horizontally. Surfaces can then change the body structure by emphasizing the overall body mass or deemphasizing body parts.

**FIGURE 5.16**

*Apparel changes the appearance of the body structure by altering body relationships. In this example the hood creates a frame for the face and head that alters the head-to-shoulder relationship.*

Designed by Fendi. Courtesy of Fairchild Publications.

## Body Parts

The body parts in relation to each other also affect how we view the apparel-body-construct. The body, whether tall or short, wide or narrow, in overall height and mass, can affect the contextual association of body parts. Often when we speak of the ideal body we are referring to the proportions of body parts in context.

The natural physical relationships of body parts can be exploited by the design of apparel to provide a visual connection or point of emphasis. For example, the position of shoulders to head is used for focus in collars and necklines. A turtleneck not only creates a longer line of the torso, it can also function as a visual transition between the torso and head, especially if it is designed as a cowl and falls away from the neck so that the resulting width is similar to the head width. The waist may be a focus when indented by a belt or be ignored with a jacket that skims the waist, eliminating some of the contour between upper and lower torso. The position of the end of a sleeve affects the horizontal appearance of the trunk—the line of the sleeve can continue the bottom line of a jacket.

The head and face are usually dominant in our viewing of the body. Examples abound where the head is used as an area for focus with the modification or treatment of materials placed upon it. Mathis and Connor (1993) recommend that the shape of the head repeat the neckline shape (Figure 5.17). The face may be framed by a hood or a hairstyle. Many details that attract the viewer are found around the face, such as brightly colored hats, earrings, and necklaces.

Body parts can appear very much segregated as visual components. The cape that at one time appears to visually unify the body torso and limbs can also cause the head to appear as a separate part. If the cape was a dark-value blue and the person wearing it had yellow hair and pale, yellow-toned skin, the visual separation of the head would be quite distinct. On the other hand, a hood of the same color worn covering the head with dark hair would unify the head with the torso and limbs, framing the face for visual focus.

The apparel-body-construct, by design, can emphasize one part of the body while at the same time minimizing or ignoring another. A body segment, such as the head, legs, hips, or trunk, may be emphasized. In the 1920s, the female extremities, exposed for the first time in a century, became a point of emphasis that has persisted intermittently in the twentieth century (Figure 5.18). Often an emphasis on a body part is accomplished by contrasting one portion of the

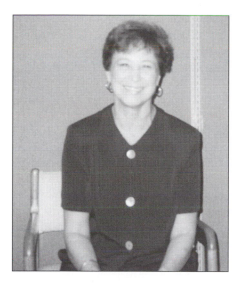

FIGURE 5.17

*This model is wearing a neckline that repeats the shape of her chin. If a horizontal line is imagined at the widest part of the face, the shape of the chin below that line can flatter the wearer when repeated in the neckline.*

Courtesy of Marilyn Revell DeLong.

a                                    b                                    c

## FIGURE 5.18A, B & C

*In the 1920s the image of the flapper (a) called to mind stockings rolled to expose legs and knees. This leg emphasis contrasted with the short hemline of the skirt. Exposed arms were also seen frequently. The miniskirt (b) that again emphasized the legs, but with more exposure, was made possible by the innovation of pantyhose. Often the extremities were further emphasized with shiny boots of the same color or a contrasting white. A 1990s short denim dress (c) that again emphasizes the leg and lower extremity, this time with sandals and the crisscross of the straps.*

Courtesy of: (a and b) UPI/CORBIS-BETTMANN and (c) Fairchild Publications.

body with another beside it or a shape placed upon it. A big, oversized shirt could contrast with a narrower treatment of the hip area, such as close-to-the-body opaque tights. Contrast of a body feature with other shapes can emphasize the difference and thus modify the appearance of the body segment.

## Extending the Body

The body is inherently vertical—longer than it is wide. This verticality is often repeated, enhanced, and extended with the form of the apparel-body-construct. Examples include such emphasis in a long caftan, trousers, and skirts. Treatment of the body silhouette as a triangular shape, a gradation from wider at the bottom narrowing to the head, is also a way to emphasize and extend the body vertically as well as grounding the image, creating stability.

The center front area of the body is often used for a focus to repeat and therefore emphasize the verticality of the body. A panel of buttons or pleats or even a collar coming together at center front are examples of use of this centered area for visual detail and focus. Such treatments at the center of the body often call attention to a center line or area and the breaking up of the space reduces the effect of the mass or volume of the entire body. An interesting example of centering is Korean traditional dress where the opening of the neckline of the *chogore* or top is centered but the line extends diagonally beyond center front and is tied on one side (Figure 5.19).

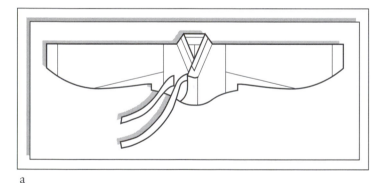

a

### FIGURE 5.19A & B

*Korean traditional dress features a neck opening, centered upon the body but with the line extending beyond center front in a crisscross effect. The opening is fastened with long fabric bands, tied with one loop that crosses center but hangs with a long double tail. Achieving the proper effect takes practice.*

b

The body limbs are more truly cylindrical than the trunk, and thus their curves are more pronounced. Often this curvature of the limbs is utilized in the apparel-body-construct. Pants often emphasize the continuous rounded surface of the leg (Figure 5.20b). Small checks or a reflecting surface call visual attention to the rounded cylinder but a dominant pattern can flatten out the body cylinder (Figure 5.20a). Seams or ruffles spiraled around the arms or legs are another way for a designer to call attention to the cylindrical nature of the body.

The limbs can create more space for the apparel-body-construct by extending outward from the horizontal or vertical axis, depending upon how they are positioned. Photographers sometimes utilize the effect of horizontal space by having models extend their arms horizontally to increase the visual space of the apparel-body-construct. This would particularly display the full and massive effect of a large coat or cape. Religious vestments often employ a robe with large sleeves, specifically designed to extend visual space, incorporating the space of the arms outstretched horizontally.

Vertically, the use of tall hats or shoes with a high heel can extend the body upward. At times in history, both men's and women's shoes have added 3 to 6 inches to the height of the body. Hats have been combined with a hair shape that extends not only the actual height, but also creates an added illusion of head height.

The formal wedding dress and train offer an interesting example of body extensions. The front, side, and back all may be in full view of a large number

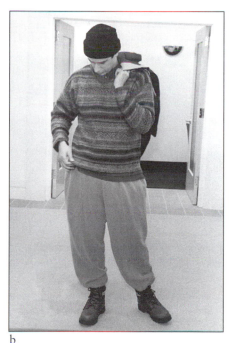

**FIGURE 5.20A & B**

*In Figure 5.20a, fabric surfaces with a dominant surface motif often call attention away from the rounded body surfaces. Fabric surfaces in Figure 5.20b can call attention to the rounding of the body cylinder, especially those in light to medium values and without dominant surface patterns.*

Designed by: (a) Valentino and (b) Gant. Courtesy of Fairchild Publications.

a                                    b

of people at any one time. In addition, the dress is often designed to trail behind to extend the effect. Either the headdress and veil or the dress itself sweeps outward from the body, extending the body of the wearer both horizontally and vertically. Visually this reinforces the importance of the bride in this ceremony as she moves down the aisle.

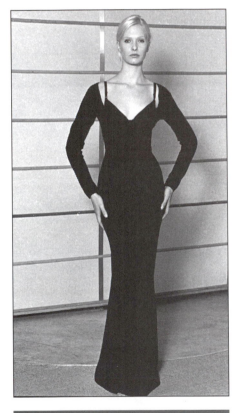

**FIGURE 5.21**

*A body surface covered with a nonreflecting matte dark surface can appear to flatten the body cylinder, but calls attention to the body surfaces not covered.*

Designed by Isaac Mizrahi. Courtesy of Fairchild Publications.

## Body Surfaces

The surfaces of the body offer variation to viewing and can be treated in various ways in the apparel-body-construct. They can be smoothed with oils and creams or highlighted with color cosmetics. They can be reflecting and shiny or may be presented as matte surfaces. They can be covered and modified with a fabric surface that closely follows the body contour, such as a leotard or swimsuit, or obscured or subtly revealed as under a silk charmeuse blouse or a flowing sleeve that reveals the arm when movement occurs. The surfaces of the body interact significantly and characteristically with the surfaces placed upon the body.

Surfaces of the apparel-body-construct can be structured so the body surfaces are viewed as contrasts in flat and round. Use of a matte black surface is one way to make the body appear to have a flattened surface in those covered areas. Even though the material may follow the rounded surfaces closely, to the viewer the body appears flattened like a paper doll. Then the body surfaces not covered by the matte black can provide contrast as rounded surfaces (Figure 5.21).

All body surfaces are composed of both texture and color that can contribute to the design of the apparel-body-construct. Skin has a texture that may appear relatively smooth to somewhat rough, as in a freckled surface or the surface of the elbow joint or kneecap. Other body textures are those of the toenails and fingernails. Hair can range from smooth and straight to curly or kinky, from matte to shiny, from thick to thin. Each type of hair serves a different visual function. Head and facial hair can create shapes because of density and length, while body hair, more sparsely positioned, only provides surface interest.

Body colors include skin colors, hair colors, and eye colors. These colors can be very similar to each other in hue, value, and intensity or offer visual contrast in one of the three attributes. Body colors may be maximized, minimized, or ignored in relation to clothing colors. Identifying colors found upon the body is a good start in developing a color palette for an individual because there is an automatic relationship. Placement of clothing colors next to body colors has a profound effect on both because colors viewed in context with each other can become different than those colors viewed alone.

The relationships of skin, hair, and eye colors are an important part of the body context for an apparel-body-construct. Consider the effects of similar values of dark brown skin and black hair, or the effect of the contrast of cool, blue-white skin and black hair. The latter offers value contrast and a natural focus for the viewer, while the former would contrast with lighter surfaces placed upon the body. Though most people can wear many hues (color name), the other attributes, value (light-dark) and intensity (bright-muted), have just as profound an influence in contextual relationships.

Relationships of similarity between body colors and colors worn on the body can be noted. When the relationship is similar, the body colors do not become a focus. They blend with the colors of clothing and accessories. An example of such a subtle difference would be use of a less intense and lighter value but similar hue in clothing as hair color, for example, brown eyes, hair, and skin and beige clothing. The more intense, darker value body colors would attract the viewer to the head.

Body hues of skin, hair, and eyes can range from being similar or opposite (contrasting) in position on the color wheel. For example, a contrast in body hues may be yellow tones in hair, red tones in the skin, and blue eyes. Some contrasts in hue, value, and intensity are present in small areas of the body, for example, the eyes and lashes. Though skin covers the largest area, people are often least aware of its color because of its subtlety of hue. However, the body colors and the surfaces placed upon the body do affect each other. This relationship may be the reason why the wearer can appear pale and sickly, with "health" vaguely identified as the culprit. Being aware of the relational effect of body and clothing colors and wearing colors that relate to the body colors could give the skin a chance to glow.

Select a photograph where the colors of the apparel-body-construct are apparent. Now analyze the effect of the use of color. How are surfaces placed upon the body similar or contrasting with body colors? What affect do they have on your viewing of the apparel-body-construct?

*Application Exercise 5.4*

## Body Movement

The apparel-body-construct is often designed with body movement in mind. For example, a wedding dress can extend backward as the bride moves down the aisle. A skating costume with a circular skirt takes advantage of the circular movements of a female skater, creating a circle outward from the body. By contrast, the male skater is often traditionally treated as a distinctly contained silhouette.

Body locomotion can vary greatly in direction, speed, and economy of movement. Large, slow, sweeping motions and small, quick, jerky, motions can occur with little warning of the change for the viewer. Forward movement is most common, but the body can move in all directions.

An important aspect of the body is that as it moves about it changes position. Such movement can appear unbalanced depending upon the actions of the arms and legs. When the arms are swinging they can create a diversion for the observer. Hollander (1978) links 1920s flapper fashion not only to the exposure of the arms and legs, but also to their distinctive movements in dances such as the Charleston. The arms in a hugging position increase the emphasis on the body cylinder but can create an effect of instability. The body can create another kind of visual effect when bent over at the waist or contorted into a twisting movement. What other variations can the body present by moving about and changing position, and what effect can they have upon clothing?

The body's potential for movement has to do with gravitational effects on the body. The body's response to gravity is also important to its overall visual effect. The torso and limbs relate to gravity and maintenance of body balance, especially when the body moves. The body usually appears to be in dynamic equilibrium and when it is not, the viewer often feels tension in his or her own body. The lower limbs can be spread to gain and maintain balance; the trunk and upper limbs can be adjusted as well.

The body through movement can interact with the materials placed upon it. The effect of body movement on various weights of fabric can offer much visual variety and can attract the viewer (Figure 5.22). Body movement can be affected, for example, by a crisp fabric that hangs from the shoulders, skimming the body surfaces. The effect achieved can be one of stately elegance because body movements often become restricted to slow, sweeping motions. The Japanese kimono hugs the legs and affects the way the wearer moves. We somehow expect the body movements to follow those that we anticipate from the movements of the fabric. During World War II when women worked in factories, they adopted a one-piece coverall that allowed freedom of movement, and the close-to-the-body fit provided protection from clothing getting caught in machinery.

On the other hand, imagine a buoyant, lightweight fabric, such as chiffon, which moves with the body, resisting the immediate body contours but following the body with a slight lag. A body and fabric in motion can achieve a floating, butterfly effect, as in the work of the designer Hanae Mori, called the "butterfly designer." A silk scarf in a breeze can create a lilting, flowing movement away from the moving body, thus extending the space of the body.

a                                                          b

**FIGURE 5.22A & B**

*Body movement can interact with the materials placed upon it and offers greater visual interest than when the body is still.*

Designed by Yves Saint Laurent. Courtesy of Fairchild Publications.

Body movement is a considerable attraction for the viewer. In fact, body movement is such a strong attraction that it may be more stimulating than the arrangement of the materials upon the body. Thus, body movements may play a large role in attracting attention to the apparel-body-construct.

An apparel designer expects varying degrees of movement from the wearer—walking, raising the arms, bending. However, body movements may be encumbered or restricted, as with a long, tubular skirt that limits the stride or the miniskirt, which restricts bending. The historic period of clothing often reveals something about what body movements are characteristic and acceptable. In the mid-nineteenth century the confinement of the body by the wearing of a floor-length, full skirt with numerous petticoats and/or crinoline was coupled with the restrictions of the corset and the body appeared to float. A few decades later the effect of the bustle created yet another kind of restriction of body movement. The silhouette that followed was perceived to be more freeing than its predecessor, though it was still restricted through corseting and long skirts.

An apparel-body-construct that allows for uninhibited body movement may rely upon the natural arrangement of the body structure. For example, the most uninhibiting material would be a substance that stretches over the body and moves with it, like a leotard. Such a material allows a minimal obstruction of body movements. However, if the ultimate goal of all apparel-body-constructs were to allow for the most body movement, the eventual solution might be no clothing at all.

In the 1990s emphasis on comfort would seem to make severely limited body movements unacceptable. Can you think of some restrictions on body movements that are not comfortable in the clothing you wear? What do you consider the most optimal way for clothing to interact with the body? Example: unrestricting, supporting.

# MEANINGS ASSOCIATED WITH THE BODY

Certain parts of the body are associated with various processes and functions that affect the observer's viewing. How we view the apparel-body-construct and associate meaning depends upon the area of body emphasis. Consider clothing without any body and think of the difference this makes in viewing the apparel-body-construct.

Sometimes the meaning association depends upon the way the body is treated by such aspects as shaping and coloring. Body features often associated with youth are long, slender limbs and body curvatures minimized by the shapes placed upon the body. Colors placed upon the body are often light values or intense primary hues. On the other hand, those associations that suggest maturity stress body curvatures and the use of a belt to change the shape of the figure and create visual focus, for example. Colors that suggest maturity have traditionally included dark values and muted secondary hues.

**FIGURE 5.23**

*This couple in Korea wear traditional dress to celebrate life and the man's sixtieth birthday.*

*Courtesy of Geum, Key Sook, Seoul, Korea.*

Expectations and past experiences of the viewer have an effect on body associations. For example, blue jeans—worn by so many and seen so often in the twentieth century—have become a standard item in our viewing, an equalizer of the lower torso. We no longer need to notice them, until the details begin to be worth noting, for example, labels, stitching, color, fit, holes, rips, and tears. Adding such details has caused the observer to reexamine with new eyes, searching for subtle changes.

How the body serves as a medium of expression can vary with cultural context. Our expectations of the body vary with time and age of a person. We often have certain expectations about what is appropriate to wear at different ages. How a culture considers the elder is important to the way the body is used to express age. In a culture where age is revered, the body is often considered differently than in a culture where youth is revered.

Ideals associated with the body is a cultural perspective. Whether a culture emphasizes individuality or being a group member influences the ideal. For example, in Korea the elder is respected and revered. In Figure 5.23 this couple, celebrating the man's sixtieth birthday, are both dressed in traditional dress. How the body is considered by the individual varies from culture to culture (Benthall in "A Prospectus" Benthall and Polhemus, 1975). This could include ideals related to modesty, size, and importance of various body parts—which are covered and which are not and how much of the body is covered. Some ideals can change over time and others remain embedded within a culture's identity.

## The Body as a Social Metaphor

There are many references in advertising media and in daily discourse that originate from our experiences with the body. Such references may be related to the apparel-body-construct and create a direct relationship with cultural associations. Though this is a very large and complex topic, a few examples will illustrate and then you may examine the references at the end of this chapter for a more complete discussion. MacRae in "The Body and Social Metaphor" (in Benthall and Polhemus, 1975) suggests that being upright is a universal and that from this erectness are derived such directional categories as up-down, left-right, before-behind, over-under, and beside. Forward is active and backward is slow, perhaps because of the speed with which human beings can move forward relative to the awkwardness in stepping backward. Thus, is the term "fashion-forward" related to the ease with which people move forward?

Many terms people use are derived from our bodily experiences. For example, "on the other hand," or "even-handed justice," are in use perhaps because of the balancing we believe is involved in "weighing" both sides equally. Measurements of scale often relate to the body, a foot, an arm's length, or an arm's throw. People's concepts of spatial relationships come not only from their binocular vision, which is necessary for depth perception, but also from each person's eye level related to what is seen and how it is then described. For example, a person short in height has a different idea of how high "tall" is than a tall person. Body size may be used to refer to other meanings. For example, "a perfect 10" could mean "perfection" but also reference the idea of desirable size through women's apparel sizes.

Clothing features are often related to the body and gender. In Eastern cultures, yin is red and female, whereas yang is blue and male. Wearing such colors is often then associated with gender. Red may be associated with menstrual blood, a female premenopausal experience. Warm tints in combination are often associated with other related details such as delicate fabrics and trim and a silhouette of soft shoulders, small waists, and full skirts on a gown or coat, which describe the "feminine" characteristics of the court dress of Louis XIV (Cunningham, 1994). Banner (1983) believes that it is useful to compare the male and female silhouettes and shapes of the apparel-body-construct in the nineteenth century, that is, you can learn about the one by referencing the other. For example, a lady of small stature, tiny mouth, and pale skin pictured with a gentleman of similar appearance (p. 226). Many alternative ideals of male and female appearances prevailed throughout the nineteenth century, and the notion that the male should be characterized as aggressive and manly and the female as beautiful did not occur until later in the nineteenth century with the increasing differentiation of male and female roles.

In communicating, you can be aware of double meanings related to the body and clothing. For example, the advertising caption in a prominent magazine, "Great Expectations," referring to a picture of two babies, has a double meaning, especially if the intention is to focus upon the brand of baby's clothing or the flexibility of baby furniture to accommodate more than one.

| *Application Exercise 5.6* | Think about what colors you commonly associate with babies. Do you think such colors are the same in all cultures? Why or why not? |
|---|---|

## Body-Clothes Interactions

In summary, to understand specifically how the body is utilized in the apparel-body-construct requires that the viewer analyze and compare the differences and similarities between the body as a preexisting structure and the visual form presented by the apparel-body-construct. It is useful in viewing the apparel-body-construct to ask: What is the body bringing to the organization?

When one perceives the apparel-body-construct, the body or clothes may vary in amount of viewer focus. At one extreme are clothes related directly to the display of the body, its curvatures, or one body part such as the head (Figure 5.24a and b). At the other extreme, the body may be used only as a hanger for garments, as with robes where the actual body curvatures are min-

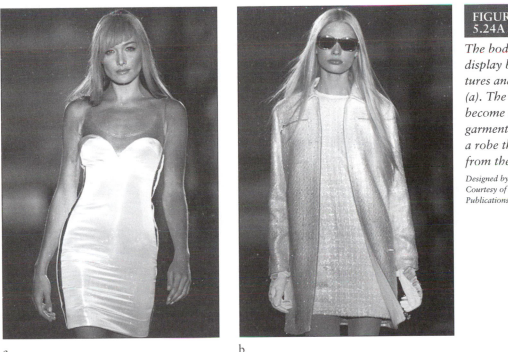

a                                    b

**FIGURE 5.24A & B**

*The body used to display body curvatures and body parts (a). The body may become a hanger for garments (b), such as a robe that hangs from the shoulders.*

Designed by Gianni Versace. Courtesy of Fairchild Publications.

imized (Figure 5.24b). Shapes of the clothes can make the body appear to expand in a horizontal or vertical direction. The variation between a display of body and a display of clothes causes a difference in the general visual effect. What visual relationships do we need to be aware of in order to understand how the body interacts in the apparel-body-construct? When, for example, does the body become ground for the figure of the clothing or the clothing become ground for the body as figure? How does the context of a particular body influence what is placed upon it?

The visual interrelations of body and clothing can be considered as to their relative dependence versus independence. In essence, the primary viewing focus may be provided in three ways, mainly by the body, mainly by the clothing, or by the interaction between the two. Flugel (1969) uses the term "confluence" to define the relationship of body to clothing when the viewer perceives neither as a priority. This would include an instance of complete interaction and probably also relate to the fashionable image and what is emphasized in the figure-ground relationship, the body or the clothing. Rubenstein (1995) suggests that a contemporary version of confluence is the suit. The question is, has the suit taken on background characteristics as an ever-present apparel-body-construct of our time? If it is resisted, will it still provide such an example of confluence? By contrast, when clothing is oversized for the body, the body may seem insignificant in comparison and thus clothing

*When clothing is oversized, the body curvatures may become less significant.*

Designed by Bill Blass. Courtesy of Fairchild Publications.

will take on a relationship of priority (Figure 5.25); when the clothing is undersized, the body curvatures may take on greater significance. This is especially perceived when the fashionable image suddenly changes in terms of the fit of clothing upon the body, from loose to more closely fitted or vice versa.

A combination of sizes of clothing worn on the body is often a useful tool in calling attention away from actual body sizes or emphasizing a body part. Earlier in this chapter, reference was made to Joan Crawford's Letty Lynton dress, which superimposed a large sleeve shape on her broad shoulderline (Figure 5.9). The close-to-the-body tank top and small waist emphasize the contrast of a voluminous circular skirt.

The apparel-body-construct involves variations that occur because of the placement and emphasis of surfaces and the relationship of these surfaces to the body structure. Circular lines in clothing may emphasize body contours. Focus in one area in a part-to-whole relationship calls attention to a particular body part. Many types of clothing are designed to emphasize the body in motion. If the body is still, a diagonal line can create a feeling of movement within the viewer. If the body is actually in motion, the clothing can flow with the body in synchrony, as in the dancer who wears a fabric that languidly flows from the body during a waltz.

Consider the body as a generalized structure in responding to the apparel-body-construct, that is, how the viewer who is engrossed with the apparel-body-construct as a visual form becomes aware of the similarities of one human body to another and at the same time of the differences that create individuality. The form of the apparel-body-construct is always fascinating because it is modeled on our human form and we are personally connected to it via our own humanness. The analysis of the apparel-body-construct is distinguished from the analysis of other visual forms because of the pervading sense of the human qualities present. By considering the body's characteristics as a form, we can also understand the potential for variety in the apparel-body-construct.

## Summary

• The body as a basic visual structure influences how clothing is designed. In each era there are characteristic ideals of the body structure. There are certain givens of body structure—for example, the body is a vertical, convex unit.

• Body views—front, back, in-the-round—affect how clothing is designed. These views can be related to the function of clothing—for example, dance attire is viewed in-the-round.

• Planar and depth effects are related to apparel design.

• The body affects the apparel-body-construct design; for example, the body may be extended, body parts may be revealed or concealed, body surfaces may be bared and emphasized through the use of makeup, skin tone may relate to the color of clothing, body movement may affect the cut of clothing.

• Cultural meanings are associated with the body—for example, a youthful look emphasizes long, slender limbs; darker hues are associated with maturity.

• The body also serves as a social metaphor—for example, red clothes in the Orient are associated with the feminine principle (yin), and red is related to menstrual blood.

## Key Terms and Concepts

bilateral symmetry
body views

depth effects
planar effects

## References

Arnheim, R. *The Power of the Center*. Berkeley: University of California Press, 1982.

Banner, L. *American Beauty*. Chicago: The University of Chicago Press, 1983.

Barnette, M. "The Perfect Body." In Roach-Higgins, M., Eicher, J., and Johnson, K., eds., *Dress and Identity*. New York: Fairchild Publications, 51–55.

Benthall, J., Polhemus, *The Body as a Medium of Expression*. New York: E. P. Dutton, 1975.

Cunningham, R. *The Magic Garment: Principles of Costume Design*. Prospect Heights, IL: Waveland Press, 1994.

Flugel, J. C. *The Psychology of Clothes*. New York: International Universities Press, l969.

Hollander, A. *Seeing Through Clothes*. New York: Viking Press, 1978.

Mathis, C. M., and Connor H. V. *The Triumph of Individual Style*. Cali, Colombia: Timeless Editions, 1993.

McCracken, G. *Culture and Consumption: New Approaches to the Symbolic Character of Consumer Goods and Activities*. Bloomington and Indianapolis: Indiana University Press, 1988.

Rubenstein, R. P. *Dress Codes: Meanings and Messages in American Culture*. Boulder, CO: Westview Press, l995.

## Chapter Six

# MATERIALS OF THE APPAREL-BODY-CONSTRUCT

After you have read
this chapter, you will
be able to understand:

- The materials used to make
the apparel-body-construct and
how they are arranged upon the body
to obtain exciting visual effects.

- The three sources of visual structuring: **layout structuring, surface structuring,** and **light and shadow structuring.**

- The ways in which surface, layout, and light and shadow structuring interact.

ATERIALS OF THE APPAREL-BODY-CONSTRUCT include all that we use upon the body to create a visual effect— fibers and fabrics, as well as paints, films, and metals. Paints and powders, dyes and sprays may be applied directly to the skin and hair as cosmetics. Every material has a certain visual potential based upon its salient characteristics. For example, metals and plastics may be used for jewelry, buttons, zippers, or shoes. Fabrics can be manipulated into a myriad of surface effects due to their pliable character.

Why is it important to be aware of the visual potential of materials? The designer manipulates materials to create visual results. The manufacturer who has decided to maintain a certain price selects among various qualities of materials and may have to choose between using less expensive finishings, such as buttons, or a different fabric than originally planned. The retailer must discern subtleties in buying just the right products to attract purchasers and provide a consistent store image. Such decisions will be easier if the apparel professional is aware of how materials influence the apparel-body-construct.

The majority of materials used for the apparel-body-construct are physically relatively flat with more length and width than thickness. Materials offer a great variety of characteristics and potential and when arranged upon the body can create exciting visual effects. A wide range of substances is available in today's marketplace. Substances can be woven, knitted, crocheted, felted; they can be fibers, fur, feathers, wood, metal, plastic. They range from soft to crisp, from transparent to opaque, from matte to shiny, and from bright to muted hues. The surface can be one color, printed with a floral motif or a large single flower, or woven into an all-over plaid. All of these characteristics influence the material's visual potential.

Becoming aware of the influence of materials allows an individual to manipulate visual effects. A customer placing an order for velvet wants white but has only a middle value red for a sample. This red sample is a richly shaded surface with wonderful highlights and lowlights. The customer, seeing this sample, decides to go ahead and order it in white. Not a problem! But the material that is ordered and finally arrives does not appear the same as the red, in a number of significant ways. The potential for nuance from light and shadow is not present in the white velvet as it was in the red sample because of the difference in light reflectance. This is because red, as a middle value hue, is a carrier of light and shadow in a manner entirely different than white. Therefore, some changes in the ultimate design of the garment were required as a result of the fabric substitution. Being aware of the influence of structuring, the process of creating structure, is necessary to predict the end result.

To understand the role of materials in the apparel-body-construct, you must consider their visual effect first. In this chapter materials will be discussed from the point of view of their potential for visual structuring and influence on the visual effect. The question is: How do characteristics of the materials contribute to the end result?

# SOURCES OF VISUAL STRUCTURING

In Chapter 2, structure was defined as the way parts are fitted together or arranged for the characteristic nature of the whole. Within the apparel-body-construct, the visual structure is the essential framework, and we perceive structure as organization from lines and shapes that can derive from a variety of sources. Materials are the primary means of structuring the apparel-body-construct. Surfaces that are printed with a soft but distinctive shape attract our viewing as do surfaces that are manipulated into folds or gathers. Both can serve to structure the apparel-body-construct in entirely different ways but possibly with similar outcomes in terms of viewer interest. For example, compare the two dresses in Figure 6.1a and b. The silhouette is similar and there are distinctive details with the flavor of the Orient on the surfaces of both that lead the eye throughout. However, in the dress designed by Claire McCardell (Figure 6.1a), the surface is structured by layout and light and shadow, and in the dress designed by Ralph Lauren (Figure 6.1b), the Ikat pattern is a special combination of dying and weaving and thus is surface structured.

a                                          b

**FIGURE 6.1A & B**

*This dress, designed by Claire McCardell in the 1950s (Figure 6.1a), is a classic, deep-red dress with a surface structured by layout. The resulting pleats are enhanced by light and shadow. The silhouette of this dress, designed by Ralph Lauren (Figure 6.1b), is similar to the one in Figure 6.1a a dyeing and weaving process called Ikat produces the distinctive surface structure.*

Courtesy of: (a) The Metropolitan Museum of Art, gift of Irving Drought Harris in memory of Claire McCardell Hall, 1958; and (b) Polo/Ralph Lauren. Photograph from The Metropolitan Museum of Art.

The three sources of visual structuring of an apparel-body-construct can be characterized as surface structuring, layout structuring, and light and shadow structuring. **Layout structuring** involves the three-dimensional variation in the way the surfaces appear because they are manipulated upon the body, that is, in, out, and around the body. **Surface structuring** results from variation of the two-dimensional surface caused by the difference in the dye or dyes used, or from printing or weaving that can create lines and shapes. **Light and shadow structuring** occurs because of the varying illumination of the environment as it interacts with the apparel-body-construct, creating light and shadow effects for the observer.

Every apparel-body-construct involves all three sources of structuring in their interaction. However, one source can dominate. For example, surface structuring can visually negate the layout structuring. We can observe the difference between a pocket shape (layout) that is made more or less important because of the surface it is placed upon. In one instance the pocket may be dominant, and in the other the pocket may be hidden because surface structure has camouflaged the pocket shape. Shadow can be a direct or an indirect influence on the apparel-body-construct under ordinary circumstances and is influenced by both layout and surface structuring.

By now you may be asking, "Why must I understand structuring?" Obviously a designer needs to be aware of structuring, but everyone involved in the apparel profession needs to be able to first recognize the sources and results of structuring, and second to separate the various sources, one from another. Much of the inherent quality of the apparel-body-construct rests in your awareness of the nuances of surface. The sophisticated and dedicated viewer cannot ignore the effect of one source of structuring on the other. By first separating their effects, the role of each and eventually the interaction of all three are understood. Let's look at each one in turn.

## Layout Structuring

Many apparel-body-constructs get their primary identifying character from **layout structuring** or the shaping that results from the physical arrangement of the garment on the body. As a result, garments are often named according to their layout structuring. When you think in terms of some apparel items, such as "slacks," "kimono," "blazer," you are considering a particular layout structure of lines and shapes on the body. Layout structuring is created by the three-dimensional manipulation of materials in, out, and around the body. In layout structuring, the surface is more than incidental to the visual effect. Layout can involve cutting, sewing, and draping.

Structuring through layout can include a combination and manipulation of materials to create lines from pleats and yokes, shapes of pockets and collars, and even some textural effects from gathers. Layout structuring appears in Figure 6.2 as shapes created by lapels and collar, set on sleeves, lines of pockets, buttons, and edges of hemlines and front closing with a tailored result. In

**FIGURE 6.2**

*(Left) In surfaces structured by layout, lines and shapes are created by manipulation of materials and include collars, pockets, yokes, and edges of hemlines.*

Designed by Valentino. Courtesy of Fairchild Publications.

**FIGURE 6.3**

*(Right) This surface, structured by layout, is dramatic in the effect created through an asymmetric overlay.*

Designed by Christain Lacroix. Courtesy of Fairchild Publications.

Figure 6.3 layout is illustrated in an overlay placed diagonally from one shoulder and cascading to the hem and soft-edged gathers distributed along the upper torso and skirt waist to create a textural effect. Lines and shapes of the silhouette can create a dramatic effect.

The body is three-dimensional and the materials of the apparel-body-construct become three-dimensional when used on the body. Some materials and layout structuring mimic the body contours. A soft, thin material can be used to create shapes that interact with the body. The effect created by a soft, single-knit T-shirt that hugs the body contours as it glides across the chest and falls to the hemline is an example of this interaction. Materials and layout structuring may take on many other shapes and lines than those that follow the body. A crisp material can be used to create a shape somewhat independent of the body that hangs from the shoulders, skims the upper torso, and then falls straight to the hem. The designer Charles James often used layout structuring and crisp materials to create garments that superimposed alternative shapes on the human contours.

When a woven fabric is used in the layout structuring, the silhouette is affected by the placement of the grain of the fabric on the body. **Grain** refers to the warp (vertical) or filling (weft or horizontal) yarns of the fabric. Lengthwise grain is located at any position along the warp yarns and crosswise grain is at any position along a filling yarn. When the lengthwise yarns of the fabric correspond to gravity and are placed on the length of the body, they hang straighter and create a more vertical line than one created when the same yarns are placed horizontally on the body, leaving the crosswise grain to interact with gravity in a potentially different manner. If the number of threads between lengthwise and crosswise grain is similar, placing the crosswise grain on the body lengthwise will not affect the visual result. However, if the threads are different, the lines created by the fabric may not be as crisp as when lengthwise grain corresponds to the length of the body. **Bias** is the diagonal of the grain. Since lengthwise yarns are kept firmly taut in the weaving process and thus have the most stability and least amount of give, placing the fabric on the bias provides the most stretch. A fabric cut on the bias (diagonally across the grain) often appears to follow body curves more closely. This body hugging effect became desirable during some fashion periods and in certain types of garment, such as the bias-cut dresses of Vionnet and other designers popular in the 1920s and 1930s (see Figure 6.4) or the bias-cut effect of sarong skirts of recent periods.

Two important ways to manipulate layout structure on the body are by draping or cutting and joining of flat shapes. Draping is the process of manipulating and incorporating materials onto the three-dimensional body, easing to create gathers, bending to create folds, and creasing to create edges such as tucks and pleats. The cutting and joining of pieces also affects the structure and appearance of the apparel-body-construct. A seamline resulting from the joining of two materials can be an important source of line or shape in the viewing of the apparel-body-construct, not necessarily because of the seamline itself, but because of the resulting three-dimensional shape. Cutting and sewing seamlines can create lines and shapes such as collars, lapels, belt, and pocket flaps. Such lines are created by enclosing the raw edge of the seam in upon itself. Hemlines can also be sharply defined lines and edges.

A two-piece Western business suit is a tailored product where flat shapes are cut and sewn to fit the body. Materials that are capable of holding a crease or pressed-in edge lend themselves to the effects of crisp tailoring. Materials that are soft and pliable lend themselves to draping and a fluid effect. An Indian sari is an example of creating layout structure without cutting for shaping because it uses the entire length and width of fabric arranged upon the body. A Japanese kimono combines both—geometric rectangular shapes for the sleeves and body of the garment for a minimum of cutting and joining—thus maximizing the effects of both cutting shapes and draping onto the body.

The lines and shapes of the layout structure depend upon the physical nature of the materials, that is, the characteris-

**FIGURE 6.4**

*This bias-cut dress of the 1920s is body hugging, and reflectance from the surfaces creates emphasis upon a rounded body cylinder. This effect produced a desirable look at the time.*

Courtesy of Charles Kleibacker.

tics of the fabric that can be manipulated into three-dimensional results. In the creation of an apparel-body-construct, materials can be transformed from surfaces that appear flat and uninteresting to wonderful, elegant, three-dimensional effects. In viewing the materials of an apparel-body-construct, the observer needs to be reminded of the potential for their transformation upon the body through layout structuring. Though the potential of the material often depends on its character when flat, and the inherent surface structure of the material is an important consideration, the visual effect is ultimately the result of how it is manipulated upon the body through the layout structuring. A firm, crisp fabric can be cut and sewn. The example in Figure 6.5a is a wool fabric that falls into soft folds in the skirt. The upper torso is molded with the fabric to define the waist.

In addition to more traditional fabrics, many different materials can be used, creating a myriad of different outcomes—lace, feathers, beads, coins, leather. For example, leather cut into long strips and placed upon the body can create fascinating results, especially when they are free to move with the body.

Layout structuring is closely aligned to the potential of the materials for physical manipulation. A term used to describe the physical nature of many woven and knitted materials is **hand**. "Hand" actually refers to the way the material feels. However, it is also a way to describe the potential for manipulation, which includes weight and drape—that is, how the material will hang

a

b

### FIGURE 6.5A & B

*In Figure 6.5a, the firm and crisp hand of this wool fabric is cut and sewn to reflect the body curvatures in the upper torso. In the lower torso, the fabric falls into soft folds. Figure 6.5b illustrates how the silhouette can change to a more horizontal line when fabric weight is removed by shortening the skirt.*

Designed by Claude Montana. Courtesy of Fairchild Publications.

and fall from the body. Crunch up a fabric in your fingers to see how wrinkled it becomes, and then think about the uses of the fabric based upon this property, for example, in travel, in design. Hand influences how the material can be manipulated into various lines and shapes, whether shapes will stand away from the body or cling to it. Certain materials ease very well into small spaces, while others do not. Some materials are excellent for pressed pleating because they can maintain a sharp crease, while others are better used only for soft, unpressed pleats. The hand of the material fundamentally affects its use within an apparel-body-construct, and this understanding and preplanning on the part of the designer is critical to the results.

Weight influences the way materials interact with the body and gravity. The intimate relation of the weight of material to the silhouette can be demonstrated rather dramatically by altering the physical dimensions of an article of apparel that hangs from the body, for example, the length of a flared skirt. Before hemming, the skirt appears too long when it is tried on. What is viewed in the mirror could be described as follows: all the flares (wedge-shaped folds) interact with the body in a silhouette that appears quite vertical, as in Figure 6.5a. In the process of cutting off several inches and hemming, the silhouette changes (Figure 6.5b). When the skirt is tried on again, the silhouette looks more horizontal as in the insert. The flares are more independent, less interrelated with the body curves. How could this happen? The hemming and lesser weight of the total skirt changes and reduces the pull of gravity and consequently the silhouette appears somewhat different. This type of alteration of visual effect can occur with what seem like minor changes in the physical dimensions of the material.

Manipulative characteristics of materials that most affect silhouette have been discussed by Helen Brockman (1965), who concludes that the character of the silhouette is influenced by the tactile qualities of the materials chosen and the interrelation of the characteristics of soft-crisp and thin-thick. A thick, soft material can be manipulated differently than one that is thin and crisp. A thin, soft material will create quite a different silhouette from a thick, crisp one. The fabric dimensions used in each of the pairs of skirt shapes in Figure 6.6 are the same; they vary only in thin-thickness and soft-crispness. Examine the results carefully across each pair from left to right to determine the differences.

The apparel professional experiences the visual influence of all kinds of materials on the body. This can be accomplished by relating the tactile character of the fabric with the visual result. Though some relationships are very subtle, the effect of fabric on layout structuring is direct and influential. The physical dimensions of draped or cut and joined pieces may be identical, but the apparel-body-construct visually appears quite different when the fabrics used vary in hand. The very different tactile character of fabrics in Figure 6.7 used in combination create very different visual results. The linen jacket and crepe de chine pants create some significant visual differences in the type of lines and silhouette created in the upper and lower portions of the body.

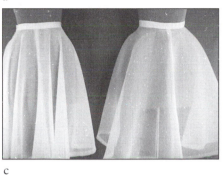

a

b

c

## FIGURE 6.6A, B & C

*The surface dimensions of these skirt shapes are the same, but the silhouette varies because of fabric that differs from thin to thick and soft to crisp.*

## FIGURE 6.7

*The tactile character of fabrics used in this ensemble varies from the crisp and opaque character of the jacket to the softness of the full pants. Used together they create a unique ensemble that has coherence because of a continuous silhouette line and similar surface color.*

*Designed by Oscar de la Renta. Courtesy of Fairchild Publications.*

Using the apparel-body-construct in Figure 6.7, picture how the ensemble would appear with the same fabric used for both the jacket and pants, and think about how the surfaces would appear upon the body. This will take some thoughtful imagining!

## Surface Structuring

Surface structuring begins with the characteristics that materials have as two-dimensional surfaces of the apparel-body-construct. Visiting a fabric store to look at bolts of fabric with their myriad of textures, colors, and prints available can help us become aware of the visual variety of surfaces, as in Figure 6.8. The surface can be colored and defined by hue, value, and intensity. It can be a smooth matte surface or a luminous shiny one. It can be smooth and thin or thick with a pile. It can be physically textured from weaving a number of colored fibers together or visually textured from printing.

### FIGURE 6.8A, B, C, D, E & F

*These surfaces are structured from various sources and provide for differences in visual effect.*

Courtesy of Marilyn Revell DeLong.

Even though surface structuring occurs on the two-dimensional surface of a fabric, the perceptual effect may involve organizing several surface levels or planes. This causes the flat, two-dimensional surface to appear to have visual depth. If a motif appears on one level as figure, then the other level is ground that appears to surround and lie behind it. The viewer may organize in terms of figure-ground relationships. For example, a polka dot can appear as figure on an otherwise plain surface, as in Figure 6.9a. What is viewed as figure appears to lie in front of the ground. If we group a number of larger circles, and then a number of smaller ones, we can create two levels of figure and one of ground. How far the figure appears in front of the ground depends upon its contrast and clarity, that is, the distinctness of its edge. In Figure 6.9b, the irregular edges and meandering lines spread out from the flower motif. This makes for a more

a                    b

**FIGURE 6.9A & B**

*Shapes as figure can be closed or more open to the ground in a fig-ure-ground relationship. A surface with polka dots (a), which are sim-ple and enclosed shapes, creates figure-ground separation. A more complex shape is the one in (b), which creates an effect of figure-ground integration.*

a                    b                    c

**FIGURE 6.10A, B & C**

*The degree of contrast in value influences the appearance of figure-ground integration to separation. In Figure 6.10a, figure-ground integration occurs because the figure, i.e., surface shapes, is similar in value to the ground. One way to determine value contrast is to squint your eyes partially closed, and the motif almost disappears when figure and ground are close in value. The moderate amount of value contrast creates the appearance of some figure-ground separation in Figure 6.10b. The most value contrast in figure to ground is exhibited in Figure 6.10c, and the resulting appearance is that of figure-ground separation.*

integrating motif in the figure-ground relationship. The degree of contrast in value also influences the figure-ground relationship. For example, a white motif one-half inch in diameter on a black ground is more distinct than the same white motif on a light yellow ground. In Figure 6.10a, b, and c, the way the surfaces appear is dependent upon the degree of light-dark contrast exhibited.

A flat surface that is printed or woven to include lines and shapes can have a direction and an order. Variations in how a surface can direct the eye across the plane appear in Figure 6.11a, b, and c. In addition, the shapes can be characterized as forming a figure-ground relationship, creating depth by grouping into planar levels. In the surface in Figure 6.11c, the larger dark squares group and the smaller dark squares and light squares in the center of the larger squares can also be viewed as figure. Even though this depth of surface is apparent and not actually three-dimensional, it influences the spatial organization and visual effect when used in the apparel-body-construct.

| *Application Exercise 6.2* | Think about how Figure 6.2 appears as pictured in terms of layout and surface structure. Then select a different surface from the fabrics featured in Figure 6.11 and compare how the surface will appear based upon the same layout and different surface structure. Here layout structure is a constant and the variation in visual effect could include both the surface structure and hand. |
| --- | --- |

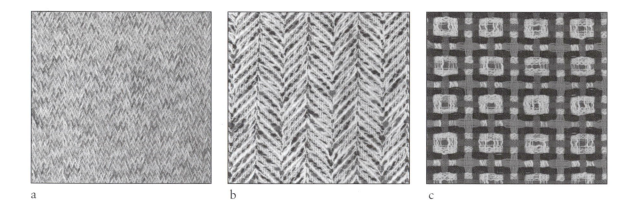

a                               b                               c

### FIGURE 6.11A, B & C

*In Figure 6.11a, surfaces can vary in direction and order. In Figure 6.11a, visual texture creates direction and surface thickness. Surface direction includes vertical and diagonal lines, and the visual texture is more prominent in Figure 6.11b than in Figure 6.11a. Shapes that group as figure in Figure 6.11c create apparent planar levels.*
Courtesy of Marilyn Revell DeLong.

There are some surfaces on which the figure-ground relationship is not separate and distinct. Pattern, defined as repetitious shapes upon a surface, can provide an example. The pattern in Figure 6.12 does not readily separate as figure from ground because of the irregular nature of the lines and shapes. They appear more integrated with the ground and therefore not as distinct from it. Such a pattern may also mask layout structure. Transparency of surface can create indeterminacy by softening edges of surface motifs. Patterns can blur as they are manipulated into folds or gathers in creating a dress, as in Figure 6.12a and b.

Small protrusions from a woven or knitted surface create a **micro surface** provided by actual three-dimensional surface relief. A surface, defined by all-over color, may be varied with a textural effect, which is part of the weave or knit structure or smooth, as in Figure 6.13a and b. A micro surface can be a regular weave or knit, such as the pile of corduroy fabric, or irregular slubs or yarns incorporated into the surface, such as the slubs that characterize linen or raw silk. Such a textured surface does not separate into a figure-ground relationship; instead, the highpoints of the texture separate only enough to appear to thicken the surface and create the appearance of a visual energy above the surface. Such visual energy often results in an indeterminate effect, as in Figure 6.12. Visually such surface effects can derive from either actual protrusions from the surface or from woven or printed venues where the surface appears three-dimensional. Either venue can appear to create a similar visual result.

**FIGURE 6.12A & B**

*In this dress, pictured as viewed from front and back, the pattern or motif does not readily separate from ground due to similarity in value of figure and ground and also because of the irregular and complex nature of the lines and shapes.*

Courtesy of The Goldstein Gallery, University of Minnesota.

a

b

**FIGURE 6.13A & B**

*A surface with all-over color (Figure 6.13a) may vary only slightly because of a smooth surface. In Figure 6.13b, a surface may have a textural effect based upon three-dimensional protrusions that are part of the weave or knit structure.*

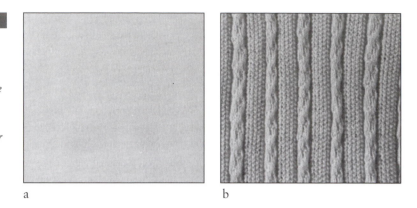

a                                                  b

Surfaces can be patterned by printing or weaving, producing a variety of surface structures. Refer to Table 6.1 for a description of a range of simple to complex surfaces. Pattern can derive from an all-over, repetitious, simple motif, as in polka dots or irregular and complex shapes such as in Figure 6.9.

Size or scale of a surface shape as it relates to the size of the human body is influential in the apparel-body-construct. The surface can involve a few, large motifs, dividing it and creating a structure that is nonrepetitious because its large size would not repeat when used upon the body, as in Figure 6.14. The surface can involve a large border with a simple and distinct figure-ground relation or with a more complex motif on many levels. The placement of a large motif on the body needs to be planned carefully as the structure becomes influential in leading the eye. The effect of size and placement of large shapes on the body can cause them to appear to encircle the body cylinder.

As we have seen, the surface structure can include all-over repeated surface shapes, irregular repeats, and large singular shapes. The viewer is directed depending upon the nature of the shapes and how they are used. The direction of viewing can be horizontal, vertical, or diagonal on the flat surface but may change when placed upon the body due to orientation of the shapes to the body's verticality.

| TABLE 6.1 | | |
|---|---|---|
| *Visual Effects of Surface Structure* | **Simple** | Smooth matte surface, all-over minute points of color |
| | | Irregular pigment or optical mixture of minute points of texture |
| | | Regular repetition of small-sized shapes; large quantity of polka dots, pleats, or gathers; similar value figure-ground integration |
| | | Regular repetition of shapes, small in size, but contrast of value that creates figure-ground separation |
| | | Large-sized shapes, regular repetition, planar levels |
| | **Complex** | Large-sized shapes, irregular repetition, complex structure of several types of directed viewing; organization both on one plane and in-depth levels |

Color can be used to define surfaces. The materials of the apparel-body-construct can appear simply defined by an all-over color on a smooth surface. A one-color surface used by itself can interact with the lines, shapes, and colors of the body. Surfaces of several combined colors interact not only with the body, but also in combination with the other colors. Combinations of color in patterns can also direct our viewing and provide spatial levels of organization. Bringing together several separate surfaces in gradations of value, intensity, or hue can direct our viewing. Each of these surfaces provides a sequential relationship that provides structure. From this structure the viewer perceives the graduating order.

The degree of boldness of a surface or pattern influences its priority for the viewer. Motifs that are determinate because of a distinct and hard edge are a visual priority for the viewer, as in Figure 6.14, and with direction can direct the viewer. Surfaces that are more subtle can also direct the viewer, such as the more indeterminate motifs in Figure 6.15.

**FIGURE 6.15**

*(Right) Surfaces that have soft-edged and indeterminate motifs can direct the viewer, although not in the same way as hard-edged. This all-over motif on the dress surfaces and the trim at the neck and hem edges are indeterminate, but create a horizontal direction nevertheless. The horizontal outline of the dress contributes greatly to its horizontal direction.*

Designed by Nicole Miller. Courtesy of Fairchild Publications.

**FIGURE 6.14**

*(Above left) A large-scale shape, when placed upon the body, may divide and create dominant structure that does not repeat.*

Designed by Moschino. Courtesy of Fairchild Publications.

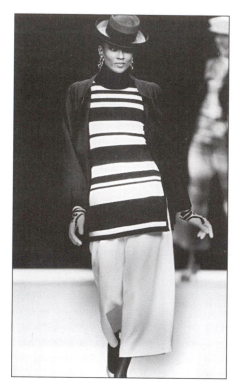

**FIGURE 6.16**

*The irregular stripes in this ensemble by Christian Lacroix are placed within the design so that the viewer can trace their horizontal or vertical direction. But direction is the result of gradations. The gradation of the three widest stripes creates a vertical order and, because of the jacket opening, their length is also graduated from narrower at the neckline to wider as they progress to the hem.*

Courtesy of Fairchild Publications.

Many patterns, such as a series of stripes, direct the eye, that is, horizontally, vertically, diagonally. Stripes on a flat surface often direct the eye along the stripe. Depending upon how such patterns are placed upon the body, the viewer can be directed along the stripes or across the stripes, from one to another as occurs in Figure 6.16, where the placement leads your eye along the stripe and from stripe to stripe. A line that changes in some measured aspect, such as size or shape, can direct the viewer. When stripes vary in width and provide a gradation from wider to narrower, the potential for directing the viewer from one stripe to another increases. In Figure 6.16 the stripes gradate from wider at the hem of the tunic top to narrower at the neck. Additionally, placement of the stripes leads the eye vertically.

When two or three differently colored materials are combined on the body to create a spatial arrangement, it is called **color blocking**. Surfaces of colors of similar intensity and little texture are placed adjacent to each other, and the result provides the effect of color in distinct shapes that share similar or equal attention, as in Figure 6.14. Color blocking draws immediate attention to the edges of the shape as a block of surface color when the surfaces are not textured. In Figure 6.14, the black bands surrounding the primary red, white, yellow, and blue areas intensify these primary hues even more. Another example to imagine is a child's jacket of teal, dark blue, and fuschia colors of similar value, with fuschia collar, teal body, and blue wrist- and waistbands. The similarity of intensity and value is important to placement of colors.

Surface structuring increases the opportunities for visual variety at several stages—by a designer working with fabrics arranged upon a dress form to plan the visual effect of the apparel-body-construct, as in Figure 6.17a, b, and c. The three jackets are similar in layout, but the visual effect is quite different because of the surface structuring. The jacket in Figure 6.17b is viewed as part-to-whole due to the varying size of the geometric motif, while the dark, all-one-color jacket and pants in Figure 6.17a and physical coloring of the model create a more whole-to-part ensemble. The jacket in Figure 6.17c is noted for layout and other parts of the ensemble. A merchandiser planning a window display that publicizes denim jeans should attract the viewer's attention, as in Figure 6.18 when the stars and stripes are arranged differently on each leg. A variety of surfaces structured to include both figure-ground integration and separation may be the solution.

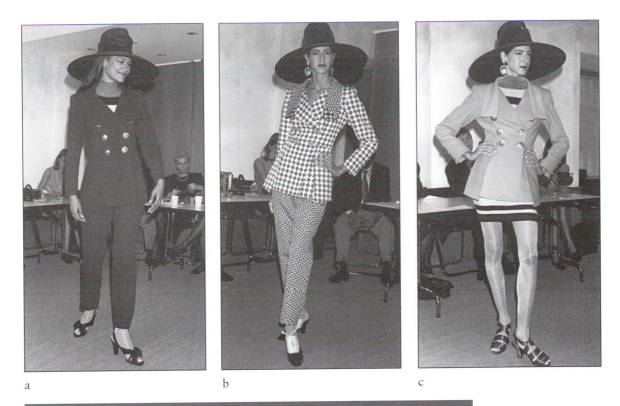

a                                        b                                        c

## FIGURE 6.17A, B & C

*The jackets in these photos are similar in layout, but the visual effect of the apparel-body-construct is quite different because of surface structuring and what other parts are included in the ensemble. The part-to-whole relationship varies. The jacket in Figure 6.17a is a dark, all-one-color jacket and pants. Thus, the visual effect is a more whole-to-part relationship, with the parts being the shirt, buttons, and shoes. In Figure 6.17b, the jacket has two patterns: the larger regular motif used for the majority of the jacket and the smaller pattern on the collar. The pants here repeat the small motif on the collar and the buttons are not as noticeable as in Figure 6.17a. The jacket in Figure 6.17c is light in value. However, the jacket is worn over a dress with dominant horizontal stripes that create a strong part-to-whole relationship that includes body parts, i.e., the legs as well as the hat and shoes.*

*Designed by Christian Lacroix. Courtesy of Fairchild Publications.*

It is important to remember that surface structuring does not operate in isolation. It is the interaction of the surface structure with the body through layout that always influences the visual effect of the apparel-body-construct. As we will see, shapes created by the layout structuring of the apparel-body-construct can change the surface structure. We will examine the effects of layout structuring in greater depth in the next section.

FIGURE 6.18

*The jeans on the left are familiar blue denim, but the ones on the right have the stars and stripes printed upon each leg respectively.*

*Application Exercise 6.3*

Select a photograph of an apparel-body-construct, but picture the garment as if it were a sewing sketch for a pattern with just the outline of the silhouette and other details. Select two fabrics that vary in surface structuring. Think about how the surfaces could appear differently depending upon which is used.

## Light and Shadow Structuring

Surfaces are partially defined by their reflecting character. They can range from dull and matte to shiny and luminous. A surface may present a potentially rich source of surface definition, greatly enhanced by light and shadow structuring. In Figure 6.1a the parallel tucks crisscross the bodice area and the medium value carries the light and shadow. The clothed body, when lighted from a certain point, has a potential for casting shadows because of layout, as in Figure 6.3. In this ensemble the medium value and crisp pleating create optimal light and shadow effects.

The viewer who ignores light and shadow loses a major source of visual effect of the apparel-body-construct. Light and shadow effects may be ignored because of the early perceptual experiences that form our viewing habits or because the effect is not considered important in our culture. You may ignore the rich contribution of light and shadow variation because you have programmed your perception to that which has the most meaning for you. Frequently you find it easier to view something that is more tangible and constant. You may ignore those aspects of objects that are not constant; this includes light and shadow that is inconstant in our ordinary circumstances. In order to perceive the transitory effects of light and shadow you need to view the apparel-body-construct with new eyes and new expectations. You also need to accept the changing or transitory nature of light and shadow, rather than discount it.

To concentrate on how the apparel-body-construct looks from our immediate visual field is to perceive light and shadow effects. Only when you concentrate on the field immediately in front of you do you actually take notice of the nuance of what is there. For example, in Figure 6.19 it is the shadow in the folds that carries the viewer's eye vertically. To pay attention to light and shadow as a variable can greatly influence the impact of the apparel-body-construct on the viewer. Clothing designers specializing in the category of women's evening wear may design for maximum impact through light and shadow. In this way the transitory effects of the evening shadows are echoed in the surfaces of the dress.

The capacity of surfaces to carry light and shadow can be influenced by their color value (their degree of lightness or darkness). The surface value affects its potential as a carrier of light and shadow. A relatively homogeneous dark-value surface has different potential for influencing the form than a similar light-value surface, as in Figure 6.19. A medium-value surface has the most potential for carrying light and shadow effects because of its inherent capacity to reflect light.

Light and shadow structuring are important to the apparel professional who will encounter its effects over and over again. In order to sell a garment, how it is photographed, displayed, and worn to attract the eye are critical. Manipulation of layout, surface, and light and shadow structuring is instrumental in this process. This is different from attributes of surface and layout structure viewed alone.

**FIGURE 6.19**

*Value influences capacity for surfaces to carry light and shadow. The middle value on the left carries light and shadow very well. The dark example in the middle is the least able to carry light and shadow, and the light one on the right requires deep folds for the shadow effects to occur.*

Courtesy of Marilyn Revell DeLong.

Practice viewing in terms of light and shadow. Think about a type of clothing that is dependent upon light and shadow, or find an example in a photograph where light and shadow structuring have been used to good advantage.

Light and shadow structure can be controlled when the illumination is directed for special effects. The extent of control in lighting varies since the apparel-body-construct moves about under normal circumstances. Even though light sources are not usually controlled, an ordinary light source comes from above. The presentation of a costume on a mannequin in a gallery exhibit, in a display, or in an advertisement would be an exception to this lack of control. Here the staging of the light and shadow structure can help produce a constant and consistent visual effect.

Even though shadow is not ordinarily under complete control, some control can be achieved by understanding the surround in which the apparel-body-construct occurs. How differently the surfaces of a visual form can appear under different lighting—incandescent, fluorescent, or daylight! Successful designers consider the different types of lighting in selecting surfaces and in designing the layout of an apparel-body-construct. For example, the visual result will be affected if a particular apparel-body-construct is viewed primarily in daylight, intense sunlight, or evening where artificial lighting predominates.

Select an apparel-body-construct from a current fashion magazine. Imagine and think how different it would be if it were all beige, smooth surfaces that could be varied only by layout and shadow! Now think about how colors and textures can define surfaces of the apparel-body-construct to create spatial effects. Finally, choose one color and surface pattern and imagine a plan for the apparel-body-construct you selected.

## INTERACTION EFFECTS AMONG SURFACE, LAYOUT, AND LIGHT AND SHADOW STRUCTURING

The three sources of structuring—surface, layout, and light and shadow—all influence the apparel-body-construct. As sources of structure, all can be used to create lines, shapes, colors, and textures. As you consider the contribution each brings to your viewing, you will become more aware of what it takes to view the richness and nuance of all that is in our visual field. The sources of visual structuring need to be separated in viewing the apparel-body-construct and analyzed for their influence. One or the other may predominate, or the three

**FIGURE 6.20**

*This ensemble has evidence of all three sources of structuring. The different surface structures, that is, the patterns of the jacket, top, and full culottes, are optimized by the layout. The light and shadow, though often masked by dominant patterns, is evident in the full folds of the culottes.*

sources may interact with none taking priority. In either case, it is useful to consider how each responds in creating their respective visual effects. In Figure 6.20 the visual effect of the apparel-body-construct includes all three sources of structuring. The surface structures are optimized by the layout; the contribution of the light and shadow structure is apparent mostly in the silk pants.

In order to understand what role the sources of structuring play in visual effect, we continually must ask the question and consider the interaction. For example, a textured, tweedy surface used in an apparel-body-construct can appear to fill the space differently than an all-over colored and smooth surface. The texture appears to thicken the surface and mask some seamlines, as in Figure 6.21. Thus, there is a certain ambiguity in the way edges appear. For this reason such a surface structure is often considered a good selection for a beginning tailor. By contrast, the seamline of a smooth, matte surface would become more important because the eye would not pause or stop but would proceed quickly to the edge created by the seamline. Any irregularity in design or execution would be readily apparent.

The qualities of the materials influence their potential in the apparel-body-construct. Materials are defined as two-dimensional surfaces before they are incorporated into the apparel-body-construct. For example, a material can appear relatively simple—smooth surface, all-over color, medium weight, and midway between soft and crisp in hand. A material with no dominant surface structure is often used for its hand where the layout structure will be emphasized, possibly manipulated with pleating, folding, or gathering. The visual effect of the apparel-body-construct in Figure 6.21 can be compared with Figure 6.2, both of which are primarily a result of layout structure. The viewer is indirectly influenced by the nature of the surface, which acts as a visual carrier of layout. A medium value allows the maximum visual effect from the layout structure.

### FIGURE 6.21

*What role do the three sources of structuring play within the apparel-body-construct? Here the surface structure, that is, the texture of the suit surfaces, masks some layout structure, such as the lapel and collar and some seamlines. Light and shadow highlight the jacket hem and the areas where folds occur because of the movements of the body at the bent arm and crotch.*

*Designed by Valentino. Courtesy of Fairchild Publications.*

Structuring from surface and layout influence each other and the visual effect of the apparel-body-construct. A surface that is initially structured by distinct shapes to create a figure-ground effect could become a viewing priority. In this interaction, the layout and light and shadow structuring can be masked to some degree because of such a surface structure, as in Figure 6.22a, b, and c. This type of ordered surface structure could be used in layout structuring to contradict itself, in a curved shape or on the bias. Also, a surface that is geometric and ordered according to the vertical-horizontal orientation of the material could be repeated in the layout on the body according to this same orientation. In Figure 6.23 the shapes become curved in silhouette and the surface appears to have more depth.

Even though a surface structure may be simple or complex in its appearance before its incorporation into the apparel-body-construct, it will be further transformed in use on the body. A simple surface structure can appear more complex with both layout and light and shadow structuring strongly defined, as in Figure 6.20.

The surface structure can reveal or camouflage the layout structure. A napped fabric has a built-in source of highlight because as the pile receives light it reflects in a variety of directions. The example in Figure 6.12 shows the result of a surface structure with a pattern of irregular shapes that camou-

a                                    b                                    c

**FIGURE 6.22A, B & C**

*A surface structured with regular lines and geometric shapes (a) can be used to contradict the order when placed on the bias grain (b) or emphasize the vertical-horizontal orientation of the material (c).*

FIGURE 6.23

*Surfaces that, when flat, appear ordered and oriented to the vertical-horizontal because of the structure parallel to the grain can be designed with deep folds and appear curved in silhouette.*

Designed by Gianni Versace. Courtesy of Fairchild Publications.

flage some aspects of layout. Layout structure can also either reveal or minimize surface structure because of its action as a carrier of light and shadow structure.

The source of lighting of the apparel-body-construct can interact with layout and surface structuring. For instance, if the light source is ordinarily from above, a horizontal overlap from the layout structure of a jacket of medium value may produce a shadow most of the time. Under ordinary circumstances, shadow effects may be planned in relation to an ordinary light source. Layout that utilizes overlapping can be further revealed and enhanced by shadow from overhead illumination. Photographers can further control this means to create various effects, directing viewing by use of different sources of lighting. For example, directing the light source from below could create different light and shadow effects.

All sources of visual structuring can define and describe space and therefore direct viewing. Lines can be created by printing or weaving, an effect of surface structure. In layout structure a line can be created by the manipulation of surfaces into edges or by combining two different surfaces. By asking what is the visual effect from each, one can assure an awareness and understanding of all sources of structuring in viewing. Lines, shapes, colors, and textures can be made visually distinct or indistinct, whether produced by pigment on the two-dimensional surfaces of the apparel-body-construct or created through layout and/or light and shadow effects.

Cultural priorities often greatly influence what we see. For example, in Western cultures layout has been a predominant means of analyzing what has been worn within a certain historic period. In the nineteenth century, Western men's suits were often identified by silhouette shape and such details as lapel, length of coat, and width of front button closures. If cutting and sewing are predominant, we pay more attention to that aspect. Think about the difference in what would be noticed in a culture where one particular layout structure is the constant source of structuring, such as in Japan where the kimono shape is consistent over many historic periods. When layout is a constant, then meaning tends to arise from other sources of structuring than layout. In the case of the kimono, surface structuring becomes more predominant, as illustrated in Figure 6.24. Think about the richness of symbols that arise from surface patterns and motifs on some Korean traditional dress, another culture with consistency in layout structure of the *hanbok*. The *hanbok* can be profusely decorated with symbols of nature, such as flower motifs, birds, or cloud patterns (refer to Color Plate 12).

**FIGURE 6.24**

*When layout structure becomes a constant, surface structuring often becomes dominant and motifs used may become symbolic. The Japanese kimono, consistent in layout structure of rectangular shapes, is often dramatic in its surface structure.*

Courtesy of The Goldstein Gallery, University of Minnesota.

Think of the relationship of layout structure to body ideals and ideals of beauty. How does cut and sewn clothing reinforce a changing ideal? Does a fixed layout structure help to reinforce a more continuous body ideal?

# INFLUENCE FROM TACTILE AND KINESTHETIC EXPERIENCES

Even though the visual effect of materials has been emphasized, the influence of the tactile and kinesthetic aspects of surfaces also needs to be discussed. Our experience with materials is more than just visual, and this influences how the viewer responds to the visual.

Visual, tactile, and kinesthetic experiences all affect our viewing of the apparel-body-construct. Many of our important early sensory experiences are tactile. A child likes to touch soft things—soft blankets, furry stuffed animals. The tactile qualities of materials mean much to us and later give meaning to our visual sense. Kinesthetic experiences that influence viewing also occur in our childhoods. The weight of a coat is experienced as different from that of a cotton shirt. In fact, the wearer may get so used to the feel of a heavy coat in cold weather, a close association may be created of heavy weight to warmth. This caused difficulties when *Thinsulate®* was first introduced to the American public to provide "warmth without weight"—an idea consumers had to get used to because of their former associations that warmth is provided by thickness and weight.

Though the visual aspects of materials and the way they can interact in viewing is a primary consideration, our other sensory experiences are very much present in our visual interpretation. A sweater may appear to be soft because we have previously experienced its softness by touch. A suede leather surface that feels soft and somewhat furry also looks shaded, with light and shadow areas on the surface. This connection between visual and tactile message needs to be recognized as a major source of the pleasure we gain in viewing materials.

Sometimes a surface structure will differ in its visual and tactile character. Often touching will reveal a discrepancy from how the surface visually appears. For example, a sequined surface is shiny visually. When touched, it does not feel smooth and slippery as one would expect if a direct correspondence between tactile and visual experiences always existed. In this case, the tactile and visual offer two quite different sensory experiences. How often have you felt a sense of disappointment or surprise when a fabric fails to meet your expectations for consistency between visual and tactile qualities?

A printed surface is another example of a surface that can appear different from the way it feels. Many types of visual definition, for example, lines and shapes, can be printed onto the surface, thereby altering it visually but changing the tactile character minimally. A contemporary example is an animal print, such as leopard. Though it looks so distinctive, when the source is surface structure, the fabric seldom feels like the fur of the animal. Some surface and layout structures can cause a conflict between visual and tactile qualities. For example, the richness of a paisley motif is primarily visual, even though when used as the patterning of a shawl it also wraps and encompasses the body. Many nineteenth century women experienced both the visual and tactile qualities of the paisley shawl that was so popular to wear. However, the visual richness of the shawl was not always matched by a tactile richness in wearing the wool material.

Materials are also influenced visually because of their kinesthetic relation to the body. How the material hangs from the body is a factor that not only influences our judgment about wearing certain materials but also influences our viewing. We may think that wool looks scratchy and heavy because of our experiences with the way it feels and moves on the body. On the other hand, silk looks and feels smooth, moves easily, and hangs fluidly with the body. The way wool and silk interact with the body can certainly influence the way they drape and thus our viewing. Empathizing with the wearer because of our past experience with the kinesthetic aspects of a material may affect our visual perception of that material. This is when we make such comments as, "That looks like it would feel scratchy!"

Body movement is a source of interaction experiences. The legs interact with a long dress or robe as we walk, sometimes impeding movement if the fabric gets caught up by the walking movement. How exciting it is for a child to twirl the body in a long garment, such as a robe or nightgown, and feel the circle of the hem extend outward and then momentarily swirl against the body! Such experiences, even in childhood, continue to affect our visual thinking as adults.

By distinguishing between the visual, tactile, and kinesthetic qualities of materials, we can recognize the potential associations of the visual with the tactile and the visual with the kinesthetic and separate them in our awareness. However, we must also be aware of their associations in interaction.

| Application Exercise 6.7 | Find an example or think about a fabric that when touched is different from how it appears visually. How could it be used in the apparel-body-construct? What difference could it make? |
|---|---|

## Summary

• A variety of materials from traditional fabrics to paints, films, and metals are used to construct the apparel-body-construct. Designers use materials to create visual effects, while retailers use them to attract customers.

• There are three sources of visual structuring: **layout structuring**, involving the three-dimensional variation of materials manipulated on the body; **surface structuring**, resulting from variations of the two-dimensional surface caused by dyeing, printing, or weaving; and **light and shadow structuring**, which occurs because of the varying illumination of the environment as it interacts with dress, creating light and shadow effects.

• Layout structuring involves the form of apparel items such as slacks, blazers, and kimonos. It involves manipulation of materials and thus the nature of the materials used is crucial—from thin silks to heavier fabrics like woolens. Fabric grain, hand, and bias are important terms, and the draping, cutting, and joining of shapes are crucial. Nontraditional fabrics such as feathers and metals may also be used.

• Surface structuring involves two-dimensional characteristics of fabric, such as textures, colors, patterns, and prints, which affect the way a garment appears to the viewer's eye.

• Light and shadow structuring involves transitory effects which are important in designing certain categories of apparel—for example, evening dresses or sportswear—and also influence how a dress is photographed and sold.

• Finally, surface, layout, and light and shadow structuring interact and influence the apparel-body-construct. You will become more aware of their interplay while training yourself to view more consciously from the visual field perspective.

## Key Terms and Concepts

bias
color blocking
grain
hand
layout structuring

light structuring
micro surface
shadow structuring
surface structuring

## References

Arnheim, R. *Art and Visual Perception: A Psychology of the Creative Eye.* Berkeley: University of California Press, 1974.

Brockman, H. *The Theory of Fashion Design.* New York: John Wiley and Sons, 1965.

Gibson, J. *The Senses Considered as Perceptual Systems.* Boston: Houghton Mifflin, 1966.

Gombrich, E. *The Sense of Order: A Study in the Psychology of Decorative Art.* Ithaca, NY: Cornell University Press, 1979.

Kubler, G. *The Shape of Time.* London: Yale University Press, 1962.

Martin, F. *Sculpture as Enlivened Space.* Lexington, KY: The University Press of Kentucky, 1981.

Myers, J. *The Language of Visual Art: Perception as a Basis for Design.* Chicago: Holt, Rinehart and Winston, 1989.

*Chapter Seven*

# VISUAL DEFINITION WITHIN THE APPAREL-BODY-CONSTRUCT

*After you have read this chapter, you will be able to understand:*

• The fundamental components—elements or visual definers—within the apparel-body-construct: line, shape, point, texture, and color.

• Linear definition—definition by line or edge, including line, shape, and point and the different categories of line—straight, curved, angular. How lines can be manipulated via fabric—by folds, pleats, distinct or indistinct edges, by the creation of different kinds of shapes, points, and silhouettes, etc.

• Surface definition—definition by surface, including color and texture, and surface texture as a visual phenomenon; the impact of color on dress and what is meant by hue, intensity, and value.

• How the elements are associated within the context of the apparel-body-construct, the natural world, and with individual and cultural meanings.

T HE VISUAL ANALYSIS OF DRESS IN THIS BOOK BEGAN with an examination of the whole, the entire apparel-body-construct, and the visual effect created; then the components were examined— the body, materials, and structuring. Now a more elemental component will be examined—the visual definers of line, shape, point, texture, and color. These are called **elements** or **visual definers** because they are the most fundamental components that shape our understanding of the apparel-body-construct; each helps to characterize the apparel-body-construct. First each element must be understood, then its function in the whole.

Elements such as shape or texture are the cornerstones of every artistic media, but how they are used and combined in connection with the apparel and the body is what makes the apparel-body-construct a unique medium. It is crucial to remember that visual definition within the apparel-body-construct combines the lines and surfaces of clothing, the accessories, and the wearer. Visual definers relate to each other and to the visual result. For example, surface texture is made more complex within the apparel-body-construct because of its interactions with lines and edges, as well as with other textures such as those of the wearer's skin and hair. Continual awareness of this overriding predominance of the whole is critical for all professionals of the apparel industry—the designer, the manufacturer, or the retailer.

Elements that provide visual definition within the apparel-body-construct are:

- Line
- Shape
- Point
- Texture
- Color

In combination, such definers can create an infinite variety of visual effects. Definers are not the only influence upon visual effect. Let us review how they link to other concepts that have been discussed previously.

Visual structuring (discussed in Chapter 6) can arise from such sources as two-dimensional surfaces and from three-dimensional layout of the surfaces on the body. However, identifying the source of structuring does not adequately describe the visual effect. Other relationships must be examined closely. How a line is characterized is important to the resulting visual effect. A line may be elegantly curving or straight, hard-edged or soft-edged. A hard edge may be created by a line printed on the surface of a material or from a hemline. A soft edge may also be created from structuring by layout, surface, or light and shadow.

The definers offer the potential for visual relationships within the apparel-body-construct. In the discussion of visual relations in Chapter 2, it was noted that the observer tends to group similar aspects and separate dissimilar aspects. Parts in the apparel-body-construct can be similar in many ways.

Definers enter into the development of parts and how they will be organized. There are characteristics of shapes that interrelate and can be grouped, such as circles with other circles. Shapes can also be similar in texture or color. Blue circles group with other blue circles in a simple organization, but what happens when some circles are blue and some are red or there are blue circles and blue squares? The response is that such phenomena must be examined within the organization of the particular apparel-body-construct.

Visual relationships can derive from many characteristics of definers from relatively simple ones to the more complex. Some of these relationships can be direct and physically quantifiable; you can describe how long, how wide, how thick. Such relationships derive from simple definer characteristics, such as long or short lines, light or dark values. Other definer characteristics provide visual relationships that are not so direct, such as hard-edged or soft-edged shapes, filled or unfilled surfaces. A more complex relationship is a color complement, that is, those hues that are opposite each other on the color wheel. Color complements also are sensory opposites. If a viewer thought in terms of wavelengths, such hues could be quantifiable; however, the viewer perceives the relation of complementary hues used within one composition or, as a result of visual fatigue, perceives the complement in an afterimage. Another way definers can be related is by inference. Sometimes the way we describe a definer involves mental concepts that only make sense because they are related to past experiences. An example is the use of an adjective such as "fashionable" or "casual" when describing a particular definer. Then interpretation is based upon an inferred relationship to such factors as culture or time period.

Visual definition of the apparel-body-construct cannot be limited to just the clothing ensemble. The entire apparel-body-construct must be our frame of reference, and this extends to any discussion of visual definers. For example, the visual effect of a shape at the neck is not just a result of the clothing but also of the interaction with the neck itself, the shape of the hair, and the shape of the body at the shoulders.

In order to fully understand the apparel-body-construct, it is not enough to identify visual definers, such as line, color, texture, shape, and point, without understanding their combination and how they can result in different visual effects. How people prioritize in the process of viewing is better understood if one can separate and describe the way the apparel-body-construct gains definition through its elements. There are basically two ways to define visually:

- **Linear definition**
- **Surface definition**

**Linear definition** is created by line and edge and derives from elements of lines, shapes, and points. An apparel-body-construct can be characterized as a result of the dominance of linear definition. **Surface definition** is the characterization of the surface by color and texture. Color is an attribute that has infinite possibilities for varying the surface. Surface texture is the perception of how space is occupied, as unfilled and smooth or filled with minute points that vary the surface. Surface texture can be physical and/or visual. The origin of physical texture is from the actual fibers or yarns, which can create light and shadow effects; visual texture can be printed. Physical texture actually has small protrusions that can be felt tactually; visual texture alone does not. As the apparel-body-construct is organized, linear definition influences how the visual result is perceived.

The visual possibilities provided by linear definition of line, shape, and point will be defined within the apparel-body-construct. Each is perceived through identifying characteristics and each functions within the apparel-body-construct in a characteristic manner. Line is the first such fundamental component influencing the visual effect.

# LINE

The term **line** is commonly used in several ways regarding the apparel-body-construct. The term "line" can be used interchangeably with a consistent style, for example, a "line" of clothing identified with a designer or manufacturer usually for a specific time period. Using line in this manner is an abstraction of what we see in any one apparel-body-construct to a number of apparel-body-constructs perceived to be similar to each other. Line is also used to describe a cut of clothing, as in a line of a skirt, like an A-line skirt, which actually describes shape. The adequacy of such a description depends somewhat upon cultural models, for example, an Indian sari forms lines not through cut, but by drape of diagonal folds when worn upon the body. A sari stored flat does not reveal the same characteristics of line formation as when it is seen on the wearer. However, a cut and sewn product may form lines when stored on a hanger that are similar to the lines formed on the body. Though one must be aware of the various uses of the term "line," what we will discuss next are its most elemental aspects—how line is perceived within the apparel-body-construct.

## Visual Function of Line

The function of line in the whole can be to provide visual interest, such as the pleats in a yoke; to give direction, such as the buttons at center front that the observer visually connects as a line; or to divide space, as does the edge of a jacket, especially if the jacket contrasts in some respect (such as shape, color, or texture) with what is adjacent to it or is emphasized by light and shadow. Line can become an important focus in taking in the apparel-body-construct, for example, the double rows of buttons in Figure 7.1 together form lines that

FIGURE 7.1

(Left) Lines are created by the double row of buttons that echo the shaping of the silhouette. On a dark-value surface, such a contrast, even though small in size, is important to the character of the whole.

Designed by Richard Tyler. Courtesy of Fairchild Publications.

FIGURE 7.2

(Right) Repetitious parallel lines become textural in effect, and change in line direction creates parts.

Courtesy of Fairchild Publications.

take on added significance because they reflect the curve of the silhouette. Numerous lines can become textural in effect by defining the surface when no one line is dominant, and they group together as in the swimsuit in Figure 7.2. Parts are characterized by the line direction and the change in orientation from one part to another. In Figure 7.3 the horizontal lines repeat and encircle the body but become gradually wider at the hem to create a graduated effect. With the narrow to wide widths of line from a visual field perspective and with the similarly contrasting buttons, collar band, and sunglasses, the eye is directed in an orderly way. Diversion is created by the rounding of the hair shape and "Liz" parcel.

## General Appearance of Line

Line in the apparel-body-construct is identified by its length and by the proportion of its length to its width. To recognize a line, the observer must perceive its length and a degree of thinness. However, a line can appear thicker

a                                    b

## FIGURE 7.3A & B

*Lines define the fabric surfaces, and in the context of the whole they define the body and give direction to the viewer in Figure 7.3a. The lines at the bottom of the jacket encircle the body cylinder and are horizontal. However, visual cues within the ensemble influence the direction. The horizontal lines are graduated from wider at the hem to narrower. Because of the contrasting outline of the collar, the buttons, and the sunglasses, the viewer is cued to a vertical direction in the jacket. In Figure 7.3b, lines are created in a fabric surface as it is manipulated into edges and folds. Such edges include the collar, center front opening, the tie belt, and the hemline. Folds of the skirt extend from the waist and are accentuated by light and shadow.*

Designed by Liz Claiborne. Courtesy of Fairchild Publications.

or thinner. A thick line boldly contrasting with its surround can appear closer to the observer than a thin line. If a line becomes very wide, we may perceive it as shape.

Line can be described as straight, angular, or curved. Line can be used to define the flat surface of fabric, as in Figure 7.3a, or the folds of a three-dimensional surface, as in Figure 7.3b. Line can be described as regular or irregular, distinct or indistinct, direct or indirect. A line may curve in one direction and be a simple curved line, or in several directions and be considered a compound curve. Such curves may be shallow and flattened or full and rounded. If the curve of a line folds in and is enclosed, visually it may be perceived as the edge of shape created by layout.

Since lines can be manipulated via fabric, they can be perceived in terms of their three dimensionality in and out, relative to the observer. For example, line can appear as the edges of pressed pleats or folds of gathers and can vary in character from decisive and sharp, to intermittent and soft. In Figure 7.3b, the lines of the skirt are emphasized by light and shadow on the folds at the hem that gradate to narrower folds toward the waistline. A variety of characteristics of line will now be explored.

Examine the use of line in Figure 7.3a and b. Then compare the lines in terms of visual priorities, relation to the body, and structuring. How does the line identified in each influence how you order each apparel-body-construct?

*Application Exercise 7.1*

## Continuous or Discontinuous Lines

A continuous line, one that is regular and does not change direction, is more easily viewed than a discontinuous line, one that abruptly changes direction or is interrupted in its path. Often a point of discontinuity will separate in viewing, as in the ensemble in Figure 7.4 in which the checkers on the vest do

### FIGURE 7.4

*Lines may or may not be continuous within the context of the apparel-body-construct. Discontinuous are the lines of the surface of the vest. However, the lapels of the jacket and vest opening create a center front line that continues to the feet.*

Designed by Alexander Julian. Courtesy of Fairchild Publications.

not continue the diagonal lines on the lapels of the jacket. Such differences can attract focus to a specific visual part because of the change in direction. On the other hand, a line that is continuous and links several shapes is a source of similarity and visual connection within the apparel-body-construct. In Figure 7.4, the center front line of this suit by Alexander Julian continues from the head, chest, waist, and between the legs.

## Line Direction

Directing the visual path is an important function of line and an awareness of it is vital in viewing the apparel-body-construct. Eye movements while taking in the visual form are the source of the sensation of direction. The observer's bodily movements and tensions may also be a source of directing, as when an observer, describing the body, traces it with the hands in midair. The viewer who traces a line within the apparel-body-construct, as in Figure 7.5, may literally feel some tension of the movement.

## Line Length

The length of a line is important to the way it is viewed: A shorter line is more immediately viewed but may not direct viewing as much because of its short length. A longer line may direct viewing because it is not all taken in with one glance.

**FIGURE 7.5**

*The numerous sources of line in this ensemble by Bill Blass create excitement, from the lines encircling the scarf at the neck; the curved line of the jacket opening, made more prominent by the contrast of the exposed, light-value vest; and the buttons repeating the curved line of the opening. Other lines include the outline of the sleeves, the repeat of the cuff banding and buttons, and the outline of the dark lower torso made more prominent by the matte surface that does not carry light and shadow.*

Courtesy of Fairchild Publications.

## COLOR PLATE 1

*The Munsell color notation is a system used to describe ten major hue families in terms of hue, value, and intensity or chroma. Hue notations are Red, Yellow-red, Yellow, Green-Yellow, Green, Blue-Green, Blue, Purple-Blue, Purple, and Red-Purple. The pigments are placed on a scale of equal visual steps for accurate specification and description of hue, value, and intensity. This color system is used to communicate accurate color information.*

*Colors have an apparent temperature. Warm hues include Red, Yellow-Red, and Yellow. Cool hues include Blue, Purple-Blue, and Purple. More intensity often increases the apparent warmth of a specific hue. Apparent temperature is a source of relationships within the apparel-body-construct, that is, cool with cool creates similarity, and cool with warm creates contrast.*

## COLOR PLATE 2A, B, C, D & E

*The selection of a color scheme for an apparel-body-construct is an important and satisfying task. Color schemes can be created and named through location on the color wheel. (A **monochromatic** (a) scheme is the use of one color with variation of value or with a neutral.) **Analogous** (b) colors are those close to each other on the color wheel and **complementary** (c) colors are opposite each other on the wheel. Other color schemes include **split-complementary** (d) where the color on either side of the complement is selected. A **triad** (e) is one in which three hues equidistant from each other are selected.*

## COLOR PLATE 3

*Value is the lightness, darkness dimension of a color. A value scale on the left side of Color Plate 3 shows a gradient of values, varying from white (0.0) to black (l0.0) with (5.0) designating the middle halfway in value between black and white. Each hue has value and each hue relates to a home value; thus some hues are normally lighter or darker than others, i.e., yellow is lighter at home value than purple. Each hue has the dimension of brightness-dullness that is called intensity or chroma. A saturated hue is intense and can evoke excitement when viewed within an apparel-body-construct. Locate the hue on the color wheel in Color Plate 1 corresponding to the number 5 YR in Color Plate 3. In this example the intensity of one selected hue, 5 Yellow-Red is indicated from its least intense on the left closest to the neutral gray of the same value at /2, to its most intense at the far right, 14. A complete color notation includes hue, value, and intensity or chroma. Colors can be re-*

*lated to the body through similarities or contrasts in hue, value or intensity. Many body colors are less intense and relate by similarity through less intense clothing colors.*

## COLOR PLATE 4A & B

*Each color influences its adjacent neighbor. In (a) colors are influenced by their surround through the effect of simultaneous contrast. Center dots are identical in size and are the same value of light gray but are surrounded by white or black. The center dot with greatest contrast appears lighter in value. In (b) colors associate with their surround. One hue can appear differently when surrounded by a complementary color or with a value of gray. Color of ground changes perceived intensity. A blue-green ring with a neutral gray ground looks different than the same blue-green ring with a complementary ground of red.*

## COLOR PLATE 5A & B

*The same item of clothing can appear different in color when worn by two persons with different personal coloring. When viewed within the apparel-body-construct, different color and surface variations can be emphasized when combined with colorcontrasts within an ensemble. For example, in (a) the dark hair tends to emphasize the dark areas of the jacket and the middle value relates to her skin coloring, whereas in (b) the light hair relates to the lighter values in the jacket. Consider what each model would wear with the coat to create a visual relationship of similarity with her personal coloring.*

Courtesy of Marilyn Revell DeLong.

## COLOR PLATE 6

*Colors selected for the ensemble are similar to the personal coloring of this young man and thus he appears whole-to-part. His own skin and hair tones appear more intense because of the less intense surfaces of the suit, shirt, and tie.*

Designed by Paul Smith. Courtesy of Fairchild Publications.

## COLOR PLATE 7

*The use of similar hues, values, and intensities in clothing and body colors makes them group and tend to stay in the same plane. The golden hue of the pants and blouse worn by the figure on the left are in the same hue family as her skin coloring but lighter in value. The dark areas of her floral jacket repeat the dark hair, while the lighter more intense yellow floral motif and her gold buttons, earrings, and hair orna-*

*ment create small areas of related accent. In the figure on the right, there are contrasting values with personal coloring in the upper torso. The white shirt advances as figure, with the ground being the black trousers, shoes, skin, and hair. He holds her hat which breaks up the dark area of trouser.*

*Courtesy of Barbara Sumberg.*

## COLOR PLATE 8

*The many similarities in the lines, shapes, textures, and colors of this young girl create order and coherence among the parts. Groupings occur because of similarity of visual definers and modifiers within the apparel-body-construct. The dominant use of curving shapes relate to this young girl's physical shape, and light values in the ground of the ensemble relate to her personal coloring. The use of complementary hues in the meandering floral motif create visual interest.*

*Courtesy of JCPenney.*

## COLOR PLATE 9

*Color relationships can be created by combining colors similar in hue, value or intensity. Such selections will create groupings and visual integration as in the young girl's white dress, hat, and shoes. Colors that use the body colors form immediate relations of grouping with the body. The young man's trousers and shoes are less intense than his skin but in the same hue family. The dark value of his hair relates to this dark belt. Combining colors similar in hue, value, and intensity will create visual groupings. For example, the contrasting colors of light blue and yellow are similar in value. Colors can define spatial position and appear to be near or in the distance. For example, a warm and intense hue seems nearer than a less intense cool version. In Color Plate 16, the gloves are a more intense and darker value blue than the dress and they appear as figure and a distinct part to the viewer.*

*Courtesy of JCPenney.*

## COLOR PLATE 10

*This ensemble by Bill Blass, with its richly varied shapes upon the surface and subtle light and dark contrasts, requires a lingering pace to view its parts after first considering the whole. The similarity of the warm peachy hue of the skin to the upper and lower portions of the dress (Notation: Hue is 5 Yellow-Red, Value 8/, Intensity or Chroma /3) contrast with the blue-purple color floral motif in the central torso area. The colors of the dress are complementary in hue, but*

*the indeterminacy created by the motif and the use of the basic neutral white carries throughout the surface.*

*Courtesy of Fairchild Publications.*

## COLOR PLATES 11 & 12

*Korean traditional dress is designed to relate to cultural traditions and to the wearer. This includes layout and surface structures. Some colors such as celadon green, blue, and burgundy in Color Plate 11 have become traditional in their meaning for certain events, age, and status of wear. In Color Plate 12, the colors are not considered traditional ones, although they may be pleasing and appear similar to the traditional to the unknowing eye of a foreigner.*

*Courtesy of Geum, Key Sook, Seoul, Korea.*

## COLOR PLATE 13, 14, 15 & 16

**Expressive effects are the resulting response to some combination of properties of the apparel-body-construct. (Color Plates 13–16)**

*All photographs courtesy of Fairchild Publications.*

**Plate 13**  *Excitement may result from viewing the contrasting lines in the upper torso, the value contrast, figure-ground ambiguity, and the part-to-whole viewing in this Ralph Lauren design. Compare the result of this dispersion of contrasting values throughout the ensemble with the large contrasting white and black areas of the man in Color Plate 7.*

**Plate 14**  *In this Bill Blass design, a response of calm may result from ordered parts, the use of a muted hue throughout, basic lines related to the body axis and silhouette, and figure-ground integration within the clothing ensemble.*

**Plate 15**  *Strength may be the feeling received from this combination of large shapes with emphasis on the silhouette, continuous vertical lines, and black combined with a hot pink coat in a closed form with determinate surfaces, as designed by Oscar de la Renta for Balmain. Compare the result of this concentration on a large intense area of color with the less intense colors in Color Plate 6.*

**Plate 16**  *A feeling of delicacy may result from small, soft, rounded, and simple shapes, light value, smooth surface, and planar integration, as designed by Oscar de la Renta. Compare this expressive effect with Color Plate 8. Both result in a feeling of delicacy, but use different means to create the effect.*

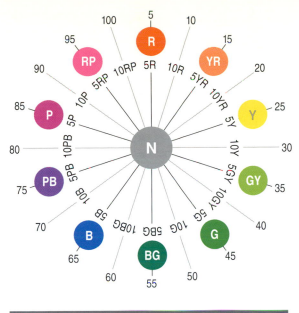

## COLOR PLATE 1

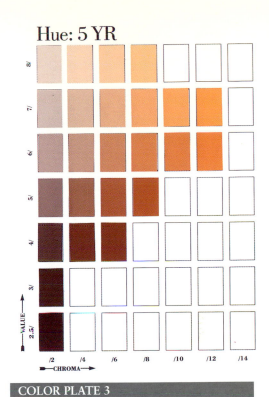

## Hue: 5 YR

## COLOR PLATE 3

2A  MONOCHROMATIC

2B  ANALOGOUS

2C  COMPLEMENTARY

2D  SPLIT-COMPLEMENTARY

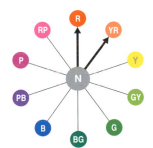

2E  TRIAD (3 HUES)

## COLOR PLATE 2A, B, C, D, E

a

b

**COLOR PLATE 4A & B**

a

b

**COLOR PLATE 5A & B**

**COLOR PLATE 6**

**COLOR PLATE 7**

**COLOR PLATE 8**

**COLOR PLATE 9**

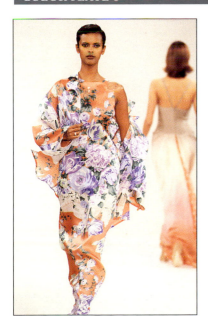

**COLOR PLATE 10**

**COLOR PLATE 11**

**COLOR PLATE 12**

COLOR PLATE 13

COLOR PLATE 14

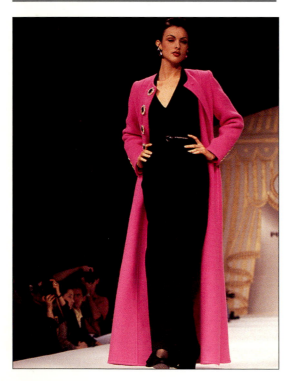

COLOR PLATE 15

COLOR PLATE 16

The length of a line in the context of the body and clothing is also significant. If the line is just as long as a body part or appears to continue a body part, it may be less noticed than a longer or shorter one. On the other hand, a line that extends beyond the body part may cause attention to be directed to that area. For example, a hat brim that extends horizontally beyond the widest part of the head offers contrast and potential focus because of its influence on the silhouette.

A line may begin and end within one body view (that which can be taken in or viewed in one glance) or extend around the body. Straight lines can be vertical, horizontal, or diagonal. A diagonal line often appears to extend around the body because it tends to cut across a greater surface area. Vertical lines usually can be taken in within one body view, and horizontal lines can be seen either as related to one body view or as extended around the body. A horizontal line that is viewed as an edge of a shape and as a part of the visual field relates to one body view. Thus, a belt worn at the waist may be viewed within one body view or perceived as a line that encircles the body.

## Actual or Implied Lines

A line connection can be actual or implied: actual when the eye of the observer traces a continuous seamline or stripe printed on the surface and implied when two points of interest with relatively clear space between them are connected visually. Examples of implied lines are shown in Figure 7.1, where the path is from one button to another or, as in Figure 7.5, where the eye traces the line at the center front opening.

## Line or Edge

Line may be perceived primarily as line or as edge. "Line-as-line" is distinguished as figure on top of ground. "Line-as-edge" is usually perceived as the boundary for a shape, belonging more to one adjacent shape than to another, as in Figure 7.6a. The buttons in Figure 7.6b may push the figure-ground relationship a bit more, but you still may view the shapes of the jacket as edge. This comprehension of line-as-edge may occur when the line becomes important in the observer's viewing, for example, in the process of viewing a transition between one part and another. Edges are related to area of shapes, but it is useful to separate the idea of edge because at times the edge of a large shape is perceived in the focusing process more as edge than as a portion of the shape. For example, hemlines are often considered in viewing first as an edge and secondly as part of a shape. This is especially true when length of a hemline is a critical aspect of fashion, as in length of a trouser pant leg. Then we may first notice its relation to where it falls on the body rather than as a portion of the shape of the trouser.

a                                          b

**FIGURE 7.6A & B**

*Line-as-edge is perceived as a boundary for a shape belonging more to one side than the other. In Figure 7.6a, the alternating black and white areas form shapes and the line is perceived as edge. The contrasting buttons in Figure 7.6b create a transition between the two prominent areas of black and white and thereby remove some of the ambiguity of the figure-ground relationship. With the white buttons on top, the dominant side becomes the black one.*

Courtesy of The Goldstein Gallery, University of Minnesota.

## Hard-Edge or Soft-Edge Lines

Lines that are simple, angular, decisive, and sharp are called hard edged, as in the collar and jacket lines in Figure 7.3a, and lines that are curving, indistinct, and blurred are called soft-edged, as in the skirt folds of the dress in Figure 7.3b. Hard and soft edges affect the character of an apparel-body-construct because of the way the observer takes them in. Hard edges are often accompanied by other factors influencing perception that result in a primacy and an immediacy in viewing, such as smooth, seemingly unfilled surfaces. Soft edges are often accompanied by filled or textured surfaces, light and shadow, or transparency. Soft edges often do not attract our attention to the actual edge—rather, our attention turns to the surface itself or to the light and shadow created by the soft edge.

Think about different hemlines. Can you think of one hemline that appears as hard edged and calls attention to the shape of the skirt or trouser? Can you think of a hemline that appears softer and incorporates a body part in a different way than in the previous example? What accounts for this identification? Example: An off-white skirt hem at mid-thigh appears differently depending upon whether stockings are nude color or the same color as the skirt.

*Application Exercise 7.2*

## Position of Line

Line is characterized by its position. Position includes the line's relationship to the body, to adjacent space (left-right, up-down), and its apparent distance from the observer (in-out, near-far). In Figure 7.7, the thick, hard-edged lines of the upper torso contrast with those of the lower torso, but the lines created by folds repeat the vertical lines of the body. They also contrast with the horizontal lines of the upper torso. Hard-edged lines appear closer to the observer than soft-edged lines, which appear farther away. For example, compare the hard-edged lines of Figure 7.3a with the softer ones of Figure 7.3b.

Where a line is located on the body is important to the way it is viewed. Since the body is basically vertical, vertical lines may reinforce body verticality. They can relate closely to the visual axis of the body, as in the case of a center front line created by a zipper or button closing. Horizontal lines draw attention away from the body verticality and may divide the body into a series of sections, depending upon their position. A bikini may be viewed as horizontal lines as well as shapes on the body.

The observer's perceptual habits influence the viewing of linear position. Many common eye movements affect our perception. In Western cultures, we often view the body from left to right, top to bottom, and come to anticipate this direction when viewing the position of lines on the body. Any lines that require a contrary eye movement may be perceived as more complex and require more energy to view. Consequently, they may be associated with more aggressiveness.

## Sources of Line

Lines in the apparel-body-construct can originate from many sources: from the clothing itself, such as from seams,

**FIGURE 7.7**

*Lines of the upper torso are thick, hard-edged, horizontal lines that contrast with the thinner but more numerous and hard-edged diagonal lines of the lower torso, as well as the softer lines created by the folds in the full pants. The character of each of the lines helps to create an order within the ensemble. There are also cues to figure-ground ambiguity created in this example. Can you find them?*

Designed by Sonia Rykiel. Courtesy of Fairchild Publications.

folds, and edges; from the body, such as the line of the chin or the arm; or the relation to context, such as the line that can be created by the silhouette because of the contrast with the immediate physical surround.

*Seams as Lines.* Seamlines are the lines made when two pieces of material are stitched together, often enclosing or covering a cutting line of fabric. Seams that are perceived as lines can vary in importance in the context of the apparel-body-construct. For example, a side seamline is considered as it divides the body proportionally, front to back, if the seam is viewed from the side. However, the side seamlines are not as apparent when viewed from front or back views and then function to create shape. The seamline itself can be less important in perception when it is primarily functioning to create shape. It can be important when located at a body position that is being emphasized. For example, a seamline is more important when it is accompanied by stripes placed at an angle, creating a chevron effect as in the pant legs in Figure 7.7.

A seamline may overlap another surface, as in a pocket flap, hemline, or lapel. If the surface is capable of reflecting light and dark, the resulting fold can become more emphatic through the increased definition provided by shadow. In Figure 7.4, note the shadow created by the jacket lapel and hemline.

*Folds as Lines.* Many of the materials of the apparel-body-construct are very pliable, and this characteristic is sometimes utilized in creating a visual effect. By easing or gathering a long piece of material into a short space, many variations can be achieved. One is the creation of lines from gathers. A fold or pleat can be a source of line that may either be short or long and extending the length of a shape. For example, trouser pleats may be the result of the fit of a localized area, that is, the difference in circumference between hip and waist, and thus only extend to the hip. Trouser pleats may also extend the full length of the trousers in a distinct full-length crease. To extend without interruption requires careful consideration of the interplay with body curvatures.

Folds can be soft-edged or hard-edged. Soft edges can be the result of folds created by a shallow inward and outward curve, such as in gathers. These edges can then be further defined by the interplay of light and shadow. Hard edges can be the result of the fold created by deep in and out curves, with the edges both soft- and hard-edged depending upon the depth of the fold and shine of the surface. Some materials can retain a permanent crease, which can be used in a pleat with a distinct and crisp edge.

*Pigment as Line.* Surfaces can be structured to create lines by printing or by weaving several colors side by side. Either

**FIGURE 7.8**

*Lines that define two adjacent areas close in value become soft edged.*

*Designed by Calvin Klein. Courtesy of Fairchild Publications.*

way, changes in pigment are creating lines. Lines created in this way can be visually as important in the apparel-body-construct as line from other sources. The line can be soft when two colors close in value are used, as in Figure 7.8. For example, two tints (light values) or two shades (dark values) can be placed side by side and create soft edges. Line from pigment can also be used to create hard edges. This occurs when black and white lines form a strong contrast that creates a figure-ground separation, as in Figure 7.7.

*Lines in Combination.* When a number of lines are placed together, their grouping needs to be considered, as in Figure 7.9a and b. The eye can jump between two lines varying in length or color or in some other measured difference, such as width or distance apart. Awareness of the way the eye proceeds along a visual path is important because the eye may follow the actual line or notice its difference from other lines.

a                                    b

**FIGURE 7.9A & B**

*The character of lines used throughout an ensemble and their variations can create subtle directions for the enjoyment of the viewer. In Figure 7.9a, parallel lines on the transparent surface of the sleeves encircle the arms in horizontal bands but create vertical direction. The vertical lines of the jacket are spaced strategically so that the shawl collar appears to have diagonal lines. These, along with pockets and the other rounded edges, create a discontinuity of vertical lines. The more widely spaced lines of the skirt keep the eye continuing throughout the ensemble, but the order is still created by the spacing and grouping of lines. Attention is first drawn to the contrasting stripes of the T-shirt in Figure 7.9b, exposed by the opening of the coat at the neckline. Then the many other lines are considered, such as the lines of the vertical bands of the coat, the crisp edge of the creases of the pant legs, the smooth line of the armscye, and even the short lines of the tailored buttonholes marching up the center line of the coat, or the sweep of the coat, as it spreads outward from the body.*

*Designed by: (a) Karl Lagerfeld and (b) Ralph Lauren. Courtesy of Fairchild Publications.*

Lines in combination can appear simple or extremely complex in their visual arrangement. A grouping of lines can create a grid effect when two sets of parallel lines cross each other. If lines are otherwise equal in aspects such as width and color, no hierarchy is created. However, when lines are used in a number of directions, they may group according to direction.

Lines creating a checkered surface with two colors can be viewed as reversible figure-to-ground when either the one color or the other can be made to appear as figure. In the suit by Armani in Figure 7.10, the lighter or darker color can appear as figure. This reversibility creates some ambiguity that can be changed in use with one or the other color predominating in other parts of the apparel-body-construct. Use of one of the colors as figure elsewhere in the apparel-body-construct reduces ambiguity and creates a more stable figure-ground relationship. In the case of Figure 7.10, the row of buttons and hair in the darker values become figure and take away some of the ambiguity. The continuous curved line that can be traced from shoulder to neckline to hem of jacket also adds figural quality. The shadowing of the line opening from waist to jacket hemline helps further define the line.

As the observer views and analyzes the apparel-body-construct, priority of line is considered within the apparel-body-construct and in comparison with other lines, as well as an assessment of line direction and position. To further create interest within the apparel-body-construct, a printed surface may be interrupted by other sources of line, for example, folds and seamlines.

Line is also considered as it relates to the body lines. In Figure 7.9a, the multiple lines of the jacket and dress and the way they are shaped to the body create an exciting interrelationship. Sometimes the body lines in a particular apparel-body-construct take priority; often it is the lines of the clothing. All of this determines how line helps characterize visual effect.

A hierarchy is created if some of the lines in a group are made to appear visually more important. Superimposing lines on top of other lines is one way of making them visually more important, especially if they interrupt those underneath. Varying the lines in thickness or boldness can create sets of lines that lead the observer into the surface through several layers of lines or in a plaid. This is different from a clear figure-ground arrangement because the surface does not separate as readily into figure and ground; instead it appears to have a certain visual depth. However, you can focus upon the more dominant lines, though the figure-ground relation is still somewhat ambiguous.

**FIGURE 7.10**

*The figure-ground relationship of the surface of this suit by Giorgio Armani can appear as darker lines on the surface or as a light checkered pattern when focusing upon the surface only. However, when also focusing on the buttons and hair, the darker value becomes a visual cue and takes away any ambiguity of the figure-ground relationship.*

Courtesy of Fairchild Publications.

Application
Exercise 7.3

One way to consider the interaction of the clothing lines with those of the body is to think of clothing on a hanger without the body. Garments are variously appealing on a hanger, and the designer or merchandiser is often acutely aware of the lack of "hanger appeal" of a bikini or bias-cut nightgown, for example, hoping that the customer will nevertheless try on the garment. Think about an article of dress you have experienced differently on a hanger and then on the body. How do the lines of the clothing and body interact?

The context of lines of clothing with lines of the body is an important interaction to consider. A different visual priority can be created by changing the direction of line on the body, for example, by relating the vertical body to horizontal or diagonal lines. In Figure 7.9a, lines flow from the vertical lines of the dress and the jacket but contrast with the horizontal lines of the arms and the diagonal line of the collar. In Figure 7.11a, the vertical lines of the suit contrast with the diagonal lines of the tie and lapels.

a        b

**FIGURE 7.11A & B**

*The tailored suit in Figure 7.11a by Giorgio Armani is associated with a degree of formality and thus is often used in a business situation. The character of the suit adds to the message of directness through definition of lines that are distinct and primarily related to the body's vertical axis. In Figure 7.11b, the casual nature of sportswear from Nautica can convey a message of activity through body exposure and multiple horizontal, diagonal, and vertical lines.*

Courtesy of Fairchild Publications.

*Line as a Source of Associated Meaning.* Line character may be associated with characterization of an object or event. A simple and direct line as related to the body and clothing shapes is immediately and easily perceived. Therefore, in a business situation associated with seriousness and directness, as in Figure 7.11a, the vertical straight line is more often used because it can be perceived and understood quickly and by extension connotes a simple directness. In sportswear a message of activity can be conveyed by the use of angular, discontinuous, or straight lines, as in Figure 7.11b. A curving or soft, full line, such as a ruffle on a shirt or a curve created by a full sleeve, is often used in eveningwear. In Figure 7.12 the curved lines are multiple: the curving lines of the collar and skirt, the soft curve of the motif of the fabric surface, as well as the hair shaped into a curve. The softening of line is associated with an event that encourages visual lingering.

It is important to note that line is always perceived in the context of the entire apparel-body-construct and that other visual definers may be significant to the visual effect.

## FIGURE 7.12

*The use of a curved and continuous line at the neckline through to the hemline, and the resulting light and shadow in the folds of the dress from Christian Dior, create a soft effect for evening wear. The curved line is repeated in the hair shape and the surface motif of the dress.*

Courtesy of Fairchild Publications.

**FIGURE 7.14**

(Right) The pockets
are prominent shapes
that contrast with the
jacket in value. Along
with the hat, which
echoes the same
shape, the pocket
shapes become figure
and lead the viewer
from shape to shape.
The repetitious lines
in both the areas of
dark and light func-
tion as texture and
create a relationship
between the two
areas.

Designed by Bill Blass. Courtesy
of Fairchild Publications.

**FIGURE 7.13**

(Above left) Shapes can focus our attention, as the round hat, sunglasses, and collar do in
this ensemble by Christian Lacroix. The hat is large and contrasts with the ensemble
through an irregular surface pattern. As such, it frames the face and creates focus.

Courtesy of Fairchild Publications.

# SHAPE

## Visual Function of Shape

The function of shape in the apparel-body-construct can range from providing a source of figure to a source of ground. Shapes can be the focus of attention when singular and isolated from other shapes, as are the contrasting
round hat and sunglasses in Figure 7.13. A large, bold shape often becomes a
focal point when contrasted with its surround. When shapes are small in size,
numerous, and regular, such as checks, diamonds, or dots, they can be viewed
as an area of visual texture or pattern because they are not all perceived one
by one but in their relationship. In Figure 7.14, the shape of the pockets is
regular enough that they are noticed for their regularity and contrast from the
jacket. Shapes that occupy space distinctly and boldly can become a priority

Consider a shirtwaist dress, named for its resemblance to a basic shirt, and how lines can interact differently when different fabric surfaces are used. Consider it in a plain surface with only the layout of the collar, front-button shirt tab, sleeves, etc., to be perceived as line. Then consider the same shirtwaist dress, but in a fabric printed with stripes. How did line priority change? Did associated meaning change, too?

and often lead the viewer from shape to shape. In Figure 7.14, the darker value of the pocket shapes becomes figure and a viewing priority in the figure-ground relationship of the jacket. The hat shape adds to the viewing priority.

## General Appearance of Shape

Shape is perceived as a bounded area with a defining surface, or as a definitive outline with or without a defining surface. An example of a shape perceived as figure is a solid gold button, and one perceived as an outline is a circle pin that is placed upon a collar. A shape whose surfaces are perceived as figure is usually quite a different surface than its surround, as in Figure 7.14. If the surface of a shape is similar to its surround, it may be defined more by line, as noted in Figure 7.9a in the vertical and diagonal lines at the chest. The outline at the neck can become figure, and both the surface of the collar shape and its surround can

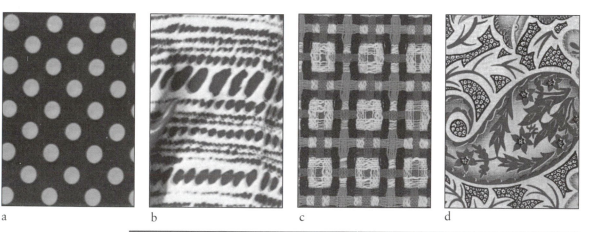

a               b               c               d

**FIGURE 7.15A, B, C & D**

*Shapes may be regular (a), irregular (b), geometric (c), or organic (d). Regular and geometric shapes are often easier to perceive.*

Courtesy of Marilyn Revell DeLong.

be perceived as ground. The figure-ground relation is different in these two instances depending upon what appears as figure—the shape and its surface or the outline.

Shapes within the apparel-body-construct may be categorized as regular or irregular, geometric or organic. Regular shapes are bounded by straight or curved lines and are often viewed as simple figures separated from ground, for example, circles, squares, triangles. Geometric shapes often have a regular repeat and appear ordered. Irregular shapes may be bounded by a combination of straight and curved lines and are often viewed as more fluid and less separated as figure. Regular and geometric shapes are usually more immediate, familiar, and simpler to perceive than irregular and organic shapes, as shown in Figure 7.15a, b, c, and d.

The entire apparel-body-construct is the viewing reference when identifying shapes. Shapes within the silhouette include the head and the shapes created by the hair, eyeglasses, makeup, and jewelry. Earrings, for example, can define a new shape apart from the head shape or they can repeat the head shape. The head shape can close off at the chin, as when paired with a turtleneck or other high collar contrasting in color with the skin and hair. The head shape can extend to include the neck, as with a flat "jewel" neckline, or even include the neck or shoulders, as with a neckline sometimes called a portrait neckline, in Figure 7.12. Such a lowered neckline serves to outline a curved shape upon the body and define it for viewing.

## Simple to Complex Shapes

Simple shapes of the apparel-body-construct are geometric shapes that include the circle, square, triangle, and rectangle. Simple shapes have continuous or definite contours, as in the shape of the neckline in Figure 7.9a. Simple shapes are easily viewed and recognized and occur frequently as pockets, buttons, cuffs, and in surface shapes such as polka dots (when large enough to be perceived as circles and not points). The shape of the arm in Figure 7.9a is made somewhat less simple because of figure perceived as either the arm, the dark shapes, or the spaces created by the skin of the arm showing through.

Shapes can also be complex, with irregular outlines and edges that are more difficult to trace and therefore difficult to perceive. In Figure 7.16, note the irregular outlines and edges of hat, neckline, and jacket. A complex shape

**FIGURE 7.16**

*The plaid surfaces are similar but made more complex by the varying shades of light to dark values. A level of indeterminacy is created by the use of three plaid surfaces. The hat, stockings, and shoes are surfaces of dark value that appear as shapes without textural variation to define the body extremities. The jacket is also dark but is quilted with light gray parallel lines (lining shows on one side). The rounded hat, lace collar, and neckline opening contrast with the geometric regularity of the plaid surfaces. Viewing the plaid surfaces as distinct parts is difficult, and therefore the viewer may concentrate on their difference or upon the parts with more contrasting shapes, such as the darker hat, jacket, and legs.*

Courtesy of Fairchild Publications.

## FIGURE 7.17

*Indeterminate surfaces can add to the complexity as well as the pleasure of viewing the soft edges repeated in adjacent surfaces and shapes. Emanuel Ungaro repeats such rounded shapes as neckline, scarf, and necklace in the surfaces of the ensemble and enhanced by the light and shadow effects. The dark hair repeats the rounded shapes but contrasts in value with the remainder of the ensemble.*

Courtesy of Fairchild Publications.

might be a jacket, trouser, or hand. A discontinuous contour may occur in such complex shapes because of the overlap of one shape with another, as when a jacket overlaps trousers or skirt. This creates depth levels and complexity of shapes that may be more difficult to view as distinct visual parts.

Complex shapes may be complex because their edges are not discrete, as in an indeterminate surface such as Figure 7.17. When shapes are adjacent, they may be touching and have shared outlines where either side may be perceived as a shape, as in Figure 7.18a and b. Picture the effect of a large honeycomb, as in Figure 7.18a. This is a more complex shape than if an edge more clearly belongs to one side of the shape or the other and not to both, as in Figure 7.18b. Some shapes become bounded or enclosed by the interaction of a seamline with the body. For example, the head may appear as figure because of a hood closely encircling the face. From the front, this could be viewed as a shared contour, that is, the edge of the hood could be viewed as belonging to either the face or the hood.

Complex shapes within the silhouette may be an upper torso shape, such as a jacket or shirt, or a lower torso shape, such as pants or skirt, legs, and shoes. These shapes can include within them other shapes, such as layout of pockets, collars, cuffs, or surface prints such as a floral or geometric motif. The degree to which these shapes take on importance as parts of the whole depends upon their nature: their difference from adjacent visual parts, their color and texture, simplicity and clarity of boundary.

As a shape becomes larger and more complex, the outline may become less important in our perception and other aspects will take on more importance, such as how its surface is defined. The shape may be noted for its similarity to the silhouette shape or for its direction related to the visual axis of the body.

## Planar Shapes

The term *plane* means flat, and a shape that appears smooth and flat is a planar shape. Even though the body is a rounded surface, shapes can appear smooth and flat on it for a number of reasons. A shape may be small and positioned on the body so that its surface appears relatively flat with the boundary as an important characteristic. An example is a patch pocket positioned close enough to the center front axis of the body to appear flat. When a surface is devoid of complexity or has a highly contrasting edge, the three-dimensional nature of the body may not be noticed. Then the main visual characteristic of the shape will be its outline. This can occur for a small shape within the apparel-body-construct or for the entire silhouette of that ensemble. This phenomenon is viewed and remembered as a flattened cookie-cutter effect. The shape of the silhouette can become predominant when the surface of the clothing is matte black, as in Figure 7.1. Since

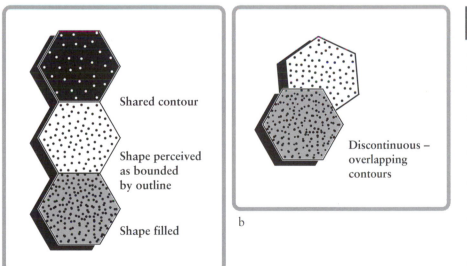

Shared contour

Shape perceived
as bounded
by outline

Shape filled

Discontinuous –
overlapping
contours

b

a

FIGURE
7.18A & B

*Shapes that touch at an edge have shared contours (Figure 7.18a). Shapes can appear bounded by an outline or filled and without an outline. In Figure 7.18b, shapes that overlap can appear in a figure-ground relation with the continuous shape appearing as figure.*

such a surface is nonreflecting, it does not pick up light and shadow from the body, such as the curvature of the ribs or muscles.

## Depth Shapes

Some shapes on the body appear to be rounded. A dirndl skirt, one gathered on straight grain at the waist, emphasizes the three-dimensional character of the surface. Depth shape is viewed when a shape appears to be contoured through the manipulation of the surface to create gathers and folds, as in Figure 7.19. A surface that is flat can appear thicker visually because of a pattern printed on the surface, as in Figure 7.7. An ensemble fitted close to the body with a small, regular print may call attention to the body as a rounding surface, as in Figure 7.10. Some three-dimensional shape is then viewed because

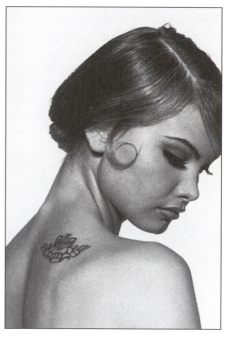

FIGURE 7.19

*Depth shape occurs when surfaces are manipulated to create shaped folds. These gradate from narrower at the waistline to deep and wide at the hem and thus maximize light and shadow on this middle value surface.*

Designed by Christian Dior. Courtesy of Fairchild Publications.

FIGURE 7.20

*Position of a shape is important in determining how prominent it will be in viewing the apparel-body-construct. A tattoo of distinct shape placed upon an otherwise bare shoulder attracts attention.*

Courtesy of Fairchild Publications.

of the interaction of the print with the body surface. However, if the motif on the surface is very dominant, it will mask the body surface and create a strong figure-ground relationship. Depth shape is also viewed when the surface appears thick because of selection of color and weave, such as a tweed filled with minutely varying points, such as an indeterminate surface.

## Position of Shape

Important to shape is its use in relation to the body—its size, number, location, and direction. For example, one large circular pin positioned near the head, or a tattoo with rounded edges placed upon the shoulder, as in Figure 7.20, can become noteworthy. A small button placed on a contrasting shoulder tab may not be prominent except from the top-down point of view. Several buttons may appear more important together as they circle a pocket or create a grouping on a double-breasted suit. A number of buttons arranged down the center front or side of a skirt or diagonally across the shoulder may create an implied line, not a shape. The placement of an irregular animal print influences perception of the apparel-body-construct. Such a noteworthy print demands attention wherever it is placed, whether it is used in the lower or upper torso or on both the upper and lower torso.

A shape may have an inherent direction, such as that of a rectangle or an oval. When positioned on the body, it may coincide with the verticality of the body or extend horizontally across the body. Circular shapes, because they do not have an inherent direction by themselves, may appear to be ordered or randomly placed on the body. In Figure 7.21, the circles appear orderly in their placement.

A shape may be viewed in its entirety within one body view or be completed only if viewed as it rounds the body. For example, a belt encircles the body, but the observer sees only a portion of the circle, a horizontal line, from one body view. From prior experience we know that a belt encircles the body cylinder, and we can close that circle in our minds. We may even consider the buckle as the center of a brief horizontal line or as the beginning and ending of the circle. In addition, a belt may belong more to one side of what it surrounds than the other. For example, a belt the same color and texture as a skirt may appear to blend with the skirt and contrast with the shirt. This effect of the belt can be reversed if it is the same color as the shirt and contrasting with the skirt.

**FIGURE 7.21**

*The surface of this dress by Isaac Mizrahi is covered with small circular shapes— polka dots. Their regularity and lack of inherent direction as a shape make them seem almost textural in visual effect because the viewer notices the interruptions of dots more, such as in the folds of the full skirt or where the sweater, similar in color to the ground of the dress, is worn over the shoulders.*

Courtesy of Fairchild Publications.

Application
Exercise 7.5

The shape of a belt can create many different visual effects with the body; it can appear as figure or ground with the rest of the ensemble. (To assume that a belt always "cuts the body in half" without really considering how it is perceived is a disservice to the belt.) Belts can define the shape of the upper and lower torso of the body or create a blending of the two. Think of two examples of the way the same belt can appear on the body within the context of the apparel-body-construct to create a different visual effect.

## Priority of Shape

Whether a shape becomes a viewing priority depends upon its relative strength; a visual dominance depends upon how a shape relates to other shapes within the apparel-body-construct. It can be a singular contrast and immediately perceived as focus or one of many repetitious shapes. The following are characteristics of a shape that can make it a primary visual part: distinctly defined surface; isolation of a single shape; hard, defined edge; simple outline; continuous edge; no shared or overlapping edges.

## Sources of Shapes

*Silhouette.* A most basic shape of the apparel-body-construct is the silhouette, which provides a frame of reference for our perception of all its other shapes. The silhouette is the outer perimeter of the entire form and is planar in nature. Its character can be very defined and bold or undefined and subtle. It is important to note the silhouette, its shape, and character, because it can become a reference for all of the remaining parts. As a shape, the silhouette can repeat the basic verticality of the body or take on new shapes apart from the body silhouette. It can appear to be enclosing the body, to be a relatively closed form, or seem open to the surrounding space.

The silhouette forms its own relationship with its surroundings. Thus, a unique figure-ground relationship forms in which the silhouette is figure and the surround becomes ground. A silhouette that is boldly defined will detach from the surround, and attention then is easily focused within the form. Some clothing attracts attention because of bold, clear-cut boundaries, such as a crisp, dark silhouette that provides an immediate focus, as in Figure 7.1. Other types of clothing, like an evening gown, may appear more open or interrelated with the body and surround, inviting a less immediate focus, a softness, and more visual lingering, as in Figure 7.12.

Application
Exercise 7.6

Think of or find an example of an apparel-body-construct with a silhouette that does not appear as a hard-edged boundary. What type of fabric is used to create such a silhouette? How would you describe the entire apparel-body-construct? What is the influence of the silhouette?

*Shapes from Layout Structuring.* Shapes from layout include sleeves, pockets, lapels, and necklines, and these shapes can be simple or complex to view. In Figure 7.11a and b, the shapes perceived include collar and lapels, sleeve, jacket, head, trousers, and shoe. A shape from layout that is irregular and more difficult to view may not begin and end within one body view, for instance, a pocket that is placed on the side of the body or a side pleat that opens into a triangular shape gradually as it extends from waist to hem. Shapes created from folds of material that hang from the shoulders or waistline vary from being primarily tubular to triangular, depending upon how the grain of a fabric is placed upon the body. Figure-ground relationships can be created by additions to the shapes from layout, as in Figure 7.5 where the shapes of the suit jacket are outlined by contrasting banding. The dark value of the skirt and banding contrasts with the shapes created by the white at center front and zigszg lines at the neck.

*Shapes from Surface Structuring.* Shapes may be woven, knitted, or printed upon the surface. Such shapes take on many different characteristics. They can appear to be a small, isolated figure on a large expanse of ground or a large, single figure. Shapes can appear to blend with the ground in figure-ground integration or stand away boldly and distinctly from the ground in figure-ground separation. They can be grouped on one level as figure or on several levels.

Consider in Figure 7.16 how you view the apparel-body-construct. Is the way you order your viewing influenced by the regular and irregular motif? What other factors influence your viewing?

*Application Exercise 7.7*

Pattern, a term used for shapes that define the surface through repetition, may be simple, small, clearly bounded shapes repeated intermittently as figure on ground. Such a pattern may give surface definition but not enter into the part-to-whole relation of the apparel-body-construct. Instead, such definition can be part of the determinate-indeterminate character of the surfaces. Surface structure may also be shapes large enough to be considered in the part-to-whole relation. A large motif that repeats only four or five times often must be planned carefully in positioning on the body, especially if it provides a visual path. Then the viewer takes in the apparel-body-construct from motif to motif.

Shapes are often characterized by the dominance of either their surface or their edge. Perception of the outline of a shape can be altered by surface structuring. When a bounded area is filled with visual texture, the observer can become more aware of surface than edge definition. The surface can appear to have a thickness and energy not present in a surface that appears smooth.

Shapes printed on the surface are often interrupted when placed upon the body. They can be interrupted by the layout of gathers or folds or pockets. A shape printed on the two-dimensional surface and placed within the apparel-body-construct can be interrupted by the layout of the silhouette as it extends around the body cylinder.

*Shape as a Source of Associated Meanings.* A shape can direct the eye and imply meaning by its direction. A graduation robe is an example of a garment that appears stately, with the whole trailing the body in a processional march. It repeats the body verticality in silhouette and tucking that hangs from a horizontal yoke at the shoulder. Potential meaning associated with shape can derive from its basic character. Repetition of shapes that are regular and geometric, as in a plaid, is often associated with order and calm if in close values. Repetition of irregular or organic shapes is associated with an appearance of some disorder and excitement, especially if they also contrast in light-dark values.

**FIGURE 7.22**

*Comparison of three similar appearing apparel-body-constructs shows the influence of value contrast that is strategically placed.*

Designed by Emanuel Ungaro.
Courtesy of Fairchild
Publications.

*Application Exercise 7.8* | Find shapes in Figure 7.22. Compare the effect of silhouette shape, the placement of light and dark contrasts and physical coloring. Compare how you order each apparel-body-construct.

# POINT

## Visual Function of Point

The function of the point in perception is assessed within its context—the apparel-body-construct. The point may be observed as the focus of a primary visual part, the center point of a neckline or the widow's peak of a hairline. It is important as a discontinuity or contrast in the visual path where two lines meet at an angle and is thus a focal point. It may also define an aspect of the surface through texture or a continuous direction of a line, as the end of a row of buttons. Therefore, it is context that determines whether a point provides focus or is one point interacting with numerous other points, as in a textured surface.

## General Appearance of Point

Point in perception can define location on the body and position in space. Thus, it may be included in a discussion of linear or surface definition depending upon number. A single point can vary in importance based upon its context, from focal point to one that goes unnoticed. A large number of points can be perceived as pattern or texture. A point often indicates a convergence of two lines. Two lines that cross often create a corner and a point of focus at the crossing or a shape containing an angle whose tip may be viewed as a point.

## One Point Focus

Viewing a critical point in our perception may involve taking in several parts of the apparel-body-construct or only one of its visual parts. A visual point can be as precise and explicit as the tip of a stick pin or button or as implicit as a portion of the silhouette that involves two lines meeting as, for example, the point of a V-neckline or the indentation that defines the waist. In Figure 7.23, points include the crossing of the line of straps, as well as where they join the bodice. If a point is critical in perception or becomes salient in a fashion season, it can become a focal point.

**FIGURE 7.23**

*Point is illustrated in the crossing of the two straps at center front and, together with the bodice, appear to form a diamond shape connected by four points. Additional points include the fringe of the shawl that hangs away from the body to create end points that define the body in movement.*

Designed by Giorgio Armani. Courtesy of Fairchild Publications.

Imagine a focal point or find one in an apparel-body-construct. How is the point created? How does it influence how you view the apparel-body-construct?

*Application Exercise 7.9*

*Different surface textures used through-out an ensemble can provide a rich and subtle variation for viewing enjoyment. Here the face is framed by a pile collar contrasting with the white at the neck and the shiny, smooth surfaces of the jacket and gloves.*

Designed by Gianfranco Ferré. Courtesy of Fairchild Publications.

## Priority of Point

The focal point is a primary visual part because it captures our attention immediately. To do so requires contrast from the surround and as such it usually appears to be figure on top of ground. A point often becomes a focus when it is located strategically, such as along the visual axis of the apparel-body-construct or reinforcing or contradicting other important lines or shapes. In Figure 7.23, the crossing of two straps perceived as lines creates a focal point. Differential weighting of two focal points placed on either side of the body center can create a tension between them. The body is sometimes marked with a point strategically placed for attention, such as the beauty mark on the face or the red dot above the eyes and at the center of the forehead used in some cultures.

## Many Points

To the observer, the point in perception can be composed of many points creating surface effects, such as polka dots. Then the point can define a surface. If small circles repeat and cover a surface, but their repetition is interrupted by shapes created by the layout structure, the eye notices the interruption. In Figure 7.21, the circles become textural in their repetition over much of the surface of the dress and are not noticed one by one, except where the shapes of the dress and sweater interrupt the pattern of circles. Even though we tend to perceive them as constant, consider the variations in perceiving a polka dot on the surface of a material that covers the body. The polka dot can be placed on any one of a number of areas of the body, covered by a fold or gather, interrupted by a seam, shaded by light and shadow, or mistaken for a freckle.

# SURFACE TEXTURE

Thus, point becomes a transition between linear and surface definition. When point is repeated over the surface of an apparel-body-construct, it creates a surface definition called texture.

## Visual Function of Surface Texture

Terms used to identify surface effects may be smooth, shiny, variegated, heavy, thick, rich, shadowy, or grained. Surface textures can provide interest and order for the apparel-body-construct because they vary the surface and locate it in space. They have potential for providing spatial position for visual

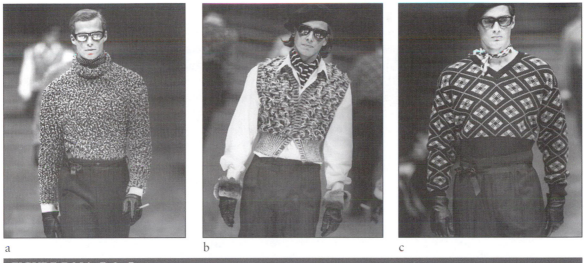

a                                        b                                        c

## FIGURE 7.25A, B & C

*A surface that appears active and full can appear closer or farther away from the viewer depending upon the surfaces adjacent to it. In Figure 7.25a, the surface of the sweater attracts attention and the boundaries within the sweater are less dominant than between the neckline and the wrist, where a contrast of light and dark is what attracts attention, or the boundary of the dark trousers. The surface of the vest in Figure 7.25b is filled with an indeterminate texture and the edges are outlined with an indeterminate ribbing. However, adjacent surfaces offer contrast and the boundaries of the vest become defined in this way. Consider how you as a viewer order the various surfaces of this ensemble, that is, what do you see 1, 2, 3? In Figure 7.25c, the prominent shapes influence the visual effect of this sweater and how the surfaces influence apparent distance from the viewer. The sweater surface becomes figure in a figure-ground relationship. The neckline and face also become figure; even though the boundary of the dark beret is lost to the surround, it is still important in framing the face. The scarf is not as prominent as in Figure 7.25b.*

*Designed by Valentino. Courtesy of Fairchild Publications.*

parts within a whole. Surface textures can provide a direction for the observer when, for example, surface parts are varied from smooth and shiny to smooth and matte. In Figure 7.24, textures that have visual priority are the shiny and smooth jacket, gloves, and shoes. The face is framed by the fur pile collar. A surface that is smooth and matte is the trouser. A surface can appear active and very full, as in Figure 7.25a. Such surfaces can take priority over other surfaces adjacent to it. In a tweedy and textured tailored jacket, the texture may even camouflage some edges.

With regard to textural effects, the eye does not view individual shapes or motifs, but instead it sees units so small and close together that they are hard to distinguish individually and appear to just fill the space. Often the surface contains a large number of tiny shapes, lines, or colors that appear to be milling about upon or above the surface. It seems to contain a visual energy and is perceived as having an apparent thickness or depth of surface (refer to Chapter 4 on indeterminate surfaces for discussion).

## General Appearance of Surface Texture

Surface texture refers to the surface variation of a shape. A surface is usually noticed because it has some variation that attracts the eye. In the apparel-body-construct, the surfaces can vary from smooth to rough, fine to coarse, even to uneven, soft to hard, matte to shiny, transparent to opaque, heavy to light, or dense to spaced. To become aware of all surfaces within an apparel-body-construct is often a visual delight.

The word "texture" is derived from the Latin for weaving and, since many of the materials of the apparel-body-construct are woven, it is appropriately applied to these surfaces. However, surface texture includes more than just evidence of weaving and applies to all visual effects, whether visual and tactile or just visual.

The terms "textured" or "textural" often refer to surface appearance created through minute variations. When one point becomes many points, it defines a surface as textured. **Microlayout** is a term for the three-dimensional effect of surfaces from such sources as knitting or weaving but also from fringe, knots, and other applied protrusions. A single minute protrusion does not necessarily create focus, but a group of protrusions can attract attention to surface. In Figure 7.25a, the surface of the sweater is varied by minute variations, whereas the trousers and gloves appear smooth and matte.

Visual texture is a source of surface energy and other accompanying attributes, such as the appearance of warmth. Visual texture may result in shimmering highlights and shadows from a reflecting surface. A printed surface appears to be textured, as in the case of very minute points of color printed overall. Surface variations can include the fading of portions of blue jeans or a shirt pattern with a floral motif so small that it may be viewed as textural. The projections and hollows from small folds of fabric may also function as texture if they remain as surface variation and do not appear as lines or shapes. In Figure 7.23, the middle value and irregularity of folds creates a rich variation of the surface. Textural effects occur from surface pile such as velvet or fur. Velvet is an example of a dense pile surface that often appears to have highlights and shaded areas. In Figure 7.17, the pile surfaces are enriched by reflection and the highlights are repeated throughout the ensemble. A thick fur pile may create its surface at the pile tips.

Surfaces that vary within the apparel-body-construct include the skin surface and the light and shadow effects that the hair can provide. Both of these are surface effects, which can include variation in light and dark values and reflectance. The skin surface can appear textured with freckles or a small quantity of hair.

## Spatial Position of Surface Texture

The spatial position of textured surfaces can vary in apparent distance from the viewer. The surface that has vague detail can appear at a greater distance from the viewer. In actual distance viewing, the impression is similar—detail appears vague. If the textured surface contains separated colors and distinct detail of tiny individual points, as in Figure 7.25a, it can appear to be thicker and denser and influence spatial position.

The distance of the viewer from the apparel-body-construct affects the appearance of texture. Seen at close range, a surface may contain a complex, all-over pattern of flowers, animals, or other shapes, intricately detailed and tiny. From a distance the observer may perceive a generalized, vague impression of indeterminacy.

## Surface Texture in Combination

Two surfaces combined that are the same in color and similar in texture will produce a soft and subtle, sometimes indefinable, edge. Surfaces can contrast in texture; a rough surface placed next to a shiny one will call attention to their differences and the transitional edge. This concept of the effect of contrasting surfaces has many applications, for example, making the face appear less blemished or freckled by planning the textures close to it, or distinguishing a body shape by creating surface interest, even excitement, through use of complex visual textures.

## Priority of Surface Texture

How much a surface is noticed because of texture depends upon the viewer's impression of whether it is filled or not filled. The filled surface can become more indeterminate in character, as the vest in Figure 7.25b. When it appears filled, surface may dominate our viewing, sometimes taking priority over linear definition because of the camouflage effect upon the lines and shapes within a garment. The surface can also appear smooth and matte and seemingly devoid of variation. This type of surface definition is determinate in character and is immediately viewed. Then the viewer is attracted to edge more than surface. Sometimes a determinate surface is the result of color, for example, a smooth surface accompanied by an intense primary color. When a seemingly unfilled surface is middle value, as in Figure 7.23, it is a good visual carrier of layout, light, and shadow. In Figure 7.26, edges and surface wrinkles of the jacket, vest, and trousers are apparent. As previously noted, surface variation is masked by an unreflecting surface such as matte black. This also calls attention to edge, not of interior edges but of exterior edges outlining the black.

**FIGURE 7.26**

*A middle value surface is a good visual carrier of layout, light, and shadow. In the jacket, vest, and trousers, surface wrinkles and edges are apparent.*

Designed by Gianfranco Ferré. Courtesy of Fairchild Publications.

## Surface Texture as a Source of Associated Meaning

Surface variations offer a wealth of associated meanings. Surfaces are often marked by seasonal variations, from smooth and flat in the hot summer to textured and thick in the cold winter. Both types of surfaces relate to our thoughts about comfort, for example, snuggling into the warmth of a soft, thick sweater on a cold evening. The formal-casual dichotomy offers another contrast of surface variation. Formal is often related to either dark and imme-diate viewed surfaces or a reflective surface with highlights from a smooth, shiny surface that invites visual lingering. An example of the combination might be a pair of black crepe pants and shimmering golden top. Casual is often marked by surfaces that vary through light to medium value shading, such as linen, denim, or corduroy.

| *Application Exercise 7.10* | Think of textures that you associate with a season of the year. What relation is there between the characteristics of the surface and the characteristics of the season? |
| --- | --- |

# COLOR

## Visual Function of Color

Color can define the surfaces of the apparel-body-construct in several differ-ent and exciting ways. It can create variety in the way we appear, sometimes simply because of a dye bath. Color can be instrumental in establishing posi-tion of surfaces, such as in figure-ground relationships.

Three dimensions of color—*hue*, *value*, and *intensity*—can be used to cre-ate coherence and integration or separation of the surfaces, one from the other. If any one dimension is similar, the colors will appear to have some vi-sual relationship in a combination of colored surfaces. Usually *color schemes* or *colorways* traditionally used within a culture have such similarities.

## General Appearance of Color

Color is perceived as a surface effect. Colors of the apparel-body-construct in-clude the body colors and those surfaces placed upon the body. The body has preexisting colors that will be influenced by other colors placed upon it. Body colors affect the surfaces placed upon the body, and the reverse is also true. What surrounds a particular color in a context affects how it appears. The apparel-body-construct can be greatly influenced by colors of the surrounding areas and by lighting.

Color has three basic dimensions that can be distinguished—hue (the name), intensity (brightness/dullness), and value (lightness/darkness). Even though the three dimensions are combined into one viewing experience, it is necessary to separate them in order to achieve an understanding of the effects of color. Visual relationships that create grouping or separation can be achieved by similarities or differences in any one of the three dimensions.

*Hue.* The name of the color as designated on the color wheel is its **hue**—the visual sensation of red, for example. This sensation can derive from pigments, which are chemical substances reflecting light rays, or from light rays themselves. Color related to the apparel-body-construct is affected by both. Color is described through a notation system depending upon its source, that is, from pigment or light. We will refer to the Munsell color notation system that was developed to describe color pigments in terms of specific hue, value, and intensity (Color Plate 1).

Each hue has an individual physical character: the primary pigment hues are red, yellow, and blue, the secondary hues are orange, green, and violet. The secondary hues are mixtures of the adjacent primary hues; thus, orange is a mixture of red and yellow, while violet is a mixture of red and blue. The hue spectrum runs from red at one end to violet at the other, but it is usually depicted as a circle of hues with the primary hues separated by the secondary. Tertiary hues result from mixing a primary and a secondary, i.e., red-orange, blue-violet.

Groups or categories of colors that share common sensory effects are often called *families.* Adjacent or analogous hues are those close to one another on the color wheel, purple, purple-blue, and blue, for example (Color Plate 2b). Such related hues can constitute a color family.

Colors that contrast are separated from each other on the color wheel. Contrasting color schemes include complementary, split-complementary, and triads. Complementary hues are hue opposites on the color wheel, such as yellow and purple-blue, and in perception can produce an afterimage of each other (Color Plate 2c). *Afterimage* means that if you stare for several minutes at one hue, when you glance away to a neutral surface you will see an image of its complement. In a split-complementary scheme the color on either side of the complement is selected. A triad scheme is based on hues equal distance from one another on the color wheel (Color Plate 2d, and e).

*Value.* The lightness-darkness dimension of a color is expressed as **value**. To determine value, a scale (Color Plate 3) with value levels is matched with the hue. A tint is a combination of a hue plus white (sometimes termed pastels); shade is a hue plus black. Some colors are named with value implied, such as burgundy, which is a dark value red, and pastels are names for tints or light values of hues.

Colors used together can affect the perception of edge in the apparel-body-construct, as in adjacent surfaces contrasting in value. For example, a light-value surface placed next to a dark one offers a strong visual pull to the difference between the two surfaces. An application to the apparel-body-construct can be found in the value contrast between light skin and dark hair or white shirt and black trousers or dark hair and skin and pastel suit. In Figure 7.25a, b, and c, the dominance of a surface influences spatial position. In Figure 7.25c, the diamond shapes of the sweater vary from light to middle to dark value and appear hard edged where the greatest contrast occurs. In Figure 7.25b, the areas of greatest contrast are the light shirt and dark gloves and trousers, while the vest is an indeterminant middle value. Two adjacent surfaces of similar value will create a softer edge, as in the vest and vest edges of Figure 7.25b.

Value contrast used throughout an apparel-body-construct in adjacent surfaces is an effective means of establishing visual order. In Figure 7.26, the two adjacent surfaces of light to medium value in the jacket and pants create a softer edge. Each surface is characterized by light and shadow because of the middle values that carry light and shadow very well. In Color Plate 6, the head becomes a focus because of the lighter value and greater intensity. In Color Plate 7, values are medium to dark and contrasting in the two apparel-body-constructs. The middle value and motif variations of the jacket create an interesting textural effect in the woman's ensemble. The contrast of value in the upper and lower torso of the man's ensemble creates a part-to-whole effect. Differences in value of the surfaces are important to the interest a viewer takes in these apparel-body-constructs.

A value scale (Color Plate 3) of light to dark is a gradation of grays, from white through black. Often presented on a 10-point scale, a value of 9.0 is close to white (11.0) and 2.5 is close to black (1). The order is usually displayed as a straight line.

Each hue has a normal or home value and varies from lighter to darker, with the home value of yellow being closer to white or light gray and violet being as dark as very dark gray. This has an effect upon colors in combination. For example, the values of the complements red and green are similar, offering hue contrast but less value contrast. However, the complementary hues of yellow and blue at normal value also offer value contrast.

*Intensity.* The relative purity or saturation of a color is its **intensity**. Saturated colors are the primary and secondary hues at their purest on the color wheel, without any dilution of their complement. A saturated hue is intense and usually evokes a response of excitement, as in Color Plate 3 (level 12). The addition of a complementary color to a hue lowers saturation toward a neutral gray. The less saturated colors are more neutralized and muted. Their muted effect is considered more subtle and restful (Color Plate 2, levels 2, 4). The effect of complementary colors can be subtle when less saturated (Color Plates 4 and 10).

Intensity is perhaps the most difficult dimension of color to discuss, especially when applied to body colors of the apparel-body-construct. The intensity of the skin is often not strong, and understanding its intensity requires noting small and subtle differences. Colors found within the body surfaces of hair, skin, and eyes are often called personal body colors. By matching, naming, and locating those personal body colors an individual can go far in understanding color relationships of the apparel-body-construct. "Highlights" in personal coloring may include areas of the hair, skin, or eyes that seem more intense than other areas. "Undertone" is a term used to describe underlying skin and hair hue, value, and intensity. Identifying both highlight and undertone for each individual helps in placing colors on the body that are related by similarity or contrast.

Identifying all of the body colors is important to understanding their role in selection and planning colors for a particular wearer. This can be accomplished by matching colors chips to those colors found on the body. Include as many colors, that is, hue, value, intensity—as you associate with each body part. Then place the identified colors on a card grouped together for skin, hair, and eyes. Identify body location and location of body colors on the color wheel. How do the colors relate to colors (consider hue, value, intensity) you often choose to wear for your clothing? (Note: Refer to the Munsell Color System or the color section of the book by Mathis and Connor.)

*Application Exercise 7.11*

## Warm and Cool Colors

Apparent temperature is another characteristic of color relationships. Red, yellow-red, and yellow are sensed as warm colors, as in Color Plate 1; purple, purple-blue and blue are perceived as cool. Color warmth may be due to the association with sunshine and fire. Warm colors are perceived as presenting an immediacy, nearness, density, a heavy impression. They are often associated with earth tones that are muted, for example, brick or red orange, ochre, or golden brown. Generally, the warm colors are considered to be yellow, yellow-orange, orange, red-orange, red, and red-violet. Cool colors are associated with air, distant mountains, and water and may present an appearance of distance, depth, shadow, coolness, and lightness. The cool colors are yellow-green, green, blue-green, blue, blue-violet, and violet. However, intensity and value can make a difference in whether a hue appears as warmer or cooler. (Refer to the levels of color in Color Plate 3.)

Think of a color you enjoy wearing. Describe the color as to its dimensions of hue, value, and intensity. How does it relate to your personal coloring? Does it blend or contrast with your hair, skin, and eyes?

*Application Exercise 7.12*

## Colors in Combination

A color is almost always viewed in relation to other colors. Colors interact in combination within the apparel-body-construct. If one area is large and surrounds another, its influence will be greater than if used in a small adjacent area. Adjacent colors can transform the appearance of a color, and the one in the combination that operates as figure in the figure-ground relationship is the one most affected.

*Simultaneous Contrast.* The influence of colors used in combination and in proximity to one another is referred to as simultaneous contrast. When colors are viewed at the same time, their differences in hue, value, and saturation or intensity are emphasized. Thus, colors in association with other colors can appear quite different from how they appear alone. Each color influences the neighbor to the extent that two colors can appear similar or one hue may appear as two distinct hues when placed on backgrounds of different color (Color Plate 4a and b).

Even when colors are viewed individually, color associations can affect our viewing. Hues viewed singly can produce an afterimage, and this affects colors on the body. For example, when the viewer concentrates on a clothing surface and then glances at the face, the skin can appear to take on tinges of the complement to the clothing's hue. After looking intensely at a green sweater, a viewer who glances up at the face may find it tinged with the complement, red.

Whether a hue is immediately surrounded by another hue or is separated in some way affects perception. When individual colors are separated by black or white, both their singleness of character and their interaction are suppressed somewhat. For example, black causes adjacent hues to seem lighter and more brilliant; a surround of white often appears to darken them.

| *Application Exercise 7.13* | In Color Plate 5a and b, two individuals with different personal coloring are wearing the same coat. How does the coat appear differently based upon the context of personal coloring? What could be worn with the coat in Color Plate 5b to increase the difference? |
|---|---|

Visual mix colors combined in very small patterns or woven together appear to mix visually. When two or more colors are interwoven onto one surface, the result can be more vibrant than a surface of just one color. Complementary hues or black and white threads woven together will create a surface that appears gray when viewed from a distance, as in the sweater in Figure 7.25a. The visual mix will make the surface appear gray, but the gray will be more vibrant than a gray created by using all the same color gray threads. If the size of the black and white threads is increased, a salt-and-pepper effect is created. As the size of the areas of value increases and they appear more clearly and distinctly, the surface takes on the more definite values of black and gray. This phenomenon also takes place with colors such as in tweed yarns.

## Spatial Position of Color

Color defines spatial position of a surface, as in Color Plate 7. Colors can appear to be near or farther away. A warm, intense yellow will seem near, while a muted, subtle gold will seem farther away. Warm colors advance and cool colors seem to retreat. An intense hue will appear closer than a less intense one. When colors similar in hue, value, or intensity are combined, they will appear related, as in Color Plate 6. When colors dissimilar in hue, value, or intensity are combined, their differences will often cause visual separation. In Color Plate 7, the left apparel-body-construct displays visual integration and the one on the right displays visual separation.

## Priority of Color

Surfaces can seem to be defined by color alone. When surface dominates our viewing, it may be that the color is primary, intense, or by combination offers contrasting value. Color is one visual definer that gains a viewer's attention and receives much consideration. Viewers have paid more attention to color because, perhaps more than any other visual definer, it seems the most easily recognizable and distinctive. Of all the definers, color is the most closely associated with the psycho-physical. We often preface a description of clothing in terms of color, for example, a red shirt, a blue dress. We often ask, "What is your favorite color?" and rarely do we ask, "What is your favorite shape?"

## Color Relationships

However, color must be considered in the context of the apparel-body-construct. On the body, color enters a relationship and the viewer needs to address this relationship by becoming aware and knowledgeable about its nuances. Similarity of any of the characteristics of colors placed upon the body can form a powerful visual relationship with the body. Colors placed upon the body that are similar in any aspect, that is, hue, value, intensity, or temperature, form immediate relationships of grouping, whereas those that are dissimilar cause separation. Similarity of personal body colors with colors placed upon the body is evident in Color Plate 6. Similarity or contrasts in personal body colors with color surfaces within the apparel-body-construct can create separating effects. For example, Color Plate 9 includes some colors similar in hue, value, or intensity to body colors and some that contrast. Which ones create grouping effects and which ones create separating effects?

## Color as a Source of Association

Color is associated with many natural objects and therefore acquires similar meaning according to that association. Colors often are associated with other objects and things of similar color, as mushroom or fawn. Sunshine is yellow and warm: yellow is warm. Blue is cool and distant, as the mountains and water. Red is exciting, like fire. White is pure, like the snow. Earth colors, the warm but muted hues found in the earth, suggest stability and calm. Mood is associated with color, that is, I have the "blues," or, "You're in the "pink."

The naming of colors reflects our perception of colors. Saturated colors tend to have unambiguous names and most viewers agree on the hue in question. Desaturated colors often have names like puce, putty, or mauve, and viewers may disagree about their identification. This may occur because saturated colors are more focus colors and desaturated ones are more often used for background.

Historic periods are often defined by specific colors preferred for use during that time. For example, in American culture, pink, worn by both men and women, is often identified with the 1950s. Men began to wear pink shirts on black-and-white television because it appeared light in value and without shadows on the screen. In the 1960s, psychedelic colors were symbolic of the decade. Combinations of color were accepted that heretofore were not acceptable together. Intense hues of pink, yellow, blue, green, and purple were combined. In the Victorian period of the nineteenth century, the preferred colors were rich, dark values such as crimson red, emerald green, midnight blue, and purple.

Colors are often associated with a culture and are important in their defined uses. Celadon green is a pastel blue-green that is considered significant and favored in clothing in the Korean culture because of its historic and traditional association with pottery and ceramics (Color Plate 11). On the other hand, hot pink, a term used to describe a particular red hue, is often associated with a Korean engagement or marriage because it intensifies the coloring of the young bride-to-be and photographs well. Though celadon green is a historically important color, hot pink has only recently been used and is thought to have its origin from Western cultures in the early twentieth century. Colors take on importance in their use within a culture. An unknowing "foreigner" can often misperceive based upon limited knowledge of the use of colors and their association with certain events (Color Plate 12).

# INTERACTIONS OF VISUAL DEFINERS

The number of ways visual definers can be combined to create part definition is virtually unlimited. One begins to wonder about ever being able to understand the extent of the possibilities. A ready visual laboratory awaits—yourself as observer. You can learn by becoming aware of how you take in the apparel-body-construct and then systematically learn to understand the reasons why. You can generalize with the understanding that no specific combination of definers will always produce the same visual effect. The relation of a part to other parts and to the whole, its relational context, must always be considered.

Using yourself as a visual laboratory, try on an ensemble and examine in a mirror the visual definers of line, shape, texture, and color. Play "what if," and consider how you could make the greatest change in visual effect with the least amount of actual change in number of definers.

*Application Exercise 7.14*

## Summary

- Elements that are visual definers within the apparel-body-construct are line, shape, point, texture, and color.

- There are two ways to define visually: linear definition, definition by line or edge; and surface definition, definition by surface (including color and texture). The function of line is to provide visual interest; lines can be straight, angular, or curved and can be manipulated via fabric—for example, by pleats, yokes, and distinct or indistinct edges of shapes. Color and texture can define the surfaces of the apparel-body-construct in exciting ways. Texture can appear to fill the surface, and if the surface appears unfilled it is often viewed as shape. Color has three basic dimensions: hue, intensity, and value. Colors can be associated with the natural world (e.g., blue recalls mountains and the sea), with moods (reds and pinks are associated with vitality), and with cultural meanings and associations (e.g., black is associated with mourning in the West).

## Key Terms and Concepts

color
edge
elements
hue
intensity
line
linear definition
microlayout

point
shape
surface definition
surface texture
texture
value
visual definers

## References

Geum, K., and DeLong, M. "Korean Traditional Dress as an Expression of Heritage." *Dress*, 19, 1992, 57–68.

Marx, E. *Optical Color & Simultaneity*, New York: Van Nostrand Reinhold, 1983.

Mathis, C., and Connor, H. *The Triumph of Individual Style: A Guide to Dressing Your Body, Your Beauty, Your Self*. Cali, Colombia: Timeless Editions, 1993.

Meyers, J. *The Language of Visual Art: Perception as a Basis for Design*. Chicago: Holt, Rinehart & Winston, 1989.

Munsell. *A Book of Color: Neighboring Hues Edition, Matte Finish Collection*. Newburgh, NY: Kollmoregen, 1973.

# Chapter Eight

# ORGANIZING THE APPAREL-BODY-CONSTRUCT

*After you have read this chapter, you will be able to understand:*

• How the apparel-body-construct is organized by the viewer—the interplay between the viewer and the form. This includes understanding the visual effect, starting with the Gestalt or the immediate visual effect, and consciously initiating a process of analysis.

• The difference between simultaneous, successive, or separated viewing and to understand visual perception, the separating and grouping of visual parts, and the principles of similarity, closure, proximity, and continuation as they affect visual organizing.

• How number, pattern, and other part modifiers affect viewing, as well as proportion, direction in the experience of movement of the apparel-body-construct, gradation, symmetrical and asymmetrical balance, spatial position of visual parts, figure-ground ambiguity, and color as a visual definer.

• The viewing path, entry, viewing tempo, viewing priority, integration of visual parts, and the causes of visual effect as these factors affect viewing the apparel-body-construct.

Previous chapters concentrated on the whole form and its visual priorities, broken up into materials of the apparel-body-construct and the potential of the body and surfaces placed upon it. Then parts and their details were considered, that is, how parts are defined and characterized by line, shape, color, and texture. This chapter returns to the form as a whole and examines its impact. As you remember, the Gestalt is how the apparel-body-construct is organized and those relational factors that impact the whole.

The organizing process is an interplay between the viewer and the form. The viewer is actively involved in taking in the form, relating various distinguishable parts to other parts and to the whole. The viewer compares the degree of connecting based upon similarity and difference of one part related to another, and to the whole. To be aware of and understand the organizing process means first considering the immediate visual effect and then pursuing the underlying causes.

Why is it necessary to consider how the apparel-body-construct is organized? Much of the organizing process takes place in the subconscious and people organize automatically based upon the structure. Each apparel-body-construct is unique, but processes such as organizing principles of grouping and separating and how they function in patterns of perception help the viewer to understand his or her response and even whether he or she is attracted enough to bother to perceive a particular apparel-body-construct. Initially people are attracted based upon the Gestalt of the whole and then they may be involved on deeper levels. Attraction depends upon how the viewer interacts with the form as properties, that is, the kind and degree of definition and those qualities that make one form different from another. Sustained attention is a result of the initial response of the viewer to the apparel-body-construct and the relationships among its visual parts.

## KINDS OF ORGANIZATION

The **visual effect,** as noted earlier in this book, is the cumulative effect on the viewer produced by the distinctive way materials are arranged within the apparel-body-construct. Forms differ in:

- Their visual priorities, that is, the extent of and degree to which sudden breaks occur and the extent to which they are linked or related again.

- The amount of space they occupy and the definition and character of that space, whether they appear immediately as a whole or to have parts that break up the visual space.

The apparel-body-construct is defined by particular lines, shapes, colors, and textures. How the definers are combined and interrelated affects viewing. For example, if a certain shape is similar to one shape but different from another, particular kinds of relationships will characterize the apparel-body-construct. The two similar shapes will create a unit and the different shape will stand apart. When shapes are more visually equal, but not similar enough to group, they will remain more independent as parts. These parts can direct the viewer's gaze from one part to the other. If parts are unequal visually, they can create an order or a sequence that also directs viewing. For example, the form is viewed differently in Figures 8.1 and 8.2. In Figure 8.1 the parts are organized in a hierarchy. The light values of the jacket and hair color and their contrast with the dark dominate viewing. Subordinate parts are the black V shapes at the center front that create a centering and the dark full-length pants in the lower torso. The area of the shoes offers variety and interest in the repeat of the value contrast, but the size of the area means it is not the first attraction within the apparel-body-construct. Another example is in

**FIGURE 8.1**

*(Above left) The viewer compares contrasts in shapes of hair, suit jacket, and contrasts of light and dark, i.e., the dark surfaces of the pants and top and light areas of jacket. The placement, such as the contrasts in the upper torso and head and the smaller area of the bicolor shoes, creates a hierarchy of viewing based upon size of areas of light and dark. A figure-ground relationship is also established with the light-value jacket and head as figure and the dark areas as ground.*

Designed by Ralph Lauren. Courtesy of Fairchild Publications.

**FIGURE 8.2**

*(Right) The viewer focuses on areas of light and dark throughout the form. Body parts are important in the examination, i.e., head, arms, and legs. The surfaces are determinate and offer a contrast in value. A source of focus is the rounding shape created by hair and dark sleeves draped over the shoulders and tied. The horizontal lines are also important in establishing the order, especially the continuous line of the sleeves, and waistline with its adjacent surfaces of light and dark, and the hemline of the skirt that creates a proportion of about half light and half dark areas.*

Designed by Ralph Lauren. Courtesy of Fairchild Publications.

Figure 8.2, where value contrast is again an important definer. The viewer focuses on the head and dark hair, which connect with the sweater draped over the shoulder with sleeves tied at center front. The short skirt, however, creates another part and the legs yet another. Though the shoes are the same as in Figure 8.1, in this instance they attract less attention because of the number of more independent parts within the rest of the apparel-body-construct.

Some apparel-body-constructs are easier to view than others. Some are viewed as a whole immediately. Some have a clearly established viewing order and each part has a place. An apparel-body-construct that appears less orderly usually contains parts that are independent and more equal. Such a form requires time for viewing and separating into parts.

Easy viewing is not necessarily the final goal of all visual forms. Some apparel-body-constructs invite an immediate viewing of the whole because of a blending of interdependent parts, possibly with one part dominant as a focal point. In Figure 8.3, dominant is the head and neck area, which is coupled with the dark value of the remainder of the body. There is a similarity of value of hair and suit. Other forms with a definite order may have more parts that lead the eye of the viewer throughout the form. Such a form may have parts that are both independent and interdependent within the whole. In Figure 8.1 the viewer compares the shape of the hair with the more contrasting shapes of the suit jacket. Other parts to notice include the areas of the dark shirt and pants and the bicolor shoes. Still other forms may invite attention to contrasting parts that appear equal and more independent; these forms are seemingly more separated. In Figure 8.2, areas to view include the head, arms, and legs; the determinate surface of the light-value top; the black skirt and sweater; and bicolor shoes. These are not necessarily viewed in any particular order. Table 8.1 is a descriptive summary of the way the apparel-body-construct may be organized.

By beginning with the immediate visual effect or Gestalt, the viewer can initiate a process of analysis without necessarily understanding the causes. For example, sometimes the parts of the apparel-body-construct appear ordered but the cause is not at once apparent. Continued effort to comprehend the causes behind the way the apparel-body-construct appears can broaden one's viewing experience and aid in understanding the form. The organizational process involves strategies for viewing the apparel-body-construct.

| TABLE 8.1 Categories of Apparel-Body-Construct organization | Simultaneous | Successive | Separated |
|---|---|---|---|
| | View whole first, many secondary foci | One primary focus and/or several secondary foci | Several primary foci, view parts first |
| | Blending parts dependent upon position in whole | Some parts unequal weight and some equal | Parts equal weight, independent and contrasting |

The process can be described in objective terms based upon the interaction of the viewer with the form. The visual relationships within the apparel-body-construct can be understood in terms of their effect on this organization.

There are types of order from which we can generalize and learn. The apparel-body-construct may appear to have a definite viewing order or may appear less ordered, even random, as the viewer takes in separate parts. We can organize the parts by grouping like units in levels, one in front of the other. The apparel-body-construct may also be organized with one surface related to an adjacent surface in a side-by-side comparison. These types of order are considered in the following section.

## Simultaneous, Successive, or Separated Viewing

The viewer may find either the whole or the parts simpler to perceive. The viewer will tend to perceive first that which has the most clarity. Whether the person viewing the apparel-body-construct is attracted to parts or the whole, surfaces or edges, single focus or multiple foci, has much to do with the ultimate visual result.

When the immediate whole is the simplest form to perceive, it is called **simultaneous viewing**. Often such an apparel-body-construct is similar in surface in terms of texture and color, and the entire apparel-body-construct at first appears as a whole, as in Figure 8.3. This does not necessarily mean the whole is all there to see. Often the surfaces may have intricate interrelationships involving light and shadow or subtle and indeterminate relationships of these factors inviting side-by-side comparison. In Figure 8.4a, the strong triangle of dark from head to toe, alongside the equally strong black-and-white patterned surface of the cape, creates a side-by-side comparison in which both command the viewer's attention.

In the process of perceiving the whole apparel-body-construct, the viewer may find that some parts are dominant and others are subordinate. When a part has dominance it becomes a priority; an order is thereby established in our viewing, and this is called **successive viewing**. When two people compare their respective visual paths in an apparel-body-construct and identify the same parts as first, second, and third in priority, these parts are viewed successively. When parts exist in such a hierarchy, the whole can appear simple because each part has its place in the order. Parts that have unequal visual weight, some being dominant and others subordinate, can create such an order. In Figure 8.4b, the

**FIGURE 8.3**

*The viewer focuses first upon the whole form. Body parts such as the head contrast with the dark, two-piece suit. However, the hair is similar in value to the suit and creates a shape that continues with the upper area of the suit.*

Designed by Jil Sander. Courtesy of Fairchild Publications.

a    b    c

## FIGURE 8.4A, B & C

*Organization is considered in these apparel-body-constructs. In Figure 8.4a, viewing is simultaneous because of the side-by-side comparison of the patterned, black-and-white surface of the cape and the strong, black, triangular area from head to toe of hat, hair, top and pants, stockings, and shoes. The shapes of the black area and cape are vertical and encourage first a visual sweep, and then a horizontal comparison of surfaces. Viewing is successive in Figure 8.4b because of the order in which the two sizes of black-and-white checkered pattern command attention. First, the large size, then the smaller pattern, the dark hair, dark legs, and feet. Thus, the viewer is encouraged to encompass the entire form. In Figure 8.4c, viewing this apparel-body-construct involves discrete parts of the black-and-white checkered pattern of the jacket and skirt; the circular effect of the black hat, hair, and collar area; and the black side panels of jacket, gloves, legs, and feet. Since the parts are interdependent but also independent, they can be viewed more as separate parts. The organization is ordered, but separated into parts.*

*Designed by Oscar de la Renta. Courtesy of Fairchild Publications.*

patterns continue throughout the form in two different sizes, but the larger pattern of the jacket commands more attention than the smaller size pattern of the skirt, shawl, and gloves. The slit of the skirt, exposing the dark stockings, and the dark hair are both additional parts to be considered. Thus, the order of jacket and head, then shawl, skirt, stockings, and shoes becomes positioned in our viewing.

An apparel-body-construct organized first as parts that are more equivalent and often distinct may be viewed as more **separated**. The parts are more independent and give the viewer a part-to-whole impression. When the viewer considers a visual path, this apparel-body-construct is often viewed more casually. For example, two people may discuss the visual path but not agree on the precise viewing order. Both individuals may start the viewing process at different points but proceed in a similar manner. Such an apparel-body-construct is still ordered, but some parts are equal and some are unequal and independent. Thus, this apparel-body-construct is ordered but less definite in its order. In Figure 8.4c, parts include the hat, head, and neckline area; the patterned suit; the black stockings and shoes; and the black gloves. The areas of solid black vie for attention with the areas of black-and-white pattern. The figure-ground relationship is somewhat ambiguous in that solid black areas can be perceived as both figure and ground. When the viewer focuses on the suit, it is figure, but the viewer can also focus on other areas as figure, such as the hat, hair, and neckline area or the dark legs and feet. Thus, parts located throughout the apparel-body-construct share similarities but also differences that create discrete parts, and the viewer may be drawn to one and then the other part.

An effect of separation may occur for a variety of reasons. For example, the silhouette of the apparel-body-construct may be a continuous straight line, and the parts are viewed in a curving path. Or the shapes of the silhouette and the parts may be about equal visually, and the option of beginning with either of the two impacts an effect of randomness to the viewing process. Irregular and organic shapes on the surface that separate as figure can also be viewed individually.

As you consider organization in the apparel-body-construct, remember that there is a three-way interaction of form, viewer, and context. The form is not always viewed in exactly the same manner, but the task remains to view it as a Gestalt. Sometimes one viewer will perceive differently from another based upon differences in their respective experiences, education, and preferences. If your only interest is the shoes and you automatically begin there, you need to realize this influence. However, it does little good to become frustrated and stop your viewing process; instead, try to examine and analyze how you are viewing a particular apparel-body-construct. The types of order—simultaneous, successive, and separated—are primarily a tool for analysis. Additional examples of these types of order are Figure 8.3 (simultaneous), Figure 8.1 (successive), and Figure 8.2 (separated). It is by considering the organizing process that you will discover the causes behind how you view an item of clothing.

# THE ORGANIZING PROCESS

In the organizing process, the viewer perceives order whenever possible. Similar visual parts are grouped; contrasting or different visual parts are separated. Grouping and separating occur automatically for the viewer, but to understand organizing, the viewer must become aware of the process.

**Visual perception** involves both scanning and focusing. The viewer can only focus on small areas of a visual field at any one time, but the apparel-body-construct itself plays a role in what becomes focus or figure. People first scan and separate what they are going to view. When you focus on a part, the remainder of the apparel-body-construct becomes ground or periphery in your perception. As you continue to examine the entire apparel-body-construct, the relationships within the form become evident. In this process, the way the form is structured directs the viewer—where the viewer focuses first, how strong the focus is, and how many foci are perceived.

Areas in the visual field that are sources of focus and priority attract attention first. For example, the closed silhouette plays a dominant role in organizing because it attracts attention and influences the relationships of parts. If the silhouette is open and interacting with the surround, it may play a secondary role, especially if there is a more contrasting part that becomes the focus of attention.

The viewer's first task in understanding a form is to scan the whole, that is, to determine how much space is occupied and how the eye is directed within the form. The viewer's second task is to determine the relationship of parts. This involves finding the focus of visual attention and determining the nature of the visual relationship in the form.

## Steps in Understanding the Organizing Process

1. Scan the whole. What is the type of order: simultaneous, successive, or separated? What attracts attention first, second, third? Is the whole or part viewed first? At what pace does this occur (e.g., immediately or in a more lingering way)?

2. How many centers of focus are there—the whole, one point of focus, many?

3. Examine the following:

   - Viewing path: How is your eye directed within the apparel-body-construct: vertically, horizontally, diagonally? Are you directed to surfaces of the body cylinder or to silhouette?

   - The space of the apparel-body-construct: Does the silhouette offer closure for the viewer (closed or open)? Is the space within the silhouette solid or broken up (part or whole, figure-ground integration or separation)? How do the surfaces appear (flat or rounded, determinant or indeterminate)?

   - The point of entry visually: What is the location and source of your first focus? Is viewing contained within one area or carried throughout?

   - Function of parts: How many parts are there? How are parts similar to each other and to the whole? What is their nature—contrasting, blending, independent, interdependent?

| *Application Exercise 8.1* | Select an apparel-body-construct from Figure 8.5. Follow the process outlined above. How does considering the organization of your visual response help you to understand your overall visual perception of a given form? |

# ORGANIZING FACTORS

What is set off for viewing is significant to the ensuing perceptual organization, affecting whether we see the part or the whole first, whether you see one layer or many. People tend to perceive the organization that is the simplest and best. This has special meaning in perceptual terms. For example, the best order may be the one that appears the most stable and unambiguous; the simplest may be the one that has the most or the fewest levels to process. Since the viewing process is efficient, people want to see what makes the most sense and gives the clearest meaning to them.

Viewing the apparel-body-construct involves both the **grouping** and **separating** of visual parts. These processes occur automatically for the observer, that is, the act of grouping requires focusing, yet in this process separating or detaching is also occurring. Thus, the entire process necessarily involves both at the same time.

The observer organizes parts to give them a place in the whole: grouping when there is similarity in shape, color, size, location, direction, and separating when visual definition involves difference and contrast or when one part is more distinct visually than another.

**FIGURE 8.5**

*The process of organizing can be examined using one of these apparel-body-constructs. Select one and pursue the process.*

Courtesy of Kmart.

## The Visual Part Revisited

**Visual parts,** as pointed out in Chapter 2, are units that have a measure of separation or distinction from their surround. A part in some way both separates from and defines how the whole is organized. Understanding how the apparel-body-construct is organized requires responding to its visual parts and analyzing how each part is defined and related to the whole.

How the part functions in the whole is dependent upon its visual definition within the apparel-body-construct. A visual part is affected not only by its own characteristics of line, shape, point, color, and texture, but also by what surrounds it. To fully understand the function of a part within the whole requires taking all of the parts into account, regardless of their visual primacy. Any discussion of a visual part involves consideration of its position and function within the apparel-body-construct.

---

Examine the apparel-body-construct in Figure 8.6. How many parts do you see? Be sure to consider body parts in your count. How is each part defined and characterized? What uses are made of line, shape, color, texture?

*Application Exercise 8.2*

*An apparel-body-construct with a number of visual parts. What are the similarities and differences among the parts?*

Designed by Ralph Lauren. Courtesy of Fairchild Publications.

The visual part can define and integrate within the space of the apparel-body-construct or define and divide the space. The part that is intimately coordinated with the whole is described as blending, and its function is that of integration within the whole. The part can also be related to the whole through contrast, becoming an independent source of focus in the apparel-body-construct. A contrasting part is viewed as a more independent unit. While we can appreciate the experience of visual parts based upon their similarity to other parts, often we first notice the part that acts as focus, the one that offers contrast and demands our attention because it separates from the whole. How a part functions within the whole is dependent upon the viewing processes of grouping and separating.

Some parts are noticed before others and are dominant within the apparel-body-construct. This means they have a visual primacy. Other parts are subordinate to the dominant ones. The function of such a subordinate part may be to act as a transition between one part and another or as a repetitive pattern that helps direct or sustain attention. The visual effect is based upon the special characteristics of each apparel-body-construct that await the viewer's participation and response.

## The Whole—Gestalt

Through a series of visual experiments, Gestalt psychologists established principles of organization: **similarity, closure, proximity,** and **continuation.** Through their experiments these psychologists observed what happened when viewers perceived numerous simple geometric figures. They noted what was perceived and what took precedence over what. At first they enumerated many organizing factors, but then they consolidated them and arrived at a few principles. Gestalt psychologists found remarkable consensus among viewers in the organizing process. Differences were usually traced to some unique experience of a particular viewer or to ambiguities within the form itself.

The Gestalt principles occur automatically and are not usually a conscious part of our thinking. Therefore, to learn about them, you must take yourself off of automatic pilot. Nothing can be taken for granted! The underlying causes of grouping and separating of visual parts need to be understood within the visual field. We will refer to the following Gestalt principles: similarity, closure, proximity, and continuation (see Figure 8.7).

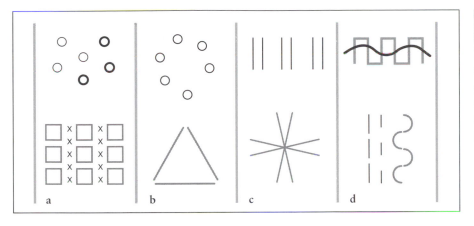

**FIGURE 8.7A, B, C & D**

*The Gestalt organizing factors are: (a) similarity, (b) closure, (c) proximity, and (d) continuation.*

*Similarity.* **Similarity** refers to the relative degree of sameness among visual parts. Parts that appear similar will be grouped in perception; parts that are dissimilar will be separated. Parts that are similar in one or more aspects have a perceptual connection and tend to be organized into groups based upon the degree of connection. For example, in Figure 8.8a, groupings of similar lines on the center front band, and continuing at the hem and the upper and lower pockets, all group and become figure on the ground of the dress. In Figure 8.8b the pocket lines, neckline, and hem are double lines and the center front line is just one line with the buttons. In Figure 8.8a, the sets of pocket lines may be considered easier to group with the center line than the pocket lines in Figure 8.8b because they are more similar to the center front of the garment. However, they are also positioned differently—horizontally rather than vertically. Which similarity wins?

Similarity is the most inclusive principle and therefore perhaps the one most difficult to understand in all of its applications. Applications include similarity in visual definers: color (hue, value, intensity), shape, line, texture. For example, in Color Plate 8, a number of similarities are noted: the light color values throughout; the curved line of the hat, neckline, sleeves, and skirt; and the curving shapes of the hair ringlets and dress. The application of the similarity principle also includes a series of "modifiers" of the whole, which will be discussed in this chapter, such as similarity of size, number, and spatial position. Similar parts can become a grouping on the same level in space. Parts that are dissimilar tend to separate and may form other groupings.

Similar, as pertaining to parts within an apparel-body-construct, does not mean identical. Even visual parts that treat the left and right sides of the body as mirror images are not identical because they are placed differently on the body. Six buttons that are identical before use may still seem identical when they are spaced in pairs equidistant from each other down the center front of a jacket. The buttons in this context, however, are not identical because they all have different positions upon the body.

a                                                    b

**FIGURE 8.8A & B**

*Groupings (Figure 8.8a) are formed of similar and parallel lines at center front and continuing around the hem, and also upper and lower pockets. These become figure on the ground of the dress. However, their vertical and horizontal orientation and positioning create separate groups. The center front line (Figure 8.8b) may be grouped with the buttons and continuing double parallel lines at the neck and hem edges. The similar orientation of the pockets in the upper and lower torsos make these vertical lines easier to group together.*

Designed by Chanel. Courtesy of Fairchild Publications.

When the apparel-body-construct becomes more complex, parts may relate in several or even many different ways within the whole. For example, in Color Plate 8, parts include the area of the head, the stockings and shoes, and the dress. Groupings are created due to similarity of the shapes of the hair; the floral pattern printed on the dress, the light values of the entirety; the striped pattern used in small areas at the neckline, waist, and hemline; the bow motif at the waistline and shoes; and the ruffle at the neckline, hem, and on the stockings. Groups and the way the observer connects parts are a source of order and coherence within the apparel-body-construct. For example, a part may be similar in color with one part and in shape with another. In Color Plate 8, grouping of the curving shapes of the hat, hair, and dress provides order and coherence within the apparel-body-construct. Parts are also grouped based upon other similar characteristics, such as hue and value. If parts are similar in two characteristics, the degree of connection will be stronger and will influence the organizing process. The clearest, least ambiguous grouping will be perceived first.

A myriad of variations can occur and awareness of the visual result is your best clue to spotting the effect of similarity. One way to see how this phenomenon works is to vary one visual definer while keeping the remainder constant. Then ask yourself: "What difference does this variation make?" For example, two shapes are both blue, but one is a circle and the other is a triangle. In the apparel-body-construct this could be the circle of a pin and the triangle of a tie or pocket handkerchief. Are they still grouped by color, even though the shapes differ?

---

Vary one visual definer in Color Plate 8 and imagine what influence that alteration will have on the apparel-body-construct. For example, imagine the shoes to be black so that they are a value change from the stockings.

*Application Exercise 8.3*

---

While we experience the wholeness of visual forms based upon similarity, what we focus upon may be the part that is dissimilar. But keeping the whole as the reference for viewing is a must in establishing similarity among parts. A part that is not similar to other parts is viewed as separated and is often a source of focus by itself, and what first separates as a part is significant within an apparel-body-construct.

*Closure.* **Closure** refers to the perception of detachment or separation of a visual part because of edge. This can occur because a shape has a clear, simple, and continuous outline, creating a part that separates to some degree from the whole. In Figure 8.2, the dark hair falling about the shoulders may be perceived as connecting with the dark sweater tied over the shoulders, creating a sort of lopsided circle. A part can be as large as the silhouette or as small as a pin placed upon the lapel of a jacket. In Figure 8.1, a triangular shape is created at the neck by the closing of the jacket, and together the angular shapes of the lapels and collar can group with the dark V shape created by closure.

Closure can be perceived even when a figure is not actually closed. This concept of closure implies viewer participation in filling in the blanks. Already noted is that line can be implied by the viewer and thus does not actually need to be connected to be perceived as a line. When a visual part is not entirely closed or bounded, the observer will fill in the outline if it provides a clearer meaning. For example, lines and shapes that are nearly complete can be perceived as completed and closed. The observer who fills in to create a closure

FIGURE 8.9A & B

*In Figure 8.9a, closure is perceived resulting from the continuous line of lapel, collar, hat, and head. Closure in Figure 8.9b is perceived from the shape created by the boundaries of dark hair and T-shirt within the area framed by suit collar and lapel.*

Designed by: (a) Hugo Boss and (b) Joe Soto. Courtesy of Fairchild Publications.

a                                                              b

may group buttons into a rectangle or even connect the lines created by pockets and buttons, or collar and lapel. In Figure 8.9a, the lapel, collar, hat, and head can be perceived as a shape that is separated from the remainder of the apparel-body-construct. However, if the outline does not provide a clearer meaning, the viewer may not fill in the blanks to create closure but may perceive the parts as separate. In Figure 8.9b, closure is created by the shape observed in the contrast of dark hair and T-shirt with the jacket lapel and collar line.

*Application Exercise 8.4*

Examine the suit jacket in Figure 8.9b. The line created by the edge of the collar and lapel, though notched, could appear continuous and create a point of focus. Imagine a change in the collar and lapel that would create closure and focus for their edges.

As noted, visual perception is a process of scanning and then focusing. We focus on manageable portions of our visual field at any one time. Thus, we must first create closure to separate what we want to view, then focus upon what we have closed off. The process of closure can require grouping as well as separating. What has the most contrast and the greatest detachment from the surround will create the strongest closure. This may be the whole apparel-body-construct or a part may separate first. If a viewer is looking at the apparel-body-construct in its entirety, a sharply defined silhouette will separate and become a reference in his or her viewing, especially if no part within it is as sharply defined. Then what is within the silhouette will group, but if the silhouette is not as dominant visually, the part may take priority in the viewing process. In Figure 8.9a, although the hat and collar are the same hue, value, and intensity, the similarity of their textures and their placement around the head can be perceived as a closure and viewed separated to a degree from the coat.

*Proximity.* Parts that are located close together will group in perception. **Proximity** is a special instance of similarity of location, or close spatial placement. As the distance between similar parts varies, those that are close spatially will tend to group. The viewer is more likely to group two parts that are close together and that are also similar in one but not all characteristics. In Figure 8.10, the vertical buttons and banding group because of proximity. For another example, picture a silk necktie and pocket handkerchief of the same color. Though the necktie and handkerchief are the same color and texture, they are a different shape. Their proximity increases their potential visual relationship. Given the complexity of the apparel-body-construct, grouping of physically close visual units may occur when only one aspect of the units is similar, for example, hair and neck scarf that are similar in color but different in shape and size. This occurs especially when the parts are in close proximity.

The observer is less likely to group parts that are far apart unless they are similar and contrasting enough with the remainder of the apparel-body-construct. An example would be contrasting black shoes and hair that have no other such contrasting parts. On the extremities of the body, dark shoes and hair are about as far as they can be from each other. Yet, because of the extreme contrast in color, they may form a distinct connection. If the black hair were to be located close to another part, such as a similar black jacket, then this grouping would take precedence over the potential grouping with the shoes, because of proximity. However, the black shoes would still play an important but secondary role in directing the attention of the viewer.

Proximity also relates to apparent distance from the observer in forward/backward space. Similarly, indeterminate surfaces will group because they appear to be located a similar distance from the viewer. Two surfaces that differ in degree of determinacy, that is, an indeterminate and a determinate surface as in the veil and dress in Figure 8.10, will tend to separate as parts since they will appear to be different distances from the viewer.

Visual parts can be spatially close in a number of ways in the apparel-body-construct. Boundaries of each can touch, overlap the other, or be detached but close together (see Figure 7.18). When boundaries of two parts are detached or touch, they will easily group if similar in surface treatment. The same occurs when the boundaries of two visual parts touch. When two or more parts overlap, other characteristics

**FIGURE 8.10**

*Proximity, that is, similarity of location, aids in grouping of the vertical and asymmetrical buttons and banding on this wedding dress.*

Designed by Chanel. Courtesy of Fairchild Publications.

*Continuation is perceived in the curved neckline continuing the shape of the hair.*

Designed by Chanel. Courtesy of Fairchild Publications.

being equal, the part with the most continuous border usually appears to be in front. Such parts may group if the outline of both is simpler to perceive together than the outline of one alone. When the two parts are transparent, there may be a visual penetration of one part by another or the formation of a new part where the two parts coincide, especially when the overlap creates another distinct color or texture.

*Continuation.* **Continuation** is that connection of parts in perception which occurs because parts follow a similar direction. The horizontal placement of the braid on the pockets and lowered waist in Figure 8.10 are an example. Visual parts arranged in a straight or curvilinear path result in perception of continuation, and the vertical line created by buttons that extends from neck to the hem is a continuation in Figure 8.10 also. A curved neckline that continues the shape and visual path of the shape of the hair, as in Figure 8.11, is another example.

Lines and shapes with more connecting and continuous contours tend to be more definite configurations than those with discontinuous contours. A discontinuous contour occurs when there is an abrupt change in direction, which tends to create separate visual parts. A point of focus often occurs at the place in the line where a contour changes direction. This discontinuity in the line may create a separate part. A skirt hemline changing the vertical line of the leg to the horizontal edge of the skirt tends to be viewed as separated. However, if the skirt is similar in color and texture to the legs, and repeats the vertical line, the skirt and legs are perceived as more continuous.

Context can aid continuation. If the continuation is reinforced by a similar meaning, the grouping is stronger. A series of horizontal stripes placed within a vertical shape on the body could be viewed as a continuous vertical path. The eye would be directed up by moving from the edge of one stripe to another. Also, the reverse is true. That is, if a discontinuous outline is reinforced by a change in meaning, it will be more strongly separated. For example, a jacket edge that changes direction from the verticality of the body is perceived as more separated than a vertical line that does not change direction, such as a dress silhouette. The change in orientation in stripes from vertical in a jacket

Think of a way that the head might be treated visually to continue and unite with the upper torso, for example, with a hood or haircut. Imagine the colors, textures, and shapes that would create such a continuation.

to horizontal in a skirt, even though the silhouette line does not change abruptly, would create a separation of parts.

Relatively dissimilar parts can be grouped by continuation, but the parts must be perceived as going in the same direction. For example, in a row of buttons, if one button were unbuttoned in the middle of the row, the buttons could still be perceived as a continuous grouping. The eye could follow the direction of the other buttons and would be less likely to stop. However, if the unbuttoned button was the one that ended the point at an angled juncture of two lines of buttons, it would be more difficult to perceive as a grouping because the line would be discontinuous.

Continuation also may depend upon past experiences. For example, continuation may be perceived when a line extends around the body. If the viewer does not actually see the line all the way around, it could be imagined because of the viewer's past experience with the cylindrical surfaces of the body. In Figure 8.12, the viewer expects the continuation of the lines around the body, and this expectation is increased because of the asymmetric floral motif.

## Interaction Effects

Organizing is the process of combining and relating the visual parts, and the four Gestalt principles can occur together within the same apparel-body-construct. Thus, visual parts that are similar, provide closure, are in close proximity, and are continuous will group, and those that are not will separate as parts. Which principle will dominate when more than one is present? The stability of the relationships depends upon their clarity and simplicity. In Figure 8.13a, the interaction works to strengthen the relationships. The similarity of the color of the hair and upper bodice create a grouping, but also the continuation of the ends of the hair flip and the neckline add to the effect. The contrast in the remainder of the dress, the light and shadow of the diagonal lines converging at center front also with the neckline of the bodice and breasts, the graduation effect of the dark of the skirt, the combination of dark and light in the upper bodice, and the light but similar hue and value of the hair add to the organization.

When the organizing principles compete within a visual form, the most clear and stable solution is the one that will prevail for the viewer. The way to determine which principle prevails is to follow the steps in the organizing process and learn for yourself which principle dominates in the visual result. You can determine which prevails from using your own awareness of the principles of organization. As you make your discoveries, consider the influence of your culture and the time in which you live.

**FIGURE 8.12**

*Lines may be perceived as continuing by encircling the body, even though the viewer does not actually follow the lines around.*

Designed by Dries van Noten. Courtesy of Fairchild Publications.

a                                                          b

**FIGURE 8.13A & B**

*Relationships are strengthened when more than one organizational principle is at work, as in Figure 8.13a. The relationships of similarity of hair color and upper bodice, as well as the continuation of the neckline with the ends of the hair, aid in grouping. Proportional relationships can be examined following an analysis of visual parts within an apparel-body-construct. In Figure 8.13b, an approximate ratio of 2:5 is created following this process.*

*Designed by Balmain. Courtesy of Fairchild Publications.*

*Application Exercise 8.6*

Find an example of an apparel-body-construct in this book or one you have collected. Follow the visual path and record what you see in the order you perceive it—what you notice first, second, third, fourth. Then apply the Gestalt principles to determine which are operating. (Note: At first this exercise may be tricky because the organizing principles operate in your subconscious and you must remember to make them part of a conscious effort.)

# PART MODIFIERS

Any visual part is affected not only by its own makeup but also by what surrounds it. The character of a visual part is influenced by how we compare the part to other parts and to the whole. A **part modifier** alters a part's interaction within the apparel-body-construct. The interaction of visual parts in the whole is influenced by such modifiers as number, size, location on the body, and position in space.

## Number

The significance of a visual part changes with **number**. A single, isolated unit is perceived differently as a visual part than is a quantity of the same unit. According to Barratt (1980) in his book *Logic and Design*, the maximum number of similar visual units a viewer can take in without counting or grouping is around seven. The number any viewer can take in without counting is called a **number threshold**. When we are confronted with one to seven items, we can easily assess the number and respond with an awareness of their separateness. In Figure 8.14, the six buttons can be viewed easily as six buttons.

Past a threshold of seven or so, we must group or order the parts to comprehend. For example, twelve units may be grouped into four rows of three units each. In the case of eight buttons, the viewer may group into two rows of four or four rows of two. Even in the case of the six buttons in Figure 8.14, the viewer may group them all together or into pairs. Past seven groups of seven, we begin to experience numerical dazzle until the groups of units evolve into pattern.

**Pattern** is experienced as an ordered repetition of shapes on a surface. Once one motif of the pattern is examined, the repetition may become textural, that is, motifs are not grouped but operate as numerical dazzle and define space by becoming ground. Pattern may also involve a grouping process and a consciousness of repetition. Then the pattern is assisted by easily comprehensible repeats, or a grouping of groups. The groupings on the body involve an order, and one grouping can become more important than another, depending upon their use.

As we group like shapes or lines, they can become more important in several ways depending upon how they are treated and their location. For example, six buttons can be perceived as a rectangular shape, as in Figure 8.14, or as

**FIGURE 8.14**

*Buttons will group if they number eight or fewer and form a simple shape. Such a shape becomes figure upon the ground of the jacket.*

Designed by Donna Karan. Courtesy of Fairchild Publications.

Think of how a pattern can be perceived differently on various parts of the body. For example, imagine a surface imprinted with groups of small, regularly repeated motifs such as circles, squares, or triangles. In a skirt, for example, the motifs lose their separateness. The gathers take on visual priority if they supersede the motifs. If a portion of the same surface is placed flat on the body, then those shapes gain added importance in viewing and introduce an order. Imagine how you would view this apparel-body-construct, or think of another example of ways to place a pattern onto the body to create order.

following a line with direction or continuation. If the left and right sides of the body are treated similarly with shoulder tabs or epaulets, for example, then one side is not more important or dominant in the viewing process. When working with two mirror-image shapes, such as symmetrical lapels, we can create a hierarchy, that is, one becomes more important than the other by placing a pin on one lapel. This asymmetrical treatment makes the side with the pin more important visually.

When two or more similar parts or units are perceived, a space or an interval may appear as ground between the two units that group. However, the space between may be perceived as yet another unit, that is, as figure rather than ground. An example is similar bands of stripes that are contrasting black and white. If either the black stripe or the white one can become figure for the viewer, then ambiguity may occur because the viewer can switch from one to the other. In Figure 8.4a, the central vertical black area is surrounded by the black-and-white checkered cape. Both are strong in their attraction, and the result is that the viewer may compare the areas in a side-by-side comparison of equal attention to unit and interval.

## Size

Parts may vary in size in relation to one another, and they are compared for similarities and differences. Similar size is one factor in grouping. In Figure 8.4b, the similar black and white checks on the jacket, skirt, and shawl group but then separate from each other by like sizes. However, initially the similarity of motif does influence their connection. Remember in the apparel-body-construct the sizes of parts are also compared to the size of the body.

**Proportion** refers to the size relationships of the parts to each other and to the whole. The size of a shape enters into a proportional relation when it is read in the context of other shapes. However, the apparent size of the shape is also influenced by other factors, such as surface color and texture.

What we judge as proportional with regard to the apparel-body-construct changes with time, though absolute rules have been developed through actual physical measurement for what is considered a "good" proportional experience. Historically, proportions of parts within the whole have been examined and certain ratios have been designated as more appealing over time. One ratio of note is the 3:5 ratio, often called the Golden Mean, because over time this ratio has been satisfying to many viewers.

When viewing an apparel-body-construct, one cannot stop to take precise measurements to determine proportional relationships. What can be concluded from such rules is that unequal sizes are more interesting than equal ones. With unequal proportions the viewer must consider the parts in relation to each other and to the whole. If one part is much larger than others, it may separate and not appear related at all. If the larger part is perceived as clearly dominant, it can become a focus within the apparel-body-construct.

If the apparel-body-construct is taken in as a whole first, we make proportional judgments based upon that reference. In a culture oriented to fashion and regular changes in proportions, the key to making judgments is to be aware of the proportional change. When the size of the lapels of a suit change in width, our judgments of proportion adjust accordingly. When the fit of clothing becomes larger and looser, its relation to the body changes in our view of the apparel-body-construct. This changed relation may require an increase in the size of all the parts in order to be proportional. Another way to influence the relation is to contrast the larger fit on one body part with a close fit on another.

One proportional reference viewers always have is their own bodies. We compare our own body height to those of others we are viewing. Concepts such as short can mean "someone shorter than I am." As we grow taller as a society, the concept of tall changes. Models of the apparel-body-construct used in illustration or photography are often nine to ten heads in height. While this proportion has been useful for the proper hang and drape of fabrics on the body, it exceeds the average. Viewing this proportion in fashion images surely can affect the viewers' expectations of their own bodies and our frame of reference for proportion in other apparel-body-constructs. What looks "good" proportionally on a model may need to be adjusted to meet the proportions of another wearer who is not of the same proportions.

From a magazine, trace the outline of a model who is nine or more heads high. Now compare with the proportions of a different wearer who is less than eight heads. A good way to do this is to draw both apparel-body-constructs to the same scale. What adjustments might you need to make in the shorter figure?

*Application Exercise 8.8*

Manipulating the elements of design according to the Gestalt principles can create different proportional relationships. To apply the concept of proportion to the apparel-body-construct, the entire body must be accounted for. For example, black opaque stockings may be perceived as united with black boots, and this influences the way an apparel-body-construct and its parts are perceived. Hair and upper torso may be similar in hue, value, and intensity and may be grouped by proximity and similarity, as in Figure 8.13a. Then the part to be considered in a proportional relationship is that grouping with the remainder of the apparel-body-construct. If the lower torso is completely dark in value, such as a floor-length skirt, a proportion approximating a 2:5 ratio may be created when comparing one part to another and 2:7 when comparing the part with the whole (see Figure 8.13b).

The size of a part and its use within the apparel-body-construct can alter its appearance and place within the whole. For example, a very large shape may not be viewed totally within one body view and may curve around the body. A very small shape with a regular repeat can become almost textural in effect, especially from a distance. The sizes of accessory items can change proportional relationships. Items such as purses, backpacks, and jewelry all relate to the body through their sizes and can change the proportional relationships of the remainder of the apparel-body-construct. A large belt can then become more of a focal point than a small one, especially if it also has a large metal buckle. The ratio of parts within the whole as they relate within an apparel-body-construct is well worth your attention.

## Direction

**Direction** refers to the experience of movement while taking in the apparel-body-construct. This occurs because seeing takes time. This type of movement is not actual movement but has to do with the apparel-body-construct in a standing and stationary position. The impression of movement is largely temporal since it occurs in the mind while the viewer is experiencing the form. The viewer is usually involved in perceiving a number of visual parts in a process of scan, focus, scan, focus and is led visually throughout the apparel-body-construct. Focus is an arrest or pause; scanning is moving from one visual unit to another. How a part is experienced in the focus and scanning process influences its place in the whole.

Movement within the apparel-body-construct involves the direction the visual parts take in relation to the basic axis of the body. Thus, a line or shape on the body expresses some direction, either related to the vertical-horizontal axis of the body or departing from it. The buttons in Figure 8.14 create a strong up and down direction when the viewer compares and groups them. A vertical line often reinforces the vertical axis of the body. A diagonal line, which opposes the body axis, is experienced as having more energy than a vertical line. A shape such as a rectangle, seen by itself, has a direction, that is, length greater than width directs the eye. When placed on the body the long way, it reinforces the body verticality. If placed horizontally on the body, it may reinforce or contrast the basic vertical axis. It may also create parts on the body, depending upon other factors such as number or clarity; in other words, its relationship within the apparel-body-construct. A series of diagonal parallel lines group to form a vertical rectangle or two rectangles in the upper torso and leg below the knee in Figure 8.15. This creates a dynamic vertical directional pull for the viewer.

In addition to directing the viewer within the apparel-body-construct in a horizontal, vertical, or diagonal direction, visual parts can also direct the viewer's attention in a forward-backward or in-out movement from the surface of the apparel-body-construct, as in Figure 8.4b. This creates an impression of depth when parts are organized in levels or when light and shadow play on the folds of gathers. Ask yourself when viewing the apparel-body-construct: How is my eye directed? The eye may be directed on the upper torso horizontally because of a horizontal neckline, and on the lower torso vertically, due to a tubular silhouette. In Figure 8.15, in addition to the diagonal lines grouping, the dark hair, dark lapels, pocket flaps, and cuffs visually connect with the dark leggings. The figure-ground reversal of black on white in the upper torso, and the white-on-black reversal in the lower torso, also helps to determine which area receives your attention first.

**FIGURE 8.15**

*Direction of lines and shapes and their relationship to the body axis influence perception of the apparel-body-construct.*

Designed by Future Ozbek. Courtesy of Fairchild Publications.

***Direction by Rhythm.*** Direction can be aided by repetition of similar parts, often called **rhythm**. Rhythm is defined as the ordered recurrence of parts that leads the eye. It makes use of an observer's expectations of a regular pattern, for example, repeated pleats in a skirt or motifs printed on a shirt. If a grouping of pleats is centered on the body, the eye will be directed there. Then the eye moves from one part to another in a repeating movement that the viewer finds satisfying.

Rhythm is never an exact repetition of the same part in the apparel-body-construct, since the identical part repeated on the body cannot occupy the same space. For example, in Figure 8.15 each of the diagonal motifs is similar and is rhythmical, yet its placement on the body influences the viewer. The motif curving around the legs because of the body contour is different than the presentation on the upper torso where the area is relatively flatter.

**FIGURE 8.16**

*Rhythm is illustrated in this 1930s design by Elsa Schiaparelli through numerous lines forming a concentric circle upon the body, resulting in a triangular drape flowing to the hem. The pattern of circles lends a degree of indeterminacy by being printed on an already textured surface.*

Courtesy of The Goldstein Galley, University of Minnesota.

The repetition that occurs in patterns printed on surfaces can be interrupted when they are draped into folds and through the interaction of the material with the body's contours and movements. Pleats may group by similarity, even though the pleats encircling the body are not totally similar, for they occur differently on the various planes of the body and in different body views. The eye may see the continuous line made by the row of pleats rather than the pleats themselves.

When the unit and interval are perceived as two distinct parts, rather than as figure-ground, we scan alternately between them. This occurs when the eye is led from a black to a white stripe placed vertically on the body or from the highlight of the top of a pleat to the shadow of the recess. Often variation in unit and interval gives the eye something to take in more separately, thus directing the eye from unit to interval, unit to interval, rather than simply to the grouping of units. In Figure 8.15, the eye is directed from white to black, unit to interval.

An example of rhythm is the centering effect of lines in a concentric circle. This not only creates rhythm from the lines converging and then radiating outward, but also can create focus on a body part. The evening dress from the 1930s designed by Schiaparelli in Figure 8.16 is an example of such rhythm through centering of lines on the body.

***Direction by Gradation.*** Another type of directing occurs because of **gradation**, which is a measured change from one part to another. The viewer experiences a progression from one part to the next because of a just-perceptible difference in the parts. For example, colors may gradually change in value from dark to light, or shapes may progress in size from large to small, as in the ties in Figure 8.17. This provides order that directs eye movement.

Direction is experienced in the apparel-body-construct because the body structure itself involves gradation of size and shape, such as from smaller limbs of the upper body to larger limbs of the lower body. The natural draw of the head at the top of the body is often a good starting reference for a graduated effect. An example is a caftan that begins with a motif of small size at the shoulders and gradually gets larger all the way to the hemline, or an ensemble that begins with lighter values at the top and graduates to darker values at the lower body. Body parts may combine with clothing details for the effect of a gradation, for example, crisp pleats may vary in width from narrow at the waist to wider at the hip and interact with the female body, which follows the same shape.

## Visual Weight

In the process of viewing the apparel-body-construct, the observer is continuously involved in comparing one part with another. This process occurs with size and proportional relationships, but also with other aspects of parts, such as surface texture, color, and the like. This comparison involves an unconscious visual weighting. A surface that appears dense and filled may be weighted visually more than one that appears empty. When one part is experienced as weighing more than another, a hierarchy is established. When one part is experienced as approximately equal to another, we perceive a balance.

Two types of **balance** are **symmetrical** and **asymmetrical**. Symmetrical balance is the result of treating identically the two sides of the body—left and right sides. Asymmetrical balance is the result of considering the visual weight of the two sides, but not treating them identically. Compare the balance in examples of skiwear in Figure 8.18a and b. In Figure 8.18a, the left and right sides are similar with the scarf the only variation, the result being a centering influence from the scarf and the division between the legs. The bands of the sweater are viewed separately and sustain symmetry. However, in Figure 8.18b the stripes and their differences in value make them asymmetrical left to right in both the jacket and lower leg. The result is that the viewer perceives each side as a somewhat more separate entity, and the stripes in the jacket may appear to continue around the back in a spiral effect.

Skill in developing balanced relationships, either in symmetrical or asymmetrical arrangements, means an awareness of the center, that position from which we can achieve balance in visual weighting. In Figure 8.19, the collar is large and asymmetrical, and comparison with the body's center is important in viewing. The visual center is usually the actual center of the body from one body view. The center can also be moved to a position of the body that is not the actual body center. Think about body center and the difference between the front or back body view and the body viewed from the side. Clothing is often asymmetrical upon the body when viewed from the side.

Balance is a perceptual condition, and preference for symmetry or asymmetry depends upon each apparel-body-construct, as well as the cultural context and time period. Habits of perception affect how we view a visual form, and treatments of the apparel-body-construct take this factor into consideration. For example, many languages are read from left to right. Often the left side of the apparel-body-construct is balanced with the right, with this left-right viewing order in mind. In Figure 8.2, the arrangement of the tied sweater at center front takes into account left-right viewing, with the slightly shorter end

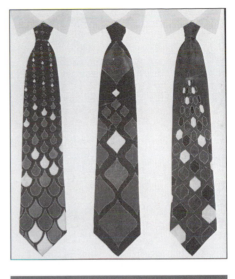

**FIGURE 8.17**

*Ties that direct the viewer's eye through a progression of sizes, gradually changing from smaller to larger.*

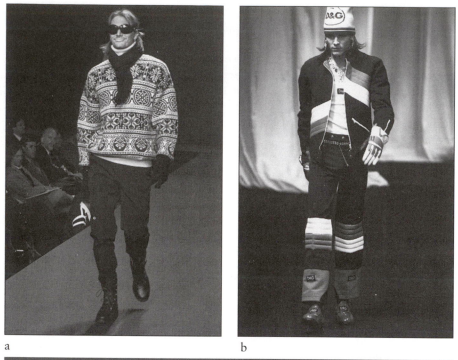

a                                                        b

**FIGURE 8.18A & B**

*The left and right sides of the body in Figure 8.18a are treated similarly with the clothing placed upon it, except for the scarf that provides a degree of asymmetry. In Figure 8.18b, the left and right sides of the body are treated asymmetrically because the prominent shapes or their colors do not continue left to right within one body view. However, balance may be achieved by taking into consideration the unseen body views where the bold stripes could continue around the body.*

Designed by: (a) Hugo Boss and (b) Dolce & Gabbana. Courtesy of Fairchild Publications.

on the viewer's left and longer on the viewer's right. An interesting detail on the left can lead the eye into the rest of the apparel-body-construct across to the right, as read from the viewer's perspective. Therefore, applying this direction of visual movement from reading, it is often more comfortable recording visual information from left to right than right to left.

Asymmetry prevails more in some historical periods than others. For example, during the 1920s in the United States asymmetry from the front, side, and back body views was frequently used. Some cultures prefer asymmetry more than others. For example, the Japanese are noted for their use and preference of asymmetry in floral arrangements, landscaping, and architecture, as well as clothing.

Visual weighing is not just for the purpose of noting similarity. Dissimilar parts are also viewed in comparison to each other. For example, a coarser-textured surface will appear to be heavier by comparison with a smoother one. The contrast between the two is what is noticed, and each surface affects the viewer's experience of the other. In Figure 8.18a, the visual texture of the sweater surface compares with the smoother surfaces of the skin and hair, as well as the surfaces on the lower body.

The concept of a balanced apparel-body-construct is based on its apparent visual weight. Balance by visual interest is achieved by varying the amount of attention of the parts. Even though all parts of the apparel-body-construct exist at an equal distance from the observer, some may appear to come forward and some recede. A part that appears to advance gains attention. Visually we compare one part of an apparel-body-construct and weigh it against others. In Figure 8.18a, the light-valued parts, sweater, skin, and hair are compared to the dark value of the scarf and lower body. A grouping of parts (those similar in color, texture, size, shape, and location) will often appear heavier, or to have more visual weight, than a single part. In Figure 8.8a, the grouping of dark braid on the dress provides more visual weight than if just a single line of braid outlined the center front.

Balance includes weighting in terms of body views, that is, the silhouette plane parallel to the observer, left-right, top-bottom. In Figure 8.4c, the dark stockings help to balance the jacket, lapels, collar, and hat and help to lead the eye in a vertical direction. Balance also is seen in terms of the body in the round when an apparel-body-construct is in movement. In patternmaking, a designer is often concerned with the balance of the drape of a skirt, trouser, or jacket in the way it hangs from the body—left to right and front to back. If an item of clothing hangs askew, an imbalance will occur. This physical imbalance, which affects the actual hang of the garment, also affects the visual balance of the apparel-body-construct.

The easiest way to achieve balance in the apparel-body-construct is through bilateral symmetry, where the halves are treated similarly. This type of symmet-

**FIGURE 8.19**

*Awareness of the body center in viewing helps a designer balance this large and asymmetrical collar.*

Designed by Claude Montana. Courtesy of Fairchild Publications.

From a historical point of view, think of silhouettes that offer a pronounced side view, for example, the bustle of the later nineteenth century or the skirts of the 1970s with front full pleats and smooth back.

*Application Exercise 8.9*

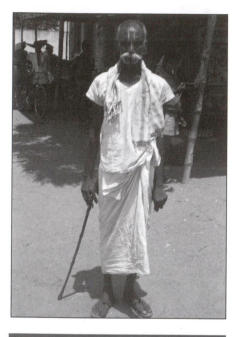

**FIGURE 8.20**

*An Indian sarong is an asymmetrical treatment of the lower torso through an elaborate draping of folds.*

Courtesy of Barbara Sumberg.

rical balance is very easy for the observer to take in. It requires a minimum of effort, especially when body symmetry is repeated in the clothing, for example, in a suit with similar lapel and pocket treatment on the left and right sides. However, there are many other possibilities in visual weighting.

Asymmetrical treatment, the balancing of two sides that are not treated similarly, is more complex but also can provide a visually satisfying balance. Balance by visual weighing is a type of asymmetrical balance that requires a comparison of the visual demands of two or more parts. Often an apparel-body-construct that is basically symmetrical will include an asymmetrical accent. An example includes a pocket handkerchief arranged in the upper pocket of a woman or man's suit jacket, a logo or pocket on one side of a T-shirt, or a large pin or even silk flower on a dress. If, additionally, the hair is styled asymmetrically, then the accent and hair need to be considered together. Not all asymmetrical accents are on the upper torso. In Figure 8.20, this man is wearing a sarong, an asymmetrical treatment on the lower torso that is often worn with an otherwise symmetrical arrangement on the upper torso.

Where a part is located on the body affects its visual weight. The body is already a hierarchy for viewing, and the viewer tends to give more attention to the upper portion of the apparel-body-construct. A grouping of parts may combine adjacent body parts, for example, the head and upper torso. In perceiving the body we may experience weighting of the upper-lower body treatment as symmetrical or asymmetrical. In Figure 8.15, there is a symmetry of upper and lower body, with the dark hair flowing upon the shoulders, making a continuity with the V shapes at the neckline and continuing to the end of the bodice on the upper torso. This ties the head and neck together at the center of the upper body, which balances with the lower body, the dark, fitted leggings continuing the centering and similar diagonal patterns on the lower leg, creating a connection with the upper torso. If the upper portion of the body is perceived as dominant because of a strong horizontal line across the shoulders contrasting with the head size and the rest of the body, more attention will be given to this line. On the other hand, in a comparison of similar colors or patterns throughout the body, the observer may experience a dominance not of one body part but of the whole apparel-body-construct. A border print placed at the shoulder area and repeated at the hem requires eye movement over more of the body. The amount of border print at the shoulder may be smaller than the amount at the hem, but position alone may create a visual balance between the two areas.

Balance can also refer to the actual body position of the apparel-body-construct. If the body appears off-balance literally, as though it would not stay in its current position for long, the observer feels a tension, as in Figure 8.18b. A designer can create tension through asymmetric treatment of the body and can thus attract and direct the viewer's eye in a dynamic way. However, if the body appears stable, then the observer becomes aware of the symmetrical balance within the clothing, as in Figure 8.18a.

## Spatial Position

A part or a grouping can vary in position in space. Whether perceived as close to the viewer or farther away depends to some extent upon the surface aspects of the part in relation to the whole. It matters where you, as a viewer, position the part spatially, because this has to do with how you organize the apparel-body-construct.

*Levels of Parts in the Whole.* An observer needs to consider how parts group—on one level or several. If visual parts are similar, they can group on one level or plane, as figure on ground. Examples of this type of grouping are created by a simple surface pattern or a repeated motif or shape. Often similar lines or shapes are experienced as a grid slightly in front of the ground. Grouping on one level includes everything that appears equidistant from the observer, as is seen with the diagonal lines grouped at the chest in Figure 8.15.

The figure-ground relationship may be quite clear-cut and unambiguous for the viewer, that is, what is perceived as figure appears in a spatial position in front of the ground. In Figure 8.8a, the bands at neck, sleeve end, and hem can appear in a spatial position together and before the remainder of the dress. Ambiguity in spatial position can occur when the viewer is able to reverse the figure and ground. Competition between figure and ground can provide an energy and tension. What at first appears as figure can become ground in an ambiguous figure-ground relation. This is termed **figure-ground ambiguity** and can be controlled. When a surface is ambiguous as to figure-ground, other visual cues may reduce the ambiguity. For example, figural cues elsewhere on the body can make clear what is figure and what is ground. In certain situations some ambiguity lends interest. Designers often experiment with the use of figure-ground ambiguity, especially for eveningwear. In Figure 8.21, parts that can be perceived as figure, in turn, are the light-value hair and

**FIGURE 8.21**

*The figure-ground relationship may involve perceiving several areas as figure within the apparel-body-construct, first one and then another. This results in some figure-ground ambiguity for the viewer. Here figure can be viewed as the light values of hair and skin, or the dress itself.*

Designed by Balmain. Courtesy of Fairchild Publications.

**FIGURE 8.22**

*When surfaces vary from opaque to transparent, from determinate to indeterminate within one ensemble, then the judgment of distance will be affected and the result may be a bit of mystery.*

Designed by Karl Lagerfeld. Courtesy of Fairchild Publications.

skin, the transparent portions of similar middle value of the sleeves and legs, or the darker lace of the body of the dress. Photographers often use figure-ground ambiguity to create interest and some duality in perception.

In the organizing process, there may be distinct levels of two-dimensional or three-dimensional surfaces. Grouping can occur on more than one level. Similar motifs on a two-dimensional surface can be grouped as figure-ground. When surfaces gradually curve in and out or are gathered, they become three-dimensional through use. For example, if a piece of lace is viewed before it is placed upon the body, it is seen mainly as a linear tracery in two dimensions. However, lace worn as a veil or trimming may appear as lines or as flexible shapes. It is constantly moving and may fall into soft folds on the body. The openings may reveal additional layers underneath, which are composed of skin or another fabric. Here, grouping on distinct levels does not occur with the lace motif, and instead the surface appears thicker and indeterminate.

In the apparel-body-construct, indeterminate opaque surfaces may appear thicker for a variety of reasons, due to indefinite shape, texture, or the play of light and shadow. Often the indeterminate surface appears farther away from the observer, and this factor is used by the viewer in ordering within the apparel-body-construct. Such levels may not be very insistent in the ordering process. On the other hand, a determinate surface is clearly defined and definite in its relation to the observer. It is often relatively free of three-dimensional light and shadow effects and often has sharp edges. There is little doubt as to where and how a determinate surface is positioned in space. In Figure 8.22, the determinate surfaces of the upper torso may cause them to be perceived sooner than the transparent surfaces of the underskirt in the lower portion of the body.

*Apparent Distance.* Our judgment of an object's distance is affected by our early experience in giving meaning to what we see, as in Figure 8.22. By the time we are adults, the means by which we estimate distance are quite unconscious. However, making them conscious will help in understanding the part-to-whole relation in the apparel-body-construct.

Normally our assessment of distance in the ordering process is simplified and approximated in near-far space. Within the viewer's personal space, distance is judged precisely and objects usually appear clearly positioned. The size of this personal space varies with activity and expectations. Beyond this space, we are concerned mostly with similarity and comparisons of "more than" and "less than."

The apparent spatial distance of attributes is directly related to our past experiences with identifying the spatial relations of both things and people. There are a number of attributes of shapes in space that cause these shapes to appear in certain positions as they relate to each other. From a distance surfaces appear blurred and therefore distance viewing is associated with indeterminacy. A sharp edge is experienced as more immediate and a blurred edge as farther away. A larger circle will appear closer to the viewer than a smaller one, as in Figure 8.23, if other aspects such as color and texture remain equal. This may be related to our experience with stargazing, where the larger the star, the closer it is to us in the sky.

It is important to think about what characteristics of an object make it appear to be a given distance from the viewer. As shown in the example of large and smaller circles, size is a factor in distance viewing. Several objects of the same size, shape, and color will appear to lie on the same plane. A greater difference in size creates a greater difference in apparent spatial position. If a large star is accompanied by a similar-sized star in our visual field, the viewer will organize them on similar planar levels. People group similar sizes. However, if the large star is accompanied by some stars of much smaller size, the viewer begins to see the stars as existing in unlimited space, being unable to judge how far away the stars are from each other, thus perceiving indeterminacy.

When viewing patterned surfaces, one begins to realize their potential in spatial positioning, as in Figure 8.24. Patterns can appear as all-over texture

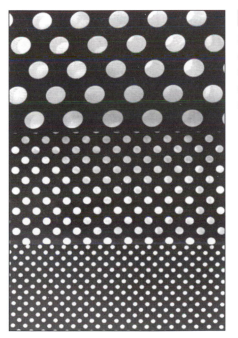

**FIGURE 8.23**

*Size is a determining factor in judging apparent distance. A large circle will often appear closer to the viewer than a smaller one, if other characteristics such as color and texture remain equal.*

when they do not appear as a definite figure-ground relationship, as in the jacket in Figure 8.24. The surfaces of jacket and trousers appear textural in effect and indistinct in figure-ground. The similarity in color, and at the same time the slight difference in size of the pattern, could influence the distance surfaces appear to be from the observer. But the gold curved embroidery motif and buttons of the jacket help to create more balance of visual weight between upper and lower areas. Do not overlook the influence of the darker hat, legs and feet, and gloves as figural cues. Patterns with repeated but more individual shapes can be viewed in a figure-ground relationship, as in Figure 8.25. If they are similar in shape, but gradate from smaller to larger in size, the shapes will group with each other and at the same time separate from the ground and direct the eye through their size gradation. Such distinct surfaces appear closer than those surfaces with indistinct figure-ground relationships.

Consider the apparent distance between the levels of the groups of figure, that is, whether the levels appear to lie close together or farther away. The grouping may appear to be quite close to, and integrated with, the ground, or it may appear to separate from the ground. When it is said that a surface has a "spotty effect," this usually means that a number of figures appear to be closed and separated and a considerable distance from the ground. This makes them appear less connected to the surface. Such a surface is not considered a good choice to wear for a photograph because it demands more attention than the person who is wearing it.

### FIGURE 8.24

*A variety of surface patterns within one ensemble can create a variety of interesting visual effects, from surface texture to figure-ground relationships. All surfaces are considered in the visual weighting of the surfaces upon the body. Here the upper and lower body balance, though two sizes of pattern are used, through figural cues that include the dark hat and gloves and the gold, curved embroidery pattern and buttons of the jacket.*

Designed by Christian Lacroix. Courtesy of Fairchild Publications.

The same figure-ground experience occurs with different sizes and shapes when the layout of the apparel-body-construct is considered. People group what is similar and separate what is different. Thus, the apparel-body-construct can be viewed as having a finite number of levels or, if there are too many different sizes and shapes, the observer may not try to order it in this way. After a certain number of levels, the observer does not continue to group; he or she simply notes the degree of indeterminacy. The surfaces in Figure 8.16 include a similar motif to that of Figure 8.23, but of different clarity of definition or determinacy. Degree of determinacy of surface is a cue in perceiving the apparel-body-construct.

Apparent distance can be applied to other visual definers, such as color. Cool colors appear to retreat and warm colors to advance. If a blue shape is placed adjacent to and surrounding a yellow one, the blue will look as if it lies behind the yellow, especially if the boundaries are blurred somewhat. This order is due to our previous associations in viewing distance, that is, blue is not only cool but is also associated with the sky or water, and yellow is associated with the stars and sun, which are usually figure in our perception. However, a middle value, low-intensity yellow can appear farther away, as in Color Plate 6 than the more intense yellow of his hair.

Refer to Table 8.2 for some generalizations that can be made concerning attributes that affect the apparent location of a visual part in space.

To apply these principles to the apparel-body-construct, one attribute listed previously will be considered—edge. Edges make a difference in the visual character of any object. What edges are possible in the entire apparel-body-construct? There are the edges within the items of apparel themselves: a shirt has pocket and collar edges; edges can derive from a surface pattern. There are edges created by the relation of the shirt perimeter to the body, as in the meeting of the neck of the body and the neckline of the shirt. Finally, there are edges in the relation of the apparel-body-construct to the immediately surrounding space, for example, the edges created by the sleeve of the shirt and the adjoining space. All of these edges are possible, but which are viewed as closer and therefore of greater priority will depend upon how distinct each appears. Distinctness of edge makes a difference in what is more immediately viewed within the apparel-body-construct. First the viewer would be more aware of the parts with greater edge definition.

The nature of the adjoining space affects what types of edges are created. White tennis shoes, for example, would have soft edges when surrounded by snow and hard edges when surrounded by black dirt. When worn with white socks, they would have a soft edge between the sock and tennis shoe, and when worn with black socks, a hard edge.

**FIGURE 8.25**

*Gradation from wider to narrower directs the eye.*

Courtesy of The Goldstein Gallery, University of Minnesota.

| | |
|---|---|
| | |

| | |
|---|---|
| Hue | A warm hue appears closer than a cool hue given similar value and intensity. |
| Value | Surfaces contrasting in value appear closer than surfaces similar in value. |
| Intensity | An intense, bright hue appears closer than one less intense. |
| Shape | A shape that appears self-contained and enclosed appears closer than one that is open and integrated with the ground. The simplest shape to see is a circle, and it usually appears to be closer than a shape with a more complex edge. |
| Line, Edge | A line or shape with a clear boundary appears closer than one that is not clearly outlined or is blurred. Opaque surfaces usually have more clearly defined lines and edges than do transparent surfaces. |
| Surface Texture | Rough or coarse textural effects appear closer than fine texture. |

The part with its many definers and modifiers must be considered within the context of the whole apparel-body-construct. Exceptions can always be found to the spatial position, or apparent distance, of a specific attribute of the apparel-body-construct when it is considered as a separate visual phenomenon and not a part of the whole.

What difference does spatial position make to visual result? Some separation is created if surfaces appear at different distances, as in Figure 8.5 in which the shirts and pants are of different values. Those contrasting in value are viewed first in a part-to-whole relationship. Grouping occurs with similar surfaces and creates a more whole-to-part effect. To attract attention to the whole apparel-body-construct, consider surfaces that appear to lie in close immediate space to the body or cover the entire body. Parts that appear in the distance can create a mysterious and ethereal effect. In comparing the examples of Korean traditional dress illustrated in Color Plates 11 and 12, the colors of the dress on the right are more related in value and to the colors of the model. However, in the example on the left, the top of the dress is much lighter and more muted than the coloring of the model and the skirt and, therefore, appears less immediate to the viewer. The dark tie provides the balance and immediacy of the contrasting values of the upper and lower torsos.

# VIEWING THE APPAREL-BODY-CONSTRUCT

If the process of organizing parts is followed routinely, awareness of visual relationships should become second nature in viewing a form. Knowing about these relationships can lead to discoveries about the visual effect of an apparel-body-construct. The steps in the organizing process discussed earlier will now be reviewed.

## Viewing Path

The direction taken while scanning the apparel-body-construct is the viewing path. If the viewer numbers the parts in order of viewing, the path can be noted. The visual path may encircle the apparel-body-construct and/or remain within one-body view (Refer to Figure 5.6 of man and child). The cues of the apparel-body-construct greatly influence the direction you take. In Figure 8.15, the viewing path could be considered within one body view, because the lines of the apparel-body-construct create interesting figure-ground relationships throughout. However, the diagonal lines pique the curiosity of the viewer as to what the other side is like.

The visual path can take a number of different directions within a one-body view. The path may be related to the vertical or horizontal axis of the body, with the dominant direction being either vertical or horizontal.

The body axis plays an important role in the scanning process, and the vertical central axis of the body often serves as the reference in viewing the apparel-body-construct. Even when a vertical line is placed slightly off-center, the resulting tension is a reference to the vertical center. The vertical reference can be indicated by an implied line. It can be composed of shapes forming a continuous line on the vertical axis through size variation, or it can be made up of color or texture gradation. Color gradation, beginning with a light value on top, progressing to medium to dark value on the bottom, can be the source of the viewing path. Thus, the viewer needs to consider broadly what could suggest direction.

Horizontal lines and shapes contrast the basic verticality of the body and are often strong viewing references to mark the viewer's direction. But the viewer needs to consider the direction of the viewing path and not the direction of the lines. For example, if a series of horizontal lines extend to the silhouette and vary from wide to narrow, their gradation may be what directs the viewer. Then the viewing path would be more vertical than horizontal. When horizontal lines are viewed as extending around the body cylinder (often accompanied by rounded surfaces), the viewing path would be horizontal. In Figure 8.25, viewing may be both vertical because of the gradation created by the narrowing silhouette and horizontal because of the bands encircling the body.

## The Entry

Where we first enter the apparel-body-construct—our first focus—is important to note. This is often the area of most contrast, either in terms of part properties or our expectations that make us take notice.

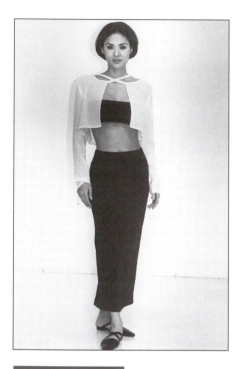

**FIGURE 8.26**

*The viewer enters
this apparel-body-
construct in the
upper torso based
upon simple and
well-defined shapes
and the white trans-
parent overwrap
with crossed straps.*

Designed by Sylvia Heisel.
Courtesy of Fairchild Publications.

The observer's visual scan may be concentrated within one part that has viewing priority. Certain parts or part properties may take priority in viewing an apparel-body-construct, and this priority can influence the way the apparel-body-construct is perceived. When part-to-whole viewing occurs, the cause may be clear edge definition of simple shapes or a contrast of surface that overrides the effect of the silhouette. In Figure 8.26, the entry is in the upper torso and is based upon well-defined but simple shapes. The relationship between the white transparent overwrap with the focus on the crossed straps is echoed later in the shoes, the rounded shapes of the hair, the neckline, and hip curves and the contrast of the horizontal lines of the tube top, overwrap, and long skirt. All follow through from the entry.

The apparel-body-construct may be viewed as a whole first because of the interdependence of the parts or because of the distinctness of the silhouette. A closed silhouette can become a viewing priority. The degree of correspondence between the frame of the apparel-body-construct and its details or parts can make a difference in whether a part stands out in perception. A repeated shape that covers a large area can refer the viewer to the whole. Then the viewer does not attend to each shape as a separate part in a distinct figure-ground relationship.

## Viewing Tempo

The rate at which the viewer takes in the apparel-body-construct is the **viewing tempo**. This term refers to the amount and type of activity taking place within an apparel-body-construct and the resulting effect on the viewer. The pace can be immediate and abrupt or lingering.

An apparel-body-construct that is simple and bold, viewed as a whole first, with a hard-edged determinate surface and a centering, as in Figure 8.14, is likely to have an immediacy in viewing and its visual path clearly marked. The viewer takes in such an apparel-body-construct quickly. On the other hand, an apparel-body-construct that has several contrasting and more independent parts is viewed at a slower pace than the first example. Even though such an apparel-body-construct is ordered, there is more complexity because of the viewing of parts. The viewer gets caught up in a process of spotting the similarities and contrasts within the whole. In Figure 8.6, the dark and light value contrast and numerous and discrete parts involve the viewer in parts, the geometric patterns of the tie and skirt, and the contrast of the shirt and pocket handkerchief with the dark jacket and hair. Such an example is successive in organization, based upon value contrast and differences in dominant patterns and sizes of areas.

An apparel-body-construct with many complex surfaces, such as in Color Plate 10, is often viewed as a whole first, but then taken in at a more lingering pace, as shapes and color are compared one with another. Even though parts in a figure-ground relationship are not as distinct, the apparel-body-construct is richly varied and takes time to perceive and comprehend.

## The Function of the Part

Parts function differently. The viewer organizes the form in the process of comparing the similarities and differences in parts and then the part with the whole. When part relationships compete in an apparel-body-construct, the clearest, most stable relations are the ones that will prevail. The viewer is initially attracted to those parts that offer the most contrast within the apparel-body-construct. The organizing process is also controlled by the similarities and differences among parts and their relation to the whole. Therefore, the viewer is directed from one part to another through relationships.

*Viewing Priority.* While you experience the wholeness of visual forms based upon similarities within them, what you first notice is a difference, a break from similarity. This difference can originate from the form itself or from the associations presented.

Parts viewed as separated are unlike their immediately adjacent surround, but the degree of separation varies. Parts can be different in any one or several of the visual definers or modifiers. A part that controls viewing is often essential to the visual order and meaning of the apparel-body-construct. Priority can be achieved by placement on the body, by contrast in size, or by intensity of color. A part may look large because it is next to a small part. This contrast, which includes contrast of many features, such as horizontal with vertical and light with dark, sharpens the perception of both elements.

To *contrast* means to stand against. In comparing dissimilar parts, the viewer receives a clearer message of both parts if the dissimilarity is distinct. Rough next to smooth sharpens the meaning of both surfaces. Regular shapes next to irregular shapes intensify the difference. All three of the dimensions of color—hue, value, and intensity—offer potential for visual contrast. A light value next to a dark value will create a distinct visual separation. Bright next to dull, cold against warm produces contrast in spatial position.

Contrast sets up counteraction in perception, a break in linkages. The viewer attempts to give the clearest meaning to what is seen. Parts that are clearly in contrast are given viewing priority. If you desire to call attention to a smooth skin surface, place a rough surface next to it. If you desire to call attention to a body part, put a part that is clearly different in shape and size next to it. By heightening the differences in visual parts, contrast can create a counterpoint.

As the viewer continues to become aware of the visual part, its function in the whole becomes more clear.

*Focus.* We have discussed the fact that visual parts can function within the whole as a source of focus. To serve in this way, the part must be different in character from what surrounds it. The relation is one of contrast. In Figure 8.18a, pattern and value contrast make a visual priority of the upper body area, but the similarity in overall value of the hair, turtleneck, and sweater and contrast with the scarf and trousers is also important to the balance overall.

Any part of the apparel-body-construct can serve as a source of focus, but certain factors tend to be influential. For example, the strength of the part influences how it is viewed—as a primary or secondary source of focus. Parts may be grouped within a large area of the body and may be separated from the remainder of the apparel-body-construct. In Figure 8.15, the diagonal pattern in the upper torso groups and also separates from the coat, leggings, and edges of the silhouette. A part that is small but very isolated and different from its surround is a likely source of focus. An example is the crisscrossing effect of the straps in Figure 8.26.

The widest areas of the body are an important horizontal reference. One horizontal reference of the body is the shoulders. This area becomes a focus when the head, with closely shaped hair, contrasts with shoulder width or when a large shape on the head is similar to the width of the shoulders. Shoulder pads will further emphasize this horizontal shoulderline. Another natural horizontal reference is the hip area when the hands or wrists hanging down continue the hipline horizontally at crotch level. Clothing can emphasize such a horizontal reference or diminish it.

*Centering.* Viewing the apparel-body-construct as having a convergent center creates a type of focus and reference. This can be a visual axis created by two lines crossing strategically on the body or a group of lines radiating out from a center in a rhythmic effect. These lines may be actual or implied. Centering can occur at a balance point, located because of the body lines and shapes and how they relate to the clothing lines and shapes. The shape of the silhouette helps to determine this centering at the hip, and the configuration of visual parts is also a determining factor.

Centering can occur because of lines radiating from a central point. The shapes of lapels can appear to converge as they angle into the first buttonhole. Triangular or wedge-shaped folds placed on the body often create a center by converging to an apex. If they do not quite converge, the lines may still be viewed as doing so. In Figure 8.16, the lines of the folds in the skirt appear to converge at the hip and drape to the hem in folds.

Centering can describe the visual axis created by the interaction of parts within the apparel-body-construct. Placement of a group of parts, a line of buttons, or a fold of the fabric close to the central vertical axis of the body attracts the viewer's eye to the center of the body. A vest with contrasting blouse, but which is similar to the value of the pants, can create a centering effect on the body. In Figure 8.27, the viewer can group the centered lines created by the collar, the triangle of center front buttons, and the shape at center front of the jacket hemline.

## Integration

A visual part that functions as a source of integration does so because of its similarity to other parts. This creates coherence within the context of the apparel-body-construct. The particular visual part may not attract attention to itself but functions to group with another part or direct attention within the apparel-body-construct. During the 1950s in the United States, women often wore matching hat, shoes, a purse or an umbrella, and gloves to create visual similarities between the body extremities. This practice was distinctive enough visually to continue to be associated with that time period.

Integration and coherence result from visual parts that are viewed interdependently. Similarity promotes integration. If a number of similar shapes are viewed throughout the body, the apparel-body-construct will appear integrated because the viewer will be directed to the whole. If some of those shapes were different in color, this would direct the viewer to group similar colors. A similar shiny texture of black, patent-leather shoes may be repeated in a satin stripe defining the trouser seam of a tuxedo. Reflection from each surface integrates the whole because the viewer compares the similarity of shine. Three types of part integration are: *blending, gradation,* and *transitional.*

**FIGURE 8.27**

*Centering is when a group of parts are placed at the body's vertical axis to attract the viewer. The deeply rounded collar overlaps and is focused with an inverted triangle of buttons of the same value as the skirt. The hemline of the jacket forms another triangle, and yet another is created by the shaping of the jacket silhouette. The light-value stockings call attention to the cylindrical nature of the leg and focus the eye on the shadowing between the legs. Shadowing also enhances the pocket flaps on the jacket.*

Designed by Bill Blass. Courtesy of Fairchild Publications.

*Attention is directed to the whole with the gradation of colors from upper torso to hemline, as well as the folds graduating from a convergence at the breast to become wider as they cascade to the hem.*

Designed by Bill Blass. Courtesy of Fairchild Publications.

*Blending.* Integration results from parts that blend, that is, when one part is viewed as not more dominant than another. Soft edges help to blend visual parts and can result from similarity in any one of the definers. For example, two visual parts that are similar in value or texture may not attract attention to themselves as much as to the whole form, especially if the whole form is closed from the surround. Yet the intricacy of viewing such a subtle relation is important to the visual result. In Figure 8.28, the gradation of color in the upper and lower torso, in conjunction with the light and shadow effect in the skirt folds, adds intricacy but still directs attention to the whole.

*Gradation.* Gradation was defined as a measured difference in a part-to-part relation. Gradation can be a source of integration by directing the eye either within the one-body view or around the body. Examples can occur using many visual definers and modifiers—light to medium to dark values, hard to soft edges, small to large shapes, rough to smooth textures. The visual measure varies in graded intervals from one part to the next; the parts vary by degree. When this happens, the eye is directed by the difference between the parts and the properties of the parts from one adjacent part to another. In Figure 8.27, red hair, light-value gray jacket and dark skirt, gloves, and shoes set a vertical direction, though there are the contrasting horizontal hemlines of the jacket and skirt.

*Transitional.* A transitional part functions as an interval between two otherwise contrasting parts. It can become transitional by softening their contrast with a repetition of one of each of their attributes. For example, black and white placed side by side are viewed as separate. However, a necklace of small areas of both black and white can serve as a transition between the two parts. In Figure 8.14, the white buttons function to integrate the contrast of the darker suit with the white blouse.

## Controlling Relationships

The viewer's task in understanding organization is to determine what is causing a part to group and/or separate and, furthermore, what controls the relationship between parts. This involves observing their degree of similarity.

In any one apparel-body-construct there can be a number of visual parts with varying degrees of separation. A visual part that is viewed as very independent, very much separated within the apparel-body-construct, is likely to be functioning as a point of contrast and focus. A substantial degree of separation of the part is critical in establishing its priority.

A part may be separate enough to create focus but still be similar enough to another part to direct the viewer in the organizing process. A visual part that is similar in one visual definer, such as value, can still direct the viewer to its similarity with the next visual part. The boy in Color Plate 9, with the contrasting hues but similar values of the pants and shirt, directs the eye. The small area occupied by the tie contrasts in value and becomes the focus.

A visual part that is viewed as interdependent with its surround is often being grouped in perception with other parts and functions in an integrating sense. Parts are often related in several or even many different ways within the whole. As has been shown, an observer may first connect a visual part with one that is similar in color and then with another visual part that is similar in shape. The degree of similarity will influence the viewer's organizing process. To become aware of the possible ways a part will group takes time, effort, and a motivating curiosity.

## Cause of Visual Effect

What causes the viewer to organize the apparel-body-construct? The activity of organizing may result from one visual part that has priority or from a property, such as a dominant surface or edge. In viewing the whole apparel-body-construct, you may first concentrate on the shape of a large part but then focus on some unexpected surface treatment.

As one visual part is compared with another, the viewer can read the apparel-body-construct primarily as a two-dimensional surface with the variation of the parts occurring on one level or several levels in the space between the apparel-body-construct and the viewer. The viewer can take in the entire apparel-body-construct or remain in one area (whole-to-part viewing or part-to-whole viewing).

An examination of similarities and differences in visual parts within the whole helps the viewer understand the cause of the visual effect. You should continue the analysis, comparing uses of color, shape, and texture and their interaction. A viewer can be directed by a definer or a modifier. It can be the difference in a part, perceived at entry, that causes the viewer to compare the part with another. A viewer can be directed by a visual part or parts, including body parts.

At first, it is often not obvious what is directing the viewer. For example, the influence of variations in light and shadow could be missed. A surface that is structured with a figure-ground contrast may be used in the apparel-body-construct. If the shapes are redundant, the viewing path may be influenced by the shapes as figure, i.e., collar, buttons, pockets, and cuffs, as in Figure 8.27. Sometimes the visual part is similar to another part in all respects except one (e.g., location within silhouette) and it takes some thought to analyze exactly what is directing the viewer.

| *Application Exercise 8.10* | Examine the apparel-body-constructs in Figures 8.1 and 8.2 and consider the viewing order. Number the areas of focus, and then analyze why you viewed each the way you did. What differences did you note in the viewing order of Figure 8.1 as compared to Figure 8.2? |
|---|---|

The time it takes for a visual part to come into the viewer's awareness depends on the **viewing order**. By numbering the areas of focus as they are viewed, you have a good indication of visual priorities.

At first the apparel-body-construct may appear quite simple. Upon further examination the subtleties—those parts that integrate with other parts—become evident. One part can connect in a number of ways with other parts, and the viewer takes in these connecting links in the order in which they attract attention. The viewer may perceive several or many groupings in a jacket and shirt considered with the body coloring. For example, an apparel-body-construct may be viewed first in terms of complements of red and green, with dark red hair complementing a light green shirt and pocket handkerchief. Another grouping may be the navy blue jacket with a contrasting row of brass buttons at center front and with similar buttons on pocket flaps. Still another grouping might be the similarity in the value of red hair and jacket.

To perceive subtleties, the viewer needs to be aware of the entirety. An apparel-body-construct involving a middle-value gray suit and worn with an off-white blouse or shirt can be used to demonstrate this principle. The wearer in this case has light-value skin and gray hair. The head is grouped first with the blouse, and then the similarity of gray hair and suit is noted. The rest of the body is skimmed and the contrasting silhouette is noted. However, the viewer does not simply dismiss the image, but in continuing the examination notices the similarity in the shapes of the pockets and the shape of the sleeves and lapels. Thus, the viewing order in an apparel-body-construct is not only what first attracts a viewer's attention, but also what sustains it.

## Summary

• The process by which the apparel-body-construct is organized is an interplay between the viewer and the form. The **visual effect** is the clothing form's cumulative effect on the viewer. The apparel-body-construct is defined by particular lines, shapes, colors, and textures—the visual definers. Some forms are easier to view as wholes; in others, the component parts are the starting point.

• **Simultaneous, successive,** and **separated** viewing are three major ways of perceiving the clothing form.

• Visual perception, important in the organizing process, involves both scanning and focusing. Viewing involves **grouping** and **separating** of visual parts.

• Gestalt psychologists established the following principles of organization: **similarity, closure, proximity,** and **continuation.**

• A visual part is affected by what surrounds it. **Part modifiers** alter a part's interaction within the apparel-body-construct. Such modifiers are: number, pattern, size, proportion, direction, visual weight, including symmetrical and asymmetrical balance, spatial position, and distance, including the effects of hue, value, intensity, shape, line, edge, and surface texture.

• In viewing the apparel-body-construct, important concepts are: viewing path, the entry, viewing tempo, the function of the part, viewing priority, contrast, focus, and integration, controlling relationships, and cause of visual effect.

## Key Terms and Concepts

asymmetrical balance
closure
continuation
direction
figure-ground ambiguity
gradation
grouping
number threshold
part modifier
pattern
proportion
proximity

rhythm
separated viewing
separating
similarity
simultaneous viewing
successive viewing
symmetrical balance
viewing order
viewing tempo
visual effect
visual parts
visual perception

## References and Suggested Readings

Arnheim, R. *Art and Visual Perception*. Berkeley: University of California Press, 1974.

Barratt, K. *Logic and Design*. Westview, NJ: Eastview Editions, 1980.

Berlyne, D. *Conflict, Arousal and Curiosity*. New York: John Wiley, 1960.

Bloomer, C. *Principles of Visual Perception*. New York: Van Nostrand Reinhold, 1980.

Collier, G. *Form, Space and Vision*. Englewood Cliffs, NJ: Prentice-Hall, 1980.

Dondis, D. *A Primer of Visual Literacy*. Cambridge, MA: Massachusetts Institute of Technology Press, 1973.

Eisner, E. *Educating Artistic Vision*. New York: Macmillan, 1972.

Ellis, W. *A Sourcebook of Gestalt Psychology*. New York: The Humanities Press, 1955.

Forgus, R. *Perception*. New York: McGraw-Hill, 1966.

Gibson, J. *The Senses Considered as Perceptual Systems*. Boston: Houghton Mifflin, 1966.

Gombrich, E. *The Sense of Order*. Ithaca, NY: Cornell University Press, 1979.

Kepes, G. *Language of Vision*. Chicago: Paul Theobald and Co., 1969.

Kubler, G. *The Shape of Time*. London: Yale University Press, 1962.

Martin, F. *Sculpture and Enlivened Space*. Lexington, KY: The University Press of Kentucky, 1981.

McKim, R. *Thinking Visually*. Belmont, CA: Wadsworth, 1980.

Meyers, J. *The Language of Visual Art: Perception as a Basis for Design*. Chicago: Holt, Rinehart and Winston, 1989.

Munro, T. *Toward Science in Aesthetics*. New York: The Liberal Arts Press, 1956.

Peckham, M. *Man's Rage for Chaos*. New York: Schocken Books, 1965.

Scott, R. *Design Fundamentals*. New York: McGraw-Hill, 1951.

Thiel, P. *Visual Awareness and Design*. Seattle: University of Washington Press, 1981.

Wertheimer, M. "Gestalt Theory." *Social Research,* vol. II, 1944, 78–99.

Zeisel, J. *Inquiry by Design*. Belmont, CA: Wadsworth, 1981.

*Chapter Nine*

# INTERPRETING THE APPAREL-BODY-CONSTRUCT

*After you have read this chapter, you will be able to understand:*

• How the apparel-body-construct is interpreted—to grasp the role played by the form with its many associations of color, texture, and shape; the context, including the time, culture, and the specific locale, season, and event; and the viewer, with his or her varying associations arising from past and present experiences.

• How shared meaning is communicated and the importance of repetition.

• The significance of codes, consisting of conventions and the three types of signs—icons, indexes, and symbols.

• The source and level of meaning within the apparel-body-construct— recognition, association, and conception.

• The concepts of attraction and attention as related to communication.

• The aesthetic codes of the apparel-body-construct and how its meanings change over time; how "looks" can recycle and again be part of the fashionable image.

• How varying expressive effects, such as calmness, excitement, etc., can be conveyed by shape, line, color, texture, and viewing priority.

• How the viewer's reaction is important to how the apparel-body-construct is perceived and affected by expectancy and surprise, individual and shared meaning, the effect of tradition, and the factors of geographic locale and season.

TO INTERPRET MEANS TO CONSIDER HOW WE PERCEIVE and give meaning to a particular apparel-body-construct. The form, the context, and the viewer all contribute to the interpretation. The form is the source of many associations: the particular color, texture, and shape and the method of organization can all result in distinctive visual effects. The context, including the time, the culture, and specifics of locale, season, and event can influence how people perceive and give meaning to the apparel-body-construct. In turn, the viewer can interpret the form through associations that come from past and present experiences. This chapter will concentrate on how the apparel-body-construct is interpreted.

The apparel professional is aware of what and how the viewer is attracted. Clothing design is very much tied into what attracts a particular audience and often this means what is new or fashionable. From a couture designer to the designer of mass-produced clothing—all deal with varying degrees of the expected and unexpected, the familiar and unfamiliar. They rely on knowledge of their audience. A marketer can often sell products based on how they are displayed, that is, a very basic T-shirt combined with other clothing in an unusual way to provide a degree of the unexpected. In marketing, it is first necessary to attract the viewer's attention.

What is promoted is dependent upon the characteristics of the particular market segment. Age, for example, may make a difference in what is promoted. Bright colors and simple shapes, as in Figure 9.1, attract the attention and interest of some very young viewers. However, bright colors and attractive but simple shapes also communicate a childlike message to an adult who may share such preferences in dressing children. The audience for such a product increases because the child who wears it and the adult who ultimately purchases it are both attracted to the cheerful yet functional message. What a win-win situation!

People interpret based on their perceptions and the many associations they must make to relate a particular apparel-body-construct to self and situation. Associations can range from those that are unique to the viewer, to those that are shared. An apparel professional, such as a designer, buyer, or store manager, is an educated viewer who can interpret and therefore predict how a specific apparel-body-construct will communicate a shared message. The focus of the professional may differ, and interpretation will depend upon this focus. For example, a designer may focus upon an inspired, new image from the play of color, light, and shadow on the surfaces or how to create clothing that solves a problem in a different way. The buyer, on the other hand, may

**FIGURE 9.1**

*Children enjoy being dressed for play in bright, attractive, and simple clothing, and this communicates a message to the adult who makes the purchase.*

Courtesy of Target Stores.

be focusing upon how many units to buy based upon how customers will receive the message and be inspired to purchase. The store manager may consider how this apparel-body-construct relates to others in the store and therefore how best to display it.

# SHARED MEANING = COMMUNICATION

Though people's responses to any given apparel-body-construct are personal, the research on perception and communication indicates that human beings react in much the same way to many types of objects. The more people share with other human beings, the more experiences they will have in common. For example, people who are similar in age, location, profession, and religion are presumed to share a common bond of interests, motivations, and preferences. Such common bonds create a basis for similarity in response. In a market segment for apparel products, those who have common interests tend to group together and respond similarly. This shared meaning is the basis for communication to take place. The fields of marketing and advertising are especially based upon such common bonds.

To communicate shared meaning, we must rely on repetition to establish communication with an audience, and the wider the audience, the greater the need for repeatable and repetitious use of definers, modifiers, organization of the apparel-body-construct, and so forth. This sets up a base of the familiar and expected within which to operate. Repetitive means recognizable—not boring—consistency. Think of how many things you can name that, due to repetition, communicate a visual image to you? For example, a beret, a tweed blazer, a letter sweater, black stockings, or penny loafers may be familiar clothing products. How many of these together create a visual image that you could share with others? Repetition plays a role in creating an ensemble, those items of dress that you see together that form familiar associations, such as a sweatshirt with blue denim jeans and canvas shoes or satins, laces, and the smell of cologne. Associations can relate to ways to organize the body for an event such as a summer picnic, a hike up a mountain, or skiing down a mountain on a cold winter day. All of these have a consistency that helps in sharing a message and creating communication with others.

In his writing about communication, Fiske (1990) discusses a number of models of communication. These models are based on the premise that the viewer/creator communicates in part because of cultural influences and that cultures have different underlying codes. He defines a **code** as a system of meaning common to the members of a culture. A code provides a means of organizing and understanding data, but it also functions as a communication device. All codes convey meaning and depend upon common bonds among viewers.

A code then, is a collection of rules or guidelines. It is a communication system in which definite meanings are assigned that may be used for such purposes as brevity or secrecy. A convention is defined as accepted rules or guidelines established by general consent or custom. A code consists of both **conventions** and **signs**. *Conventions* are the guidelines or rules we use to interpret and evaluate the apparel-body-construct. Conventions rely on conformity and similarity of experience, and on redundancy or repetition, which helps make decoding and interpretation possible. Conventions determine how and in what contexts signs are used and how they form messages. A *sign* is defined as a unit, component, or object that refers to, represents, or stands for something other than itself (Berger, 1992). Conventions determine how and in what manner signs will be used and how they will combine to form more complex messages.

Signs are of three types: **icon, index,** and **symbol.**

- An *icon* is a sign that directly resembles what it stands for—a photograph looks like a person.

- An *index* is a sign that can be determined because it is inferred by causal connection—smoke is present because of fire.

- A *symbol* is a sign that must be learned—a word such as car stands for a category of object.

The connection of any one of the types of sign with an object is based on convention within the culture of use. It can go beyond that culture but often becomes misinterpreted if cultural context is not considered.

Let us consider examples of dress using these three signs. Some clothing items may serve as **icons**—a T-shirt with a picture of the person wearing it printed on it. Doll clothes are icons of the clothing worn during the historical period to which the doll belongs. Doll clothes are an icon because they resemble those worn by people, oftentimes children. Much of the code of dressing is unstated and falls into the sign type of **index**, that is, we can determine by inference—a watch associated with a time-conscious culture, gray hair with a mature person, or manicured and painted fingernails with restrictions of certain types of activity. A few clothing types have definite meanings by themselves, that is, they involve a stated agreement among users. When they do, they are often of the sign type that is termed **symbol**—a badge, a club pin, or a uniform—that all refer to, or stand for, something that we must learn. For a person "in the know," a pin worn on the lapel may be for perfect attendance at school or represent membership in Rotary, a service organization. To an outsider such a symbol may mean nothing if that person has no knowledge of its meaning.

Categories of clothing types, for example, tie, shirt, jacket, stockings, are units from which people select each day, that on their own do not necessarily communicate a message. However, when an individual combines clothing types, he or she makes a statement that conveys meaning about himself or herself as the wearer of the clothes. In terms of communication, what we choose to wear each day is a process of encoding a message—by our clothing selections we exhibit our perception of relationships with people we expect to meet and signify our status or role within the social situations we will encounter. A clothing ensemble often works by index because you can infer meaning from the combination, as an indicator of the wearer's mood, social position, and respect or lack of respect for social conventions. The male business executive who is also a "deadhead" (a fan of the Grateful Dead music group) may wear an expensive suit while keeping his hair longer than expected, an earring in his ear, and wearing a tie designed by Jerry Garcia. By combining formal and casual aspects in his dress, he is making a statement to the viewer about himself, one that combines codes as it communicates information about his lifestyle as well as his music preferences. One object may be composed of more than one type of sign. Blue jeans made of sturdy, blue-denim fabric and copper rivets resemble what they stand for: ruggedness. In this respect they are an icon, because blue jeans are physically sturdy, durable, and look rugged. Wearing jeans is also an index because they infer the Wild West and casual living. In the United States blue jeans also may have associations with freedom, tradition, and self-sufficiency, as well as democracy and social consensus (Fiske, 1989). In this respect they are a symbol because the connection is based on agreement or convention. Another example of products that involve a combination of signs is in brand names or designer clothing. For the person who recognizes the clothing as being a designer label—Ralph Lauren or Dolce & Gabbana—there is communication at a different level than for the observer who does not go beyond seeing the directly perceptible aspects of fabric, tailoring details, color, and so forth. Some designers make sure the viewer recognizes the clothing is his or hers by the signature on some noticeable part of the apparel-body-construct, as in the initials "D&G" on the tie in Figure 9.2. This tie can be a sign in three ways. It is an *icon* because the letters D and G resemble those used in the labels inside the clothing and in advertising for Dolce and Gabbana. For those who know the label, then the "D&G" on the tie is an index to the wearer's ability to purchase the designer tie and that it is a high fashion tie. The "D&G" is a symbol of the designer's style and kind of clothing, but only to those who recognize the sign's reference and are "in the know." In order for the tie to act as an index or a symbol, it must be recognized by the viewer as something other than a well-made garment.

Dress has both a communicative and noncommunicative aspect. The noncommunicative aspect has to do with its function, such as how it performs as protection. Most cultural artifacts have such a dual function, that is, a physical or technological one, as well as a design or communicative one. Some products incorporate both aspects. The seam-

**FIGURE 9.2**

*A message for those "in the know" is communicated with the small initials "D & G" on the tie advertising designers Dolce & Gabbana.*

Courtesy of Fairchild Publications.

lines on the back of women's stockings used to be a necessary part of production technology, but today they are also a design and communication cue. No longer necessary for production, they now serve as a cue from past decades, when the seam was a necessary part of production. Today the cue may provoke nostalgia in one viewer who remembers wearing them, or a certain sexiness because they are something different that causes another viewer to be newly attracted to the leg.

The objective of material culture studies is to discover how meaning is generated and conveyed by objects or artifacts. Berger (1992) defines material culture simply as objects or artifacts made by human effort. He believes we can study such objects that surround us because they are not simply functional; they also serve as a mirror reflecting of our image. The apparel-body-construct as material culture includes both the incorporation of articles of apparel designed and produced by humans and the wearer who designs his or her body through an ensemble of articles of dress, reflecting a desired image sought by the wearer.

Objects communicate, providing us with information and insights. When people interpret objects, they evaluate them according to various codes, connect them to values and belief systems, and relate them to the state of economical and political systems of the society creating them (Berger, 1992). Establishing a thorough description of what is considered to be fashionable clothing, the "look" or "looks" of the year acceptable to the majority, is often difficult enough due to the all-encompassing nature of the task and the variations that arise because of location, that is, culture, region, city, school. To further consider how such "looks" relate to our value system is even more complex because people are often imbedded in such a system unconsciously. Such an exercise is highly rewarding, and if you trace the relationship of the object of clothing to the various systems of values—for example, economic, political, and social—you will rapidly become very curious and wish to continue your exploration of this fascinating subject. The first time you trace the relationship will be the hardest.

Aesthetic codes, for example, those we use to respond to the apparel-body-construct, are sometimes hard to understand because they are defined loosely, are not explicit, or are not defined at all. Aesthetic codes that become conventions acquire agreement amongst their users from shared cultural experience, but not from explicit discussion. The more conventional and redundant such codes are, the more they are likely to relate to the majority of society. Such a code would be based on highly predictable messages and would depend on a background of common assumptions, shared interests, experiences, and expectations. However, an aesthetic code is also often considered in terms of a more changing, fluid, and impersonal form of communication. The development of a code through abstractions and generalities creates more dependence upon education and formal training.

Aesthetic codes are often complex, inviting, and allow a negotiation of meaning. An apparel-body-construct can either follow or break with conventions. The more popular a code is with a wide audience, the more pronounced the patterns of repetition and redundancy that are so critical to the satisfaction of many people. Repeatable does not necessarily mean static, because the apparel-body-construct often breaks with existing conventions and establishes its own convention that must then be learned and accepted. Once learned and accepted, the apparel-body-construct can become accessible to a wider audience.

Let us examine treatment of the female leg throughout the twentieth century and its effect on the entire apparel-body-construct. At the turn of the century, women wore cotton, wool, and silk stockings held up with garters, a belt, or a foundation garment. Stockings were usually an opaque black or white and were worn under long skirts and dresses to coordinate or blend with the remainder of the female ensemble. As such, they were not meant to attract attention to the legs. Then nude stockings were introduced, first of rayon and then nylon, and they were accompanied by a greater exposure of the leg and more attention to the lower extremities in ways of wearing them. At first, only a few women wore them, but gradually they became more widely accepted. In the decade of the 1960s, pantyhose helped allow for the shortening of the lengths of the hemline to the miniskirt. Today the female leg can be the center of attention because of the option of wearing stockings or tights that are brightly colored, highly patterned, or textured with metallic threads. They may be worn to create a line below the hem of the skirt or create no lines and the smoothing over of the area between the waist and toes. With each introduction of variations, the effect is at first skepticism but eventually wide acceptance. Each variation introduces a change in the influence of the leg and the viewing of the apparel-body-construct.

Designers who care about communicating by necessity build repeatable patterns into their work. This is a way to achieve a consistency of look so that shoppers will recognize their products as distinctive from that of other designers. The retailer will be successful in building an audience if the importance of communication is understood. An image can be built in much the same way as the designer creates a series of identifiable garments or accessories. The only difference is in the means available for meeting the needs of clientele.

## Sources of Meaning Within the Apparel-Body-Construct

People's initial responses to the apparel-body-construct are often based on their emotions and the emotional attachments they bring from past experiences. One responds to an apparel-body-construct based on one's level of emotional attachment, that is, the degree to which what one sees is favored, familiar, loved, or hated. The emotional reaction to a particular apparel-body-construct often influences how much you will attend to what is shared. The response will be based on past experiences, such as, cultural origins, parents, friends, and likes and dislikes. Initially people may respond based on emotions, but to understand meaning also involves reflection.

There are a number of sources and levels of meaning possible within the apparel-body-construct—recognition, association, conception. When a shape within an apparel-body-construct is identified as figure separated from ground, the figure is given meaning. This is meaning in its most basic sense—perceptual recognition. **Recognition** involves separating figure from our visual field for attention and then identification of colors, shapes, and textures. Recognition includes naming, and how observers name is related to how we give meaning. Recognition is the first step in the process of giving meaning to the apparel-body-construct.

**Associations** are those ties or relationships you make to what you see. Associations occur after recognition and can include simple associations within the form, such as blue circles with red circles or vertical clothing lines with the body line. At another level, people may associate categories of clothing with contextual matters, including where they are worn or with what they are worn, (for example, hat and head, shirt and tie), or this is fashionable for spring and that for fall. If such associations are familiar and expected, people are likely to feel comfortable and at ease in making them. These associations range from very simple to complex ones.

An important association we often make in the apparel-body-construct is to the person wearing the clothing. This is why fashion models become celebrities. If a person we know is an integral part of an apparel-body-construct, people may never go beyond a recognition of that person to an awareness of the entire apparel-body-construct. People respond intensely to living things and to people they know and approve or disapprove of, either directly or indirectly. Circumstances can also change one's attention greatly, particularly if you are searching for a specific person or object. A father searching in a crowded railroad station for a daughter he expects to meet soon is focused upon recognition cues such as red hair or a certain height or walk. The process of association is revealing of the emotional response—surprise, approval, or resentment—and the associations may be highly complex. That same father may seldom notice what his daughter wears unless he objects to the connotation or message of her ensemble. If what he sees contradicts his image of his daughter, he may suddenly become very aware of it! If the father thinks of his daughter as a child, but suddenly realizes she is mature and attractive to her friends, he may take more notice of her dress than he did previously.

Even if some components that people often associate with each other are not actually present, they may still connect them. At a complex level of association, one may associate a clothing object with a type of person who wears it, such as brand-name tennis shoes with younger males and loafers with older males. Then just seeing a certain brand of tennis shoe may cause the association in one's mind. Something may cause people to change their minds or they may find ways to discriminate in a more complex way, for example, white tennis shoes with young males and black ones with older males. Such associations are spontaneous and are often not a conscious act, especially if they are based upon associations that meet people's expectations.

**Conception** is an idea that occurs primarily in the mind. We have already discussed the concept of signs. Symbols can be used to create ideas with minimal detail and have been used for an entire apparel-body-construct or its parts. Symbols are highly dependent upon cultural context for interpretation. For example, a certain color or combination of colors may stand for a holiday or a season. Why in America do clothing colors with such names as forest green, burgundy, rust, and gold appear in stores in August and September? Such colors for clothing are not only associational, but they may also symbolize autumn and the ending of summer, or even the impending winter. Depending upon one's emotional level on seeing the colors of fall, one viewer may feel joy while another feels sadness.

Conceptions may occur from memory of the past and meanings may get wrapped up in terminology that relies upon that past. Referring to a woman we believe to be a bit rigid in her thinking as "straight laced" is a historic reference to how tightly a woman laced her corset, which caused her to move in a rigid, controlled manner. Meanings may change based on current interpretations. If a person has lost the familiar meaning associated with corseting, such terminology may take on a life of its own or become meaningless.

Consider a past decade or historic era with which you are familiar. Now think about what clothing or persons from that period could be symbols of the time. For example, what about the 1970s could be recalled as symbols—psychedelic colors, bellbottom trousers, polyester pantsuits, large hoop earrings? Are some examples better than others? What makes one example better as a symbol than another?

*Application Exercise 9.1*

## Attracting and Attending

Attraction and attention are two concepts that link in communication. For something to have meaning, first we must be attracted to it. **Attraction** is tied to psychological behavior, that is, it is a fact of what happens in the mind—how much the viewer is drawn to what he or she sees. People must be attracted before they can attend. **Attending** is the act of giving attention, noticing the details of what one sees. How much people are attracted and then attend to an object depends upon how much importance they attach to it, and that importance is tied to its meaning. People are drawn irresistibly to make meaning from their visual field—from their emotions, associations, and past experiences.

From the standpoint of the marketer or advertiser, it is efficient and effective to consider attracting a viewer's attention through meaning of the apparel-body-construct. Since emotions are strongly attached to what we see and are elicited instantaneously, they are a primary means for attracting the viewer. However, to capture the viewer's sustained attention, whatever is presented in an apparel-body-construct must be consistent with the message that was first conveyed which, due to its spontaneity, may be on a superficial or even subconscious level.

We must also consider how much we are attracted by what follows in further attention to details. A detail may attract and draw the viewer's eye in, and then the viewer pays attention to the entire apparel-body-construct. All of the physical characteristics, such as color, texture, and size, need to be considered in this process—ordinarily larger size is perceived as closer while smaller looks farther away; warm colors are perceived before cool; rough surface textures before smooth. All of these aspects, which have been discussed in previous chapters, can be applied to the idea of visual attraction and attention. For example, the vests in Figure 9.3 are identical in shape and size in terms of layout, but the colors are different and the surface motifs send different messages. In Figure 9.3d, the motif portrays an icon of an actual cowboy on a bucking bronco, whereas Figure 9.3b contains a motif, perhaps reminiscent of the Old West, but more subtle in association, especially if it was not displayed among the other vests or would not be worn within the context of an ensemble reminiscent of the Old West. What do Figure 9.3a and c portray? The viewer may have to infer associations to receive the same message of the Old West. What other differences would you consider important among the vests?

Holding the viewer's attention often requires the introduction of a new association or a new idea. Associations that have become tired clichés do not attract the viewer's attention. However, too much change that disrupts our customary way of perceiving the world is threatening to many viewers. Change often attracts if it is experienced in a familiar context. In Figure 9.2, the three-piece suit, white shirt, and dark tie are all familiar, but the signature tie is the detail that attracts attention. Such a change in a small detail can attract attention, especially one that is inconsistent with past experiences and expectations.

Associations the viewer makes with the form of the apparel-body-construct are the key to how change is accepted. New ideas often are introduced detail

**FIGURE 9.3A, B, C & D**

*Though identical in overall shape, these vests portray somewhat different messages. Taken together they infer an association with the Old West, but what about each taken alone? Does each portray the Old West equally well?*

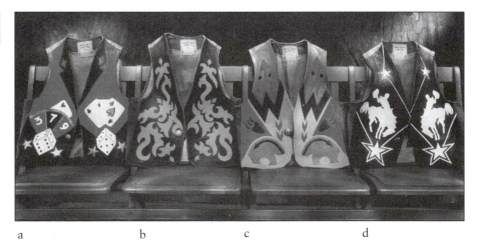

a               b               c               d

### FIGURE 9.4

*Elsa Schiaparelli designed this hat, often referred to as the shoe hat, because of its resemblance to a high-heeled shoe. Her work in the 1930s was often whimsical and caused the viewer to consider unexpected associations.*

by detail, one new association and then another, rather than a total change that would require a complete alteration in our viewing path. How a form is organized influences people's attention, and thus people's viewing path can influence associations. An apparel-body-construct with a dominant and clear visual path directs our attention based upon how it is ordered.

Some viewers like change more than others. The viewer who is creative may enjoy associating dissimilar objects and inferring from them a new idea or association. Such unexpected associations that elicit surprise and delight may become important in viewing. For example, in the 1930s designer Elsa Schiaparelli created a hat in the shape of a woman's high-heeled shoe (Figure 9.4), disconcerting to some because of its unexpected association of the shoe with the head. Her designs were often linked with the Surrealist art movement, which capitalized on gaining the attention of the viewer through such unexpected associations. This caused the viewer to sort through and order associations in a new way. In like manner, display of many contemporary products delights the viewer because of such associations. Recently in the Midwest, surfaces resembling the pattern on a cow's body have been painted onto T-shirts. The definitive shape is recognized because of its resemblance to not just any cow, but to the Holstein with its contrast of black figure on white ground. The shape is characteristically an irregular, organic, rather large motif.

## Message from Shared Meaning

Acquiring meaning from what we see is quite spontaneous and is a primary aspect in perceiving the apparel-body-construct. Meaning can result from

a                                                b

**FIGURE 9.5A & B**

*The slip—a bias-cut undergarment not meant to be worn publicly—was often attractive enough to be worn in public. This photograph of Rita Hayworth (Figure 9.5a) became popular as a pin-up during World War II and encouraged the public wearing of slips. Today, the slip dress (b) is still a bias-cut garment with tiny straps. In its rebirth, it retains many characteristics of the early versions, but still manages to look like both the 1940s and the 1990s.*

Courtesy of: (a) UPI/CORBIS-BETTMANN. (b) Designed by Christian Lacroix. Courtesy of Fairchild Publications.

many sources and levels, that is, recognition, association, or conception, as was discussed earlier. For example, in Figure 9.5b the dress pictured is called a slip dress today. We recognize it from the past—a bias-cut dress with skinny straps and bare chest of a slippery satin texture. The famous pin-up of Rita Hayworth from World War II (Figure 9.5a) resembles the slip dress of today but was actually considered underwear or lingerie at the time, and not to be exposed except in the bedroom. Then we may think of the slip dress as a symbol of American ingenuity in taking a relatively simple silhouette and layout structure and wearing it publicly. In addition, wearing such a slip dress requires a very firm and slim body. The wearer may then symbolize womanhood as sexy, daring, and with "chutzpah." The apparel professional needs to consider all of these levels of meaning; however, depending upon the focus, one or the other meaning may become primary. An apparel-body-construct that has specific visual relations resulting in a distinct visual effect can have meaning on a number of levels. Such meanings can develop and remain in the subconscious, in which case one does not examine their relation to the form. A problem in interpretation is to find some way for levels of meaning to be consciously considered.

The use of the term "meaning" does not imply message. A **message** is shared communication, whereas meaning that we gain from an apparel-body-construct may or may not be shared. Message is at a more complex level of communication in which meanings must correlate with a specific structure or context for the purpose of transmitting an idea. A look or particular image that is held in people's minds is based upon such a common idea and cultural coding. A shared image that becomes message results when all related visual components are coordinated. When used creatively, such visual components can reinforce and strengthen people's emotional responses.

There is abundant potential for associations to be made while perceiving the apparel-body-construct. An expected combination of visual definers or modifiers, or a viewing path repeatedly pursued by the viewer, can become a look for a season—a seasonal convention, so to speak. Some forms are the source of more distinctive meanings than others. Such a look can be established based on an association of the form as it relates to a time or an event. For example, the twin sweater set resurfaced as a major look in the mid-1990s. In the 1950s, twin sweaters were popular knitted in angora or cashmere, but today they can be of cotton, silk, or a combination of fibers. Depending upon the merchandiser, the exact look and price point varies from Ralph Lauren's twin set in his 1995 spring collection to a less expensive version from The Gap. Fiber content, color, and other details may make the difference, but the noticeable aspect is that it still appears recognizable as a seasonal convention. To be knowledgeable about such combinations and ways of viewing means the observer is not only consciously aware of their existence but is also constantly in the process of discovering the combinations that occur repeatedly, that is, the code that makes up the convention. Other cultures also have codes, such as what constitutes formal dress. For example, the Indian woman in a sari wears matching colors of all parts of her ensemble. This is a cue to more formal dress. In the Korean culture there are a variety of definers and modifiers that influence a traditional code. For example, Koreans consider the garment pictured in Color Plate 11 to exemplify their traditional dress because of the colors and color combinations used, the lines and shapes, and the proportion of parts.

Some designers capture a share of the clothing market because of their consistency in creating forms that elicit similar and distinct meanings, acceptable to a certain cultural group at a particular time. Think about the difference in the designs of Christian Lacroix, Liz Claiborne, or Donna Karan. What is the look of these designers' clothes, and who are they appealing to—what kind of people make up their target market? It is very revealing to study forms of a particular designer or manufacturer according to their consistent meanings and potential messages. In Figure 9.6a, the image Guess cultivates for denim jeans is youthful, mischievous, and impish, while by contrast the one cultivated by designer Tommy Hilfiger in Figure 9.6b is more conservative, with strong associations to tradition.

All emotional responses must be effectively coordinated into a coherent image or look to produce the strongest result. Such coherent images provide a theme for the apparel-body-construct, which results in similarity of meaning, which in turn reinforces communication. To become attuned to what creates a coherent image, one must return to the question of what is unique in one's response and what may be shared. One's personal response must be examined and recognized when asking: To what degree is my response to that image unique because of my own personal experiences? An experience that seems very individual can still be a source of shared meaning.

Whether or not a person approves of or agrees with a particular coherent image is not necessary for one to understand it as a code. The code may be understood in part based on those who follow it or resist it. For example, in the 1970s young males and females in London who felt disenfranchised from mainstream society developed a manner of dressing that included spiked, brightly colored hair; body piercing; and black leather clothing with elaborate metal ornamentation. Although this look was not shared by the majority of the culture, it was a coherent image called "punk" and was recognized by certain form characteristics. The look was recognized and attracted global media attention.

**FIGURE 9.6A & B**

*Advertising often reflects the look of a designer or manufacturer who appeals to a particular target market. A comparison of advertisements cues the viewer to consistent messages meant to be associated with the clothing.*

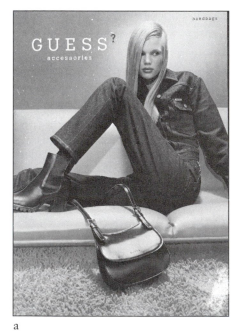

a                              b

Learning to communicate means becoming aware of what experiences one shares with others. This involves understanding the basis for the coding system. Apprehending the meaning of clothing involves understanding the conventions and signs related to the current operating code. What are the form components and relationships of the clothing form? What items and categories of clothing are ordinarily worn together? Specifically, what visual definers and elements are often connected? What categories of clothing are often related? What is the theme of the current look? How is the "current" look or fashion translated within the form and context?

Understanding the current look often means examining the basis for the coding system. For example, the business suit today comes from a male tradition of black, dark gray, or blue two- or three-piece suit of trousers, jacket, and optional vest, all of the same fabric. The jacket hangs from the shoulders, skimming the upper torso, and the trousers hang from the waist in vertical columns. The apparel-body-construct is viewed as a closed silhouette, with part priority at the neck from a contrasting shirt and tie. Suit details may vary from single- or double-breasted, pin-stripe or plain, buttons numbering from one to six, a back center or side vent or pleat, with or without trouser cuffs or trouser pleats. Shoes and stockings are usually the same value so they vary only in texture and therefore receive little extra attention. However, in the specific choices of suit, shirt, and tie, the wearer is usually considered regarding his or her physical coloring, body size, and shape. In Figure 9.7a, b, c, and d, variations of this look are shown, more or less following tradition. Figure 9.7a displays the very traditional example as described. Figure 9.7b is a version that changes the viewing pattern to more whole-to-part because of less contrast and an increased emphasis on textural variations from one surface to another. Additionally, the dark hair and shirt group and the neckline is uncharacteristic. In Figure 9.7c, the business suit is worn by a female and is still recognizable as such but with variations. The viewing pattern is again more whole-to-part. The jacket is buttoned to the neck with an attached collar and no lapel and fitted at the waist with a skinny belt. Her hair also creates a more whole-to-part effect because it is worn shoulder length to surround her face and overlays her jacket, which is the same value. The shape of her head is then more integral than separate from the jacket. In Figure 9.7d, a female again is wearing what is recognized as a business suit but also with significant variations. The priority is her head, which contrasts with the remainder of the ensemble in several ways. Her light hair is a contrasting value and her dark sunglasses give the celebrity status similar to what emerged in the 1930s movies. Her neck is surrounded by a contrasting striped tie, as in Figure 9.7a, but very different in end result. Her suit is a subtle tweed with a fitted vest and no collar or lapel at all. Thus, though the viewing pattern has changed, the 1990s look of Figure 9.7c and d is still recognized as evolving from the twentieth century business suit.

a    b    c    d

### FIGURE 9.7A, B, C & D

*The current look of the business suit is examined for the coding system as well as its variations. The traditional business suit (a), historically male, is usually a closed form of two or three pieces, including jacket, trousers, and possibly a vest made of wool, silk, or linen. Tailored jacket details include lapels, collar, button front closing, either single- or double-breasted, two or three pockets, and back vent. The trousers usually hang from the waist or hips in vertical columns with or without pressed-in pleats. As an apparel-body-construct, it is usually viewed whole-to-part with the neck area as the dominant part with the white shirt and contrasting tie. Variation on the traditional (b) includes a more casual result with more surface texture and less contrast between shirt and hair. The shirt and tie of the same color are not characteristically worn. In Figure 9.7c, a female is wearing a softened version of the traditional suit with jacket buttoned to the neck and thus no exposed shirt and tie. In Figure 9.7d, a female in a three-piece suit resembling the male business suit, but with a scarf encircling the neck combined with her Hollywood look of sunglasses and bleached hair.*

Designed by: (a and b) Alexander Julian, (c) Linda Allard for Ellen Tracy, and (d) Emanuel Ungaro. Courtesy of Fairchild Publications.

*Application Exercise 9.2*

Think of an image that is clear and strong for you, and then describe it using the terms and concepts of the apparel-body-construct. This could be a movie character or a particular fashion that comes to your mind in enough detail to allow imaging and a complete description.

# AESTHETIC CODES OF THE APPAREL-BODY-CONSTRUCT

Now that a basis for understanding how people interpret the apparel-body-construct has been discussed, the basis for aesthetic coding will be examined. Aesthetic response involves both individual and shared meaning. How does shared meaning come about? The past experiences of the viewer in perceiving the apparel-body-construct establish certain viewing relationships and paths. A viewer who recognizes established viewing patterns becomes more knowledgeable and able to recognize more subtle associations. The more the viewer searches for such viewing patterns, the easier it becomes to recognize them. By exercising the ability to make such associations, the apparel professional finds that what was subtle becomes explicit. For example, a series of associations in Figure 9.8 can be described. A geometric print of red, yellow, and black is placed asymmetrically on the child's body to create a diagonal direction that seems to envelop the trunk. The sleeves are slightly puffed, which is a type of layout structure often used for a female child. The hemline of the dress is asymmetric and related to the diagonal lines of the printed surface. Colors are repeated in the beads in the child's hair, shoes, and stockings. The red geometric shapes create figure in a figure-ground relationship on the surface of traditional geometric motifs. Meaning within this ensemble relates to the designer's African heritage. This ensemble is also within the convention of what a child would wear in the United States and reflects the African heritage of the child.

The degree to which an object suggests meaning can vary from exaggeration to a mere hint. In Figure 9.9a, the dramatic effect of the Gestalt of the apparel-body-construct represents an Oriental theme, whereas in Figure 9.9b the hat offers only a hint of the Orient. In examining Figure 9.9a, the surfaces are structured with large motifs of flowers, birds, and butterflies. Though the voluminous wrap is draped low on the arms, the effect is still that of a large robe. The turban-like hat is asymmetric and repeats the dark and light contrasts of the figure-ground relation of the dress motifs. The small touches of complementary color in the red-orange of the ribbon band of the robe and yellow-orange of the shoes with the overall blues of the remainder of the dress and robe is also quite Oriental. The theme of the whole appears Oriental, even though the details only reflect Oriental motifs without copying them. In Figure 9.9b, upon exami-

**FIGURE 9.8A & B**

*Associations of dress can originate from many sources. They often arise from the designer's heritage and become definitive characteristics of the apparel-body-construct.*

Courtesy of Isa Freeman.

a                                                    b

**FIGURE 9.9A & B**

*Meaning within an apparel-body-construct can range from a hint to prominence. In Figure 9.9a, the Oriental theme dominates, with surfaces structured with large motifs of flowers, birds, and butterflies in complementary hues of blue, red-orange, and yellow-orange. The layout, the large robe, possibly resembles a kimono but the details reflect the Orient without copying them. In Figure 9.9b, the hat offers a hint of the Orient.*

Designed by (a) Oscar de la Renta and (b) Christian Lacroix. Courtesy of Fairchild Publications.

nation the hat is similar to one historically worn more often by males than females, but still the round crown and upturned brim with the upward twisted tassel on the top offers a suggestion of the Orient.

The viewer who notes a subtlety of form is often the one who knows enough to pick out the specific details required for interpretation. For example, the curved stitching on a pocket may represent a brand of jeans widely known within a culture, but a slight elaboration of the stitching is understood only by a specific group. The meaning may be known only to a few, or will be ignored because it involves only one small aspect of the apparel-body-construct. As more and more viewers learn to pay attention to the detail and its association, it will become visually more important. An example would be a minute label on a T-shirt that designates an exclusive brand, as in Figure 9.10, or during wartime the increased recognition of heroes by reference to a small shirt decoration, such as a star or pin. The viewer learns to notice and interpret the small detail because of the importance of doing so. In a culture

**FIGURE 9.10**

*Designers and manufacturers often adopt an identifying characteristic uniquely their own that communicates their association to their audience. This can vary from a small logo, such as the one of Ralph Lauren, to a very prominent sign, such as the designer's name printed as an all-over surface motif on a jacket. Of course, many customers can tell who designed the clothing or accessory by the overall look alone.*

Reprinted with permission from Polo Ralph Lauren.

that places great importance on similar mass-produced clothing, this is a way fashion spreads through an audience.

Differences need to be recognized between associations that are commonly shared by other viewers with similar experiences and those that are unique to one person. Details of the apparel-body-construct may mean something because of personal associations, but may also be shared more widely among many people. For example, in the United States a ring on the third finger of the left hand is associated with attachment; it has both a personal and a shared meaning—personal because on one level it symbolizes attachment of marriage to one individual, but on another level shared, because the ring represents this attachment experience of many. Another example is related to color preference. Blue may be your favorite color, and that is an individual preference, but blue is also the preferred color of many Americans, and therefore shared. In addition, the experience of having a favorite or preferred color is shared by most people. Thus, meaning exists on several levels—what is individual can often be shared among many people and can exist at another level of meaning.

Over time the apparel-body-construct changes, associations change, and related meanings change. What was once obvious becomes insignificant and a cliché. For example, associations of blue denim jeans change and affect the current interpretation, such as the exact color and degree of wearing of surfaces; whether pressed or not; whether bearing signs of the designer, such as designer labels or not; and how they are assembled into an apparel-body-construct. People keep current in their interpretations only by maintaining an awareness of what is up-to-date and fashionable. Such relationships involve specific surfaces, edges, and spaces of the form itself, within the context of

a                    b                    c

## FIGURE 9.11A, B & C

*Certain looks are recycled from the past into the mainstream and are increasingly being recognized as such. However, in comparison with actual garments from the past, the exact apparel-body-constructs may never be recycled. Compare the actual 1920s dress (a) with this 1990s version by Jill Stuart (b). Look back at suits from the 1940s and compare with this 1995 version by Isaac Mizrahi (c).*

Courtesy of: (a) The Goldstein and University of Minnesota. (b and c), Fairchild Publications.

time, culture, and locale and within individuals as viewers of the apparel-body-construct. For instance, black has historically been used for mourning clothing, but today it is interpreted by its use as a strong, dramatic statement often worn by female and male members of a wedding party. It is not necessarily associated with funeral garb or the process of mourning.

Certain looks can recycle from the past back into the mainstream. Historic periods can be defined by coherent images, and such images have recently been defining current fashion, as in Figure 9.11a and b where there is a direct association to a previous decade of the twentieth century. An actual dress from the 1920s is pictured in Figure 9.11a. Now compare this with the one in Figure 9.11b, designed in the 1990s to resemble a look from the 1920s. How do they compare? In the 1940s suits looked something like the suit in Figure 9.11c, but a comparison with an actual 1940s suit may reveal some differences. Characteristics that once appeared well-defined can be further developed and can reoccur, such as with the exaggerated makeup that made the eyes appear wide open and childlike. In the later 1960s, a dominant fashion trend was typified by the creations of Mary Quant, originator of the miniskirt and simple, doll-like dresses (Payne, Winakor, and Farrell-Beck, 1992). The 1960s model, Twiggy, with her straight, noncurving body, wore such simple shapes of clothing and the effect was a leggy look that drew upon our already formed associations of an immature, childlike body (see Figure 5.1c). Her big eyes and simple, geometric haircut further provided a coherent image of innocence. Such a look is immediately recognizable on one level, but to delve further one must ask: Why was such an image of childlike naiveté so popular at a time of sexual, political, and cultural upheaval? What meaning associations can be related to such an image? Why might it become popular again in the 1990s?

At times, the use of various items that were once popular becomes a definite part of the fashionable image. Sometimes an item of clothing, such as a jacket or coat, that is reminiscent of the past will be used in a different way, and in combinations that result in different looks. President Harry Truman and casual entertaining, such as the backyard barbecue, became so popular in the late 1940s and 50s that it helped spawn a type of shirt called the Hawaiian shirt—a short-sleeved, cotton shirt of a bold floral print worn outside the trousers. Eventually this type of shirt for men became a cliché. So, too, did the synthetic, psychedelic printed shirts of the 1970s that became a sign of that time and then waned in popularity. However, both looks are featured in current men's sportswear lines and have been recycled in a slightly different form. The floral print shirt is now a more complex motif of interrelated flowers and made of Lycra, and the psychedelic print is now still boldly colored but offered in cotton. These shirts, which are reminiscent of the past, may take on new meanings in the process of recycling their slightly different forms. Though aspects of a form can recycle, does the meaning necessarily recycle too? Using past fashions in this way may capture some of the look of the past, but they are still being worn in another era with different meanings. Asking what is the

**FIGURE 9.12**

*President Harry Truman (left), following World War II, wore the Hawaiian shirt, a bold floral print, outside his trousers and helped to launch a casual fashion popular with men throughout the 1950s.*
Courtesy of UPI/CORBIS-BETTMANN.

Think of a convention in clothing you grew up with and then explore it in terms of your thinking today. (Example: "When in doubt, leave it out.") What could have been the reason for its origin? Check it out with family members or friends. Do you still believe and follow it today? Why or why not? Is it an individual or shared association among those you know?

*Application Exercise 9.3*

FIGURE 9.13

*Age of the viewer influences perception and nostalgia. Past experience viewing the movies starring Esther Williams and her synchronized swimming may or may not help to make this image appealing.*

Designed by Isaac Mizrahi. Courtesy of Fairchild Publications.

meaning behind the look is often revealing. When nostalgia for the past becomes a priority, bringing items back that remind the viewer of that time can be a result. The age of the viewer, however, influences the degree of nostalgia that is felt. Figure 9.13 has a resemblance to the swimsuit image of Esther Williams that became her signature in the movies of the mid-twentieth century featuring her synchronized swimming routine. If such a film experience was not a part of your past, you can hardly experience the nostalgia and you may just find the look appealing for itself. Recycling nostalgic images can also represent other symbolic messages, for example, a reworking of the past, a kind of resistance to the present, a belief in recycling to save the earth, or simply a thrifty use of recycled clothing just for the fun of it.

The educated viewer needs to be aware of the associations of the features of an apparel-body-construct. In addition, the apparel professional needs to understand levels of individual and shared meaning and must be particularly aware of shared meaning and how it can interrelate with the personal.

## Single or Multiple Properties

Meaning can be related to single or multiple properties found in the form. A single property, such as a warm color like red, may directly express a feeling of gaiety. Properties—such as the warm color along with a smooth texture—can combine to make multiple properties that further the expressive intent.

The way properties of the form are combined into specific surfaces and edges to create a particular visual effect may require association. For example, a vertical line repeats the upright position of the body and, if stretched out, can be associated with the dignity of upright posture among humans. Perhaps the vertical lines of the academic gown are an outgrowth of this association of verticality and dignity. Many such associations are so common that they are taken for granted or never made explicit. To stop taking such associations for granted and to uncover their meaning, they need to be discussed, defined, and made explicit.

The way in which the apparel-body-construct is organized involves multiple properties and is a further source of a distinct visual effect. People give labels to definitive patterns of organization that result in common meanings, such as elegant, sophisticated, or sexy. Sometimes meanings are related. For example, we may think that elegant and sophisticated are closer in meaning than elegant and sexy. Exploration of such meaning relationships is more informative if it involves an inquiry into the values behind them.

Consider how you would imagine an apparel-body-construct described as elegant. What specific form properties would you consider important in carrying out the message of elegance? If this is difficult, what form would you label "elegant" if you were a fashion editor? What would its specific properties be?

*Application Exercise 9.4*

One multiple association is the character of the form as it relates to the wearer, that is, how it identifies an apparel-body-construct as belonging to a specific age, gender, occupation, or ethnic group. Such multiple associations are often taken for granted, even though they are crucial to recognizing what social groups people belong to—a very important task. In fact, most of the time people do not even notice what specific surfaces, edges, and motions are associated with each nuance of meaning. One looks and creates meaning without really analyzing its cause. For example, we could take the category of "woman" and we could further specify young and friendly. How does an apparel-body-construct look young and friendly through color, texture, shape? What combinations of visual form trigger a particular meaning? How does cultural coding enter into the associations, that is, how is such meaning conveyed differently from one time to another, from one culture to another?

The viewer may become involved in understanding several elaborated codes in order to interpret an apparel-body-construct. For example, "androgyny" is a term applied to an apparel-body-construct that combines male and female characteristics. But understanding androgyny requires first understanding what it means to appear female and male at a particular time and place. What explicitly will result in the visual effect of femaleness or maleness? Curved shapes and soft pastel colors are expressive of a softening of the body and are often associated with the female gender, while angularity and value contrast are often considered male. In the United States, traditional female form characteristics include openness of silhouette, figure-ground integration, light surface values, and simultaneous viewing. Male form characteristics include closed forms, figure-ground separation, determinate surfaces, and successive viewing. Androgyny in the apparel-body-construct could result from a mixing of any of the male and female form characteristics. But does just any mixing of male and female form characteristics work? The resulting meaning, both historically and presently, must be considered. In Figure 9.14a and b, there are some examples of what could be considered the present-day exemplification of female and male characteristics. Name them. Do you agree? If so, how could mixtures of these form characteristics result in an androgynous appearance?

## Perceptible or Inferred Properties

Meaning can be derived from properties directly perceptible in the form. We recognize and name based upon such features. Meanings can be explicit

**FIGURE
9.14A & B**

*A male and female
as exemplifying
categories of the
apparel-body-
construct can be
examined and
described to better
understand
conventions.*

Designed by: (a) Giorgio
Armani and (b) Claude
Montana. Courtesy of
Fairchild Publications.

a                                    b

because they correspond directly to readily perceived features such as line, shape, color, or surface texture. Such directly perceptible properties can help to determine the meaning of the apparel-body-construct.

Previous experiences with clothing can allow us to infer associations. You categorize basic articles of apparel, such as shirt, blazer, and trousers, because of your experience of the separateness of these items in dressing and in purchasing. Such basic categories can be combined—you can mix and match. In dressing, you have experienced the processes and different body motions of putting on a shirt or jacket and trousers or socks. People often purchase apparel as separate items, labeling them accordingly. However, this labeling may continue even when these items make up an ensemble. Thus, even though the apparel items are not perceived individually, but as a portion of a whole, the separateness may continue to be inferred. How do you name what you see in Figure 9.14a and b, for example? Do you see clothing separate from the body as a result of the experience of dressing, or do you see a Gestalt first? It may be easier to view in terms of the whole and its parts if you ignore the dressing experience for a time.

Associations can derive from characteristics found in other natural or artificial objects and property relationships within the apparel-body-construct. In present viewing, we continually look for similarities to previously experienced objects. A common example is the continual search for meaning in cloud formations. We see a similarity to horses, bells, people, etc. In the apparel-body-construct, a shape can resemble a leaf or a leopard spot. The viewer can refer to a color as blue as the sky, red as a rose, or earth tones similar to those found in nature. When an association derives from something observed before, we often compare the similarities and label the apparel-body-construct accordingly and feel better for doing so. In Figure 9.15a and b, the shapes of the motifs are representative. How does such resemblance affect your naming and your response?

The apparel-body-construct can become symbolic of cultural values and their constant reevaluation and continual change of meaning. For example, a "look" has been established from the following combination: a two-piece suit with a determinate medium-to-dark value matte surface, a light-colored shirt, and darker tie. A business look often includes a suit color repeating one of the body colors of the wearer. This look is not only distinctive as an apparel-body-construct, but to adopt this look, to wear apparel of this type, has come to signify an acceptance of traditional American values—part of the code for career wear. However, over time this look has evolved and changed to include additional variations. This look has been identified as the kind of suit only a male would wear for business, to one worn by either gender. It has also been termed "power dressing," and dressing for the public. Also, this type of dress has been labeled dressing to show respect, or clothing to be avoided because of its overt connotations. Whether we accept or resist such a code, it is still

a                    b

**FIGURE 9.15A & B**

*Shapes used in the apparel-body-construct often resemble familiar shapes we find in everyday experiences. How does resemblance in (a) and (b) affect your naming and response?*

Designed by: (a) Todd Oldham and (b) Karl Lagerfeld. Courtesy of Fairchild Publications.

*"Love the bag, Stell! Very career."*

FIGURE 9.16

*In this cartoon, career dressing has extended to backpacks, and it assumes an understanding of a code for its humor.*

Drawing by Crawford; ©1996. The New Yorker Magazine, Inc.

relied upon and used by fashion editors, marketers, and designers and must also be understood implicitly by viewers. In Figure 9.16, this code is at the base of the joke. Here the boundaries between career dressing and casual have blurred. In the cartoon, the shift to casual clothing that has occurred is so casual that backpacks are considered "career." Another example of the reference to career dressing is the writer of an article on the collection of Giorgio Armani, who recognized the need to point out unexpected associations: "Giorgio Armani also advocates mixing sporty elements together: A formal dress shirt, for instance, is paired with a sport suit, while a dressy suit is paired with a high-V rayon shirt" (*Daily News Record*, July 19, 1995, p. 5). Such "unexpected associations" can really only be understood as an outgrowth of the code of formal business or career dressing.

The apparel-body-construct may combine both perceptible and inferred associations. For example, in the United States a young boy is identified as a Cub Scout when he wears a dark blue shirt with many badges of gold and other multicolored patches. The association identifying the young boy as a scout is directly perceptible in the form, based upon similar past experiences of the viewer. But such a form has also become associated with trustworthiness, perhaps because the organization is commonly known to promote trust. Thus, the Cub Scout as a sign type would designate a combination of index and symbol.

*Application Exercise 9.5*

Some terms that are used in explaining properties include the following. Select one and think of an example of how it could be used to describe properties within an apparel-body-construct.

- *Analogy*: Pointing out the logical correspondence between certain attributes of dissimilar things
- *Metaphor*: Qualities of one thing are transferred to or presented as characteristics of some other thing for the purpose of making clearer meaning
- *Pun*: A humorous metaphor
- *Paradox*: A contradictory statement, situation, or image that defies logic, for example, as found in surrealistic art
- *Synthesis*: Making a new image out of a combination of two or more existing properties or signs

Becoming aware of all of the *sources* of meaning is necessary to the interpretation of the apparel-body-construct. Associations that are automatic and unconscious need to be brought to awareness. The viewer who becomes skilled in recognizing them can begin to understand the apparel-body-construct and its potential for meaning and message. To identify these sources does take practice, but the ability can be developed. Now let us look at how knowledge of the sources of meaning can be applied to specific considerations of the form, the viewer, and the context.

## The Form

Coherence involves order in the apparel-body-construct. Human-made objects or artifacts have been described as a necessity—for making order from chaos. We have talked about the need for repetition and redundancy, not only in communication, but in satisfying the viewer aesthetically. Interpretation involves understanding those traits that summarize the form itself, that distinguish it from other forms. This is the unifying idea of the apparel-body-construct—the fusion of the separate parts into a whole. This unifying idea is referred to as coherence and involves its form properties and its meaning.

Characterizing the apparel-body-construct involves a recognition of unifying ideas or themes, even though the specific form properties that make them recognizable may vary. For example, an apparel-body-construct recognized as a Western look will usually have a range of acceptable associated properties, as in Figure 9.17a. The viewer would be able to recognize such a look even though details change. This may require generalizations about the Gestalt, and in some instances the combination of Western with business still allows for identification of the cowboy Western look, as in Figure 9.17b. The color may therefore vary within a range of colors. Identification of a unifying theme is not one color or one line but the way they are related—the way they fuse into an idea.

What characteristics of the apparel-body-construct can be interpreted as unifying or fusing ideas? Sources of fusion can arise directly from the form itself or through associations and the conventions of developing and combining articles of dress, that is, what fabrics, colors, lines, shapes go with what. Though these conventions are continually changing, one must be aware of them to understand, emphasize, accept, or resist them.

---

Examine the apparel-body-constructs in Figure 9.15a and b and describe each in terms of a unifying theme. Describe several form characteristics that are apparent. What sign type might you designate to describe the apparel-body-construct?

*Application Exercise 9.6*

---

## Expressive Effect

The way people view the apparel-body-construct involves not only how people look with their eyes and minds but how they feel about what they see.

**FIGURE 9.17A & B**

*The Western look involves such details as a confident-looking wearer of a ten-gallon hat, a string tie, a fitted plaid shirt with curved yoke and pearl button snaps, a fringed leather vest, chaps, a chain or leather belt with large metal buckle (with Western motif), and pointed boots. In Figure 9.17a, though the number of Western details are few, the apparel-body-construct may still look Western to the viewer. In Figure 9.17b, a non-Western suit is combined with remnants of a Western look that still may appear more Western than the details should entitle and provides a unifying theme.*

Designed by (a) Donna Karan and (b) YOHJI. Courtesy of Fairchild Publications.

Expression is a characteristic of the apparel-body-construct whereby emotions result from our direct experiences with the form. **Expressive effect** results from basic elementary mental states that can be linked directly to the feelings from perceiving the apparel-body-construct. Expressive effects arise from those properties of the apparel-body-construct that are perceptible to the viewer and have been identified as the definers and modifiers in previous chapters. The way these form properties associate in the whole influences expressive effect.

What feelings can be elicited from the way the form is organized by the viewer? Expressive effects are those fusions that lead us to such feelings as excitement or calmness, strength or delicacy. Below is a listing of some form properties that can work together and often bring about expressions of excitement, calmness, strength, or delicacy.

|  | Excitement | Calmness | Strength | Delicacy |
|---|---|---|---|---|
| *Shape* | Simple, contrasting, several, to many | Few with little contrast between or clear hierarchy of many ordered shapes | Large, with silhouette emphasis | Small, rounding, soft edge |
| *Line* | Discontinuous, diagonal, zigzag | Continuous and most related to the body axis and silhouette shape | Continuous, directed, dominant, thick, bold | Curved, discontinuous, lightweight |
| *Color* | Intense, warm, primary hues, contrast in value | Muted, neutrals, cool colors | Value contrast, dark colors, neutral light | Clear warm colors, tints of warm or cool colors |
| *Texture* | Smooth surfaces that do not interrupt edge viewing or filled surfaces that interrupt viewing of edge | Smooth surfaces with uninterrupted edge viewing, subtle background | Smooth surfaces to edge, very coarse textured areas often used in combination with smooth, dark surfaces or in unusual combinations | Minute variations, often printed and blurred |
| *Viewing Priority* | May be open form, part-to-whole, figure-ground separation, rounded, and determinate and indeterminate | May be closed form, whole-to-part, figure-ground integration, rounded, and determinate | May be closed form, whole-to-part, figure-ground separation, flat, and determinate | May be open form, part-to-whole, planar integration, rounded, and indeterminate |

The interaction of the form properties can result in an expression that is a powerful influence on visual effect. That is, the meaning derives from form properties and the associations they create within the whole. The form can be described as relating to separable components. For example, an apparel-body-construct can be described as red, vertical, or softened by the curves of a shape. In Color Plate 10, the apparel-body-construct is open and Color Plate 15 is closed, and this influences expressive effect. The form in Color Plate 13 creates excitement and could be described as contrasting shapes, value contrasts, and filled and contrasting surfaces, whereas the form in Color Plate 14 creates a calm effect by the muted cool colors, textured surfaces that are subordinate to the dark lines at the waist area and connecting with the dark hair and shoes. In both the viewer is led successively throughout the apparel-body-construct, but in comparison the expressive effect is quite different.

Expressive effects may be influenced by the ordering of the apparel-body-construct. For example, the observer would tend to perceive part-to-whole for the exciting effects in Color Plates 13 from black and white contrasts used throughout. In Color Plate 14, the part-to-whole viewing gives a calm effect, with small shapes creating a clear order, lines related to the body axis and silhouette of the apparel-body-construct, and rounded surfaces. In Color Plate 15, the more whole-to-part viewing aids in a strong expressive effect, with flat, dark, and smooth surfaces and a large shape of the closed silhouette.

We derive meaning as a result of the expressive effects of the apparel-body-construct. The form can be better understood by an explicit consideration of just what form properties are involved in the formation of a specific expressive effect. When an apparel-body-construct is described as dramatic, expressive effect is being considered. Such an effect is the result of a fusion of form properties. Dramatic may describe a fusion of the whole, combining properties of both exciting and strong categories, as in Figure 9.18a. Excitement derives from the surfaces that are filled with diagonal lines and circular shapes, but the strong effect derives from the value contrasts and figure-ground effect that includes the

## FIGURE 9.18A & B

*Basic expressive effects can be combined with new categories resulting. In (a), categories of "exciting" and "strong" combine for expressive effect in one apparel-body-construct. In (b), there are both delicate and calm characteristics of expressive effect. Does one category of expressive effect dominate?*

Designed by (a) Todd Oldham and (b) Susanna Moyer. Courtesy of Fairchild Publications.

a

SUSANNA MOYER

b

body parts. In Figure 9.18b, the effect is delicate and calm because of the rounding shapes of the silhouette, the horizontal lines of the neck and hem edges, and the subtle motif on the transparent surfaces. As we consider meaning, such basic expressive effects and their associated form properties need to be kept in mind.

Expressive effects have cultural connotations and are frequently looked at in terms of categories important within the culture, for example, gender. In Color Plate 8, the light coloring of the small child contributes to the expressive effect. Expressive effects are also bound by historical context. If you examine an apparel-body-construct that was worn in an earlier century, the same expressive categories would not necessarily repeat along with the same form properties, nor would they be interpreted in the same way.

## The Viewer

You must consider, as viewers, both yourself and the client you serve. However, to apply the concepts, the apparel professional needs to separate each perspective—that of self and the other.

*Predictability and Surprise.* If an apparel-body-construct is to attract and hold attention it requires both of the following to be present: (l) expected or predictable visual relations accepted by the viewer and (2) surprise, or the reliance on some unexpected part or combination of parts to achieve interest, newness, or freshness. Expectations arise from past experiences, and the formation of these expectations is influenced by how much and what type of attention the viewer has given to the apparel-body-construct.

Each person has in his or her viewing repertory a set of expectations for a number of types or categories that form an underlying code. Categories derive from one's knowledge and past experiences and how they are organized. For example, casual clothing, formal clothing, clothing for fun and entertainment, clothing to wear home to visit Mom and Dad—these would all be categories based upon relation to event. We may also have a different way of ordering forms of dress that we wear. Clothing may be categorized based on color or what it is worn with, for example, my yellow shirt that I wear with my blue trousers. Categories may be based upon time and include fashionable clothing of the 1990s, haute couture, vintage clothing, out-of-date clothing—or however you categorize time. Categories may relate to emotional response—so-so clothing, cool clothing, comfortable clothing, etc. Pay attention to how you relate to clothing, because such categories give you the basis for how you characterize forms of dress. Then ask yourself what conventions go along with each category, that is, how would I differentiate one category from the other?

Think about how you categorize clothing in your wardrobe. What is the basis for your groupings? Do you have more than one way to organize your clothing? How does this relate to how you value clothing?

*Application Exercise 9.7*

Predictability arises out of the pleasure a viewer gains from recognition of fulfillment of a type or category. A satisfying experience is something we like to see repeated. However, with repetition can come boredom if the object of our attention includes nothing stimulating or unexpected. After too many repetitions of identical stimuli, the object becomes ground noise or background—that is, it no longer stimulates at the same level.

How do these two, predictability and surprise, work together? An example of how they interrelate is a standard shirt. It is expected to have certain layout features: a collar, a yoke, a center front button closing, pockets in a horizontal line across the upper chest, short sleeves or long, with a buttoned cuff. Surfaces predictably would be a light value and possess a small background pattern in a cotton broadcloth. People expect such a shirt to be worn under a sweater or jacket. Now what could be considered a surprise? A subtle change could be made by lowering the yokeline in the front and back. Such a change would affect the predictability, but the shirt form would not change so much that one would no longer recognize "shirtness." What could be a more major surprise? The shirt could possess an unexpected surface and be worn differently on the body, perhaps two sizes too small. The observer would still have to recognize the "shirtness" for this to remain in the predictability-surprise domain.

Many apparel-body-constructs have predictable aspects: The viewer has collected images of expected properties and relations. These are used as a base to speed up the perceptual process. Whether the viewer chooses to concentrate on these expected patterns or on the surprising components is somewhat dependent upon point of view. The surprising aspects will be noticed by the viewer who has chosen to become knowledgeable about that form as a category. Think about a wedding dress for a formal, traditional wedding. What characteristics do you think about? How do these characteristics relate to the wedding itself? Do they symbolize the wedding in any way? Now examine the two wedding dresses in Figure 9.19a and b. What is predictable and what is surprising?

Predictability is based upon learning and knowing expected patterns of the apparel-body-construct. These patterns are the codes based upon conventions and signs that represent a system for organizing and understanding data. How does a viewer learn to recognize expected patterns or codes? First the viewer must become aware and interested in understanding the basis for such codes. In the two wedding dresses, what do they tell you about a wedding? Why is one predictable and one surprising? Because no set of expectations stays static, the viewer must learn to follow the visual transformations of the apparel-body-construct. An editor of fashion is skilled in comparing past forms with new ones. Descriptions are couched in terms of comparison relative to what has been, such as "a softer, more fitted look." "What does that mean," you ask, "softer than what?" The fashion editor is assuming an audience who has followed identifying features of fashion over time and will understand the comparison, even though subconsciously. Perhaps visual examples are included, photographs or sketches; then the reader can also surmise from examining them what is meant by softer and more fitted than what existed before.

a

b

**FIGURE
9.19A & B**

*To consider the idea
of the wedding dress,
we can compare the
formal and tradi-
tional wedding dress
in (a), with the more
informal and non-
tradtional one in (b).
What comes to mind
as you compare
them?*

Courtesy of: (a) Fairchild Publications and (b) Ed Keating, NY-
Times Pictures.

If the observer is interested in a particular form and has followed its transformations, an expectancy develops from this experience. For example, a jogger knows about running shoes either because of experience or education—how one pair fit, how long they lasted, how they never looked clean, or how the upper portion pulled away from the sole. Such ideas include both the function of the shoes and the way they look. An article on the new ideas in running equipment adds to knowledge about running shoes. Sales personnel tell customers about the features of the particular shoes they are selling and assure them that they are surely superior to previously owned shoes. Seeing a favorite athlete wear them in a television commercial and performing superhuman feats caps the experience. The reference again is to the observer's accumulated past experiences and knowledge of the shoes.

Part of the pleasure and satisfaction you get from viewing the apparel-body-construct is how it relates to your individual anticipations and to your shared conventions. For that particular type or category, people have established a code that influences their anticipation. This, too, is often shared among one's friends, through continual communication—"This is cool, that is not." Then, if the form fulfills in a superior way, one is more than satisfied. Satisfaction, discussed at length in Chapter 10, is an outcome of fulfillment of type and the understanding of the underlying code aids in that fulfillment.

*Degree of Expectancy and Surprise.* The relation of expectancy to surprise is one of degree—at one extreme is total surprise and at the other complete predictability. The apparel-body-construct may include mostly predictable associations, with a new color combination being the only varying feature. The focus is then on the color or the proportion of the color, since the other aspects of structure follow expectations of the audience and have not changed. The surprise of a new color combination will attract more attention than the predictable aspects.

The surprising aspects of the form may be subtle or blatant. There is pleasure in being able to pick out the subtlety of a form, in following the nuance of change that occurs in a product. It demonstrates, to oneself or to others, a certain knowledge of the product. A viewer who doesn't know the product would not necessarily recognize a subtlety unless it was pointed out. Such recognition gives a measure of satisfaction. The change could also be relatively blatant, such as a way of relating clothing to the body never seen before. Dior's New Look at the end of the 1940s was evidently a change of this magnitude, because almost every shape and proportion of the apparel-body-construct changed from what had existed previously—length of skirt, shape of skirt, narrow shoulders, fitted waistline. So, too, did the maxi-mini controversy of the late 1960s, which combined extremes of length in one ensemble, i.e., a miniskirt with a maxi coat.

If the element of surprise is blatant, the observer may be required to change the way he or she views the apparel-body-construct altogether. An example would be when dress that resembles clothing worn in another century is worn today, as in a reenactment of a particular historic period and location in a living history museum setting. Figure 9.20 is an illustration of museum guides clothed in dress similar to that in the painting to capture the attention of the child who visits the museum. Instead of focusing on the surface details as a priority, the observer may have to focus on silhouette to get the intended message. The observer may not be ready for the change and may not have adjusted viewing patterns or meaning associations. Understanding the form may require a major change in observations. This factor could influence the success or failure of an apparel-body-construct. How much change can the viewing audience tolerate? Certainly in a museum setting a great deal of change can be tolerated and even enjoyed!

**FIGURE 9.20**

*Reenactment of a specific historic period through clothing of museum guides is aptly illustrated in this student's project for the Minneapolis Institute of Art.*

Courtesy of Colleen Gau.

*Message Congruity.* Messages arise out of the predictability and surprise the viewer experiences. These messages can originate from one definer of the apparel-body-construct or from the whole form. For example, expectations for combining visual texture may be the combination of some determinate with indeterminate surfaces. Then, when the

**FIGURE 9.21**

*Missoni is well-known for distinctive surface structuring that has long been associated with their knitwear.*

viewer perceives something different, the message is not congruous with expectations and the apparel-body-construct may appear at first chaotic.

When expectations are met, the viewer experiences message congruity. A tuxedo is congruous when it meets our convention of a man's two-piece black jacket with satin collar, white shirt, black bow tie, and black trousers with stripes down the sides. The observer would also expect black shoes and socks. However, the message is incongruous when laced with a surprise—the tuxedo is all there but neon-colored socks or high-heeled shoes are worn on the feet. The viewer's expectations are met, except for the feet, which jar the observer out of his or her unconscious expectations.

Often the apparel-body-construct relies on incongruity for timeliness. An apparel-body-construct could involve a white satin shirt with blazer and blue jeans in one time period, or a frilly lace collar on an otherwise traditional khaki military uniform at another. You may recognize the stimulating knitted surfaces of Missoni as unifying the apparel-body-construct without being conscious of the unusual figure-ground relationships, as in Figure 9.21. The observer is thus jarred from the viewing reverie that arises out of the convention that he or she perceives as message congruity.

*Individual and Shared Meaning.* Although the difference between individual and shared meaning has been discussed, the differentiation between the two is a necessity. To focus on shared meaning, the difference between individual and shared meaning must be considered from the viewer's perspective.

The educated viewer needs to be aware of the difference between a personal but shared experience and a merely personal one. You can distinguish from your own experiences those that could have similar meanings for other observers. Visual forms throughout history have been based on the premise that visual forms can communicate shared meaning to a particular culture as well as being meaningful to an individual. Perception of meaning is rarely a totally individual and personal experience of the viewer. Questions to ask in sorting out the distinctions are: How is meaning shared? How does communication take place? To answer these questions one must recognize and sort out which meanings of the apparel-body-construct relate to uniquely personal experiences and which relate to culturally shared experiences. Individual experiences may be unique but similar to the experiences of others. Often a basic similarity can be observed in several viewers' responses toward the same apparel-body-construct. When observers can agree upon an interpretation of its basic form, social usage establishes convention and a code. If one person wore a baseball cap back-to-front it might be a personal statement. If many people do it then it is becoming a convention.

The observer can distinguish which associations are shared and socially established. Distinctions come from the observer's own past experience. Remember that to perceive and interpret associations from the perspective of communication means to emphasize the aspects that could have similar meanings for other observers. To say not only, "This is what it means to me," but also, "This is what it means," implies a generalization of (social) meaning—"This is what it means to this society," however identified, i.e., traditional, contemporary, casual, formal, regional, national, popular, or elite society.

## The Context

Commonality of experience occurs within a group, be it a small group or a larger social group. People's similar experiences lend shared sources of meaning to the apparel-body-construct, and these sources of shared experiences are very influential in forming people's responses to the apparel-body-construct. They are the contextual associations related to a viewer's surroundings or milieu. The influence of **culture**, **time**, and **event** is discussed in the following.

*Culture.* Unifying ideas of the apparel-body-construct are related to that which is important and therefore seeks expression within a culture. If youthfulness is valued, visual cues will be developed that express the idea of youth. They may include minimal makeup and clothing that follows body shape in the torso with the arms and legs exposed. If maturity is valued, visual cues will develop for that characteristic as well. For example, cues for maturity may include shorter, more carefully groomed hair, coordinated and layered ensembles with surface intricacy. Cues for youth and maturity will vary with the culture.

Since associations of the apparel-body-construct are usually centered around an important cultural value, an understanding of these associations means bringing these cultural factors to conscious awareness. If casual informality is striven for in a society, this will be reflected in the apparel-body-construct. The influence of casual, comfortable clothing is demonstrated in Figure 9.22.

To interpret the apparel-body-construct the viewer must ask, "What factors are especially important to the society?" Then, what are the important form images and how do they relate? If exercise and health are valued, examples will be found demonstrating this concern, not only in the forms themselves but in the publicity surrounding them. If exercise and health are believed to be important, look for examples directly related to this value such as jogging suits and new looks in exercise leotards. If fashion is a value for all, look for an extension of what is fashion to all body sizes. You may also discover that the value appears in more general categories of apparel. An example would be extending the influence of exercise and health to other categories of casual clothing, as when Norma Kamali expanded the use of cotton knits previously used mainly for sweatsuits. The cultural value in question may then be more pervasive than is initially apparent.

To communicate through the apparel-body-construct involves a shared identification within a social group. In any social group related visual forms emerge. For an insider who identifies with a particular apparel-body-construct, there will be more individuality within the identifying characteristics than for an outsider who tends to see undifferentiated sameness. This shared identification can be a single item, wearing specific beads around the neck such as love beads of the Hippies, or involve the whole apparel-body-construct, as in the white, two-piece costume of the student of karate. The

**FIGURE 9.22**

*Cultural values within the United States of casual clothing for sport, are demonstrated here.*

Courtesy of © John P. Kelly/The Image Bank.

karate student would differentiate the meaning of the color of the belt because it is a measure of ability in karate.

Identifying features can be subtle and only identifiable to the social group sharing them, or very visible and obvious to anyone within or outside the group. How obvious the identifying features are can depend upon how knowing the audience, the viewers of the apparel-body-construct. For example, to some people who wear designer clothing, the success of the experience is dependent upon others recognizing the designer's clothing signature.

Established usages are never completely definite or rigid. Sometimes meanings are ambiguous, and situations or events must be considered in order to determine the meaning intended. Sometimes, if the form is vague in its message, the context provides the interpretation. In Figure 9.23a, b, and c, the context is Morocco, but the identifying features of each apparel-body-construct vary in subtlety. One wonders whether the features would communicate a shared message within the culture of origin—Morocco. Individual apparel-body-constructs take on different meanings given new situations. New meanings will constantly appear within a culture, and old signs can take on a new meaning.

a    b    c

### FIGURE 9.23A, B & C

*When designers borrow a theme from a particular culture and country, what characteristics from an apparel-body-construct are selected to portray the theme? Morocco is the borrowed country here, but would the borrowed characteristics be recognized within that country or is there just a general exotic quality that pervades?*

Designed by (a) Ralph Lauren, (b) Karl Lagerfeld, and (c) Christian Lacroix. Courtesy of Fairchild Publications.

*Time.* Timeliness of the apparel-body-construct is called fashion. From the perspective of perception, fashion is usually a progressive succession of interconnected ideas. The concept of fashion is very influential when it is an ideology within a cultural group. There is a dynamic involved because the image at any one time is perceived as in a slow but constant state of evolution. There is consistency amid the change, which is part of the unifying idea.

Fashion is perceived from different viewpoints. For example, viewers may have to adjust their viewing from reference to the edge of silhouette to surface texture or color. Audiences choosing to be fashionable must keep abreast of such changes in how they view the apparel-body-construct or they will no longer be current. How does a body part such as the leg become figure or ground in different looks and different periods, or what is a current combination of viewing relationships that looks "up-to-date"?

Within a given culture, the term "traditional" can bring to mind a system of associated features, some of them changing over time, but overall the form can be quite enduring. In Turkey, traditional female dress consists of variously patterned woven fabrics in simple geometric shapes and layered onto the body, creating many overlapping edges. In many societies traditional calls to mind a form of traditional dress, but in the United States how is traditional dress defined? The identifying features of tradition, in one instance, may be use of symmetry, tailored details, and contrasting color within a whole that includes a definite ordering of parts, as in Figure 9.24a. Tradition may also simply be blue denim jeans, as in Figure 9.24b. At any one time the traditional apparel-body-construct may be fashionable for many within a group or for only a few. An apparel category may be enduring, with the associated features only changing somewhat with time. Or, when features are definitive, they may be borrowed for other purposes, as in Figure 9.24c.

The audience for timely forms also varies. The fashion focus of a group of young people may be quite different from that of an older generation. Within two such groups the criteria of timeliness can be different. A younger age may accept more body exposure than an older group. In Figure 9.24c, all three bodies can be viewed as figure in the figure-ground relationship. If degree of body exposure is considered fashionable, and fashion is a priority within a culture, then either a tension will exist between the generations or the older group will adopt their own look.

During any one fashion season different apparel-body-constructs with different looks are described. These may be publicized as single feature orientations or whole expressive patterns. Single feature emphases are useful because they indicate apparel-body-constructs are being compared and a message related to one association among them is stressed. Examples include: "Color is this season's message!" or "It's all about shape!" or "The essential edge!" This approach has the effect of allowing focus on and interpretation of that feature within an apparel-body-construct. Another category of terms used is expressive, such as sensuous, sweet, confident. These terms refer to combinations of form properties of the apparel-body-construct. For example,

a          b          c

## FIGURE 9.24A, B & C

*How is "traditional" defined within the United States?*

*a. Is tradition defined as tailored cut-and-sewn separates in contrasting shapes that are ordered parts within a whole and designed by Ralph Lauren?*

*b. Is tradition defined as blue denim jeans?*

*c. Is tradition simply anything made of blue denim that could be worn by a variety of ages?*

Designed by: (a) Ralph Lauren, (b) Sergio Valente, and (c) Chanel. Courtesy of Fairchild Publications.

"confident" may be translated in an apparel-body-construct to describe a combination of "strong and calm" in expressive effect. Whole expressive effects are often publicized as romantic, nautical, dramatic. These holistic effects are often associated with one or just a few designers, as one message in the total fashion picture.

Time may permeate every aspect of the apparel-body-construct if newness is an important cultural factor. Apparent newness may include such single features as the worn look of the surface, associated features reflecting the manner in which parts are put together (for example, the way a blazer is worn, collar up and sleeves pushed up), with a two-piece separate part look, or a one-piece look of top and bottom and more conventional contrasting shirt and tie. Fashion involves the entire apparel-body-construct, the wearing and shaping of hair, the application of cosmetics, and body movements. At any one time, the influence of time pervades all aspects of the apparel-body-construct, requiring the viewer to be comprehensive and flexible.

The recognition of time relations includes past, present, and future, therefore we may use such terms as "historic," "up-to-date," and "space age." We describe a "gentleman," an "old-fashioned girl," or a "thoroughly modern Millie." These terms all change in reference to the apparel-body-construct. In Figure 9.25, a form is illustrated that is recognized as resembling a sailor suit, a service uniform of the U.S. Navy. Once considered traditional and male, here it is presented as modern and female.

Time affects many facets of the apparel-body-construct, such as the biological change of the body from youthful to mature. When the youthful look is superimposed upon the effects of aging, the representation of youth may be altered. For example, what is considered "fit" at a young age may be body surfaces exposed to show smooth skin and body shapes. However, "fit" for an older age could be translated as a well-groomed body, well-fitted but unexposed body shapes, and up-to-date colors. When any look becomes a fashion, if it is to be adopted by the multitudes, the form must be translatable to many different groups. Thus, the specific form may take on variations within the unifying idea.

*Event.* The specific event at which an apparel-body-construct is viewed affects the visual form as well as our expectancies of that form. The event may involve certain anticipated features and combinations of features. What is worn in a place of business is different from what is worn socially, and our expectancies for each can vary. Consider such terms as "night dressing," "sportswear," and "career dressing." Each term relates to a general or specific event associated with the apparel-body-construct. Now close your eyes and imagine forms of the apparel-body-construct that associate with a particular event. How specific can you make your image of the apparel-body-construct for each event? Does one image come to mind or several?

Often what one wears depends upon many factors surrounding the event—location (town, region of the country), weather, season, place (theater, restaurant, health club), mode of transport, companions, number participating, and one's mood in anticipation of the event. The visual form of the apparel-body-construct may be very location specific, for example, what visual forms are being worn this year for the Central High School prom in Wobegon, Minnesota? The code acceptable for this event may be a relatively loose set of conventions or restrictive. What about the dress in Figure 9.26? Expectations for prom attire may become more form specific as those planning to attend communicate before the event and establish conventions.

**FIGURE 9.25**

*A women's suit resembling the sailor suit previously associated with a male service uniform of the U.S. Navy.*

Designed by Isaac Mizrahi. Courtesy of Fairchild Publications.

Application
Exercise 9.8
Challenging the assumptions of a "look" identified with any audience is a useful exercise. Ask several people you consider different in age from yourself about what they consider in the way they want to look. If in the interview you find the person being interviewed unable to describe a "look," ask them to focus upon a particular clothing ensemble and describe what they like and dislike wearing.

When people begin to anticipate spring, they watch not only for its signs on the landscape but also in apparel-body-constructs they observe. Viewers have expectations of apparel-body-constructs that relate to season, especially in regions with definite seasonal patterns. Even though people may accept many apparel-body-constructs that cross over from one season to another, they often adopt new forms specific to the season.

Travel makes people aware of regional patterns of dress that influence their perceptions. Since people are aware of different conventions of dress pertaining in other parts of the country or world, they often ask others for advice on how to dress in areas to which they plan to travel if they don't have any previous experience of those places. They may also adapt their present wardrobes or buy new clothing in anticipation of travel.

What other activities and events also affect people's expectations of the apparel-body-construct? You can often think of different expectations to accompany different versions of the same general activity—whether you eat pizza or cordon bleu, whether you attend a movie or live theater, etc. Who we go with influences our expectations, as does whether one goes alone or with a group. An individual in a group will often dress in reference to other group members, rather than dressing in clothes strictly appropriate to the event. Someone who goes to a baseball game or other sports event after work with co-workers may still be wearing office attire, not casual clothes.

*Single-Event Forms or Multiple-Event Forms.* Clothing may be considered to have inherent event features, such as when an apparel-body-construct is described as formal or casual. For example, "white tie and tails" signifies a category of formal event. The suitability of an apparel-body-construct can vary from being very event-specific to being event-nonspecific or multiple event. Event-specific apparel-body-constructs include a bride in a wedding dress or a drum major in a marching band costume. A nonspecific casual summer dress is often considered appropriate for a number of different events.

The expectancies associated with an event are in a constant state of flux. Time and experience change people's conventions. What is considered appropriate to wear in a given situation depends on what one has experienced in the past. If you were one of this group deciding what to wear, you might base your decision on what you observe as well as past experiences. If you have much experience in a given situation, you feel more confident; you know the expected patterns of appearance and can either choose to match them or resist them. If, on the other hand, you are entering a new situation, you may choose a conventional multiple-event clothing form. When starting a new job, a man may wear a suit and tie all through the day; later when he is more comfortable in the job, he may change to shirtsleeves and no jacket.

Time often influences viewing, especially in expectancies of multiple-event clothing forms. At one time, an acceptable multiple event form will be designer blue jeans, a white shirt, and tweed blazer. At another time, this form may appear time specific or dated as a multiple-event form, with some other form taking its place.

When an individual quits updating clothing for various events, the apparel-body-construct he or she wears can become very time specific. Often the time-specific, "frozen" apparel-body-construct reveals the last time an individual paid any attention to image. Readers of fashion magazines are often fascinated with makeovers, which explicitly reveal how to update an image.

Which events have you experienced that require single-event clothing forms and which require multiple-event forms? A formal wedding would require single-event forms for the members of the wedding party. On the other hand, many different apparel-body-constructs could be worn to a grocery store in a large city. At such a grocery store, what would people's ex-

**FIGURE 9.26**

*What would be a code for acceptable prom attire at Central High School? Would it resemble something traditional, such as this dress?*

Designed by Isaac Mizrahi. Courtesy of Fairchild Publications.

pectations of dress be? Would someone wearing a bridal gown be acceptable? What about dressing in paint-stained jeans and tank top at a fancy food emporium?

***Expectations Related to Others.*** The role an apparel-body-construct plays in an event will influence how much attention the wearer receives. If a person is attending a wedding as the bride or groom, expectations for viewer focus would be greater than if he or she were attending as an invited guest.

To address attention expectancies of an event ask yourself, what forms attract? What would a person wear to fade into the background? An apparel-body-construct that fades into the background in one situation may stand out in another because of physical context. For an event at which multiple-event clothing forms are expected, the single-event form may attract attention. Consider the attention you would receive if everyone else was wearing casual comfortable clothing and you came in very formal dress.

Form associations are specific to the contextual milieu of culture, time, and event. In terms of color, red can mean stop or may be used in upbeat holiday wear, depending upon context of viewing. Red, white, and blue can be associated with patriotism or with spring fashion. However, if stars and stripes accompany the red, white, and blue, the reference to patriotism is clear. It is important to consider the influence of specific contexts on the apparel-body-construct.

## Summary

• To *interpret* the apparel-body-construct means to give it meaning. The form with its many associations elicited by color, texture, and shape; the context, including the particular culture, historical period, locale, even season; and the viewer, with his or her varying associations coming from present and past experiences—all these factors influence how an apparel-body-construct will be interpreted.

• Human beings react in similar ways to many objects, including clothing. Shared meaning equals communication, and the message is reinforced via repetition—this is particularly important in marketing.

• Conventions and signs (icons, indexes, symbols) make up a code—a system of meaning particular to a culture.

• Meaning within the apparel-body-construct has various levels: recognition, association, conception; meaning may involve references to history, emotion, social movements (e.g., hippie, punk, New Romanticism), and is important in understanding the current fashionable "look."

- The apparel-body-construct has an aesthetic code—this is related to single and multiple properties, associations to nature or human-made objects, and cultural values.

- Expressive effects, such as conveying emotional states like calmness, strength, etc., can be achieved by means of shape, line, color, texture, and viewing priority.

- Fashion and clothing are perceived with reference to context—shared meaning; cultural emphases such as youthfulness, tradition, or iconoclasm; and the influence of geographic locale and season.

## Key Terms and Concepts

associations
attending
code
conception
conventions
culture
event
expressive effect

icon
index
message
recognition
signs
symbol
time

## References

Berger, A. A. *Reading Matter: Multidisciplinary Perspectives on Material Culture.* Transaction Publishers, New Brunswick, NJ: l992.

Evans, C., and Thornton, M. *Women and Fashion: A New Look.* New York: Quartet Books, 1989.

Ewen, S. *All Consuming Images: The Politics of Style in Contemporary Culture.* New York: Basic Books, 1988.

Fiske, J. *Understanding Popular Culture.* Boston: Unwin Hyman, 1989.

Fiske, J. *Introduction to Communication Studies*, 2nd ed. New York: Routledge, 1990.

"Giorgio Armani, Le Collezioni." *Daily News Record.* July 19, 1995, 5.

Hollander, A. *Seeing Through Clothes.* New York: The Viking Press, 1978.

Hollander, A. *Sex and Suits.* New York: Alfred Knopf, l994.

Kidwell, C., and Steele, V., eds. *Men and Women: Dressing the Part.* Washington, DC: Smithsonian Institution Press, 1989.

Payne, B., Winakor, G., and Farrell-Beck, J. *The History of Costume from Ancient Mesopotamia Through the Twentieth Century*, 2nd ed. New York: Harper Collins, Inc., 1992.

Pepper, S. *Principles of Art Appreciation*. New York: Harcourt Brace, 1949.

Prown, J. *Mind in Matter: An Introduction to Material Culture Theory and Method*. Winterthur Portfolio, 1–19, 1982.

Schlereth, T. *Material Culture: A Research Guide*. University Press of Kansas, 1985.

Steele, V. *Fashion and Eroticism: Ideals of Feminine Beauty from the Victorian Era to the Jazz Age*. New York: Oxford University Press, 1985.

Steele, V. *Paris Fashion: A Cultural History*. New York: Oxford University Press, 1988.

Wilson, E. *Adorned in Dreams: Fashion and Modernity*. London: Virago Press, 1985.

Wolfe, T. *The Purple Decades*. New York: Berkeley Books, 1983.

# Chapter Ten

# EVALUATION WITHIN THE AESTHETIC FRAMEWORK

- The "wow" in the aesthetic response. How do people evaluate what they see? What is the relationship of likes and dislikes to the process of evaluating the apparel-body-construct? What is the role of cultural preferences, and also of individual experiences, thoughts, and feelings in aesthetic awareness?

- How one can broaden one's likes and dislikes; how can your individual repertoire of likes and dislikes be expanded, particularly in regard to color, intensity, and hue?

- The cultural cycles of liking that occur in historical periods—for example, formal versus informal, close-to-the-body versus loosely fitted clothes. Why certain clothing forms become overexposed and passé.

- The role of evaluation in the four-step framework for analysis of the apparel-body-construct: (1) observation, (2) differentiation, (3) interpretation, and (4) evaluation.

- The role of the form in the evaluation process; the relationship of the aspects of the form to meaning in the apparel-body-construct; the role of the form to the wearer and to cultural ideals.

- The role of the viewer and the target audience in evaluation.

- The role of sensory experiences— visual, tactile, kinesthetic, auditory, and olfactory—in evaluation.

- The concept of typing and the various types: natural, functional, and formal—as related to viewer satisfaction; the role time, culture, and event play in evaluation of the clothing form.

- The role of communication in analysis of the apparel-body-construct, especially with regard to marketing; to grasp why it is important for apparel professionals to develop visual and synectic thinking—the ability to connect diverse things into cohesive forms or structures.

ADOPTING THE SYSTEMATIC APPROACH PRESENTED IN this book leads to the development of perceptual skills and an ability to reason explicitly. You have learned to identify and describe the visual specifics of an apparel-body-construct through an objective language. Extending this approach of visual analysis to evaluation is essential for understanding how the apparel-body-construct is valued—as a statement of what was, what is, or what is to come; as a statement of the ordinary or extraordinary; as a source of pleasure and delight, or displeasure and dismay.

Aesthetics was defined earlier as involvement in looking at a form and learning to understand the resulting experiences. Understanding your response means learning about how you are attracted to the apparel-body-construct and make evaluative judgments. Such experiences include the excitement, pleasure, and satisfaction that focus perceptions and actions. Reasoning must then follow excitement in order to complete the evaluation process so vital to aesthetic response.

From a professional perspective, understanding aesthetic response must be something more than the excitement you get from seeing an apparel-body-construct you personally care about. As you work with clients in their quest to dress for greater satisfaction, you will learn to critique based upon reflection, reasoning, and an understanding of their points of view. Working with a client on a specific problem is a particular challenge because he or she will often look at an apparel-body-construct through associations gleaned from a lifetime of dressing that are different from your own. You will need to stay aware of the process of evaluation taking place within yourself and at the same time with your client.

## WHAT IS THIS "WOW"?—AESTHETIC RESPONSE REVISITED

Every day you make judgments based upon first impressions. Most people have no difficulty expressing opinions about most anything that crosses their path. Expressing feelings about what gives pleasure or dissatisfaction is extremely important because this is the link to what you evaluate as excellent and having value in your life. Such expressive judgments related to apparel are primarily reflexive in terms of meaning. The challenge is to learn to see more and become more aware of what you see.

Likes and dislikes can narrow or expand what we pay attention to, and we can expand what we pay attention to by expanding the range of what we enjoy. One way to broaden aesthetic pleasure is to expose yourself to a wider range of things and experiences than just what you like presently. As the range of liking is increased, the potential for enjoyment and understanding is increased. Stephen Pepper (1949) illustrates experiences of like-dislike at the ends of a pleasure-to-displeasure continuum with neutral existing in the middle as follows:

**Continuum of Pleasure-Displeasure**
**Aesthetic Response and Experience of Like-Dislike**

| Pleasure | Neutral | Displeasure |
|---|---|---|
| ← | | → |
| Like | Little awareness or feeling | Dislike |

The key to aesthetic response is your awareness through experiences of like and dislike. Neutrality—where you experience little awareness or feeling—is not a desirable state for aesthetic response.

## The Formation of Likes and Dislikes

Preferences are generalized expressions of people's likes or dislikes when choosing among alternatives. What you like and dislike becomes a source of pleasure and satisfaction or displeasure and dissatisfaction, expressed in comments such as, "I detest this," or "That is truly enjoyable." Preferences and attention are related, that is, how much you like or dislike an apparel-body-construct is often related to how much attention you give to it.

The development of what we like and dislike is closely tied to early perceptual experiences and associations that result from these experiences. Our early preferences often are very focused upon a few selected properties of the form and upon what we personally would wear. This could include a preference for a certain combination of colors, because you always get compliments when you wear them, or liking a vibrant-appearing image because this is how you really like to look. If you develop your curiosity, you may get involved with the dress of a few select people—self, family, and close friends—and your preferences broaden by their influence. You observe what others are wearing, where and how they are wearing it, and what they are wearing with what. Such associations influence formation of our likes and dislikes, whether or not they are made consciously. If a conscious effort to evaluate ensues, your aesthetic response will broaden.

A very limited view of aesthetic response is that appreciation, that is, our sense of beauty or the "wow" in our life, is totally in the eye of the beholder. This implies that what gives pleasure is absolutely personal and subjective. In one sense this is true, because feelings are very personal. Aesthetic response is also contextual. One's aesthetic awareness must be viewed as embedded within the cultural protocols and roles played by individuals within that culture. The traditions and customs of a culture help to determine one's preferences and tastes, that is, what one likes and dislikes. This influence is not always obvious, and most people do not realize how much their own culture and its associations influence the formation of their ideas about what they enjoy looking at.

Sometimes you have to address past associations in order to change thoughts and feelings. For example, one individual realized that he always associated a particular color combination with his school colors. This association so overshadowed his enjoyment of the combination that he did not know he liked the combination for itself. When he reflected upon the association, he came to realize that he liked the combination immensely. Think back upon colors you have experienced and how associations influence that enjoyment. What are some that come to mind? Does an association such as a certain blue that you disliked but your mother always selected for you to wear as a child mask the possibility that you may like other shades of the color blue? When you are open to your past association and a fuller range of blues, you may have discovered you could select a more desirable blue that gave much pleasure.

What you appreciate can arise from instinctive preference—from your uniqueness as an individual. However, such instinctive preferences for certain colors or textures should not be left unexamined. Just as a person who is color blind does not develop an intense fondness for colors he or she cannot differentiate, one who does not differentiate his or her preference in dress is often blocked from experiencing further pleasure.

Conditioning is a process whereby sensations that may originally be disliked become liked as a result of our experiences with them—a process of "getting used to it." A man who repeatedly wears a shirt he truly dislikes may with time and exposure learn to like it. At first he wears his shirt only because he happened to win a baseball game in that shirt and then considers it lucky and begins to wear it every time he plays another game. However, one day he realizes that he has learned to enjoy the shirt for itself and not just for its association with winning. Some pleasures can result from a process of means-to-end conditioning. For example, when one is tired, the simple routines at the end of the day are a pleasure because they suggest a winding down and there is the knowledge that rest will follow. In clothing, a means-to-an-end example would be when you wear a certain color you dislike because you always receive compliments about how you look and so continue to wear it. Thus, you become conditioned by receiving compliments to wearing the color and begin to like it.

## Crossing the Line from Dislike to Like

Learning to like more and more, expanding your repertoire of what you like, establishes flexibility and increases the range of what you enjoy. If you consciously expand and expose yourself to the unfamiliar—the apparel-body-constructs just beyond your liking—you can experience those you like and, at the same time, be exposed to what you almost like. Repeated exposure may result in increased awareness and enjoyment. Think of instances where you are exposed to something a little different, like a new length of trousers. At first they are very noticeable and may even look odd—like something is amiss.

You think they should be floor length or shorter, but you see them often worn just above the ankle, in magazines, on television, and on people on the street. Your friends begin to talk about the new length in casual conversation. Eventually, after repeated exposure, you have crossed the line from dislike to like.

## Expanding Your Aesthetic Field

The aesthetic field of a person—the range of what he or she appreciates—can be narrow or broad. If it is narrow, an individual appreciates either very specifically or very little, and a desire to understand or a curiosity rarely occurs. The more and varied things you like, the more you are aware and the extent of your ability to enjoy and experience delight is greater. With some persistence it is in your power to expand the range of what you like and dislike. Many people participate in color analysis to learn of its effect in combination with the body colors. Persistence in maintaining this awareness will help you experience their combination more fully. Then you are more likely to enjoy those colors in new and effective uses.

Many tasks that at first seem to totally occupy one's conscious attention can become routine, freeing one to move to a new level of awareness, i.e., learning to ride a bicycle. At first the rider is aware of every sideways movement because each one causes the bike and rider to tumble. Eventually, as the habit of balancing is acquired, you ride without being aware of every small movement and are free to look where you are going in traffic, enjoy the breeze, or even to concentrate on something else. This can happen when observing the apparel-body-construct. At first you concentrate on one thing you like, such as the delicacy of the lines, but this awareness may lead to further notice, this time of the delicacy of color, then you further notice the delicacy of the young girl wearing the delicate lines and delicate colors. Each new level of awareness can lead to further discoveries.

## Sequences of Liking

To expand the range of what you like, consider potential likings as in a sequence—at one end are those that are easy to appreciate and at the other are those that are hard to appreciate. You will need to focus on one particular characteristic or product to establish an order according to a sequence of potential liking. For example, you might order five designers according to a sequence—going from those who design simple forms to those who regularly design more complex forms that are harder for you to appreciate. Exposure to each designer's work in this sequence means you are giving yourself the opportunity to become accustomed and conditioned to each in turn. The idea is that with exposure you may develop a liking for more designers in the sequence.

Sequences are also involved in understanding varying characteristics of the apparel-body-construct as well. Color and its combinations may progress from easy to hard to learn. In what order do you learn to appreciate color? Examine the following list.

- Copy color combinations exactly as you see them.
- Match hues surface to surface; then print (one motif) to plain surface.
- Group colors in traditional combinations of analogous, complementary, triads, etc.
- Distinguish and relate according to hue, value, intensity.
- Combine closely related warm colors of high intensity, then cool and warm colors of low intensity.
- Examine close relationships of hue, value, and intensity: warm colors/cool colors.

Do you recognize yourself anywhere on this list? Would you reorder the sequence according to your learning experiences? What now seems simple to know and like? What is still to learn?

In a lifetime, an individual who is unaware may never complete the entire sequence and therefore may never appreciate the full range of colors and their combinations. Those, however, who work continually with color awareness do learn to appreciate a fuller range of colors and color combinations.

*Application Exercise 10.1*

Map your aesthetic appreciation of colors on the like-to-dislike continuum following. If you imagine this simple continuum you can locate your position in terms of aesthetic appreciation. Select what you are currently "into" in your aesthetic response and place it along with examples of colors or combinations that would be categorized as neutral and disliked. Consider how your aesthetic appreciation changes and expands as you move along in the sequence.

**Mapping Aesthetic Appreciation: An Example**

| Like | Neutral | Dislike |
|------|---------|---------|
| Color contrasts | Matching | Combinations of high intensity |

## Cycles of Liking

Another way to consider expansion from the familiar to the unfamiliar is to consider a cycle of liking. In studying the history of fashion, think of continuums of form characteristics that repeat in cycles. For example, a swing may occur from female dress that is simple to clothing that is more complex, or from clothing worn close to the body to oversized. Cycles based upon such extremes are often mentioned in fashion news and include casual to formal, classic to romantic, retro to modern. Also included in cycles may be other form-related references, such as layout to surface structuring or part-to-whole separates to whole-to-part matching ensembles. Such examples are cyclic because the pendulum swings to one extreme and then back again: Simple becomes simple to the extreme and then the look swings to the more complex and ornate. Those looks in the middle, neither extremely simple nor ornate, tend to become popular more often than the extremes because the pendulum passes through the center twice as often.

Such a cycle may be considered on a continuum from one extreme to another, with you as a viewer swinging back and forth in your liking. You select certain points along the sequence to focus upon and like intensely. The range is great enough or extreme enough that you cannot focus upon the entire cycle at once. Within the cycle you may currently like one extreme and dislike the other.

An individual must find ways to gain exposure to what is just beyond liking and raise awareness of the unfamiliar to expand his or her aesthetic field. Such a viewer is in a state of readiness to find as many available pleasures as possible and be exposed to much richness and variety. By contrast, in a state of neutral, a viewer may access little and get excited over nothing. However, to pursue a conscious understanding of the relationships of visual stimuli and meaning, it is necessary to reach a new level of awareness.

Think of or find apparel-body-constructs you consider middle-of-the-road and ones you consider contrasting forms in terms of like-dislike. Can you trace a pattern in your acceptance of these forms? How does your acceptance relate to fashion cycles?

*Application Exercise 10.2*

## Stimulation Through Change When Monotony Has Set In

As you become used to something new, you take pleasure in experiencing it and seek it out. With continual exposure, you may find less delight and instead find that what was once new and exciting is getting monotonous. Then the item may pass from awareness—there will be "a dulling of delight." Alas, boredom and fatigue have set in.

Some of the result of exposure is a natural dulling process. For example, as a teenager I remember experimenting with a new clothing color each season, but I only selected one hue at a time. Thus, I became intensely aware of nuances of that color and how it combined with others. The next season, having tired of the one hue, I would select another hue. This was not motivated by a conscious desire to learn to like a new color, but the variety of experiences did increase interest in color and when the pleasure was overcome with visual fatigue, it was time to select another.

Fatigue must be differentiated. Two types of fatigue are **sensory fatigue** and **attention fatigue.** An example of sensory fatigue is putting on a pair of blue-toned glasses and looking around. At first everything looks tinged with blue, but then after a time, the color change is less noticeable. The cones of the eye are no longer responding because of the continuous stimulation. Sensory experiences can be refreshed quickly with a change to the opposite stimulation. For example, looking at complementary colors such as yellow, a physiological opposite of blue, will relieve the cones of the eye. The same experience occurs with other senses. Wearing perfume at first permeates awareness and then dulls down, but one's sense of smell can respond intensely again when the perfume is applied fresh the next day. Sensory fatigue is short-term, and recovery is stimulated by a change for the senses. This change can occur for you visually as your eye travels throughout an apparel-body-construct to enjoy a change in sensory experience.

Attention fatigue is based upon an over-awareness to one stimulus that requires forgetting, as with a popular style that is seen so often it becomes stale. An example is the polyester double-knit pantsuit, so popular in the United States in the 1970s that young and old wore it everywhere. The look was neat because it did not wrinkle, was flattering to many body types, and more casual than a suit, but still presented a put-together appearance. The pantsuit was easy to produce and care for and represented a new product for both men and women, especially for many older women who had never worn trousers. But that was several decades ago. Although pantsuits of wool, cotton, or silk are worn today, attention fatigue has existed long-term for that exact combination of surface and layout structure so popular in the 1970s.

Monotony dulls sensation, puts an apparel-body-construct out of awareness, and is therefore to be avoided. Change is required to prevent fatigue. When no changes occur in what one is viewing, either sensory or attention fatigue may result. One way to break viewing monotony and again become aware is to stimulate the viewer through some unexpected addition or subtraction. Then the change may bring the viewer from neutrality to an experience of like-dislike on the pleasure-pain continuum.

The Japanese recognize the value of change to stimulate awareness. In a small area of the home designated as a family space, they plan for continual change with pictures, photographs, scrolls, and choice bits of fruit that have special meaning to the family. This one area is designated to be changed frequently to refresh awareness and stimulate interest. Those in the apparel industry also want to keep fatigue from the viewer's experience by offering enough change for continued awareness. Designers, merchandisers, and fashion editors are challenged to offer enough change to stimulate awareness, but not so much that the viewer turns away in confusion.

Expanding aesthetic response is a desirable state for a critic and a necessary step for the apparel professional. By doing so, you optimize the opportunity to be aware of many apparel-body-constructs and therefore broaden your experience base. As a professional, you are involved not only in learning to make explicit your own evaluations, but also in developing an awareness of how your clientele make evaluations. Understanding the process of evaluation optimizes the experience for you as well your clientele.

When a clothing ensemble is worn regularly, it may become almost a uniform and the wearer may not be aware of it. But when not worn for awhile and when reintroduced in a different configuration, it may become fresh again. Consider a once favorite item of clothing, such as a sweater, that you have tired of and consider how it could be worn combined in a different way—switch figure and ground or part to whole—so that it looks differently in the ensemble. Do you then see it with fresh eyes?

Now apply this experience to visual display. You find yourself needing to display T-shirts that have become pretty ho-hum to your customers. How can you freshen the experience?

*Application Exercise 10.3*

## UNDERSTANDING EVALUATION

**Evaluation** means assessing the value of something. The objective is to consider how an apparel-body-construct is valued according to its form and meaning. In aesthetic terms, this is the integration of visual stimuli (the apparel-body-construct) with personal experiences and expectations that the viewer brings to the process from culturally shared perspectives. If successful, the result is a positive aesthetic response.

Evaluation is the final step of the process of examining an apparel-body-construct. By this time the viewer is assured that evaluation will be more meaningful because it follows and completes the previous three steps. The four-step framework for analysis of the apparel-body-construct outlined in Chapter 3 and summarized in Table 10.1 is: (1) observation, (2) differentiation, (3) interpretation, and (4) evaluation. In *observation*, the apparel-body-construct was described as thoroughly as possible. In *differentiation*, the apparel-body-construct was broken up into its components and elemental aspects. In *interpretation*, the focus was on what summarized the form. Now the last step, *evaluation*, is a summarizing aspect of the framework and is dependent upon the other three steps. How does the apparel-body-construct you described and analyzed in Steps 1 and 2 relate to Steps 3 and 4? Much of your understanding of evaluation arises from completing the three steps prior to this last step but, in addition, it forces you to consider how you respond to an apparel-body-construct within a personal and cultural context. Questions to ask are: How do I as the viewer respond—with pleasure or displeasure? How does this particular apparel-body-construct form relationships within itself and with others? How is it a statement of the culture, a particular event, of the here and now or another historic era?

| | | |
|---|---|---|
| **TABLE 10.1** | | |
| *An Expert Viewer's Framework* | Adopting the systematic approach presented is necessary for the development of the perceptual skills that lead to a more discriminating response. The expert viewer has learned to identify and describe the specifics of an apparel-body-construct through a systematic process. An objective language documents perception of the apparel-body-construct. What follows is a review of the steps, incorporating the language introduced throughout this book. | |

**Steps in the Perceptual Process**

1. **Observation:** Attending to and describing what we see.

   a. Note existing descriptive information for help in understanding the form. This includes such information as designer, manufacturer, date of creation or display, country of origin, for whom intended, materials and techniques used.

   b. Focus on the entire form. (Refer to Chapters 4, 5, and 6.) Observe and describe what is there as completely as possible. How is the silhouette defined? How does the form separate from the surrounding space? Is it **closed** or **open, whole-to-part** or **part-to-whole**? What is figure and what is ground? Are they **separated** or **integrated**? Are the surfaces **flat** or **rounded, determinate** or **indeterminate**?

   c. Describe the features that define the form. How is the body defined? What is emphasized and what has priority? How does clothing create focus? What type of structuring is used—**layout, surface, light and shadow**? What **linear definers** are used? What types of points, lines, shapes? Are they rounded, angular, or straight? How many are there? What is their orientation—vertical, horizontal, or diagonal? Size—small or large? What are the **surface definers**? What types of colors are used? Describe each color as to hue, value, and intensity. What textures are used? Are they rough or smooth, crisp or soft? How do light and shadow affect the surface?

2. **Differentiation:** Consider the relations in what we see.

   In this step, the influence of one part on another is analyzed. (Refer to Chapters 7 and 8.)

   a. Order the parts. Which parts are noticed first? Number the parts in the order in which they are viewed.

   b. Examine the parts within the whole in further detail. Why were you attracted first to part number 1, then 2, and then 3? What separates from the whole for attention? How many separate parts are there? How are the parts modified within the whole? What influence do definers have in integration and segregation? Consider the Gestalt principles of organization: **similarity, closure, proximity, continuation.** Explain the significance of the modifiers—**number, direction, visual weight, size, spatial position.**

c. Describe **organization.** Is the eye directed throughout the form? If directed, is it vertical, horizontal, or circular? What causes the direction of the visual path? If undirected, are the parts separate and independent? What is **grouping** and what is **separating**? Where was the point of entry? How does it become a source of focus? Which parts refer the viewer to the organization of the whole apparel-body-construct?

<table>
<tr><td>3. Interpretation: What summarizes the form?<br><br>At this stage, look for the associations of form and meaning that seem to summarize and explain the form. This step builds upon the preceding two. (Refer to Chapters 8 and 9.)</td><td>a. Note whether the apparel-body-construct encourages simultaneous viewing of the whole, successive, or separated. How much activity is taking place? How many relationships are there? Does the apparel-body-construct appear simple or complex? What are the priority relationships?<br><br>b. Consider and record all associations. At first, record them without judgment. Consider all alternatives of interpretation. Pull from all past experiences, consider and test alternatives of interpretation. What associations are directly observed in the form? Step back from the evidence provided by direct observation and consider indirect associations. What within the apparel-body-construct relates to cultural values and priorities? What would interest viewers? How does the apparel-body-construct relate to specific situations?<br><br>c. Select the ideas that help to characterize the apparel-body-construct. Consider your first impressions from b. Which seem to be possible and probable? To what audience(s) might the apparel-body-construct appeal? What are the features that help determine your impressions? Are they different from those you originally thought were the controlling features? Consider how the apparel-body-construct is organized and how its ideas are presented. What is the message?</td></tr>
</table>

**TABLE 10.1**

*An Expert Viewer's Framework*

continued

*continued*

TABLE 10.1

*An Expert Viewer's
Framework*

continued

| | |
|---|---|
| 4. **Evaluation**: Assessing the value. | Look back over the previous steps. How does the apparel-body-construct you described and analyzed in Steps 1 and 2 relate to Steps 3 and 4? Here the objective is to consider how this apparel-body-construct is valued according to its message. Questions to ask are: How do I as the viewer respond—with pleasure and satisfaction or displeasure? How does this particular apparel-body-construct relate to others? How is it a statement of the here and now or another historic era? How is it valued within the culture? |

The relationship between form and meaning may or may not be explicit. Often the form characteristics that relate to expression and meaning require us to be aware of a sophisticated set of associations. Interpretation was discussed in Chapter 9 as a process of summarizing the essential character of the apparel-body-construct. Evaluation requires articulating rather explicitly how meaning has been tied to visual effects.

## Evaluation as an Outcome of Interpretation—An Example

You will find explicit interpretations of the apparel-body-construct everywhere to inform the viewer. You will find interpretations in catalogs, displays, exhibits, fashion shows, that is, a visual interpretation of how clothing is to be combined and worn. Written text also informs the viewer, especially in matters related to upcoming fashion. Such interpretations are highly publicized because the intention is to develop a following based upon the summary.

Often the message has the purpose of framing an overall theme—to define and give a name to upcoming fashion. Those working in the media realize the necessity of a congruent message, that is, where written text accompanies the visual. Such a message is more successful if it informs the viewer and is congruent with viewer expectations as well.

This type of message may be selected by an editor to interpret a fall fashion statement. If it is thematic, it may transcend any one of the apparel-body-constructs by itself. In Figure 10.1, a theme, "The Long View," has been selected for six Paris couture designers to summarize their fall collections. Though the message is pervasive, it is not meant to be indicative of a particular designer, because six different designers are featured. There is a consistent vertical silhouette among the apparel-body-constructs, and the viewer can easily interpret and relate the message that focuses upon the silhouettes of the six apparel-body-constructs. Identifying silhouette is always basic to recognition of the apparel-body-construct and therefore is a good reference point for development of a theme.

a *Chanel*

b *Valentino*

c *Christian Lacroix*

d *Gianni Versace*

e *Pierre Balmain*

f *Emanuel Ungaro*

**FIGURE 10.1A, B, C, D, E & F**

*An examination of editorial message and its relationship to the apparel-body-constructs of six design houses.*

Courtesy of Fairchild Publications.

Taking this theme, we will now examine the accompanying text which reads:

Paris—*Long and lean, long and strong—those were the watchwords of the Seventies. So it isn't surprising long lengths are returning as the Seventies ready-to-wear mood infuses the couture. Here are some of the best* (Women's Wear Daily, *July 15, 1996, pp. 6–7).*

Here the text gives reference to the retro look of the 70s, simplified to "long and lean," which can be quickly surmised from the silhouette. In the context of already abundant long lengths of the mid-1990s, the viewer may wonder what is new here. Is this supposed to be a message of change? The viewer would have to delve further into a visual examination to determine what is really new. A more subtle message is the infusion of ready-to-wear and couture—a cue that couture is not different in mood from ready-to-wear this season. One could expect a common theme this fall in a wide range of couture to ready-to-wear.

There are additional messages here that can be just as clear if the viewer chooses to examine the visual evidence further. There are some other striking similarities for all of the apparel-body-constructs, for example, a center front emphasis of some sort, ranging from the continuation of V neck and center front opening at the hem in some, to centered vertical rows of buttons and other lines and shapes. Also, all the examples emphasize the shaping of the body torso, that is, they are not hanging from the shoulders with no body indentations on the way to the hem. These are not "one size fits all." The wearers reflect an interest in paying attention to body with exercise and healthy diet, etc., to look right in the clothing.

There are also differences in visual definition and organization. The predominant means of structuring varies from layout being primary, with surface structure a close second, followed by some shadow structuring. In the spatial relation, the apparel-body-constructs in Figure 10.1a and f are more whole-to-part, while the remainder are more part-to-whole, and even this varies in how it was accomplished. In the Chanel (Figure 10.1a), the dark hat and leggings are perceived as figure when seen as the vertical lines, or as ground when the long, shaped coat becomes figure. The Versace (Figure 10.1d) is part-to-whole primarily because the upper torso, with the asymmetry of the curved line and one cuff and the similar light value of the skin of the face and neck. The twist of the hair also repeats the asymmetry of the curve outlined on the dress. Then there is a successive quality to this apparel-body-construct because of the predominance of the contrasts in the upper torso and blending treatment of the legs and shoes on the lower half of the body.

Now consider the individual themes of each apparel-body-construct. For example, the Valentino (Figure 10.1b) and Lacroix (Figure 10.1c) both have more surface structuring than the others, but the Lacroix (Figure 10.1c) looks a little like Western cowboy style, while the lush surfaces of the Valentino

(Figure 10.1b) are more reminiscent of the opulence and glamour of Hollywood movies in the 1930s. What themes are represented in the other apparel-body-constructs?

You can continue to examine for the similarities and differences, but the ultimate question for evaluation is: Did the editor capture the theme of long and lean for the reader? Was it successful? You will probably conclude "yes" on both counts. Selection of the theme is justified as an easy reference to remember, that is, long and lean is more memorable than saying a "close-to-the-body vertical silhouette." Both mean the same, but "long and lean" is catchy. Even though it does not capture the entire visual message, you could argue that the editor wants to give a simple message that can be shared by all, but not to state the entire visual message that remains for the curious viewer to discover and enjoy.

Upon examining other such messages, they may not be so explicitly stated. It may be up to the viewer to respond and then determine how order and stimulation occur. Sorting out an implicit message is often desirable, especially if it is there to be discovered. Then you can determine how congruent the message is and how successful the integration of form with response.

## Establishing Criteria for Evaluation

To understand evaluation means to be continually aware of the criteria used in the process. A viewer who reflects upon personal experiences and perspective to observe and evaluate can develop an awareness of what is personal and what is shared and be able to differentiate between them. For example, an awareness of the difference between personal and shared is represented in this statement, "The color would be very attractive to many, although it would not be my personal choice." By differentiating personal from shared, a viewer can move toward greater understanding of the process of evaluation. Both need to be included in an evaluative response.

Establishing criteria for evaluation is part of the process of evaluating the apparel-body-construct for individual as well as for professional purposes. If a response is an expression of an individual's point of view, then the question is how to turn such a response into interpretation and evaluation that addresses context. An example would be, "This is one of my favorite shirts because I have always loved anything with blue! Once I had a blue shirt and it gave me a good feeling when I wore it." Two of the components of evaluation are apparent here—instinct and association. Instinct may be the reason why the color blue is so desirable in the first place. It is known that certain hues are favorites of more people than others, for example, blue is an expressed favorite of many more than say, orange or green. Also voiced is the association of present evaluation with past experience: A shirt that felt good in the wearing is associated with positive feelings. If you as an apparel professional are working with a client who is expressing these preferences, you have a fairly easy task—keep blue in the next selections but point out its relationship to the whole. Referencing the entire apparel-body-construct will provide other associations for the client to consider.

Evaluation also involves an awareness and knowledge of the place of individual expectations and culturally established conventions and coding. An example would be: "The red-white-blue combination is being worn again this spring." This comment could come from an observer who is evaluating based upon knowledge of shared meaning and message and how assessing these particular colors is related to the spectrum of apparel-body-constructs within that culture. The statement reflects tradition, that is, the conventions of when this combination of colors is worn and, by implication, who might be the audience.

Identification of audience is always critical in evaluation. The retailer stocking from a line of clothing will have to evaluate a number of apparel-body-constructs for a particular audience. This means knowing the audience and estimating their collective response to the apparel-body-constructs in question and buying accordingly. The designer will constantly evaluate his or her work against that of others, as well as for an audience of potential wearers. The personal shopper evaluates for a very particular one-on-one audience and selects criteria accordingly—from making the client look his or her best, following fashion of the moment, dressing for an interview to get that new job—or possibly a mixture of all three factors.

To establish criteria for evaluation, we must again focus on the components of the aesthetic response: the form, the viewer, and the contexts. Each in turn needs to be considered in the evaluation process, but evaluation, following interpretation, of necessity involves relationships. We can understand the extent and importance of their interface if we first discuss each component separately as it relates to evaluation.

# THE FORM

The form itself needs to be considered in the evaluation process. At the end of the four-step process, the evaluator/viewer can step back and consider questions such as: Does the apparel-body-construct reflect or shape the time in which it exists? How does it relate to specific priorities within the culture? If fashion is a priority, how does it reflect the times? If individuality is a priority, then how does the apparel-body-construct reflect individuality?

## Referencing the Whole and Its Parts

Evaluation requires that we continue to reference the whole of the apparel-body-construct, as well as its parts and details. This has been a major emphasis throughout this framework, and it represents a major shift in perspective for most viewers.

The relationship among the parts and the whole is a means to assess the apparel-body-construct. For example, a man who selects a tie may not think at all about how it will relate to the whole. The tie is so appealing that the evaluation is limited to the tie alone. In like manner, a woman may select shoes and not consider the apparel-body-construct and how the shoes will influence the whole. Everyone knows of individuals who have a particular interest in shoes, ties, hats, or some portion of an ensemble—with a collector's instinct—where the excitement exists in the details of the part. By connecting the part back to the whole, new and rewarding levels of relationships can be discovered.

Consider a person who pays attention to only the combinations of clothing and not how they are worn or any of the relationships to personal coloring or body shape. What integrates and what separates may go unnoticed if the body to clothing to surround is not noted. In Figure 10.2a and b, these relationships are important to what the viewer absorbs. In Figure 10.2a, the light and shadow of the surround highlight and direct the viewer. In Figure 10.2b, the personal colors contrast in value to the tennis shoes, shorts, T-shirts, and white areas of the jacket, and they provide figure at first. Therefore, areas of the jacket call attention to the head and legs that otherwise blend with the surround.

Remember that the apparel-body-construct includes the contexts of the immediate physical surround, as well as the cultural milieu. Think how much richer the message is when you consider the contexts. Imagine a woman in an indeterminate, cool blue, satin lingerie ensemble of robe and gown in the middle of an ice field. The headline reads "On Ice" and was described as "frosty tones"—a major direction for spring and summer. Think of how much richer the message would be if you consider the contexts. First, the contrast of such a cool message with the warmer season of the year would be refreshing—like eating an ice cream cone on a warm day. Then consider ice as cool and often transparent. Now imagine the apparel-body-construct. Boundaries fade into each other, in the cool hues of the robe and gown, between similar values and intensity of the lingerie ensemble and the body, hair, and makeup, and finally the body and clothing with the immediate surround. Such a rich contextual viewing is possible only by referencing the entirety, including the contextual surround.

## Considering the Relation of Order and Chaos

Experiences of generations have taught artists and designers a number of methods of preventing viewing fatigue. These are called principles of design, with the overarching concept of "unity with variety." Sometimes such a "principle" seems vague because it covers the gamut of order to chaos. The premise upon which such a principle is based is psychological. An apparel-body-construct is built upon and around the body, and various materials are put together in such a way as to create a composition, a unity that avoids monotony through stimulating variety. The creator is caught between two undesirable results that cause the viewer to lose interest: too much order or too

a                                                                b

**FIGURE 10.2A & B**

*To evaluate the apparel-body-construct, the viewer is aware of all relationships—the
clothing, the clothing to the body, the clothed body to the contextual surround. In
Figure 10.2a, spotlight and dark in the surround define what you see. The light-value
coat stands out against the dark surround, and the dark trousers and shoes stand out
against the spotlight on the floor. The head is barely identifiable. The figure-ground
relationship is affected by personal coloring within the apparel-body-construct. In Figure 10.2b, the white tennis shoes, shorts, T-shirt, and white areas of the jacket are
viewed as figure first. The figural qualities of the white areas of the jacket then call
attention to the dark areas of the jacket. Then the eye searches for the other dark relationships of head and legs that otherwise blend into the dark surrounding areas. The
value contrasts help call attention to the dark and light values in the POLO SPORT
logo of Ralph Lauren that prominently accompanies the apparel-body-construct.*

Designed by: (a) DKNY and (b) Polo Ralph Lauren. Courtesy of Fairchild Publications.

much disorder. Either extreme may cause a negative response. The idea is to
stimulate the viewer with enough order to provide pleasure but not so much
order as to be monotonous or so little order as to cause confusion.

**Design and Viewer Stimulation**

| Monotony | Unity in Variety | Confusion |
|---|---|---|
| Too much order | | Too little order |

What sorts of forms tend to result in favorable experiences? Some are designed so that they stimulate, while others are not. To be appreciated means a product must have the power to create a vivid and satisfying human experience. To evaluate an apparel-body-construct, then, means also to consider what creates such satisfaction. Because all humans have similar instincts and similar emotional mechanisms for meeting frustration and conflict, the basic psychological principles universally enter into our evaluation. These include principles of organization, such as focus, balance, visual weight, and movement; the Gestalt organizing factors; spatial distance; figure-ground; and so forth. Throughout this book many ways have been cited to achieve visual stimulation through change and at the same time provide order through visual relationships. For example, gradation provides order and movement using perceptible changes in some definer, such as light to dark value, rough to smooth surfaces. An organization can be successive with a hierarchy established through relationships of figure-ground, and focus can be established through variations in visual weight.

Since variety carried to excess results in confusion, and unity carried to excess results in monotony, it is essential that design, by offering some of each, holds our interest steadily and continuously. What does this mean? Viewing fatigue and monotony can be stopped by bringing in a contrasting quality. But with too much variety comes confusion that may threaten the composition. If the organization breaks down, the viewer will likely turn away. An apparel-body-construct needs relationships for two reasons: to bring order for integration and to supply contrast to stimulate.

## Providing Stimulation and Order

When the focus is on the form itself, the criteria for evaluation are numerous. A basic tenet is that the apparel-body-construct must be stimulating to look at. Much satisfaction can be derived by the viewer who is educated to pay attention to some of the intricacies of the form and its relationships that provide order. How the component parts are perceived within the whole may be the subject of evaluation. Fashion writers often describe clothing as a good background piece or a good focus, for example, "This is a wonderful basic!" or "This jacket will become the focus of the ensemble this spring!"

Stimulation is a powerful influence upon attention that takes place within the form. This includes many visual definers: the colors of the fashion season, whether surfaces are printed or plain, or a certain line or shape. It also includes how an ensemble is put together and worn: the proportions of parts to the whole, the message of the look.

In a culture that values stimulation from current forms in fashion, the apparel-body-construct is continually changing in many ways, and what was so delightful to look at yesterday is predictable or passé today. However, such timeliness also implies a degree of consistency and an underlying ordering that needs to be understood. Certain properties can be identified as changing gradually while others become the focus for change, for example, a particular width of lapel or length of hem, changes from one definer to another, this year's color, next year's shape or texture. The predicament is to present stimulation without going too far. Too little change, however, in clothing is a concern of Agins (1996), a reporter for *The Wall Street Journal*, who argues that if clothes are going to sell in the fall, changes cannot be so subtle that marketers must point them out to their customers.

Still another source of evaluation is the relationship of the clothing to the body of the wearer. Is line, shape, or color selected for the full benefit of the wearer and the culture's ideal? Does the clothing selected enhance the wearer? Many wearers want to be assured that they look their very best and that means taking full advantage of their individual strengths. Often the task here is to interpret what is in the marketplace according to these individual strengths.

Associations of meaning can be powerful in viewing the apparel-body-construct in its relation to an overarching theme. Such themes often stimulate attention in the process of evaluation. The six designers featured under the theme "The Long View" have already been discussed. Sometimes fashion is identified by an entire look and is named according to our recognition of its origin: the Jackie Kennedy look of the 1960s named after the prominent wearer of the period or the DKNY look by Donna Karan, a New York designer. Other, more generalized, characterizations derived from meaning associations include, "the yuppies," "the mods," or "the sophisticated gentleman and elegant lady." If you close your eyes, the images brought to mind of each characterization will surely differ.

Other criteria may be considered for evaluating the form. Associated criteria include how much it appears to have cost and its related investment, how much it resembles tradition or history, or how useful it may be within a person's wardrobe. For example, as an investment people may exclaim: "This is worth the price!" Marketplace cost, purpose, care, and durability are often used as guides for evaluation of the form. For example, it is expensive so it must look good; it is good enough for the intended purpose; it will last and look the same through many wearings. Wearing investment apparel may give pleasure as well as status, such as when the owner exclaims, "This old thing! I wear and wear it. I am so glad you like it." However, when evaluation of the form involves such associated criteria, the way the apparel-body-construct looks is usually still a major consideration.

Thoughtful consideration is required as to which criteria are to be used to evaluate the form. Identification of the criteria based upon the message goals is critical to accomplishing a pleasing and satisfying outcome.

## THE VIEWER

Evaluation often centers around the general audience for the apparel-body-construct—those likely to appreciate it. Who is the viewer/audience to be considered in evaluation? Is it one of the following: J. Crew? Wal-Mart? Target? Victoria's Secret? JCPenney? J.Q. Public? John Doe? Is it a national or local company? Is it a designer? Who the audience is matters in the evaluation process, whether an individual or a corporation.

The audience may be an individual **client,** the one the professional works with in providing a creative solution to clothing needs. Then the client and the professional are both viewers and wearers. The perspective of the **viewer** is to consider how the apparel-body-construct appears visually, either on oneself or another. This involves some distancing if considering oneself and one's own dressed body as the visual form. A client may only be interested in clothing on his or her own body. Others appreciate the apparel-body-construct regardless of whether or not they would wear it personally. The **wearer,** however, is concerned with the experience of wearing, that is, how clothing feels physically, how it moves on the body, how it makes the wearer feel in the clothing. The two perspectives may merge, for example, the wearer looking at himself or herself in a mirror may be considering both perspectives—how it looks like it feels on the body. Or, the wearer may be able to consider each perspective separately.

Although the professional is usually concerned with the perspectives of both the wearer and the viewer, the client also needs to consider both. The client acts as viewer when he or she is primarily concerned with visual appearance and how it gets translated and communicated to others. The client acts as wearer when primarily concerned with personal feelings and needs while wearing the ensemble. Problems may arise when both viewpoints are not considered, such as when a client tries on shoes that are exquisite looking (viewer) but physically uncomfortable (wearer). Dissatisfaction and displeasure are likely to be the outcome if both wearer and viewer perspectives are not considered.

Many designers have a viewing audience in mind as they work, and then the designer centers evaluation on how to fulfill those intentions. Ask a designer what viewer he or she has in mind in the design process and you will often discover a clearly specified, articulated audience and/or message. A designer (or designer's business agent) is continually estimating a market from a viewer's perspective, usually looking for new markets for the same product, as well as determining how the product might be altered to maintain market stimulation and thus a market share. Likewise, manufacturers and retailers consider their viewer market in order to plan stock that will meet client expectations. Then the form can be evaluated for its consistent appeal, that is, whether the designer or manufacturer is appealing to the same viewer or has changed direction for a different viewer.

At some point, questions that address the relation of the viewer to the product must be asked: How many people could or would be wearers? Who would be interested in viewing the apparel-body-construct: One person? Few people? Many? Is the appeal of the apparel-body-construct to satisfy the unique-to-me needs of specific people or the collective needs of many? A paradigm of twentieth century retail that began in the nineteenth century has been to "clothe the masses." However, authors such as Peppers and Rogers (1993) believe that a paradigm shift is occurring and professionals must think more about building relationships one client or customer at a time. The personal touch has always had an appeal for the customer. Niche marketing is simply finding a match between product and viewer. For example, an athletic shoe-maker offers a customized athletic shoe by recording such customer specifications as shoe size, body weight and height, level of running ability, and intended use. Then shoes are designed and produced based upon this information. The nature of the audience for the apparel-body-construct then serves as a criterion for evaluation.

## Considering Sensory Experiences

Our sensory experiences—visual, tactile, kinesthetic, auditory, and olfactory—are a basic resource of evaluation. A viewer who particularly enjoys color and is sensuously involved in the visual aspects of the surfaces of materials will select according to color. The person who enjoys touching fur or velvet is involved in a tactile experience. The person who enjoys how the fabrics feel upon the body is influenced by kinesthetic experiences.

Our direct sensory experiences affect us. Meaning comes from active exploration of our physical environment. Very early in life, people learn from pushing, pulling, and touching objects. They are influenced by the tactile experiences of early childhood: the slipperiness of the ribbon on the binding of a blanket, the softness of a teddy bear, the pleasure of being rubbed dry with a towel, or the sensation of a mother's hair gently brushing against them.

Early sensory experiences can interact and influence each other. A visual preference for rich or deep colors may be the result of previous pleasant tactile experiences. In the process of giving a compliment, some may require a tactile reinforcement, "That's a great shirt!" Confirmation is made by touching or rubbing the surface of the shirt sleeve between the fingers.

Auditory and olfactory responses also may be influential in evaluation. Think of the effect of the swish or crackle of a crisp taffeta skirt or the marching sound of heels clicking against a sidewalk. Does the sound in any way affect other senses? A pleasant smell can affect our visual experience of the apparel-body-construct and certainly our overall aesthetic response. The scent of perfume as a person walks past is a direct sensory experience and may even cause us to look more closely. Other smells include raw silk, wet wool, or chlorine in a bathing suit that we may or may not enjoy. For example, our past experience may be called to mind of marching in a band in the rain with the unwelcome smell of wet wool permeating our nostrils.

Separating one's sensory experiences is a good reflective exercise. Sometimes an individual responds with a healthy balance among several senses and sometimes from one dominating sensory experience. For example, a child learning about soft tactile experiences may drape a piece of velvet somewhere on the body to touch at will. Certainly a person's love of weaving may arise from such an enjoyment of tactile qualities of fibers. A stronger product results if the artist learns to consider a sensory balance in creating the design, that is, integrating visual sensory experiences along with tactile.

Questioning the relation of each of our senses to our experience and response to clothing is useful. Products of clothing often appeal to several of our senses. We may respond to visual textural effects, that is, a tweed coat is often more interesting to look at than to touch, but both senses are in play. A plaid surface is primarily a visual experience, although people will sometimes run their fingers over the surface anyway. However, a surface of sequins that appears shimmering and soft may translate in touching or wearing to being scratchy and uncomfortable. The viewer's experience of sequins differs from the tactile one of the wearer.

## Considering Viewer Expectations

Expectations are a powerful influence upon the viewer because they provide a standard for evaluation. They can occur for the viewer because of associations of features or properties that usually go together so certain combinations come to be expected. This is the result of a categorization process that was discussed in Chapter 2; this process can be individually or culturally based.

**Typing** is viewing through a system of associations (associated traits, definers, meanings, etc.) that is recognizable as a whole. Type is an important concept because it affects our expectations and how much pleasure we receive from what we perceive. Two functions are performed based on typing:

1. It is a means of providing for our expectations by producing a familiar order.
2. It is a source of recognition and delight.

Type is an example of coherence, that is, a unit that holds together by a system of associations, perceived with regularity. Within one culture, a type can serve as a source of convention or code, that is, it constitutes a meaningful association that is recognized as such.

Type, however, is not stereotyping, which involves repeated action from a set of very minimal cues. In stereotyping the viewer glosses over significant differences, but in typing the viewer focuses upon the nuances that become a source of delight. Consider the example of a client who is much older than the personal shopper. After a thorough interview with the client, the assignment is to select an ensemble for a specific occasion. The client cannot understand the misconnection of the ensemble selection with the cues from the interview. Upon examination the personal shopper realizes she has been dressing her client based upon what she thought a grandmother should wear instead of paying attention to the interview and client's responses. She has been working from a stereotype that glossed over significant differences.

Variations of type are based upon their sources:

- Basic human drives
- Nature
- Function
- Technique
- Formal

Each of these categories will be described and examples given in the following discussion.

*Type: Basic Human Drives.*  An aspect of type is related to satisfaction of our basic drives. This includes relief of hunger by eating food, physical exhaustion by sleeping on a bed, and cold by snuggling under a warm blanket. Such innate drives can periodically take over our thoughts and behavior. Our experience with hunger, for example, is based upon finding food, the eating process, and other behaviors surrounding the basic drive of relieving hunger.

Translated into how we perceive clothing: Shoes may look sexy, sweaters warm, and trousers comfortable. The way clothing can function within a society includes satisfaction of innate needs, from basic physiological needs to self-actualization. Maslow (in Thorsen, 1983) developed a theory of human nature based upon certain motivations. He believed that human beings constantly strive to surpass a given state. If basic needs are satisfied, human beings can move on to actualize their potential nature or essence. He assumed that human nature shows itself in the features of self-actualizing people based on their cognitive faculties, creativity, self-knowledge, and moral actions. All such human needs are important to address, and types arise from fulfilling such needs.

| | Needs Classification | Example of Association with Wearer |
|---|---|---|
| **TABLE 10.2**<br><br>*Maslow's Needs Hierarchy and the Apparel-Body-Construct* | Self-actualization to become all that one is capable of becoming | To dress with full recognition and understanding of one's individuality |
| | Self-esteem and esteem from others | To dress with distinction and consistency |
| | Need to belong, that is, friendship, acceptance | To dress like one's friends and conform with one's associates |
| | Need for safety, security, dark, protection | To dress to disguise oneself at night |
| | Physiological needs: hunger, thirst, sex, sleep | To dress to keep warm and dry; to express sexuality |

Think of clothing you wear that relates to each of these needs.

*Type: Relation to Nature.* The viewer may respond to the apparel-body-construct based upon the degree to which it resembles nature or ideal natural forms. These are pervasive and include our concept of animals, plants, clouds, water, mountains, humans, and all natural objects.

References to natural forms within the apparel-body-construct are plentiful. Many shapes resembling natural objects have been knitted into sweaters and used in the design of jewelry and handbags—dogs, trees, plants. People refer to fibers giving a "natural" look and the criterion of "naturalness" can become part of our ecological consciousness. People associate various shapes with natural objects; surface motifs may be compared for their resemblance to nature. In Figure 10.3a, the surface of the young girl's swimsuit is an indeterminate floral motif with curving lines that repeat in the shape and texture of her hair. The young girl herself appears completely natural in the setting of shimmering water that carries out the curving lines of the surface of the swimsuit. The young boy in Figure 10.3b is wearing clothing to celebrate his

a

b

**FIGURE 10.3A & B**

*In Figure 10.3a, the natural type offers a harmonious connection between the apparel, the body, and the context. Organic shapes on the surface resemble leaves and flowers, and repeat the curves of the loosely fitted silhouette in Figure 10.3b.*

Courtesy of: (a) Target Stores and (b) Janel Urke.

heritage with motifs of curving, organic shapes resembling leaves and other natural forms. In addition, the clothing, loosely fitted, repeats these curves in the silhouette. Thus arises the natural type, and our response is influenced by expectations for this type.

Natural typing makes reference to the physical proportions of human beings, and our response to the apparel-body-construct is affected by the pleasure/displeasure response that arises from certain types within a culture. What is considered desirable—that is, a particular combination of physical and facial features and bodily proportions—changes over time and place. Certain combinations of these factors are linked to age and gender characteristics and yield ideals that are esteemed, desired, and seen as embodying the most pleasurable human forms at a particular time and place. What are considered ideal body types within a given culture? How are such ideal body types expressed? For example, the fashion model has recently been considered an ideal body type, at least for the display of clothing, but hardly representing a natural type. As the population of the United States generally gets older, will there be an ideal type represented among this group that is more natural?

The extent to which physical types and combinations that we may find attractive are related to basic instinctive drives or natural types is a question. Are males and females attracted to certain types based upon instincts of mating, nest-building, and child-rearing? What are the roles of instinct and learning in the formation of ideals of physical beauty? Certainly standards or ideals of beauty could fall under natural types. However, the ancient traditions of binding feet in China or exaggerating protruding lips in Africa are accentuations of what could be considered intrinsically attractive features related to gender. Today in the United States women redden their lips, darken eyelashes and brows, accentuate facial features and hair through makeup and use chemicals for curling/straightening. Men get hair transplants and expend time and energy working out to accentuate muscle development. Both men and women use hair dyes and get facelifts and tummy tucks. Are these part of an innate universal drive to accentuate what is sexually attractive? Are they learned behaviors that are expressed in varying ways in different social groups?

*Type: Function.*  Clothing is valued for its function, that is, how it satisfies the requirements of its intended purpose and the needs of the wearer. If a product is highly valued for those nuances of purpose, then it is a type that will become part of our experience of pleasure and satisfaction.

The degree to which clothing appears to satisfy its apparent purpose is related to our perception of its use in the past. Generalization from our past experiences with apparel helps to establish expectancies of function. This is especially the case for basic clothing categories that people have experienced regularly—polo shirt, trenchcoat—and how they perform is of uppermost importance. For example, you can view a trench coat that performs as a raincoat with the expectation not only for how it appears visually, but also with a view toward how it will keep you dry, and if indeed it does keep you dry. If this becomes a source of pleasure in our response to the product, it is indeed operating as a functional type. Figure 10.4 illustrates clothing operating as a functional type.

A premise of design in the early twentieth century was, "Form follows function." Following this premise creates a certain type of product. However, this may overlap with formal type, to be discussed later, if the traits are perceived more from the perspective of their association than in light of their function.

***Type: Relation to Technique.*** Type related to technique has to do with the requirements of skill in the production of objects. Technical types are closely related to functional types, but are not identical. Technical types often become a strong reference for criticism, and evaluating them in apparel-body-construct may require a great deal of attention. Technique, however, can be a source of aesthetic enjoyment just as other types provide enjoyment.

Production of apparel takes technical skill, and the term "quality" is often used to describe apparel produced with fine fabrics, excellent materials, crafting, and technique. Expectations based upon technical quality can be expressed, "That is certainly worth the price—look at how it is made!" Such a statement implies an expectation of a marketplace standard of technical skill relative to the appearance and cost.

A person may respond to the degree of difficulty in constructing clothing because of past personal experience with a technique—tailoring or knitting, for example. Struggling with tailoring a collar increases our awareness level and appreciation. However, developing an appreciation of technique does not necessarily require that we achieve the full ability to carry out the technique.

Use of technological qualities is important to understand, as they can become a reference to other meanings. For example, a certain status may be identified based upon hand tailoring or the European cut of a man's suit. Technical skill also can become important to meaning if traced to an identifiable designer or manufacturer. Giorgio Armani is known for tailoring, but with a twist. His tailoring is termed soft tailoring due to the fabrics he uses and the techniques that capture the soft fabric hand in an elegant way. Think of the number of times you hear people refer to a particular brand and technique that does not meet expectations of type. There is no doubt that response to clothing is affected by the expectancies of the technical skill taken to produce it. In Figure 10.4, think of the many techniques required to produce this ensemble of jacket, trousers, and T-shirt. The combination of fabrics of both natural and synthetic fibers have been dyed varying colors to create patterns. These fabrics have been tailored into the jacket and trousers and layered upon the body along with the layers of interfacings and linings not in view but critical to the overall look.

**FIGURE 10.4**

*Clothing that is functional in type is valued for its ability to satisfy a purpose.*

Designed by Dries van Noten. Courtesy of Fairchild Publications.

*Type: Formal.* The last type is related to the organizing structure of the form that has been found particularly successful and therefore becomes typed. Such a form may be used repeatedly with slight variations. Then the form may become different than it was when just viewed as an organized structure. It has attained the status of type and is recognized as an old and familiar friend.

Familiarity depends upon past experience by definition—the resemblance of the form to what one has seen before. Humans continually look for the familiar as a source of satisfying visual experiences. Successes in providing satisfaction are repeated and people respond to their continued use with the pleasure of recognition. Such forms often become part of the tradition of a particular culture.

People continually search for the familiar and respond to the apparel-body-construct favorably based upon tried-and-true formulas. People search for favorite combinations of colors and textures, lines and shapes, and even certain ways of wearing clothing. It is difficult to respond to entirely new things that require different ways of looking and responding. People enjoy familiar forms and they become a source of pleasure and satisfaction. Clothing that is recognized as a type is labeled according to structural features such as "blazer" or "shirtwaist" or surfaces such as combinations of colors and geometric lines, in a traditional plaid.

Familiar forms, with time and repeated use, may become exemplary, especially when the type is difficult to fulfill with distinction. Recognizing fulfillment of a formal type is over and above the quality and beauty of its materials, structure, and organization. It also offers a special connection within a cultural context.

The term "classic" applied to clothing has become recognized as a long-standing and consistent means of providing pleasure and satisfaction through a formal type. For example, the Chanel suit designed by Coco Chanel in the early twentieth century is a recognizable classic for the female. Its overall form is recognized: a knee length tubular skirt, collarless blouse, and cardigan jacket with textured surfaces. The basic jacket shape with long sleeves ends at the hipbone and is outlined with braid trim around the sleeves and neck. Faux (costume or fake) jewelry frequently is used to

a                    b

**FIGURE 10.5A & B**

*Chanel herself, pictured in Figure 10.5a, wearing the Chanel suit she designed, which has become a twentieth-century classic. Originally a designer of the 1930s, Chanel made a comeback in the 1950s. A recognizable 1990s version of Chanel, designed by Karl Lagerfeld in Figure 10.5b.*

Courtesy of Fairchild Publications.

fill in the neckline and sometimes the belt is a gold chain. Currently, Karl Lagerfeld is directing the House of Chanel somewhat differently, but over half a century following Coco's classic, one can look at a fashion magazine and recognize the influence of the Chanel type (Figure 10.5a and b).

## Styles as Formal Types Within a Culture

*Styles* are defined as the distinguishing way parts are put together to form a whole. Styles become cultural patterns that influence our criteria for what is liked and disliked and for what is evaluated as good and bad—they are a standard of significance. Styles as formal types occur when certain associations create an identifiable look—that is, certain lines, textures, and colors that come to mean something as a whole—and that are named and recognized as such.

Clothing innovations can become formal types of a certain period, such as the 1960s space-age simple dress shapes skimming the body and worn with long, white, vinyl boots, or the polyester double-knit pantsuit. Such conventions can become a familiar formula that is very appealing to the individual. When the look becomes a type, people gauge what they see against this type. The type becomes a standard for expectations.

Designers who are attempting to establish a name for themselves are often concerned with stylistic consistency, which is a means to establish a signature and recognition. For example, the viewer can recognize Missoni (Figure 10.6a) for knitwear of indeterminate surface, Giorgio Armani (Figure 10.6b) for soft, tailored structures on men and women, Bob Mackie for exquisite eveningwear

**FIGURE 10.6A & B**

*Repeatable images based upon some aspect of the form can become recognized as a design signature. The Italian knitwear design firm of Missoni (a) is recognized for its distinctive knit surfaces. Giorgio Armani (b) is recognized for creating superb tailored garments with softened edges.*

Courtesy of Fairchild Publications.

a                                        b

that relates to the body in special ways, Tommy Hilfiger for his contemporary casual and youthful-looking clothing. This consistency helps establish a name through a developing recognition of the associations that make up a particular designer's style.

There is nothing absolute about criteria for style changes, although as we look back upon historic periods there are some combinations that survive better than others. This phenomenon could be studied as it relates to the fatigue and the pleasure/pain continuum. Within any fashion period there are a variety of available looks that may eventually become the look of the time. Decades are often designated by such looks that become types. Understanding and recognizing these types is especially important in designing theater costuming.

## Fulfillment of Type and the Pleasure Continuum

To provide pleasure, a type must be considered being recognizable in varying degrees, from being a common type all the way to being an exceptional instance. The type can be a common one—an average specimen of the category and simply a sum of common traits; or it can be considered a good specimen—a combination of traits recognized as typical. In certain combinations a good specimen may be sought after by the collector. The exemplary specimen is exceptionally fine, either in quality of materials or overall form. The exemplary type may be recognized as an ideal, hardly attainable, except in rarefied instances. For each type listed and described previously, some instances represent common traits or features, others good features, and still other exemplary specimens, ranging from common to realize to difficult to fulfill. For example, think of a common type worn within the United States, such as, blue jeans and a T-shirt that could be functional and formal, depending upon how the combination is appreciated. What about this type would you as a viewer need to see that would provide you with a pleasure-filled experience?

Evaluation involves the viewer's expectations based upon type. When expectancies associated with an apparel-body-construct are met, a viewer experiences satisfaction, a fulfillment based upon expectations held for that type. However, some expectations are easier to fulfill than others. Expectations for a man's white shirt may be met with a standard shirt on the market, with some choices of size and other details. The viewer may not experience a high degree of satisfaction from such easy fulfillment. Expectations that are easily met do not result in the same degree of satisfaction as those that are more difficult to meet, for example, a certain kind of stitching, a special European cut, or a finer grade of cotton.

Fulfilling expectancies relates to types and the ease or difficulty in fulfilling them. The greatest satisfaction may be in fulfilling difficult expectations, as in discovering that perfect jacket you have been dreaming about in a vintage clothing shop. Less satisfaction may come from fulfilling the expectations of a polo shirt. When functional type is superimposed with the desire for natural fibers, the characteristics of a cotton or wool surface may become important for the viewer to note along with other expectations of the polo shirt.

Finally, expectancies may be ignored in full knowledge of what those expectancies are, as in a joke. People often enjoy such a denial when intended. They can usually recognize when this denial of expectancy is unintended. For example, you play along with a very young child at a tea party dressed in an adult's red satin, close-to-the-body evening gown. The message represented by her clothing is incongruous with the immaturity of her body. She is playing dress-up and is excused from the usual expectancies.

The British designer Vivienne Westwood has received international renown by capitalizing on message expectations related to formal type. In some way she revises or ignores usual expectancies in favor of deliberately creating incongruities of message and therefore demanding the viewer to see with a different set of conventions. In Figure 10.7, Westwood provides a modern version of dress of the French Revolution, called "Napoleon." If we compare similarities to late eighteenth-century France, we recognize such exaggerated details of size, the striped surfaces, the shapes, and the longer length of the trousers worn by the male revolutionaries. However, there are some fundamental incongruities involved: A female is wearing the clothing, the hat would have been similar to that worn by Napoleon but not worn cocked to one side. Napoleon probably did not wear the long pantaloons. These striped trousers were worn by extremely radical Republicans and were called "sans culottes" at the time of the French Revolution. Libertarians who wore the striped trousers often wore the liberty cap, not the two-cornered hat pictured. There are other details that do not mesh: The shapes, colors, and proportions do not quite agree with the historical models, and viewers cognizant with the historically accurate dress will be aware of this, although the look is still easily recognized as a reference to the French Revolution. Is Westwood's clothing meant to be a joke to be appreciated by those "in the know"?

Therefore, the more difficult the type, the greater the pleasure in fulfillment; the more common the type, the greater the displeasure when not fulfilled, as depicted in Table 10.3. Fulfillment of a difficult type, such as the Westwood example, if taken as an "in the know" joke, offers great pleasure in fulfillment, but if not successful, the response may be slight displeasure or even irritation. An example of a common type could be a mass-produced article such as a T-shirt. If done well according to your expectancies, you may

**FIGURE 10.7**

*Unexpected message cues relate to formal type in this modern version of "Napoleon," designed by Vivienne Westwood. Pictured is an outfit resembling what was worn at the time of the French Revolution, but with exaggerated details and incongruities that would be appreciated by those who know about the historical model.*

Courtesy of Fairchild Publications.

| TABLE 10.3 | Fulfillment of difficult type: Great pleasure |
|---|---|
| *Fulfillment of Type and Associated Pleasure* | Nonfulfillment of difficult type: Slight displeasure or none |
| | Fulfillment of common type: Slight pleasure or none |
| | Nonfulfillment of common type: Great displeasure |

respond with some pleasure; however, when not meeting expectancies, the response could be great displeasure, i.e., the neck banding is sewn on poorly or the message, supposed to be centered, is printed off to one side. Thus, expectancies of type may be exceeded in some apparel-body-constructs, adequately met in others, or nonexistent if no prior expectancy. In this way, evaluation is tied to the criteria of formal type and expectancy.

## CONTEXT — TIME, CULTURE, EVENT

When the focus is on context, the viewer evaluates the form within the milieu of time, culture, and event. Each of these factors plays a role in evaluation. In evaluation, one of these three factors may become a priority or they will interact.

When the apparel-body-construct is considered a product of **time**, or in terms of its relation to the fashion of the era, there are many related questions that address evaluation. For example, is it a creator of timeliness, that is, is the apparel-body-construct of value because it points the way to new forms? Or is it a traditional formal piece that fulfills our expectations in its combination of materials, colors, lines, or shapes? In what way is the apparel-body-construct predictable? What about it is new? How is it similar to other apparel-body-constructs of the time? What will follow? To answer these questions the viewer needs to consider what has come before and what may evolve from the apparel-body-construct in question.

Relating to **culture**, one may ask: How does the apparel-body-construct extend or intensify the cultural values and ideals of its audience, that is, both users and viewers? In Figure 10.8a and b, the T-shirts each have an explicit message that connects directly with cultural values of the time, such as stopping hatred and violence, fighting AIDS, and being kind to the environment. What would happen if the apparel-body-construct communicates a message that is objectionable to the viewer? The apparel-body-construct can communicate simple congruous messages as well as complex and incongruous messages. For what purposes might an apparel-body-construct be required to be congruous in its message? For what purposes might one stress the incongruous or the unexpected?

To address these questions we need to know something about the underlying cultural code. What is the code of the time? What is the code of place? For

a                                                          b

example, a convention of the time related to T-shirts is that messages are written on T-shirts and that the messages mean something to the wearers and are shared with the viewers.

Such messages of time and place are continually addressed by writers interpreting history. In the later decades of the twentieth century, popular culture, youth culture, and street style have been a defining feature of the United States, according to Polhemus (1994) and Breward (1995). This movement is especially noticeable in its effects upon the present generation of youth. Since these youth grew up continuously exposed to television programs, magazine articles, home movies, and slides about previous decades, they are visually literate about those decades in a way previous generations were not. Polhemus writes that the present generation is consumed with the past, resulting in a proliferation of Neos: Neo-Mods, Neo-Teds, Neo-Hippies, Neo-Psychedelics, Neo-Punks. Members of the present generation may be determined to recreate the look of the respective time or they may be reinterpreting a look from the past to create a new one, still based in history but creatively put together to update the look. In the process they may be adding a contemporary meaning to the original. Such nostalgia for the past affects the underlying code, though not necessarily making it easier to understand.

Today's marketplace is a cultural resource that becomes important in the context of the message conveyed. Market resources include stores ranging from the generalized department store, where many categories of goods can be found, to stores focused on a limited specialty product, located in downtown urban areas or malls and devoted to providing entertainment or to discounting merchandise. Some stores are for new goods and others for used

**FIGURE 10.8A & B**

*T-shirts with direct messages connect with current cultural values: stop hate and violence, fight AIDS, and be friendly to animals and the environment.*

Photographs: (a) ©1992 Marilyn Humphries and (b) ©1993 Jerome Friar. Courtesy of IMPACT VISUALS.

goods. The general catalogs that offered everything a customer needed, from tools and paint to clothing for everyone, are vanishing. Today's catalogs for the most part are designed for a limited product line, such as hosiery, or to appeal to a special type of customer, such as J. Crew offering moderately priced, casual, and youthful merchandise. Other resources, such as television and the computer Internet, are becoming increasingly important as sources for acquiring clothing. What do each of these provide for the customer? What market and focus will fit a need, and how does the type of marketplace influence the outcome?

**Events** are defined as activities that are marked by beginnings and endings. Events vary from participatory—biking on a trail—to spectator—watching a ballgame. They can be planned months or years ahead, like attending the high school prom, or be unplanned, spontaneous activities, such as stopping at a restaurant to get a bite to eat. Event and the apparel-body-construct often are linked to expected images. When we use terms such as "casual or formal" or "work or dress-up" in reference to an apparel-body-construct, we are relating clothing to event. Such event categories fluctuate, and some activities that once were "events" are no longer so. Today, terms designating specific dress for afternoon visiting and tea or for promenade have little meaning; yet, they have been replaced with terms that do have meaning. For example, now there are many forms of clothing designated to be worn for different activities: aerobics, skiing, biking, tennis, soccer, swimming, wrestling, or rollerblading.

The relation of an apparel-body-construct to an event is a common source of evaluation. The viewer is comparing what is seen with an image of clothing he or she has previously seen or worn to a specific event. People have expectations related to the event. This happens when they have experience of the event, though other factors may enter into our thinking. Sometimes events are marked more by who one is attending with than by the event itself. Think of what you do when you have no previous experience of the event. Do you wear clothing that goes anywhere, anytime? Or do you call your friends and ask what they are wearing? Evaluation of context—time, culture, event—is intricately woven and related. Since each can hardly exist alone, all must be considered.

## Identifying Values

To assess how the apparel-body-construct relates within a cultural context is difficult because cultural values are often imbedded and implicit and one may be unaware of them. To identify values, begin to ask questions like: What are basic cultural values? How does the culture view tradition and change? For what ideals do those within the culture strive? What is considered modest? What is considered "appropriate?" Is there a relation between the two?

The apparel-body-construct can be assessed according to the state of politics, economy, and technology of the society. How does the culture view its economy—as one of scarcity or plenty? Are resources plentiful? If a priority is to save the environment and use fewer resources, how does this affect how the apparel-body-construct is valued? How many objects (including apparel-body-constructs) can be acquired? How many possessions are owned by one person? What is the possibility of recycling? If technological advances are viewed positively, this value will help in assessing the apparel-body-construct. Are new fibers valued as much as traditional ones? Who creates apparel-body-constructs within the society—males and females alike? Does one gender dominate the field creatively? How does this affect the outcome? Is the wearer perceived as having a choice or as a victim? Many questions need to be raised and considered. If identifying values is too abstract an exercise, find several authors who write about cultural values. Then relate such listings to the apparel-body-construct. This may take some creative thinking. What values could be portrayed in Figure 10.9a, b, and c?

a          b         c

**FIGURE 10.9A, B & C**

*Identifying values that are embedded within a cultural context may begin with describing images of the apparel-body-construct and values that might be portrayed. A world of high glamour (a) in this dramatic velvet coat with surfaces of sequins and fur designed by Yves Saint Laurent versus a world of casual comfort (b) in this Polarfleece® jacket, nylon quilted vest, worn over a plaid pullover and jeans designed by Alexander Julian. A sheath dress designed by Steve Fabrikant (c) has become an American classic of the twentieth century.*

Courtesy of Fairchild Publications.

Now consider the individual within the cultural context. For what ideals does the individual strive? What is the relation between cultural and individual ideals? How does the use of terms such as "anti-fashion" provide insight into the relation of individual to culture? How does the individual within the culture define and value what is appealing, fine, beautiful? Is diversity valued? Do people value their individuality or conformity within the group? If individuality is valued, it follows that choice of the apparel-body-construct could have more to do with how to stand apart from the group than how to fit in. If conformity is valued, cultural context would also play a critical role in defining the apparel-body-construct.

# CONTINUING THIS APPROACH

The apparel professional needs to keep acquiring critical observation skills, learning how others respond, and asking the right questions. Understanding the aesthetic response of those you serve means learning about their particular perspectives. Become a sponge—learn to look, educate your perceptions, understand how to relate product, client, and context. Continued application can increase such essential skills as communication, imagination, and visual thinking.

## Develop Communication Skills

Analysis of the apparel-body-construct as communication must extend to a professional concern. Your task is to think about how communication takes place and how the apparel-body-construct will appeal to the intended audience. Many apparel-body-constructs are created for mass production; they influence large numbers of people, potentially affecting how they feel, think, or act. Consider what it takes for clothing to appeal to large numbers of people. Such mass market appeal means that the basic product must be attractive on many different body shapes and that the product functions in a number of different ways or for a number of events—for multiple event dressing. For example, features of this easy-to-wear ensemble include easy-fitting pull-on jerseys and cotton jeans that allow for freedom of movement and fit a number of body sizes with increments of small, medium, large, and extra large. Communication is then focused on the needs and satisfaction of one single person within a very specific context. The casual jacket in Figure 10.10 was designed for an individual who wanted to depict the message, "It takes a village to raise a child." On the other hand, think about the creation of an apparel-body-construct for one person. Such a work could be commissioned for a special and unique individual and event. Then communication is focused upon the needs and satisfaction of one single person within a very specific context.

**FIGURE 10.10**

*This jacket was designed to depict a message very meaningful to one individual—"It takes a village to raise a child."*

Courtesy of Elka Stevens.

An apparel-body-construct, thoughtfully planned and developed, can reinforce or contradict a festive or serious mood. Image consultants are often hired by people in the public view for the purpose of communicating through the apparel-body-construct. Image consulting involves a one-to-one relationship with a client in shopping and planning an ensemble, often connecting an event or a business look with a particular individual. One's image through appearance can create an impression of being friendly, approachable, or of no-nonsense control. Which is called for in this special instance? Much time and thought can go into the visual effect of an apparel-body-construct, as in the case of costumes for movie or theater performances, or clothing and cosmetics worn by men and women in political positions. Think of the many fields relating apparel design to communication, for example, theater costume, photography, personal shopper, fashion editing. The effect of viewer interaction with visual forms is important for the apparel professional to understand. The apparel-body-construct is a message carrier, and careers are based upon its communicative power.

Since communication is so vital to the marketing effort, the professional usually has an idea or image in mind of the intended customer and his characteristics. Joan and David Helpern, owners of Joan & David shoe and clothing stores, define their target market in this way: "We're not on the cutting edge of fashion. We're on the cutting edge of the real world and what's happening to women. Our designs relate to people of style, rather than people who get involved with momentary fashion" (Morais 1995, p. 45). Such a philosophy helps to define their type of clothing within the marketplace as well as their potential customer.

## Develop Imaginative Skills

Many apparel professionals need to develop imaginative skills. This means they must be able to imagine visual possibilities or visual results beyond what they know and have seen. The clothing designer will develop powers of imagination as he or she begins to think visually. A designer who begins with a sketch imagines how the raw materials of the apparel-body-construct will blend together; one who begins with the materials imagines and then sketches the resulting product from the inspiration of the materials. Either way the designer uses imaginative skills.

The apparel professional can be an interpreter of many visual forms—for example, one who is in charge of visual displays combines apparel products in such a way as to highlight the store merchandise through a congruent message. Expertise may include store promotion of the apparel-body-construct in window displays, fashion shows, and layout for advertising copy. All of these tasks are enhanced by developing powers of imagination.

A "what if" attitude helps to visualize and imagine substitutions. First the viewer examines in detail the form as it exists and creates a mental picture of it, then he or she imagines what would happen if another color, another texture, etc., were substituted for the existing one. What would the difference be? What changes in viewing would occur? The viewer who has learned to consider the effects of one color within the apparel-body-construct can expand to consider the effects of other colors of specific hue, value, and intensity. The viewer asks himself or herself what would happen if the message of an apparel-body-construct were changed somewhat. For example, how would I change this image to a more fashionable one for this season? As a viewer becomes more skilled perceptually, he or she can develop a new understanding of forms and an anticipation of new relationships.

The apparel professional who learns the effect of structuring, spatial priorities, and visual relationships can begin to think about the relationship of forms already experienced to forms as yet uncreated. Often the designer's role is to focus upon the new and as yet uncreated images, while the store manager must emphasize how to create both change and satisfaction with clientele. Such experiences must be internalized using one's natural curiosity as the laboratory for learning, asking, and reflecting continuously. The questions for each apparel professional would be slightly different. Questions the designer would likely focus upon would include, "How could I imagine changes and what would be the result?" The store manager, on the other hand, may well ask, "How am I viewing this?" and "How would another person view this?" "How would my clientele view this?"

## Make Connections

**Visual thinking** operates when sensory data from a specific object or group of objects, for example, apparel-body-constructs, are linked to our thinking processes (Arnheim, 1969). Such connections will open your awareness and curiosity and help you to create new associations. To do this, practice perceiving broadly, that is, making connections between things that cross over between categories we normally separate. This is **synectic thinking**, a term coined by Myers (1989) for the merging of different and seemingly incompatible things into cohesive forms or structures. To become involved in synectic visual thinking, you need to develop your ability to think visually and consider how one thing or product relates to another. For example, a trend in the foods people eat is away from the artificial and toward the natural. How could such a trend relate to the clothing people wear? Becoming attuned to such synectic thinking means becoming attuned to chance and change.

One needs to be able to look from other points of view than one's own to be involved in synectic thinking. This means exploring new perspectives, for example, if you are a man, what is it like to feel as a woman feels (or vice versa)? What is it like to be a member of a different racial group or to live in a different geographic locale or a different time? Explore the relationships between two categories of clothing forms. Consider the similarities and differences between a swimsuit and an aerobics suit. Consider the following questions: How do they look? How are they organized? How are they related to cultural values? How do they each function? How could each be changed to be more like, or less like, the other?

Isaac Mizrahi, a New York-based designer, explained his idea of such synectic thinking. "I am committed to being curious about everything," he said in a presentation to introduce his film, *Unzipped* (at the Walker Art Center, Minneapolis, Minnesota, spring of 1995). In this film about his 1994 fall collection, he shows the necessity of being aware of a broad range of things and ideas, from watching old videos of the Mary Tyler Moore television show to playing the piano. The film portrays explicitly how these cultural immersions influence his clothing design for the coming season.

As you understand one apparel-body-construct, then comparisons of one form to another can be made. Our repertory of clothing forms must expand to include historic forms, new forms, forms yet to be created. This ability to make comparisons is very useful. The viewer can learn to examine existing forms or create new possibilities. In the field of fashion apparel, new forms are continually offered for viewing consideration, and these often rely on both creativity and historic precedence. Flexibility in analyzing apparel-body-constructs will broaden one's viewing and enable perception, interpretation, and evaluation of familiar and new visual experiences, regardless of whether these are new trends within a culture or a comparison of forms from different cultures.

By following and applying the visual aesthetic framework introduced and explained in this book, you have developed your visual and perceptual skills. Viewing and understanding, however, is a continual, searching, interactive process. It takes hard work and motivation to continue! When an apparel-body-construct is being viewed, an active viewer continues to question the visual effect. What visual discoveries are in store if you continue your quest!

## Summary

- Understanding aesthetic response must be based on reflection, reasoning, and understanding one's personal likes and dislikes and those of clients. Your likes and dislikes will expand through exposure.

- Aesthetic exposure is contextual—it is embedded in cultural preferences as well as in personal experience and preferences. Various clothing looks cycle in popularity; extremes such as formal versus casual, classic versus romantic, are popular less often than middle-of-the-road looks. Certain looks and clothing styles—the double-knit polyester pantsuit—may become passé through overexposure.

- The four-step framework for analysis of the apparel-body-construct is: (1) observation, (2) differentiation, (3) interpretation, and (4) evaluation. Evaluation involves understanding the criteria involved—a person may love blue because she received compliments while wearing a blue outfit. Here, the criterion is emotional satisfaction. Culturally established conventions and coding also play a part.

- The form must be considered in the evaluation process: how the whole related to the parts, and vice versa. A man may select a tie because he loves the pattern, not caring about how it will relate to the suit he is wearing, or a woman may carefully coordinate her ensemble, being very aware of the contributions of skirt, hat, etc., to the total effect. Principles of visual organization, such as focus, balance, visual weight, figure-ground, order versus chaos, etc., are important. The relationship of form to the wearer's body is important—this is often related in a "look," such as the Jackie Kennedy look.

- The viewer is also important. What is the target audience: J. Crew? Wal-Mart? Apparel professionals must consider clients and wearers.

- Sensory experiences—visual, tactile, kinesthetic, auditory, and olfactory—are basic resources of evaluation. For example, to some people color is a very important aspect of a garment; for others, it is the way it feels.

- Typing is viewing through a system of associations. Natural, functional, and formal types may be distinguished. Styles are the distinguishing ways parts are put together to form a whole. The fulfillment type is associated with pleasure—when one finds the perfect vintage jacket, this is associated with great pleasure.

- Time, culture, and event play a role in evaluation of the apparel-body-construct.

- Understanding communication is important in the analysis of the apparel-body-construct and is highly relevant to marketing. Apparel professionals must develop the ability to think visually and to use synectic thinking—the ability to connect diverse things into cohesive forms or structures.

# Key Terms and Concepts

| | |
|---|---|
| attention fatigue | time |
| culture | typing |
| evaluation | viewer |
| events | visual thinking |
| sensory fatigue | wearer |
| synectic thinking | |

# References

Agins, T. "Designers Forsake Fads, Turn to Tweeds." *The Wall Street Journal*, August 14, 1996, B1 and B6.

Arnheim, R. *Toward a Psychology of Art*. Berkeley: University of California Press, 1966.

Arnheim, R. *Visual Thinking*. Berkeley: University of California Press, 1969.

Banner, L. *American Beauty*. Chicago: University of Chicago Press, 1983.

Barthes, R. *The Fashion System* (Translated from French). New York: Hill and Wang, 1983.

Breward, C. *The Culture of Fashion*. New York: Manchester University Press, 1995.

Celente, G., and Milton T. *Trend Tracking: The System to Profit from Today's Trends*. New York: Warner Books, 1990.

Craik, J. *The Face of Fashion: Cultural Studies in Fashion*. New York: Routledge, 1994.

Dickie, G. *Evaluating Art*. Philadelphia: Temple University Press, 1988.

Eisner, E. *Educating Artistic Vision*. New York: Macmillan, 1972.

Finlayson, I. *Denim: An American Legend*. New York: Simon and Schuster, 1990.

Fisher-Mirkin, T. *Dress Code*. New York: Clarkson Potter, 1995.

Feldman, E. *Art as Image and Idea*. Englewood Cliffs, NJ: Prentice-Hall, 1967.

Frazer, K. *The Fashionable Mind*. New York: Alfred Knopf, 1981.

Hollander, A. *Seeing Through Clothes*. New York: Viking Press, 1978.

Kaiser, S. *The Social Psychology of Clothing*. New York: Macmillan, 1985.

Kidwell, C., and Christman, M. *Suiting Everyone: The Democratization of Clothing in America*. Washington, DC: Smithsonian Institution Press, 1974.

Kidwell, C., and Steele, V., eds. *Men and Women: Dressing the Part*. Washington, DC: Smithsonian Institution Press, 1989.

Lurie, A. *The Language of Clothes*. New York: Random House, 1981.

Maeder, E., ed. *An Elegant Art*. Catalog of Exhibit at the Los Angeles County Museum of Art and New York: Harry Abrams, 1983.

Mathis, C., and Connor, H. *The Triumph of Individual Style: A Guide to Dressing Your Body, Your Beauty, Your Self*. Cali, Colombia: Timeless Editions, 1993.

McCracken, G. *Culture and Consumption*. Indianapolis: Indiana University Press, 1988.

McKim, R. *Thinking Visually*. Belmont, CA: Wadsworth, 1980.

Morais, R. C. "If You Stand Still, You Die." *Forbes,* January 30, 1995, 44–45.

Morton, G. *The Arts of Costume and Personal Appearance*. New York: John Wiley, 1964.

Myers, J. *The Language of Visual Art: Perception as a Basis for Design*. Chicago: Holt, Rinehart and Winston, 1989.

Pepper, S. *Principles of Art Appreciation*. New York: Harcourt, Brace, and Company, 1949.

Peppers, D., and Rogers, M. *The One to One Future*. New York: Doubleday, 1993.

Polhemus, T. *Streetstyle*. New York: Thames and Hudson, 1994.

Rexford, N. "Studying Garments for their Own Sake: Mapping the World of Costume Scholarship." *Dress,* Costume Society of America, *14,* 1988, 68–75.

Rothschild, L. *Style in Art*. New York: Thomas Yoseloff, 1960.

Stern, G. *The Wall Street Journal*. Section B1, July 24, 1995.

Solomon, J. *The Signs of Our Time*. Los Angeles: Jeremy Tarcher, 1988.

Susman, W. *Culture and History: The Transformation of American Society in the Twentieth Century*. New York: Pantheon Books, 1984.

Thorsen, H. *Peak-Experience, Religion and Knowledge: A Philosophical Inquiry into Some Main Themes in the Writings of Abraham H. Maslow*. Doctoral Thesis at the University of Uppsala, Sweden, 1983.

Tillotson, K. "Timeline of a Trend: Chasing Down a Trend." *Star Tribune*, July 18, 1995, Variety Section E, Minneapolis, MN, 1.

Wallach, J. *Looks that Work*. New York: Viking Press, 1986.

# GLOSSARY

**aesthetic response** One's involvement in looking and the resulting experiences; what one selects as an expression of preference; understanding aesthetic response involves knowing about the form, the viewer, and the physical and cultural contexts. *(See Chapter 1.)*

**aesthetics** Understanding our response to what we value, and how we view and respond to the apparel-body-construct with evaluation being the end of the process. *(See Chapter 1.)*

**apparel-body-construct** A visual form that results from the interaction of apparel on the human body; a concept of this physical object based on sensory data. *(See Chapter 2.)*

**associations** The relationships of the apparel-body-construct that create connections for the viewer within the form and between the form, viewer, and physical and cultural contexts. *(See Chapter 9.)*

**asymmetrical balance** When visual weight is perceived as unequally distributed from one side to the other of an imaginary central line or point. *(See Chapter 8.)*

**attending** Process that involves both attraction and sustained viewing by

which the viewer is engaged in viewing an apparel-body-construct. *(See Chapter 9.)*

**attention fatigue** When the viewer gets tired of viewing an apparel-body-construct for reasons such as boredom or overstimulation of the eyes. *(See Chapter 10.)*

**bias** A diagonal line of direction, especially across a woven fabric. *(See Chapter 6.)*

**bilateral symmetry** Similarity in size and arrangement of parts on opposite sides of an imaginary or actual line or center point; regularity of form. *(See Chapter 5.)*

**body view** A view of the body form from a frame of reference of visual field; a single viewpoint (front, back, or side). *(See Chapter 5.)*

**closed** Self-contained, continuous, and independent from the surround, and descriptive of the silhouette of an apparel-body-construct. *(See Chapter 4.)*

**closed-open** The range of visual spatial possibilities applied to the outer perimeter of a form and its relation to the surround. *(See Chapter 4.)*

*closure*  The process of perceiving a grouping or segregating of visual parts, including the connecting of implied lines, to create a bounded area (Gestalt principle of organization). *(See Chapter 8.)*

*code*  Recognizable patterns of perception of the apparel-body-construct; when the order of visual parts occurs with some frequency so that the viewer becomes familiar with them and their meaning. *(See Chapter 9.)*

*coherence*  A consistent unity that holds together in our perception. *(See Chapter 2.)*

*color*  The spectrum of light perception that provides definition and potential visual relationships through the dimensions of hue, value, and intensity. *(See Chapter 7.)*

*color blocking*  When colors are planned in a large enough area so that the colors become an organizing factor. *(See Chapter 6.)*

*continuation*  The extension of a visual path by a visual connection between parts (Gestalt principle of organization). *(See Chapter 8.)*

*conventions*  Guidelines used to interpret and evaluate the apparel-body-construct; patterns of perception recognized within a group of people. *(See Chapter 9.)*

*cultural context*  A person's cultural environment that influences perceptions, thinking, and overt behavior (Lachmann 1991). *(See Chapter 1.)*

*culture*  The symbolic and learned aspects of a unified societal group (Marshall, 1994). A cultural grouping may form around a nation, a race, a

school, and may vary with time and place, so that over a lifetime a person can relate to a number of different cultural identities.  Learning can be passed on through material artifacts or nonmaterial teaching and traditions. *(See Chapter 1, Chapter 9, Chapter 10.)*

*depth effects*  The impression of depth from levels of organization on the flat surface, or from the influence of light and shadow in creating a three-dimensionality of a form. *(See Chapter 5.)*

*determinate-indeterminate*  The range of visual spatial possibility applied to the surface character of the form. *(See Chapter 4.)*

*Differentiation*  The identification of the visual parts and the awareness of their relationships—how each part influences other parts and the whole. *(See Chapter 3.)*

*direction*  The viewer's impression of movement while taking in the apparel-body-construct. *(See Chapter 8.)*

*directly perceptible relationships*  The visual connections apparent in the form itself. *(See Chapter 2.)*

*edge*  Line that identifies a bounded area. *(See Chapter 7.)*

*education*  An increase in knowledge and understanding often due to directed experiences. *(See Chapter 2.)*

*elements*  The most basic components of an apparel-body-construct. *(See Chapter 7.)*

*Evaluation*  Criteria for making a judgment that includes personal and shared values. *(See Chapter 3: Step 4 in Analysis.)* A critique of an apparel-body-construct that involves explicit criteria and a recognition of what is valued. *(See Chapter 10.)*

**event** An occurance with a beginning and an end regarded as having importance. *(See Chapter 9, Chapter 10.)*

**expressive characteristics** Features seen directly in a form that result in spontaneous feelings such as excitement or calmness. *(See Chapter 1.)*

**expressive effect** A unifying idea that summarizes an apparel-body-construct; a fusion of meaning that arises from emotional states, e.g., excitement, calmness, strength, delicacy. *(See Chapter 9.)*

**fashion** A cultural phenomenon whereby "new" is perceived as favorable; appearing up-to-date. *(See Chapter 1.)*

**figure** That which we view as having object quality and appears to be in front of ground. *(See Chapter 2, Chapter 4.)*

**figure-ground ambiguity** A viewing situation in which reversals can occur in what appears as figure, i.e., that which at one time appears as figure switches and becomes ground. *(See Chapter 4.)*

**figure-ground integration** A viewing situation in which the figure and ground are viewed as if on a similar plane. *(See Chapter 4.)*

**figure-ground separation** A viewing situation in which the figure and ground are viewed as if on different planes. *(See Chapter 4.)*

**flat-rounded** The range of visual spatial possibility applied to the surfaces of a form that connect the surface as rounding the body or not. *(See Chapter 4.)*

**form** The subject of our viewing, especially the apparel-body-construct. *(See Chapter 1.)*

**Gestalt principles of organization** Four primary principles: similarity, closure, proximity, and continuation that explain the grouping and separating of visual parts in the viewing process (See grouping, segregating). *(See Chapter 2.)*

**gradation** A measurable variation of some attribute within a whole; a gradual progression of difference that provides visual direction. *(See Chapter 2, Chapter 8.)*

**grain** The direction of threads in a woven fabric in relation to the selvage, either lengthwise (parallel to the selvage) or crosswise. *(See Chapter 6.)*

**ground** The field of visual activity of an apparel-body-construct; that which surrounds and appears to lie beneath the figure. *(See Chapter 2, Chapter 4.)*

**grouping** The process of relating similar visual units in perception, an automatic, interactive viewer process that helps in understanding the organization of an apparel-body-construct when brought to consciousness. *(See Chapter 2, Chapter 8.)*

**hand** Manipulative potential of materials of the apparel-body-construct, including weight and drape; tactile qualities of materials. *(See Chapter 6.)*

**hierarchical** A relationship of order in which one part has more dominance than another. *(See Chapter 2.)*

**hue** The spectrum variation of color. *(See Chapter 7.)*

**icon** A sign that resembles what it stands for. *(See Chapter 9.)*

*index* A sign that can be determined by inferrence. *(See Chapter 9.)*

*inferred relationships* Relationships of the form that cannot be understood by directly viewing the form that involve the viewer, the form, and the contexts. *(See Chapter 2.)*

*intensity* Strength of pigmentation or degree of purity of color. *(See Chapter 7.)*

*Interpretation* Looking for themes and associations of meaning that summarize and explain the form. *(See Chapter 3: Step 3 in Analysis.)*

*layout structuring* The arrangement of the apparel-body-construct by three-dimensional means such as shaping by seams, draping, pleats, or gathers; manipulations of physical surfaces toward and away from the observer and sometimes the three-dimensional effect of surface protrusions. *(See Chapter 6.)*

*light structuring* Means of arranging the apparel-body-construct by varying the light and shadow effects of the surfaces. *(See Chapter 6.)*

*line* Actual or imagined linkages between points or areas; a contour. *(See Chapter 7.)*

*linear definition* The characterization of line and edge in the apparel-body-construct; visual appearance derived from line and shape. *(See Chapter 7.)*

*message* Receiving communication. *(See Chapter 9.)*

*micro surface* The visual effect of threads or other minute surface variations. *(See Chapter 6.)*

*microlayout* The visual effects of the microsurface. *(See Chapter 7.)*

*number threshold* The limit number of parts taken in before part grouping occurs. *(See Chapter 8.)*

*Observation* Paying attention to and describing the total visual form. *(See Chapter 3: Step 1 in Analysis.)*

*open* Indistinct and interdependent with surround, and descriptive of the silhouette of an apparel-body-construct. *(See Chapter 4.)*

*part modifier* Factors that effect the interaction of visual parts of apparel-body-construct, i.e., size, number, spatial position, direction, and visual weight. *(See Chapter 8.)*

*part-to-whole* A visual spatial priority characterized by an initial separation of and emphasis on units smaller than the whole. *(See Chapter 4.)*

*part-whole* The Gestalt as an expression of the part perceived as related to the whole. *(See Chapter 4.)*

*past experiences* A viewer's experiences that influence aesthetic response. *(See Chapter 2.)*

*pattern* Viewing an orderly sequence consisting of repeated parts. *(See Chapter 8.)*

*perceive* To become aware of, know, identify, and discover by means of the senses. *(See Chapter 4.)*

*physical context* The immediate surround of the apparel-body-construct. *(See Chapter 1.)*

*planar effects* Appearing to be on a flat surface parallel to the visual field. *(See Chapter 5.)*

*point* The dot in perception; the intersection of two or more lines; a source of focus when single and strong. *(See Chapter 7.)*

*postmodern* A body of critical theory about the nature of contemporary society, viewed either in contrast or parallel to the modern. Specifically, postmodern refers to an aesthetic expression in appearance that often embodies reference to diverse values and disparate features of clothing and a mixing of aesthetic codes (Morgado 1996). *(See Chapter 1.)*

*proportion* Size relations of parts to each other and to the whole. *(See Chapter 8.)*

*proximity* Similarity of location or close spatial placement of parts. As the distance between like units varies, those that are close spatially will tend to group; those that are different will tend to separate (Gestalt principle of organization). *(See Chapter 8.)*

*recognition* Focusing on a visual field to attend, identify, and name. *(See Chapter 9.)*

*referential characteristics* Inferred relationships of the form that cannot be understood by directly viewing the form. *(See Chapter 1.)*

*relationships* Parts that connect because of their similar or contrasting qualities. *(See Chapter 2.)*

*repetitive* Viewing similar visual units that create redundancy. *(See Chapter 2.)*

*rhythm* The pattern of movement produced by the relationship of parts within an apparel-body-construct. *(See Chapter 8.)*

*sensory data* Information taken in directly through senses, i.e., visual, tactile, kinesthetic, auditory, and olfactory. *(See Chapter 2.)*

*sensory fatigue* When the senses become tired because of overstimulation. *(See Chapter 10.)*

*separate (separating)* Units that appear to maintain their integrity as visual parts in the simplest organization; an automatic, interactive viewer process that helps in understanding the organization of an apparel-body-construct when brought to consciousness. *(See Chapter 2.)*

*separated viewing* Characterized by visually equal and independent parts that are perceived first in pattern of organization. *(See Chapter 8.)*

*separating* When parts contrast in some elemental detail such as line direction, they are viewed as separate units. *(See Chapter 8.)*

*sequential* When parts are perceived as sharing common traits and are thereby ordered. *(See Chapter 2.)*

*shadow structuring* Means of arranging the apparel-body-construct by varying the light and shadow effects of the surfaces. *(See Chapter 6.)*

*shape* A bounded area usually perceived as having at least the two dimensions of length and width (planar), or three dimensions by including depth (that which appears thick and rounding). *(See Chapter 7.)*

*sign* A unit that refers to something other than itself, e.g., icon, index, symbol. *(See Chapter 9.)*

*similarity* The relative degree of sameness among visual parts that determines their perceptual connection. Parts that are similar tend to be organized into groups by the observer; parts that are different tend to be viewed separately. (Gestalt principle of organization). *(See Chapter 8.)*

*simultaneous viewing* Being perceived as a whole first in a pattern of organization because of blending surfaces, overall surface treatment, or a closed silhouette. *(See Chapter 8.)*

*stereotypes* A standard image or category invested with specific meaning held in common by members of a group; implies perceiving a set form with conventional meaning that does not require a viewer's perceptual awareness. *(See Chapter 2.)*

*structure* Source of organization or arrangement of visual parts within context of the whole, especially of those form features that direct movement. *(See Chapter 2.)*

*style* A distinctive form structure that is consistent and recognizable over time; visual effect that includes form relations and expressive effect. *(See Chapter 1.)*

*successive viewing* Characterized by a hierarchy of visual parts, primary and secondary foci. *(See Chapter 8.)*

*surface definition* The way in which surfaces of the apparel-body-construct are characterized by texture and color. *(See Chapter 7.)*

*surface structuring* The arrangement of the apparel-body-construct by two-dimensional means, e.g., printing, weaving, color variation of materials, that may result in a three-dimensional appearance. *(See Chapter 6.)*

*surface texture* Minute surface variations. *(See Chapter 7.)*

*symbol* A sign that must be learned in place of the object. *(See Chapter 9.)*

*symmetrical balance* When visual weight is perceived as equally distributed from one side to the other. *(See Chapter 8.)*

*synectic thinking* Combining seemingly disparate things not thought of together before. *(See Chapter 10.)*

*texture* Visual definition provided for the viewer through small variations in surface such as weave structure or printed shapes that are not perceived as figure but as surface variations. *(See Chapter 7.)*

*time* Reference to a measurement of the past, present, and/or future; timeliness of the apparel-body-construct is called fashion. *(See Chapter 10.)*

*typing* When the viewer places what is seen into categories based on a system of associations recognized as a whole. *(See Chapter 10.)*

*value* The degree of lightness or darkness of a color. *(See Chapter 7.)*

*viewer* One who views, bringing to the viewing process the combined influences of slowly changing traits such as education and personality, and rapidly changing traits such as moods and momentary expectations. *(See Chapter 1, Chapter 4, Chapter 10.)*

*viewer as wearer* The perspective of the viewer that includes experiences of wearing clothing. *(See Chapter 1.)*

*viewing* The process of perceiving an apparel-body-construct. *(See Chapter 4.)*

*viewing order*  Order in which the apparel-body-construct is viewed. *(See Chapter 8.)*

*viewing tempo*  Rate at which the viewer perceives the apparel-body-construct, dependent on amount and type of activity and resulting effect on the viewer. *(See Chapter 8.)*

*visual definers*  The elements of line, shape, texture, color, that provide definition and interest for the viewer. *(See Chapter 7.)*

*visual effect*  The result for the viewer of viewing the apparel-body-construct. *(See Chapter 8.)*

*visual field*  The physical space around one from his or her stationary point of view (changes according to viewer position). *(See Chapter 4.)*

*visual part*  A unit of the whole that separates for viewing in our perception. *(See Chapter 2, Chapter 4.)*

*visual parts*  Units that separate from the whole for viewing. *(See Chapter 8.)*

*visual perception*  The action of the mind in referring sensations to the object that caused them, and forming the viewer's understanding. *(See Chapter 8.)*

*visual thinking*  A process of integrating perception, thought, and imagination about visual relationships, i.e., shapes, color, order, spatial priority signs. *(See Chapter 10.)*

*visual world*  A view of the physical space around us as unbounded, resulting in the appearance of constancy in object attributes (involves reliance on past viewing experiences to interpret constancy). *(See Chapter 4.)*

*wearer*  The person who has clothing or ornaments on the body; a perspective that can be brought to the viewing process. *(See Chapter 10.)*

*whole-to-part*  Characterized by an initial separation of the whole apparel-body-construct before the parts, resulting from a defined silhouette or an overall surface treatment. *(See Chapter 4.)*

*whole-to-part viewing*  The range of visual spatial possibilities applied to the process of taking in the Gestalt of the form first and then proceeding to note the parts and their relation to the whole or vice versa, e.g. part-to-whole. *(See Chapter 4.)*

# INDEX